The Fifth Estate

Robert Taylor is labour correspondent of the *Observer*. He graduated with a first class honours degree in modern history from Wadham College, Oxford, in 1965 and was a research student at Nuffield College, Oxford. Before joining the political staff of the *Economist* in 1970 he was a lecturer in modern history at the University of Lancaster. He became industrial correspondent of *New Society* in 1973 and moved to his present position at the *Observer* in 1976. He broadcasts regularly for the World Service of the BBC and has contributed articles to *Political Quarterly*, *Management Today* and the *New Statesman*.

Robert Taylor

The Fifth Estate

Britain's unions in the modern world
Revised edition

Pan Books London and Sydney

First published 1978 by Routledge & Kegan Paul Ltd
This revised edition first published 1980 by Pan Books Ltd,
Cavaye Place, London SW10 9PG
© Robert Taylor 1978, 1980
ISBN 0 330 25943 1
Printed and bound in Great Britain by
Richard Clay (The Chaucer Press) Ltd, Bungay, Suffolk

Then let us pray that come it may,
As come it will for a' that,
That sense and worth, o'er a' the earth
May bear the free an' a' that
For a' that an' a' that,
It's comin' yet for a' that
That man to man, the world o'er
Shall brithers be for a' that

Robert Burns
'For the Sake of Somebody'

Contents

Part two   Varieties of unionism

Abbreviations

ABT	Association of Building Technicians (now STAMP section of UCATT)
ACAS	Advisory, Conciliation and Arbitration Service
APEX	Association of Professional, Executive, Clerical and Computer Staffs
ASE	Amalgamated Society of Engineers
ASLEF	Associated Society of Locomotive Engineers and Firemen
ASRS	Amalgamated Society of Railway Servants (now NUR)
ASSET	Association of Supervisory Staffs, Executives and Technicians (now ASTMS)
ASTMS	Association of Scientific, Technical and Managerial Staffs
AUBTW	Amalgamated Union of Building Trade Workers
AUEW	Amalgamated Union of Engineering Workers
AUT	Association of University Teachers
BIFU	Banking, Insurance and Finance Union
COHSE	Confederation of Health Service Employees
CPSA	Civil and Public Services' Association
CSEU	Confederation of Shipbuilding and Engineering Unions
CSU	Civil Service Union
DATA	Draughtsmen's and Allied Technicians' Association
EETPU	Electrical, Electronic, Telecommunications and Plumbing Union
EMA	Engineers' and Managers' Association

EPEA	Electrical Power Engineers' Association
ETU	Electrical Trades' Union
GMWU	General and Municipal Workers' Union
IPCS	Institution of Professional Civil Servants
ISTC	Iron and Steel Trades Confederation
LRC	Labour Representation Committee
NALGO	National and Local Government Officers' Association
NATSOPA	National Association of Operative Printers, Graphical and Media Personnel
NFBTO	National Federation of Building Trades Operatives
NGA	National Graphical Association
NPA	Newspaper Proprietors' Association
NUAAW	National Union of Agricultural and Allied Workers
NUBE	National Union of Bank Employees
NUM	National Union of Mineworkers
NUPE	National Union of Public Employees
NUR	National Union of Railwaymen
NUS	National Union of Seamen
NUT	National Union of Teachers
POEU	Post Office Engineering Union
SLADE	Society of Lithographic Artists, Designers, Engravers and Process Workers
SOGAT	Society of Graphical and Allied Trades
TASS	Technical, Administrative and Supervisory Section (of AUEW)
TGWU	Transport and General Workers' Union
TSSA	Transport Salaried Staffs' Association
UCATT	Union of Construction, Allied Trades and Technicians
UPW	Union of Post Office Workers
USDAW	Union of Shop, Distributive and Allied Workers

Acknowledgements

This book was substantially revised and updated during the eventful winter of 1978–9 for the paperback edition. I am most grateful to the *Observer* and *New Society* magazine in particular for the opportunities they have given me over the past few years to write about Britain's complicated but fascinating industrial relations scene. Many of the ideas and developments covered in this book first originated in their pages. *Socialist Commentary*, the *Political Quarterly* and *Management Today* must also be thanked for providing me with other occasions on which to set out my views. I am also most grateful to the Fabian Society for publishing my pamphlet on *Labour and the Social Contract*, much of which has been reworked for inclusion in this paperback edition.

Trade unionists – from general secretaries and full-time officials to members of the rank and file and shop stewards – gave me invaluable help and time over the years to discuss their arduous and usually thankless work with me. Without their warm assistance, this book would never have been possible. My wife Ann gave me the necessary encouragement to see this paperback edition through to a conclusion.

May 1979

Preface

The unions are not the Robin Hoods they are supposed to be on every television programme. They are the robber barons of the system. (Samuel Brittan, *Inflation: Causes, Consequences and Cures*, Institute of Economic Affairs, 14, 1974)

British trade unionism has become a formula for national misery. (Paul Johnson, *New Statesman*, 16 May 1975)

The unions: underdogs or overmighty subjects?

Britain's trade unions are never short of critics. A large body of public opinion – rightly or wrongly – is now convinced that they wield far too much destructive power in our complex inter-dependent society and behave in an arrogant, irresponsible way. This is an unreasoning mood, but it has grown much stronger over the past decade.

In their 1970 study of electoral behaviour David Butler and Donald Stokes discovered from their survey material:

In all our surveys a four to one majority said that when they heard of a strike their sympathies were generally against the strikers. By the end of the 1960s the number who felt the unions had too much power had risen from a half to two thirds. In 1963, 53 per cent of people thought so; by 1970, 66 per cent did with less than a quarter disagreeing.

By the end of the 1970s the unpopularity of the unions had grown even more widespread. A survey carried out by Market and Opinion Research International (MORI) for the *Daily Express* in September 1978 revealed that 82 per cent of the people sampled believed the unions had too much power in Britain. Interestingly, trade unionists tend to agree with that view themselves. In the September 1978 MORI poll, 73 per cent of trade unionists surveyed thought the unions were too powerful. As many as 60 per cent of the MORI sample agreed with the statement: 'Most trade unions are controlled by a few militants and extremists', and 57 per cent of the polled trade unionists agreed with this. A MORI survey carried out for the *Sunday Times* in October 1977 discovered that the unions came only slightly higher than the nationalized industries in those institutions in Britain people were most dissatisfied with. A substantial number of people appear to believe that the unions remain the main cause of Britain's economic problems. Even a supposedly militant and class-conscious group of workers like London dockers were divided in their response to the issue of trade union power. Stephen Hill in a survey of dockers in the early 1970s found that as many as 40 per cent of those he interviewed also agreed that the unions were exercising too much power. The depths of hostility towards the trade unions were well established during the strikes of early 1979. MORI carried out an opinion poll for the *Daily Express* in February of that year. As many as 86 per cent of trade unionists agreed that there should be a ban on picketing a company not directly involved in a strike, while 91 per cent of trade unionists agreed that no stoppages should be called until there was a postal ballot of the members concerned. Even 76 per cent of trade unionists agreed there should be a limit on the number of pickets allowed at any location, compared with 71 per cent of the whole sample who believed this. While 65 per cent of the people polled thought that social security benefits paid to strikers' families should be subject to income tax, even 57 per cent of trade unionists supported that idea. A total of 78 per cent thought that the government should use troops to provide a basic service if there was a strike in a key industry, compared with 71 per cent of trade unionists who agreed. These findings suggest that trade unionists are not separate in their views from the rest of the community. But they also tend to confirm the view that sectionalist self-interest remains the chief determinant of trade union behaviour. While trade unionists are ready to condemn militant action in general, when it comes to their own specific grievance such attitudes change until it has been remedied.

But the evidence of the polls is not quite so conclusive as

it might first appear. There is a clear ambivalence about popular attitudes to the unions behind the widespread hostility. In the September 1978 MORI poll as many as 78 per cent of the sample agreed with the statement: 'Trade unions are essential to protect workers' interests' (this compares with 63 per cent in 1976 and 75 per cent in 1977). Even 77 per cent of social classes ABC1 accepted that proposition, the same proportion as the DEs. As many as 83 per cent of Hill's sample of London dockers thought the unions had as important a role to play today as at any time in the past. During both the 1972 and 1974 national coal strikes Edward Heath's Conservative Government found to its obvious dismay that public opinion was far more sympathetic to than critical of the action of the miners, no matter what damaging effect it was having on the national economy. A total of 86 per cent of a National Opinion Poll survey in February 1974 expressed sympathy for the miners, although only two months later a mere 15 per cent of a sample for an Opinion Research Centre survey expressed confidence in unions in general.

It is indisputable that the unions in Britain collectively, and a few by themselves, have the potential power to paralyse the country's economic life through industrial stoppages or other forms of action such as work to rules and overtime bans. The negative power of some groups of workers in key jobs (miners, electricity supply workers and engineers, oil tanker and road haulage drivers, water workers, British Oxygen workers) is only too obvious, and it would be foolish to suggest otherwise. Moreover the unions have won a reputation (whether deservedly is another matter) for saying No – and of being incapable of innovating. At the same time, they have proved formidable defenders of their own freedom to remain autonomous. During the first half of 1969 the Labour government – mainly under the messianic fervour of Barbara Castle, Roy Jenkins and Harold Wilson – tried to modernize the unions through a short, sharp Bill to outlaw unofficial strikes but the TUC forced this attempt to a humiliating surrender. Again during the time of the Conservatives' 1971 Industrial Relations Act, the trade union movement found the collective cohesion and unity to resist what they believed were grave threats to their independence to act as they think best. The downfall of the Heath Government at the hands of the voters in the February 1974 general election, fought mainly on the issue of union power, appeared to confirm that no modern government in today's Britain can rule without the blessing of the unions. As TUC general secretary, Len Murray, admits, the political parties have discovered the hard way during recent times that 'they fall into trouble when they try to govern in the teeth of union opposition'.

The central argument of this book is that Britain's unions are *not* overmighty subjects, robber barons of our economic system, who wish to destroy personal liberty and create a monstrous totalitarian state. The widely held views about the unions remain a dangerous myth. Even today, when the influence of the unions is certainly much stronger than it was twenty years ago, the unions are still for the most part reactive, not revolutionary or subversive. The often crude and merciless laws of the so-called free labour market continue to dominate and shape the lives and expectations of most workers in our fundamentally unequal and divided society. Shareholders and managers continue to rate higher priority for concern than the workers on the shopfloor or the office staff. Under the strains of Britain's prolonged economic crisis of the 1970s most of the material gains achieved by workers through consensus politics and the mixed economy of the post-war years could no longer be taken for granted. In most vital respects, the unions are what they always have been – defensive, voluntary pressure groups, under sporadic attack from the class bias and common law traditions of the British legal system and the blandishments of government, at the mercy of the ebb and flow of uncontrollable, impersonal economic forces.

The main purpose of this book is to attempt a redress in the balance. In my opinion, the British unions are not greedy, unthinking giants holding the 'nation' to ransom. Far from it. Their fault lies in the fact that they are simply not strong enough. As organizations for the redistribution of wealth and income, fatter real pay packets and higher productivity, social justice and worker democracy, our unions trail far behind most others in the Western industrialized world. The power of capital – either in the boardrooms of British industry or the banks and insurance companies of the City of London – remains

overwhelming. Too many union leaders of the present generation share a wholly parochial, narrow view of the function of
the unions. They have a dislike of theory and education as
well as a suspicion of the professionalism and effectiveness
displayed by unions in other Western capitalist countries. There
is a mistaken pride in the merits of self-reliance and the virtues
of working on a shoe-string. In a world of large multinational
conglomerates and government bureaucracy, such attributes are
nothing to boast about. 'Whatever is is best' should not be
a trade union slogan. The aim needs to be a more radical,
egalitarian trade union movement dedicated to social justice
and economic growth.

It is perhaps understandable that most unions in Britain rest
content to move slowly along familiar, well-worn paths. The
habit of doing little is always strong, in unions as everywhere
else. Motions are passed at Trades Union Congresses on an
impressive array of subjects every first week in September:
very few lead to practical policy-making. Yet the movement –
contrary to mythology – is full of dedicated, energetic, able
people at all levels – as general secretaries and full-time officials, stewards and branch secretaries. There is a wealth of
talent, expertise and imagination to tap in most of our unions.
For all their more obvious faults and failures, the unions remain voluntary, democratic expressions of the collective
opinions of working people. No doubt much of the idealism
and vision – seen among the pioneers of British trade unionism – has gone with the decline of faith in ethical socialism.
But looking down over the rows of bald heads and baggy suits
at annual TUCs, even the most hostile observer would have to
admit that the movement is fundamentally decent and modest.
There is far more common sense and practical experience on
display at Congress than at any of the annual party conferences
nowadays and the efforts of the Confederation of British Industry to hold annual conventions (the first was in 1977) have
been less than a resounding success, with little debate and much
bland boredom. It would be wrong to overlook the nature of
the society within which the unions have to react. At the outset, we need to remember that Britain is a country divided by
wide disparities in the distribution of income and wealth. The
reports of the Standing Royal Commission established by the

Labour Government in August 1974 (abolished July 1979) provide much statistical material which underlines these divisions. Inland Revenue figures for 1975 reveal that the wealthiest 1 per cent of the population owned 23.2 per cent of the total personal wealth; the top 5 per cent had a share of 46.5 per cent and the top 10 per cent a share of 62.4 per cent. By contrast, the bottom 80 per cent of the population of Britain owned only 23.8 per cent of the total wealth of the country. There is some evidence of a redistribution of wealth since 1960 but only from the top 1 per cent to the top 10 per cent.

Equally the distribution of personal income has grown just a little more egalitarian since 1959. Between that year and 1974–5 the share of the top income groups fell for the top 1 per cent from 8.4 per cent before tax to 6.2 per cent, with figures of 5.3 per cent and 4.0 per cent respectively after tax. The income share of the top 10 per cent of income earners fell from 29.4 per cent to 26.6 per cent before tax and from 25.2 per cent to 23.3 per cent after tax.

As much as 35.9 per cent of all privately owned land and 28.0 per cent of all privately owned listed ordinary shares are owned by no more than 0.15 per cent of the wealth owners who have estates worth over £200,000. This amounts to nearly half their total wealth. On top of this they owned 30.7 per cent of all other company securities and 24.6 per cent of listed UK government securities. During the late 1960s and the 1970s the proportion of shares owned by institutions – insurance companies, pension funds and unit trusts – rose from 20.9 per cent to 35.6 per cent, while the proportion of shares in the hands of individuals fell from 69 per cent to just under half. The top 10 per cent of earners derive 13.1 per cent of their incomes from investment, while the top one per cent gets 29.6 per cent of income from investment.

Labour's years in office from 1974–9 saw profitability of manufacturing industry rise substantially. In real terms industrial profits went up by over 50 per cent between 1975 and 1979. In 1975 gross trading profits after stock appreciation amounted to £7,295 million excluding the revenues from North Sea oil; by the third quarter of 1978 they had risen to £13,792 million (1975 index 100; by the third quarter of 1978 this was 189). These figures, compiled by Ruskin College Trade Union

Research Unit in January 1979, reveal that there was a profits recovery from just over £3,000 million in 1975 to over £8,500 million by the end of 1978 and the rate of return on capital went up from 3 per cent to nearly 6 per cent. As the unit argued: 'Even in the worst period of output slump and accelerating inflation the company sector earned a positive real rate of return and the improvement since then has been a steady and sustained one.' The more careful scrutiny of the Price Commission after 1977 did go some way to moderate the profits boom and the restraint has continued through the stabilization of the exchange rate and the inability to improve efficiency and output. Britain's economy is dominated by large concentrations of economic power in few hands. By the early 1970s the largest 100 quoted industrial and commercial companies accounted for over 64 per cent of the total net assets of all quoted industrial and commercial companies. In 1972 those top 100 firms in manufacturing shared 41 per cent of the net output in the entire sector. This compares with only 22 per cent in 1949.

As the May 1978 review of the monopolies and mergers policy for the government argued:

In 1972 the 100 largest firms in the manufacturing sector accounted for nearly two thirds of the net output of vehicles, around half the net output of food, drink and tobacco and of chemicals and around a third of the net output of engineering and electrical goods, of textiles, of bricks etc, of paper and printing, and publishing and of other manufacturing. The only sectors which still seem to be preserves of smaller concerns are leather, leather goods and fur, clothing and footwear, and timber and furniture.

By contrast during the 1960s and 1970s the small firm went into steep decline in most sectors, although there was a belated interest in their preservation and growth by 1978. These official statistics underline the indisputable fact that Britain is a country where differences of wealth, status and income remain substantial. When we read about the greed and power of the unions these facts need to be borne in mind. The social changes of the past twenty years have not done very much to alter the unequal balance of power between capital and labour, and long spells of Labour Government have made little impact on those fundamental features of our society.

Such facts are not being emphasized in order to make any partisan points, but when union leaders, shop stewards or just rank and file trade unionists are attacked in the press and by politicians for alleged selfishness and ruthless disregard of the needs of the community, we need to keep a sense of perspective. The values of our competitive, materialistic society remain acquisitive and pleas to 'fairness' by those with vast personal wealth and power over others are hollow and hypocritical.

My purpose is to provide a panoramic view of the British trade union movement as it looks to me, moving into the 1980s. In my judgement, our unions are a symptom of Britain's postwar decline, but remain far more the victims than the culprits of what foreigners like to call the 'British disease'.

Part one

Profile of the movement

1 The growth of the unions

In an unplanned, often *ad hoc* fashion, Britain's unions have grown rapidly over the past twenty years. Now well over half the workers in the country belong to a trade union. The old prejudices and obstacles to union recruitment have disappeared rapidly. The 'cloth cap' image has gone – thanks to what is one of the most dramatic expansions of British trade unionism since the early 1920s.

Strangely, this has happened during a period when the unions have become the chief scapegoats for national decline, portrayed as the cause of everything from labour inefficiency to a cultivation of envy against the rich, from threats to personal freedom to what some regard as a 'penal' level of direct taxation. Yet despite the anguished editorials about the brutish power of the unions, it has so far proved impossible to mobilize any strong anti-trade union organization with a popular following. Extreme assaults on free trade unionism still attract few backers. Objects of hatred and derision unions may have become in recent years, but such feelings do not appear to damage the rising membership figures that most unions have enjoyed since the mid-1960s. It looks as though millions of workers in Britain cannot do without the unions. They have become, not quaint anachronisms, but (in the eyes of many) welcome necessities.

How different it all looked in the 1950s. It was a worried TUC that debated the stagnation in union recruitment at the 1960 Congress. During the somnolent 1950s the movement had actually gone into decline. In 1950 there had been 44.1 per cent of the workforce in unions; ten years later the proportion was only 43.1 per cent. Back in 1952 there had been 8,029, 079 members in 183 affiliated unions. By 1960 there were only 8,299,393 members in exactly the same number of unions. Some union delegates expressed concern that trade unionism seemed to hold no attraction for the growing number of white-collar office staff entering the labour force. Unions like the National and Local Government Officers' Association (NALGO) and the National Union of Teachers (NUT) were still keeping clear of TUC affiliation. In 1960 a mere 16 per cent of TUC members (1,332,000) were categorized as belonging to the white-collar section of the labour market. No wonder Michael Shanks in his highly influential polemic of that time – *The Stagnant Society* (1961) – drew an unflattering portrait of the movement. In his view the unions had 'failed to adjust themselves to the changing patterns of industry and society'. Shanks went on to argue:

This gives them an increasingly dated 'period' flavour. The smell of the music hall and the pawnshop clings to them, and this more than anything else alienates the middle classes and the would-be middle classes from them. To be a trade unionist is to align oneself with those at the bottom of the social ladder at a time when the predominant urge is to climb it. In an age of social mobility – and social snobbery – the activities and still more the language and propaganda of trade unions seem increasingly anachronistic, dowdy, and 'unsmart'.

Shanks poked fun at the antique union structure and quoted John Osborne's anti-hero Archie Rice from the play *The Entertainer*: 'Don't laugh too loud, ladies and gentlemen: we're living in an old building.'

The picture was very different by the 1979 TUC, eighteen years on. Then just over half all the workers in Britain belonged to a union. The TUC affiliates were 12,128,078 in only 112 unions. Around a third of all trade unionists were classified as white-collar. Neither the Association of University Teachers (AUT) nor the Institution of Professional Civil Servants (IPCS) would have given a second thought to belonging to the TUC back in 1960, but they have taken their place among the ranks of organized labour. So has the First Division Association – the trade union for senior civil servants – in 1977. The social stigma of belonging to a union lost much of its real force in the Britain of the 1970s. On the contrary, to a growing number of people a trade union is seen as a necessary shelter from the arbitrary twists and turns of an economy in crisis, a protector of living standards, jobs and wages from the ravages of inflation and unemployment.

The recent expansion of trade unionism was sudden and rapid. Even as recently as 1968 only 43.1 per cent of workers were in unions, just over 10,000,000. During the mid-1960s there had even been a slight net decline in union strength, but then came the great leap forward as table 1.1 indicates.

table 1.1 Percentage of trade unionists in labour force, 1969–76

	Labour force	%	Trade unionists	%	% of unionists labour force
1969	23,603,000	−0.3	10,472,000	+2.7	44.4
1970	23,446,000	−0.7	11,179,000	+6.8	47.7
1971	23,231,000	−0.9	11,127,000	−0.5	47.9
1972	23,303,000	−0.3	11,349,000	+2.0	49.4
1973	23,592,000	+1.2	11,444,000	+0.8	49.2
1974	23,689,000	−0.4	11,755,000	−2.7	50.4
1975	23,339,000	+0.9	12,184,000	+3.6	51.7
1976	23,713,000	+0.7	12,376,000	+3.0	52.1

(*Department of Employment Gazettes*)

If you put those figures into a wider historical perspective, the late 1960s and early 1970s constitute one of the great periods of expansion for the British trade union movement, similar in magnitude to the growth between 1911 and 1913, in the early 1920s before the onset of the interwar depression and the 1940s. What is so remarkable about this recent explosion in trade unionism is that it took place during a time when British society had gone through a profound structural and occupational change, which at first sight might look antagonistic to the very purpose of the unions. Much to the understandable worry of many economists, Britain experienced a substantial growth in service employment and a relative decline in its manufacturing base during the 1960s and 1970s (see figure 1.1). In 1961 38.4 per cent of all workers had jobs in manufacturing industry; by 1974 that proportion had fallen to 34.6 per cent. Over the same period the numbers employed in finance, professional and scientific work rose from 12.6 per cent to 19.7 per cent of the workforce, while those working in public administration increased from 5.9 per cent to 7.0 per cent. There was actually a net fall in the number of workers in manufacturing industry. In 1960 there were 8,418,000 working in that sector; by 1974 the figure had dropped to 7,871,000 – around half a million less. By September 1978 there were 7,186,000 employed in manufacturing.

In many sectors where trade unionism was traditionally strong, the contraction in manpower was particularly sharp. The numbers employed in mining and quarrying dropped from 720,000 in 1961 to 334,700 in 1978. The fall in industrial workers in coal was as much as 49 per cent in the decade from 1964 to 1974 (531,000 to 271,447). A similar decline also took place on the railways over the same period, particularly after the Beeching Report in 1963. The labour force there fell from 422,167 in 1964 to 210,200 by 1978.

Such a severe rundown decimated the one-time giants of the TUC. In 1960 the National Union of Mineworkers with 638,988 members was the fourth biggest union in the TUC; by 1979 it had 254,887 members and had fallen to tenth position among the TUC affiliates. Back in 1960 the National Union of Railwaymen had 333,844 members and it was the sixth largest in the TUC; by 1979 it had shrunk to only 180,000 members and thirteenth position.

Textiles has also experienced a sharp fall in its manpower figures since the Second World War. In 1948 just over a million worked in that sector; by 1978 the number was 460,600. The contraction in the workforce in clothing and footwear has been less drastic in the post-war period. In 1948 there were 116,000 workers in footwear; by 1978 the figure had dropped to 74,600. Over that same time-span the number working in clothing fell from 498,000 to 288,300. The biggest single decline has come among workers on the land. In 1948 as many as 868,000 people still had jobs in agriculture; by 1978 that number had been more than halved to 369,200. The size of the National Union of Agricultural Workers shrank correspondingly from 135,000 in 1959 to 85,000 in 1979 (and this was probably an over-estimate).

The decline in manpower also hit other industrial sectors, which still remain buoyant and central to the British economy. In the gas industry, for instance, the workforce dropped between 1964 and 1978 from 123,119 to 103,700. The number of electricity supply workers also fell over that period from 210,403 to 177,500. The data in the Earnings Surveys underline

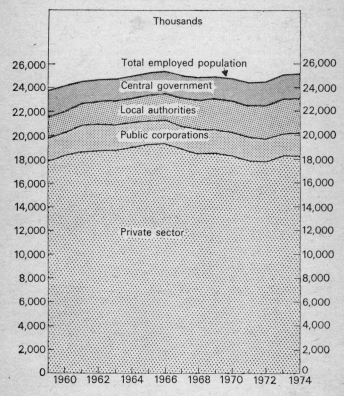

figure 1.1 Sector jobs in the UK, 1960–74 (*Economic Trends*, 1976)

the fall in the total size of the manual labour force. In 1964 there were 8,285,000 workers in the manufacturing sector; ten years later the figure was down to 7,186,600 – and it is still dropping.

table 1.2 Britain's changing occupations in the 1970s

	Industry	Employment (1,000s)			
		1970	1976	Change 1970-6	Change as % of 1970
1	Agriculture	778.9	647.0	−131.9	−16.9
2	Mining	410.9	347.9	−63.0	−15.3
3	Food, drink and tobacco	803.5	721.1	−82.4	−10.2
4	Chemicals	493.6	460.7	−32.9	−6.6
5	Metals	595.3	470.6	−124.7	−20.9
6	Engineering	3,772.2	3,299.4	−472.8	−12.5
7	Textile and clothing	1,215.8	957.8	−258.0	−21.2
8	Other manufactures	1,619.5	1,459.9	−159.6	−9.8
9	Construction	1,637.9	1,794.1	156.2	9.5
10	Public utilities	390.1	353.0	−37.1	−9.5
11	Transport and communications	1,640.5	1,557.2	−83.3	−5.1
12	Distribution	3,150.7	3,130.6	−20.1	−0.6
13	Professional services	1,483.3	1,708.6	225.3	15.2
14	Miscellaneous services	2,298.0	2,579.8	281.8	12.3
15	Social services	2,906.4	3,508.7	602.3	20.7
16	Public administration	1,852.0	1,962.4	110.4	6.0
	Manufacturing	8,499.9	7,369.5	−1,130.4	−13.2
	[1]All industries	20,290.2	19,487.7	−802.5	−3.9

(*Department of Employment Gazettes*)
[1] excludes social services and public administration

Occupational employment

		Employment (1,000s)			
		1971	1976	Change 1971-6	Change as % of 1971
1	Administrators and managers	939	1,075	136	14.5
2–3	Scientists, technologists and engineers	399	472	73	18.3
4	Education professions	761	836	75	9.8
5	Health and social service professions	727	890	163	22.4
6	Other professions	446	511	65	14.6
7	Technicians and draughtsmen	360	402	42	11.7
8	Clerical and secretarial workers	3,481	3,795	314	9.0
	All non-manual occupations	10,736	11,822	1,086	10.1
	(% total employment)	(44.2)	(48.0)		
	All manual occupations	13,540	12,799	−741	−5.5
	Whole economy	24,276	24,621	345	1.4

(*TUC Economic Review*, 1979)

If the numbers in manual work are in decline, trade unionism has extended its membership through the manual labour force at a much greater rate in recent years. In 1964, 52.7 per cent of manual workers belonged to unions, in 1970 the proportion had risen to 56.0 per cent and by 1974 it reached 57.8 per cent.

As Professor Bain and Robert Price argue: 'The level of manual union density achieved in 1974 has only been equalled once before, in 1920 at the height of the short-lived boom in union membership following the end of World War I.' The overall figures indicate the union achievement. Over the 1964–74 period there was a decline of 1,600,000 in the size of the manual labour force, but the number of manual trade unionists fell only marginally from 7,534,000 to 7,491,000. Trade union density has improved in every industrial sector. In 1948 84.1 per cent of workers in the coal industry were unionized; by 1974 the proportion was 96.2 per cent. On the railways the trade union penetration went up from 88.1 per cent to 96.9 per

table 1.3 Union density in selected sectors of the economy, 1948 and 1974

	1948		%	1974		%
	Labour force (1,000s)	Union members (1,000s)	Density	Labour force (1,000s)	Union members (1,000s)	Density
Chemicals	426.8	127.3	29.8	433.6	247.4	51.2
Metals and engineering	3,676.1	1,837.5	50.0	4,118.0	2,862.7	69.4
Glass	68.1	28.2	41.3	74.5	58.5	78.5
Pottery	75.3	31.3	41.5	60.5	56.8	93.8
Paper, printing and publishing	455.5	264.1	58.0	596.1	426.6	71.6

(G. S. Bain and R. Price, 'Union Growth Revisited 1948–76', *British Journal of Industrial Relations*, November 1976)

cent over the same time-span. In road transport the spread of union density was even more impressive, up from 60.1 per cent to 95.1 per cent over the period. Even in footwear there was improvement, up from 66.6 per cent of workers to 79.0 per cent between 1948 and 1974. In less stagnant sectors the growth of union penetration was substantial, as table 1.4 shows.

In sectors of the economy which are the most difficult for

trade unions to organize, the post-war years have brought either decline or stagnation. The most serious setbacks occurred in the construction industry. In 1948 as many as 45.3 per cent of the 1,353,700 workers in that sector were unionized (613,200); by 1974 the proportion had dropped back to a mere 27.2 per cent (388,100 out of 1,428,800). It is perhaps no coincidence that the most badly unionized part of the workforce took the full force of the Labour Government's public expenditure cuts in 1975 and 1976, when as many as 250,000 construction workers were reckoned to be jobless. Over the same period, distribution has remained hard to organize and the decline in the size of the Co-operative movement added to difficulties. In 1948, 325,300 out of the 2,167,900 in that sector were unionized (15.0 per cent); by 1974 the number was 321,000 out of 2,810,100 (11.4 per cent).

In the late 1960s the unions faced the grim prospect of real decline. If trade union membership in Britain was not to be pushed steadily downwards as a proportion of the employed labour force, the unions had to rapidly expand their unionization among white-collar workers. This is what happened and the process was aided by the mushroom growth of the public service sector of the economy, where collective bargaining was already well developed.

The total number of workers in the public sector grew only from 24.2 per cent of the country's labour force in 1960 to 29.8 per cent by 1978 (up from 5,843,000 to 7,400,000). The run-down in the older nationalized industries like coal and the railways accounts for that perhaps surprising statistic. In 1960 there were 1,865,000 workers in public corporations (7.7 per cent of the labour force); by 1977 the numbers were 2,089,000 (and the same proportion of the labour force). The re-nationalization of the iron and steel industry in 1967 brought a substantial increase in the size of the public sector workforce to offset the decline in other industries as did the public ownership of aerospace and shipbuilding in 1978.

But where the massive expansion took place was in the public services. Local government enjoyed the biggest increase – up from 1,821,000 workers in 1960 (7.5 per cent of the labour force) to 3,000,000 by 1978 (12.1 per cent). Between 1959 and 1973 there was an annual average increase of 80,000 workers on the payrolls of local councils. Such global totals are slightly misleading. A large proportion of the new recruits were women, working part-time as cleaners and secretaries. The numbers in local authority education services also rose at a massive rate – up between 1961 and 1978 from 785,000 to 1,561,000. The medical and dental service recorded a similar manpower explosion, with a rise from 930,000 in 1966 to 1,155,000 in 1978. Whatever the causes for the growth in the public services, it helped a number of trade unions to expand at a rapid rate.

The public sector service union with the largest growth was the Confederation of Health Service Employees (COHSE). In 1964 it claimed a mere 64,000 members; by 1979 that figure had shot up to 215,033. The National Union of Public Employees (NUPE) also enjoyed a phenomenal expansion in its local government and hospital ancillary manual worker membership over the same period. In 1964 that union had 240,000 members; by 1979 it was claiming to have as many as 712,000 members. Back in 1960 NUPE was the eighth biggest member of the TUC; by 1977 it had become the fourth. The National and Local Government Officers' Association (NALGO) also grew with the burgeoning of public service jobs. In 1964 – the year the union joined the TUC – NALGO boasted 338,300 members. Fifteen years later its rank and file numbered around 729,000.

The growth of jobs in the central government machine over the period was far less drastic than at council level, although the separation of the Post Office from the civil service in 1969 (when it was reborn as a public corporation) make exact statistical comparison difficult. Between 1961 and 1973 an extra 34,000 civil servants were recruited, with a net increase of 116,000 over the period in non-industrial employees being partly offset by a fall of 82,000 industrials. In the late 1970s some cutbacks occurred. The civil service unions grew correspondingly. The Civil and Public Services' Association (CPSA), whose recruitment base is essentially among the clerical grades of central government, mushroomed from 146,300 members in 1964 to 224,780 in 1979, while the Institution of Professional Civil Servants (IPCS) rose over the same period from 55,100 to 99,051.

In these areas, there was active encouragement from the

employers for workers to join an appropriate and recognized trade union, as well as an established tradition of collective bargaining machinery. Union growth in white-collar staffs in the private sector was far more difficult to achieve. Yet the expansion in employment there was just as impressive as that in the public services. Between 1964 and 1978 the numbers working in insurance, banking and finance went up from 771,000 to 1,154,100. There was a similar growth in those working for the banks – up from 209,000 to 333,400 over the same period. The vague category of 'other business services' (eg people involved in duplicating, photocopying and computer work) rose from 102,000 to 242,100 over those years. Even workers in betting and gambling went up from 70,000 to 107,200 – doubtless due in part to the rise of bingo as a mass entertainment.

One general white-collar union – the Association of Scientific, Technical and Managerial Staffs (ASTMS) – was a major agent of private white-collar growth. In 1964 ASSET (as it was then called) claimed 72,800 members; by 1979 the union (thanks partly to mergers as well as recruitment drives) boasted 471,000 members and it had become the eighth largest in the TUC. The Banking, Insurance and Finance Union (BIFU, formerly NUBE) also enjoyed an increase in its membership from 56,300 in 1964 to 116,730 in 1978.

Between 1948 and 1964 white-collar union membership failed to keep pace with the growth of employment in that sector. White-collar union density fell from 30.8 per cent in 1948 to 28.4 per cent in 1964. But over the next seven years total white-collar union membership suddenly moved upwards by 33.8 per cent, while in the next four years it had a further increase of 18.7 per cent. By 1974, 36 per cent of all trade unionists in the TUC were white-collar workers, compared with 26 per cent a decade earlier. Part of that expansion took place among salaried workers in manufacturing industry (32 per cent in unions by 1974). The Association of Professional, Executive, Clerical and Computer Staffs (APEX), whose members are mainly recruited from the engineering industry, rose from 79,200 members to just over 150,000 between 1964 and 1979, while the Technical, Administrative and Supervisory section (TASS) of the Engineers went up over the same period from 65,900 to 200,954.

table 1.4 The big unions: how they grew or shrank (1,000s) 1964–74

	Male			Female			Total		
	1964	1974	% change	1964	1974	% change	1964	1975	% change
Transport and General Workers' Union[1]	(1311.4)	1547.1	+18.0	(205.7)	279.7	+36.0	(1517.1)	1,856,165	+20.4
Amalgamated Union of Engineering Workers (Engineering section)	921.1	1022.5	+11.0	89.8	168.5	+87.7	1010.9	1191.0	+17.8
General and Municipal Workers' Union	597.8	598.5	+0.1	186.7	285.4	+52.8	784.5	883.8	+12.7
National and Local Government Officers' Association	214.9	323.8	+50.7	123.4	218.1	+76.7	338.3	541.9	+60.2
National Union of Public Employees	123.0	186.5	+51.6	117.0	321.3	+174.6	240.0	507.8	+111.6
Electrical, Electronic, Telecommunications and Plumbing Union[2]	(312.4)	361.3	+15.6	(24.2)	52.5	+116.8	(336.6)	413.8	+22.9
National Union of Mineworkers	479.1	371.7	−32.4	—	4.1	—	479.1	375.8	−31.6
Union of Shop, Distributive and Allied Workers	185.6	148.7	−19.9	166.4	204.0	+22.6	351.9	352.6	+0.2
Association of Scientific, Technical and Managerial Staffs[3]	(61.9)	277.3	+348.1	(10.9)	47.7	+339.5	(72.8)	325.1	+346.8
National Union of Teachers	82.0	68.6	−16.3	167.0	198.1	+18.6	249.0	266.7	+7.1

table 1.4 The big unions: how they grew or shrank (1,000s) 1964–74

	Male			Female			Total		
	1964	1974	% change	1964	1974	% change	1964	1975	% change
Union of Construction, Allied Trades and Technicians[4]	(361.9)	244.3	−32.5	2.2	2.6	+17.1	364.1	251.8	−30.8
Civil and Public Services' Association	60.5	69.0	+14.0	85.9	145.5	+69.4	146.3	214.4	+46.5
Society of Graphical and Allied Trades	104.3	123.9	+18.8	67.9	69.9	+3.0	172.2	193.8	+12.6
Union of Post Office Workers	137.0	147.7	+7.8	44.8	42.3	−5.5	181.8	190.0	+4.5
National Union of Railwaymen	255.9	165.9	−35.1	7.8	6.6	−14.9	263.6	172.6	−34.5
Confederation of Health Service Employees	30.5	43.4	+42.2	33.5	101.0	+201.3	64.0	167.7	+125.5
Association of Professional, Executive, Clerical and Computer Staffs	41.5	67.0	+61.6	37.7	70.0	+85.7	79.2	132.0	+73.0
Post Office Engineering Union	86.1	123.3	+43.2	0.8	3.8	+402.9	86.9	127.1	+46.3
Amalgamated Society of Boilermakers	119.4	126.8	+6.2	0.1	0.2	+42.7	119.5	127.0	+6.3
Amalgamated Union of Engineering Workers (TASS)	63.1	116.0	+84.0	2.8	9.6	+240.3	65.9	125.6	+90.7
Iron and Steel Trades Confederation	110.1	112.0	+1.7	4.3	8.2	+91.7	114.4	120.3	+5.1

National Union of Tailoring and Garment Workers	19.6	14.0	−28.5	91.6	99.3	+8.5	111.2	113.4	+1.9
National Graphical Association	84.6	105.7	+25.0	0.1	1.1	+2236.9	84.6	106.8	+26.2
National Union of Bank Employees	36.3	55.8	+54.0	20.0	44.4	+122.4	56.2	100.2	+78.3
Institution of Professional Civil Servants	53.1	94.8	+78.4	2.0	4.4	+122.2	55.1	99.2	+79.9

[1] 1964 figures include membership of the National Union of Vehicle Builders and the Chemical Workers' Union

[2] 1964 figures include membership of the Electrical Trades' Union and the Plumbing Trade Union

[3] 1964 figures include membership of the Association of Scientific Workers, the Association of Supervisory Staffs, Executives and Technicians, and the Guild of Insurance Officials

[4] 1964 figures include membership of the AUBTW, ABT, ASPD, Operative Plasterers and ASW

(Internal Teaching Aid, University of Warwick 1975)

Yet these statistics (summarized in table 1.4) should blind nobody to the severe difficulties unions are going to experience in the years ahead, increasing their penetration to the white-collar private sector, where trade union traditions and practices are still largely unknown. It was estimated in 1978 that no more than around 20 per cent of the salariat in the private sector belonged to a trade union. Where the major expansion has come from is in public services, but well over 85 per cent of those now belong to bona fide unions, and there is no prospect of any numerical expansion in that sector in the near future.

A major growth area over the past decade for trade unionism has been among women workers. In 1966 there were 2,256,000 women trade unionists, 22 per cent of all members; by 1976 the number had risen to 3,560,000, 28.8 per cent of trade unionists. While male membership rose by 10 per cent or 800,000 during that decade, female membership shot up by 58 per cent or 1,300,000. Women at work now make up 40 per cent of the total workforce (8,881,000). They outnumber men in teaching, nursing and social work, catering and distribution, banking and insurance. Of all women workers, just under a quarter have jobs in the professional and scientific sector, while a further 17.1 per cent are in the distributive trades and a further 11.7 per cent in what are described as miscellaneous trades such as hairdressing, and waitress service. The number of married women going out to work has risen from 10 per cent in 1931 to as high as 42 per cent in 1971. The figure will go on increasing further in the years ahead, as a result of social change and the pressure of economic forces. As many as 30 per cent of all working women have part-time jobs of less than 30 hours a week (3,420,000 women). In March 1978 there were just over half a million part-time women workers in manufacturing industry. A total of 40 per cent of them worked in food processing.

The present recession has hit female employment especially hard. While the number of registered male unemployed rose by 9 per cent between January 1976 and January 1978, there was a huge 53 per cent increase in the number of women registered jobless over the same period. In January 1978 women made up 28 per cent of Britain's registered unemployed. As many women seeking work do not register, the numbers untable 1.5 Where the women trade unionists are, 1977

Union	% of women members	Total women membership
Tailor and Garment Workers	88.9	100,228
Health Service Employees	74.7	149,655
National Union of Teachers	74.1	214,101
Civil and Public Services' Association	69.5	160,142
National Union of Public Employees	66.6	433,650
Union of Shop, Distributive and Allied Workers	60.7	250,508
Association of Professional, Executive, Clerical and Computer Staffs	55.3	78,315
National Union of Bank Employees	46.6	52,017
National and Local Government Officers' Association	43.6	297,973
Society of Graphical and Allied Trades	33.6	65,213

(*TUC Report*, 1977)

employed are much higher than official statistics suggest.

The unions have managed to increase their strength among the female labour force in recent years, and now nearly half full-time women workers belong to a trade union. Table 1.5 reveals just how important women have become to the organizational growth of many unions.

The big general unions have a smaller proportion of women members in their ranks. In the Transport and General Workers' (TGWU) only 15.8 per cent (305,037) of the members are women, while in the General and Municipal Workers' (GMWU) the proportion is higher at 34.3 per cent (314,272).

Surprisingly, the unions have recently also managed to recruit a sizeable number of black workers. Nearly 60 per cent of the 600,000 black labour force now belong to a union, according to a PEP survey published in February 1976 (*The Facts of Racial Disadvantage* by David J. Smith). A third of the black trade unionists belong to the TGWU, 13 per cent to the AUEW, 5 per cent to the GMWU and 4 per cent to the National Union of Railwaymen. As Smith writes:

Asians and West Indians, half of whom arrived in Britain within the past ten years, from countries having a different framework of industrial relations, have been readier than the white population to put their trust in the trade union movement.

The statistics on trade union growth reflect a complex picture. At a time of radical change in the structure of the British economy, the unions as a whole succeed not merely in holding their own, but in actually making a substantial advance in recruitment. This took place in the teeth of a net decline in the number of manual workers in manufacturing industry and a rapid expansion in the size of the white-collar labour force in both private and public service sectors – areas hitherto antagonistic to trade union ideas.

What are the reasons for the growing attractiveness of belonging to a trade union? Robert Bacon and Walter Eltis, in their influential book *Britain's Economic Problem: Too Few Producers* (London, 1976), argue the answer lies in the widespread belief of many workers that the protection of a trade union is needed to face rising direct taxation. As they explain:

What has happened since 1963 is that all too often those who sought higher living standards, or the mere continuation of car and home ownership (which have risen in cost far more than prices in general) found that they could only obtain these by making full use of their trade union power, with the result that ordinary workers turned to aggressive union leaders to produce results.

It is the massive increase in income tax on the average wage-earner which has helped to transform attitudes. In 1955 a married couple with two children with the father on an average wage could expect to pay only 3.3 per cent in tax. By 1975 that proportion had risen to a crippling 25 per cent. Even with four children to support, the average manual worker pays more than 20 per cent of his income in state deductions, compared with 2.5 per cent twenty-five years ago. George Bain and Farouk Elsheikh, in *Union Growth and the Business Cycle* (Oxford, 1976), believe the explanation of recent union growth lies primarily in the impact of rapidly rising prices and wages. In particular, they argue that this is why there was a 'membership explosion' in 1969–70.

Price rises generally have a positive impact upon union growth because of the 'threat effect' – the tendency of workers to unionize in an attempt to defend their standard of living against the threat posed by rising prices – and wage rises will have a similar impact because of the 'credit effect' – the tendency of workers to credit wage rises to unions and to support them in the hope of doing well or even better in the future.

The causal connection between the rate of price increases and the pace of change in the level of wages is seen as the key determinant in all the upsurges in union recruitment since the early 1890s.

Such an explanation looks highly plausible. Bain and El-sheikh argue that after the price level has risen over 4.0 per cent, its impact on the rate of increase in union membership continues, but at a much lower rate. So although the average annual rate of price inflation was twice as high in 1971–4 as it was in 1969–70, its impact on union expansion was not twice as great. The overwhelming empirical evidence supports the view that most people join trade unions to either safeguard or improve their wages and fringe benefits. In the eyes of union members this is what their primary function is and if the unions fail to deliver the goods, they will fall into inevitable decline. The unions are involved in what sociologists call 'instrumental bargaining'. David Lockwood and his colleagues found this was true when they surveyed Vauxhall car workers in Luton in the 1960s. As they wrote:

It is evident that in the eyes of our semi-skilled workers, the unionism of the workplace is very largely dissociated from what they regard as the official activity of the unions to which they happen to belong. That unionism should have little significance for them other than in relation to the immediate 'bread and butter' issues of their own work situation is entirely consistent with their definition of work as primarily a means to extrinsic ends : their main interest in the union, as in the firm, is that of the 'pay off'. Unionism in the style of these workers can be usefully described as 'instrumental collectivism' – collectivism which is directed to the achievement of individuals' private goals, outside the workplace.

During a period of economic stress, it is not surprising that more people at work should value belonging to a trade union as a form of protection. But another reason for that great leap forward of the unions lies in the upsurge of labour militancy between 1969 and 1974. During the late 1960s, as a result of a statutory incomes policy the net real income, of manual workers in particular, hardly rose at all. Between 1964 and 1968 the increase was a mere 0.5 per cent, though prices went up by 4.1 per cent. In the view of H. A. Turner and F. Wilkinson, 'the sharp increase in the British strike-incidence was a response to the stagnation of net real wages'. The wage explosion of 1969–70 was caused by 'frustrated – but perhaps not altogether unjustifiable – expectations'.

Up until the publication of the Donovan Royal Commission Report in 1968, the British 'disease' of strikes was essentially concentrated in the incidence of short, sharp unofficial stoppages confined to a few sectors of the workforce. Over the 1964–6 period there were 2,272 strikes involving 757,800 workers and resulting in 2,452,000 working days lost. As many as 95 per cent of those disputes were not recognized by the unions as official. The typical strike of the mid-1960s involved 300 workers and resulted in loss of production for a little over 2.5 days. Moreover strikes were primarily confined to coal mining, shipbuilding and motor car production. Pay was not usually the burning issue in those strikes. Between 1960 and 1963 'wage claims' formed only one-third of all the reasons for disputes and only 36 per cent between 1964 and 1967.

But during the late 1960s and early 1970s the pattern and nature of strikes changed significantly.

While the number of short strikes began to drop, the number of national and official confrontations in the public sector rose sharply. Between 1964 and 1966, for every official strike, backed by the union, there were thirty unofficial ones without union blessing. By 1971 that ratio had fallen to one in twelve and it dropped further still in 1972 and 1973. In the early 1970s the strike frequency and the number of strikes were nearly double the average at the time of the Donovan Royal Commission Report. The 1972 national coal strike caused the loss of more working days than all 8,931 stoppages that took place during the four years of the Donovan era (1964–8). This is not the place to examine the causes of the change in the pattern of strike activity during the period, but there seems little doubt that labour militancy and the victories won, particularly by groups of workers in the public sector between 1969

table 1.6 Strikes in the UK 1965–78

Number	Number of stoppages	Number of workers involved All industries and services Directly	Indirectly	Total	Number of working days lost
		000s	000s	000s	000s
1965	2,354	673	195	868	2,925
1966	1,937	414	116	530	2,398
1967	2,116	551	180	731	2,787
1968	2,378	2,073	182	2,255	4,690
1969	3,116	1,426	228	1,654	6,846
1970	3,906	1,460	333	1,793	10,980
1971	2,228	863	308	1,171	13,551
1972	2,497	1,448	274	1,722	23,909
1973	2,873	1,103	410	1,513	7,197
1974	2,922	1,161	461	1,622	14,750
1975	2,282	570	219	789	6,012
1976	2,016	444	222	668	3,284
1977	2,703	750	370	1,166	10,142
1978	2,349	665	274	979	9,306

(*Department of Employment Gazette*, January 1979)

and 1974, helped to widen the appeal of trade unionism for many thousands who had kept clear of any previous union involvement. Strikes can prove effective recruiting agents in sectors where trade union consciousness has been weak in the past.

In areas of low pay like local government manual work and hospital ancillary services, the radical and aggressive tactics of NUPE were an undoubted help in the massive rise in membership of that union. The solidarity achieved in a stoppage often assists the spread of trade unionism. On the other hand, the militant strategy of the AUEW to oppose the 1971 Industrial Relations Act by industrial action rebounded to the disadvantage of the union, with many hundreds of engineering workers defying union strike calls and falling into arrears in their membership dues. The strike upsurge after 1969 cannot be ignored as a factor in explaining the sudden growth in union recruitment. Whether it was a cause or an effect remains debatable. Although strikes are seen as an integral part of the

British 'disease' in the eyes of foreign observers, they are very atypical in industry. The Department of Employment estimated in a 1976 study of strikes that as many as 98 per cent of all plants in manufacturing industry – representing 80 per cent of employment – were strike-free in any one year. On the other hand, that remaining 2 per cent does contain a much higher level of unionization. But are unions as such the cause of strikes? Certainly most workers involved in stoppages are trade unionists. The 1978 Department of Employment study revealed that although non-unionists made up just over half the working population on average during the period of their investigations between 1966 and 1973, only 3 per cent of them went on strike. Almost 75 per cent of strikes on average over that period involved members of only one trade union. In an average year 87 per cent of unions had no members at all involved in strikes, but then we must remember 80 per cent of unions have less than 10,000 members. During the 1966 period members of only nine unions were involved in around 90 per cent of the strikes, although those unions accounted for less than 60 per cent of total union membership. Six unions, that on average accounted for about half of trade union membership, were involved in about 80 per cent of the stoppages. But the 1978 study did suggest that the number of unions involved in strikes was growing from the late 1960s onwards. In 1966 it found that members of 57 out of 616 unions (9 per cent) were involved in at least one strike; by 1970 the figure had risen to 89 out of 532 (17 per cent). There were 52 unions involved in strikes between 1970 and 1973 that had not had any stoppages between 1966–9, and as many as 26 of them were white-collar and professional unions. These figures confirm the growth of white-collar militancy during the 1970s and it is a phenomenon we are likely to see in much evidence during the next decade.

Yet despite this undoubted trend, the vast majority of strikes involve manual workers in a relatively small number of sectors of the economy. At least a quarter of the stoppages and a third of the working days lost as a result occur in five areas – coal mining, the docks, car manufacture, shipbuilding and iron and steel. Yet only six per cent of the entire workforce have jobs in those industries. Strikes are also concentrated in the large plants. In an average year only 2 per cent of plants employing 20 per cent of the manufacturing workforce are hit by stoppages. During the 1971–3 period eight out of ten workers in manufacturing worked in plants experiencing no strikes. There were only 15 days lost per 1,000 employees per year in plants employing from 11 to 24 workers compared to 3,708 in plants employing more than 5,000 workers.

It is hard to correlate union growth with militancy, but the 1978 Department of Employment study suggests the image of strike-prone Britain is a severe exaggeration. By international standards Britain ranks no more than sixth or seventh among western democratic countries, far behind the United States, Canada, Italy and Australia. But there are few signs that the strikes that occurred during the late 1960s and the 1970s were due to wider issues beyond the size of the pay packet. The fashionable talk of the academic sociologists about a revolt of the western workers against the capitalist system is far from the reality. As the 1978 survey states:

Data for the period 1966–76 shows that 56 per cent of stoppages and 82 per cent of working days lost concerned pay. Pay is the dominating issue as it has been since the recording of strikes began. Directly economic issues are involved in more than 80 per cent of stoppages and 90 per cent of man days lost, which is perhaps unsurprising since the cost of a strike to the striker is often considerable.

Surprisingly only 11.8 per cent of stoppages between 1966 and 1973 were about manning and work allocation; 11.9 per cent over dismissal and other disciplinary measures; 6.3 per cent about working conditions and supervision and a mere 3.8 per cent over redundancies. In as many as 88 per cent of all industrial stoppages officially recorded over the 1966–73 period the participants gave one clear-cut reason for taking strike action, usually the demand for more money. This is as it should be, because today's unions are concerned with improving pay and fringe benefits, not attacking the political and social system.

The 1978 survey on workplace industrial relations in manufacturing industry, carried out by Industrial Facts and Forecasting Ltd (IFF) for the Warwick University Industrial Relations Research Unit, suggests that forms of industrial action like work to rules, overtime bans etc are much more common among manual workers than the overall strike statistics might suggest. It is important to remember that the stoppage figures do not include disputes including 10 workers or less, those that last less than a day except when the aggregate of working days lost exceeds 100, or workers who are employed in other establishments than the one where the stoppage actually takes place. The figures in the Department of Employment data exclude workers laid off and working days lost at other plants where shortages of materials due to stoppages have occurred and hit production. Nearly a third of the plants in the IFF survey had experienced a strike by manual workers between 1976 and 1978, while 46 per cent of establishments experienced some form of industrial action. The bigger the plant, the more strike prone the workforce. The interim report of IFF said that while, 'perhaps surprisingly, the density of trade union membership seems to have little effect on the proportion of establishments experiencing industrial action' the existence of shop stewards had an appreciable impact on other forms of industrial action short of strikes. The study concluded: 'Although it may be true that the "strike problem" in terms of total days lost is concentrated in a few plants, the findings of the survey suggest that the use of some form of industrial action is remarkably widespread.'

Recent union growth was also helped by the growing concentration of companies and the decline of smaller workplace units. The larger the establishment, the more likely it is to be unionized. As John Hughes has argued in a 1976 Ruskin College Trade Union Research Unit paper: 'British capitalism has helped forward the more complete unionization of the labour force more than it can possibly understand.' The successive waves of take-overs, mergers and subsequent rationalization that took place during the late 1960s and early 1970s helped to create the conditions for union growth. Not only did the existence of the larger combines encourage union expansion, but the growth of the big monopolies made belonging to a trade union look more attractive. It seemed that the days of paternalist capitalism had gone for ever and the only real defence against deepening insecurity was trade union membership. The Donovan Commission discovered in a survey of the workplace that 63 per cent of the trade unionists in the sample worked in establishments with 100 or more workers, while as many as 64 per cent of those who worked and did not belong to a trade union had jobs in establishments with less than 100 workers.

The 1977 Bullock Report on industrial democracy reckoned over 7,000,000 people in Britain, more than a quarter of the entire workforce, were working for large firms in the public sector (defined as *The Times 1000* major enterprises). Twenty companies had over 50,000 workers on their payrolls, accounting for just over 2,000,000 people. Bullock claimed that over 70 per cent of the labour force in firms with over 2,000 on their payrolls belonged to recognized, independent unions. In smaller enterprises in maufacturing with under 2,000 workers, Bullock estimated the unionized labour force was no more than 20 per cent. Union expansion over the past twenty years has undoubtedly been assisted by the growing concentration of economic power in fewer and fewer hands.

Critics of the unions argue that recent union growth has not always been a voluntary one. There is widespread talk of moral – even physical – coercion being used against difficult people who wish to stay outside a union. Here the closed-shop bogey is raised as a real menace. In the words of Paul Johnson: 'The compulsory enforcement of the closed shop by parliamentary statute is the greatest disaster which has befallen liberty in my lifetime.' The Trade Union and Labour Relations Acts of 1974 and 1976 have certainly given statutory support to the closed-shop idea. In the past, unions have been tolerant of individuals who, for some personal reason, did not wish to join a union when the rest of their colleagues in the workplace had done so. But there are signs that such a liberal attitude is disappearing. What used to be implied or treated in a flexible, understanding manner, has become far more explicit and precise. Employers – particularly in the public sector – have written post-entry closed-shop clauses into their collective agreements with unions. Anybody who joins the company must agree to join a recognized trade union, unless he can prove that deeply held religious convictions make it impossible. A number of unfortunate cases have come to light where individual workers appear to have suffered acts of injustice. The most famous were the Ferrybridge Six, who lost their jobs in the Central

Electricity Generating Board for refusing to join a recognized trade union. Loud complaints were also brought against British Rail in 1976. Railway workers were dismissed for refusing to join an appropriate trade union. The SLADE art union – a section of SLADE – claimed its members had been driven into trade unionism by coercive tactics with threats of loss of work in the photographic art world by SLADE.

Such cases arouse much public anger against unions, but the closed-shop arguments are more evenly divided than the critics appreciate. Indeed, the major drive for 100 per cent trade unionism at the workplace owes much to an employer initiative. It is not hard to see why many managers are willing to enforce closed-shop agreements on their workforce. As Brian Weekes has written:

A manager who accepts the need for collective regulation wants to negotiate with unions who fully represent the work groups for whom they have recognition. There is also the pressure of status quo conservatism and a desire to retain existing arrangements. Managers on the whole prefer familiar and predictable situations, hence the disruption of existing closed-shop arrangements was not welcome. (*Industrial Relations and the Limits of Law*, 1975)

A Warwick University study found that during the years of the Industrial Relations Act from 1971 to 1974, 'employers defended the closed shop almost as tenaciously as did the workers'. The survey reckoned that 40 per cent of all workers in Britain in unions were in closed shops, a figure very similar to that found by Lord McCarthy in his pioneering study of the closed shop published in 1964. A closed shop is a very important way of avoiding the fragmentation associated with multi-union bargaining. Most large employers have been reluctant to encourage a diffusion of different, competing unions in their plants with all the potential conflict and rivalry that would ensue. Weekes gives other good employer reasons for backing the closed shop:

Generally managers in large companies, reared in a collectivist ethos, have little or no sympathy with the 'unprincipled free rider' who takes the benefits of union membership without paying union dues. In many workplaces the 'free rider' could be a nuisance, with some trade unionists refusing to work with him, and on occasions this could lead to a strike or other forms of industrial action.

Since 1974 there has been a dramatic extension of the closed shop in manufacturing industry. Industrial Facts and Forecasting Ltd carried out a survey in 1978 for the industrial relations unit of the Social Science Research Council at Warwick University, which found that 46 per cent of manual workers and 13 per cent of non-manuals in nearly 1,000 establishments with 50 employees or more in the manufacturing sector were covered by formal closed-shop agreements. This amounts to 37 per cent of the non-managerial workforce in manufacturing. About 40 per cent of the closed-shop agreements in the survey had been introduced between 1974 and 1978.

The critics of the closed shop argue that its growth has stemmed from the arrogant expansion of trade union power, but this is not the case. The main reason lies in the state of the law. Up until the passage of the 1971 Industrial Relations Act the practice of the closed shop was hardly touched by the legal system. Agreements were usually informal and flexible, reflecting a union tolerance for the individual who disliked joining a union. But section seven of the 1971 Act declared such agreements null and void, and attempted to provide legislative rights for people not to belong to a trade union. At the same time, the Act made provision for a redress of grievance to a worker who was unfairly dismissed by his employer. The unions were anxious to preserve that right under the law, while they sought the repeal of the 1971 measure. As Weekes has written: 'Many managers and trade unionists hoped that the repeal of the Industrial Relations Act would allow the closed shop to return to the more relaxed regime of the pre-1971 period. However once the problem of reconciling unfair dismissal rights with the closed shop became apparent, it became clear that the old-style closed shop was bound to cause legal difficulties.' The 1974 Trade Union and Labour Relations Act exempted employers from penalties for unfair dismissal when in upholding a closed-shop arrangement, they dismissed non-unionists. The 1976 case of the Ferrybridge Six led to an interpretation of the law by an industrial tribunal that meant the imposition of a precise, tightly drawn closed-shop agreement necessary to avoid charges of unfair dismissal. As Moira Hart has argued:

It established that employers would not be protected unless the requirement of union membership was imposed consistently on all workers in the groups covered by the closed shops. It is therefore in the employer's interest to make explicit in an agreement with the trade union exactly who is covered by the closed shop and who is exempt and to ensure the upkeep of union membership in the designated groups. (*New Society*, 15 February 1979)

Under the 1974 Act (section 30) a 'union membership agreement' is defined as one which a) is made or exists between one or more independent trade unions and employers or employers' associations, b) relates to an identifiable class of employee and c) has the practical effect of requiring employees of that class to be members of one of the unions which is a party to the agreement or of any other union specified by the parties. Only those who 'genuinely object on grounds of religious belief to being a member of a trade union whatsoever' can be exempt from a closed shop's provisions.

There is little doubt that many employers like closed shops for their workforce. It underpins the growth of detailed, formal workplace agreements covering a wide range of practices. A 1978 Department of Employment survey of industrial relations in eleven firms concluded that 'increased formality in the management/union relationship, with clearly written and signed agreements reducing the scope for inconsistency and misunderstanding, was everywhere seen by both parties as an important ingredient of successful bargaining reform'. Closed shops certainly mean the provision of greater disciplinary control by full-time union officials over their members in a workplace. They also provide a stability in inter-union relations, by making it more difficult for unions to compete against each other for membership. The survey carried out for Warwick University found that almost three quarters of the managers saw advantages in the closed shop for the company and only half saw any disadvantage at all.

These findings suggest that the main initiative for closed shops – contrary to popular belief – is not coming from unions intent on spreading their power, but from management who want to see order and control in their plants. The libertarian arguments, beloved of Margaret Thatcher and other Conservatives, may find support among small non-unionized employers, but in the heartland of manufacturing industry they make little impact.

Interestingly, Moira Hart questions whether the closed shop is a sensible arrangement in the interests of workers. As she writes: 'By protecting union negotiators from loss of membership or rebellion, the closed shop today provides greater insulation from shopfloor pressures. Thus, modern closed-shop agreements may be seen as part of a pervasive tendency in industrial relations today towards greater formalization and regulation' and she concludes that 'those who should perhaps be most worried about the manner of the recent spread of compulsory unionism are, paradoxically, trade unionists themselves'.

In the heat of debate, the legitimate reasons why unions seek closed shops are often overlooked. There is the argument of common obligation, which remains very powerful. Lord McCarthy quoted an Oxford printworker, who explained: 'The non-unionist benefits directly from the collective action of his colleagues through the results of collective bargaining. On what principle of freedom does he take all these things, pocket the increased wages, enjoy the increased leisure, while contributing nothing?' The argument is, in McCarthy's words, 'basing a right to coerce on a feeling of resentment that others are evading their share of a common burden'. Another potent argument is the need for the unions to establish a countervailing power to that of the employer.

Despite union participation in job regulation the initiative in decision-taking remains with employers. Generally unions can do no more than try to influence those managerial decisions which vitally affect their members. If they feel that to do this more effectively they need the extra strength and discipline which only the closed shop can provide, I do not feel that the existing balance of power in industry justifies the law in trying to prevent them.

McCarthy's argument of 1964 is still relevant. He defined the closed shop as 'a situation in which employees come to realize that a particular job is only to be obtained and maintained if they become and remain members of one of a specified number of trade unions'. Individual cases of workers being dismissed for not belonging to a union are dealt with by the Independent Review Committee, which was set up in April 1976 under the chairmanship of Lord Wedderburn, Cassel professor of commercial law at the London School of Economics, with Lord McCarthy, fellow of Nuffield College, Oxford, and George Doughty, former general secretary of the DATA section of the Engineers, as its members. This body is serviced by the TUC and meets when the need arises in Congress House.

There is a more positive way in which the climate grew more favourable to trade union expansion in the late 1960s. In the aftermath of the 1968 Donovan Royal Commission on Industrial Relations, many employers became far more tolerant of collective bargaining than they had used to be. Suddenly the unions found far less resistance to their expansion through recognition and the extension of union activities on the shopfloor and in the office. As Bain and Price have written:

The report of the Donovan commission, the White Paper *In Place of Strife,* and the Industrial Relations Bill of the Labour Government all affirmed the principles of freedom of association and union recognition. The Commission on Industrial Relations reaffirmed those principles in a series of reports recommending recognition of unions and the development of collective bargaining.

And they add:

Its reports had a significant impact on employers in general. They created an atmosphere in which the growth of unionism among virtually all levels of employees was seen as, if not desirable, at least inevitable. Many employers bowed to the inevitable by recognizing unions.

The short period of the 1971 Industrial Relations Act checked the trend, but it failed to throw back the process of trade union growth. Perhaps a major reason for the failure of the Conservative attempt to legislate on the unions stemmed from the fact that its very moment of coming into force happened to coincide with the net growth of union membership. With the return of a minority Labour government in February 1974, sympathetic to trade union objectives, new laws like the 1975

Employment Protection Act and the 1974 and 1976 Trade Union and Labour Relations Acts provided a more favourable legal climate in which to expand union recruitment. But the economic factors that helped to push along union growth between 1969 and 1974 no longer apply in a period of deep recession. With well over a million unemployed, the unions are going to find it very difficult to stand still, let alone expand their ranks. Moreover the virtual freeze on the expansion of the public service sector of the economy until at least the early 1980s makes it most unlikely the union growth areas of the past decade can expand for the time being at the same rate. All most unions can hope for is a period of consolidation. In previous slumps, unions have lost members heavily. It will be quite an achievement if they can hold their own, let alone continue to grow.

Whether the new labour laws are going to help prevent decline remains problematical. Much to the chagrin of TUC affiliated unions it does not look as though the new labour laws are going to provide TUC unions with a clear advantage over other registered unions. The problem stemmed from the work of John Edwards, the certification officer, set up with a small staff under the 1975 Employment Protection Act. His job is to decide whether organizations applying to him are entitled to certificates of independence as bona fide trade unions. Getting that clean bill of health is now of immense value to a union. It confers on the organization a host of legal immunities and privileges. Unions need the certificate in order to insist on the disclosure of information from employers in negotiations, to make closed-shop agreements and to safeguard the individual rights of their members on diverse questions ranging from industrial injury to redundancies.

The certification officer is guided by section 30 of the 1974 Trade Union and Labour Relations Act and in particular by paragraph (b) which states that an independent union is one 'not liable to interference by an employer or any such group or association (arising out of the provisions of financial or material support or by any other means whatsoever) tending towards such control'. If a body satisfies those general conditions, the certification officer cannot turn down the request for a clean bill of health. Having a certificate is not of much value without gaining recognition from an employer to pursue collective bargaining and that particular decision rests with the Advisory, Conciliation and Arbitration Service (ACAS) and the Central Arbitration Committee (CAC). An effort was made to make the definition of an independent union more precise in Lords amendments to the 1975 Act, but lack of time led to their being dropped. It was thought a code of practice might assist. The Commission on Industrial Relations suggested a union must be 'effective' as well as independent, by proving it had 'a history of vigorous negotiations' with an employer, 'an adequate income', sufficient full-time staff to service the membership and access to research and legal expertise.

Section eleven of the 1975 Employment Protection Act, which covers the question of trade union recognition, came into force on 1 February 1976, when ACAS was given the statutory responsibility for carrying out its provisions. A number of white-collar unions, notably ASTMS and the TASS section of the Engineers, have attempted to use this law to increase their influence in hitherto unorganized sectors of the economy. In the first two years those unions submitted 165 and 91 references respectively to ACAS under section eleven. Only the TGWU with 214 references lodged more than them. But this aspect of the 1975 Act has not produced rich harvests of members for the unions. In the first two years of operation from 1976 to 1978 ACAS dealt with 1,038 recognition applications from unions and reported on 93. Of these 63 were in favour of recognition, but in only a mere 10 cases had this brought an agreement with the company for the applicant union.

A major difficulty lies in the time-consuming and cumbersome procedures under the law for union recognition. To a very large extent these require the cooperation of the employer if they are to work; but it remains precisely those cases where a union faces employer hostility in its recruitment and recognition efforts that it needs the assistance of ACAS and the law. Where ACAS finds no basis for conciliation, the service institutes 'a programme of inquiries' to ascertain whether the union has enough support among the workers for being given recognition by the employer. The 1977 ACAS annual report described the process: 'Inquiries need to establish the views and policies of the employer, the referring union and any other interested

parties, as well as relevant contextual information, in particular
about existing arrangements for the conduct of industrial
relations. An employee opinion survey is an essential part of the
inquiry. It usually includes a series of questions on the subject
of union membership and support for representation in collective bargaining, together with any appropriate questions about
work organization. So that where necessary the replies of various categories of employees are capable of being analysed separately. The questions are normally presented either in the form
of a written questionnaire or in individual interviews, having regard to cost and convenience, and any preferences of the
parties.' ACAS look at three criteria to help reach a decision
on a recognition case. These are the current level of trade union
membership among the relevant group, the wishes of the
workers about collective bargaining for the terms and conditions of their employment and whether they wish to be represented in that bargaining by the union that seeks recognition.
Although the law does not stipulate that a majority of workers
have to express their approval, in practice if support falls below
40 per cent ACAS is unlikely to recommend recognition.

Under section 14 (1) of the 1975 Act, ACAS 'shall ascertain
the opinion of workers to whom the issue relates'; but the
Grunwick case caused severe problems because of the refusal
of its owner – George Ward – to cooperate with ACAS in carrying out a survey of opinion among his workers on whether they
wished a union to represent them or not. Lord Diplock and
other Law Lords in the Grunwick case agreed that this section
involved a 'statutory intention' to find out the views of all the
workers affected by the recognition claim taken as a whole. But
it was also clear that ACAS could not go ahead and make any
recommendation, if it was debarred by an employer from as-
certaining the opinions of the relevant workers. The TUC was
concerned with a growing number of legal challenges to the
unions as a result of section 11 cases. In particular there was
real anxiety over the successful move by the United Kingdom
Association of Professional Engineers against an ACAS decision not to recommend recognition for UKAPE at W. H.
Allen Ltd. The High Court declared the ACAS report was a
nullity, although ACAS found 79 per cent of the relevant
workers wanted UKAPE to conduct collective bargaining on

their behalf. ACAS had made no recommendation because of the problems this would cause for established industry-wide procedures and the need for ACAS to promote good industrial relations.

There were protracted wrangles over the recruitment ambitions of the Engineers' and Managers' Association in a number of establishments, most notably GEC Whitestone, management in shipbuilding, and Hawker Siddeley Power Transformers, Walthamstow. The TUC found itself in conflict with an affiliate union as a consequence. The recognition procedures have simply failed to achieve the promised big breakthrough in white-collar union recruitment, but provided a number of unions with endless legal problems, diverting their limited resources from their primary function. This put an added strain on the TUC's own procedures to govern inter-union relations. The TUC principles governing the relations between trade unions were established as long ago as 1939 at the Bridlington Congress and they are still in force. In the words of the TUC, 'they were drawn up because trade unionists recognized that, in situations where more than one union was capable of representing a particular grade of worker, it was necessary to prevent the indiscriminate proliferation of unions if stable and rational trade union structures and collective bargaining machinery were to be developed. Their existence has also prevented the instability that would occur if breakaway unions were formed, or if groups of workers were able to move on a whim from one union to another.' Thirteen rules cover all eventualities, with the aim of resolving inter-union difficulties within the TUC and thus avoiding any redress through the legal system. In particular, Bridlington attempts to restrict union poaching of members from one to another. Principle five states clearly: 'No union shall commence organizing activities at any establishment or undertaking in respect of any grade or grades of workers in which another union has the majority of workers employed and negotiates wages and conditions, unless by arrangement with that union.' According to principle seven no official strike should be called by a union over an issue of union recognition or demarcation before the TUC has examined the issue through the Disputes Committee.

Theoretically the general secretary of the TUC has the power to intervene in industrial disputes in order to resolve them through his good offices, if they lead to 'other bodies of work-people affiliated to Congress' not directly involved in the stop-page whose wages, hours and conditions of employment are imperilled (rule 11).

The wrangles over recognition and union certification drew attention to the fact that there are over 300 unions in existence that do not belong to the TUC. In the past, the sheer number of unions was cited as a reason for industrial conflict and in-efficiency, but parallel with the growth in union members there has been a fairly rapid increase in mergers and amalgamations. Between 1964 and 1977 membership rose on average by 15.0 per cent, while the number of unions fell by nearly a quarter. Of course, the number registered with the certification officer remains considerable. In 1977 there were still as many as 480 registered trade unions with an average size of 26,000 members. The movement towards concentration has been substantial over the past decade, mainly aided by the Trade Unions (Amalgama-tions, etc) Act, 1964, through the transfer of engagements.

At the end of 1977 there were eleven unions with over 250,000 members each and between them they accounted for only 2.3 per cent of all unions but as many as 62.9 per cent of all trade union members. At the other end of the spectrum there were seventy-four unions with under 100 members and another 144 with under 500. Both categories put together only represented 0.3 per cent of trade unionists. As table 1.7 illus-trates there has been a steady contraction in the number of trade unions during the late 1960s and the 1970s, while at the same time the proportion of people in the workforce in a union has grown as well.

Even the TUC has a number of tiny affiliates. The Sheffield Wool, Shear Workers' Trade Union claimed to have 32 mem-bers in 1978 and it contributed the princely sum of £5.44 to the coffers of the TUC. Other TUC tiddlers include the 50-strong Cloth Pressers' Society with its head office in Huddersfield, which contributed £8.50 to the TUC; the Spring Trapmakers' Society at Willenhall in the Black Country with 90 members (20 of them women) and a TUC affiliation fee of £10.80; and

table 1.7 Union concentration 1967-77

Number of unions	1967	1968	1969	1970	1971	1972	1973	1974	1975	1976	1977
Under 100 members	126	114	111	108	100	83	84	80	79	69	74
100–499	136	137	134	134	129	136	137	138	138	142	144
500–999	70	63	66	57	60	45	52	52	54	47	45
1,000–2,499	85	88	74	66	64	67	74	69	66	60	66
2,500–4,999	63	60	58	55	54	56	51	52	45	45	41
5,000–9,999	32	33	33	34	34	33	36	31	30	30	28
10,000–14,999	21	18	12	14	11	13	11	11	11	8	10
15,000–24,999	18	19	24	22	19	18	18	18	17	15	13
25,000–49,999	18	15	14	13	16	18	18	17	20	17	18
50,000–99,999	18	20	17	17	15	13	14	14	15	14	15
100,000–249,999	10	10	13	14	12	14	13	14	14	14	15
250,000 and more	9	9	9	9	11	11	11	11	11	11	11
Number of unions at end of year	606	586	565	543	525	507	519	507	500	472	480

(Department of Employment Gazette, January 1979)

the Card Setting Machine Tenters' Society with its head office at Cleckheaton in Yorkshire, 140 members and a £23.80 TUC affiliation fee.

On the other hand, the process of merger and amalgamation has gathered pace in the past fifteen years. Between 1960 and 1970 as many as 500,000 trade unionists were involved in mergers and 125 unions vanished as a result with about a quarter being wholly white-collar, acounting for 20 per cent of the total transferred membership. This amounts to the most rapid period of change within the unions since the years just after the end of the First World War. The trend was less dramatic in the 1970s.

Technological change and the growth of concentration among large companies accelerated the union trend towards amalgamations, particularly noticeable in textiles, construction, shipbuilding, printing and engineering. A growing fear among smaller unions that they would not remain viable if they stayed aloof from formal links with competitive colleagues also speeded up the process. The need to pool resources at a time of financial stringency was an added incentive. So was a belief that smaller unions were in a less advantageous position for bargaining purposes. A clash of personalities or the extraordinary obstacles enshrined in union rule-books have often thwarted attempts to merge, but since Donovan the TUC has been more ready to play the role of an honest broker and stimulate change. Even bitter rivals (as the print unions used to be in Fleet Street) have found the means of working together.

It is the 'open' general unions which have shown the greatest degree of flexibility in making themselves attractive to smaller bodies. The TGWU, in particular, grew at a rapid pace in the 1960s through a process of amalgamations. So did ASTMS. The more diverse the recruitment base of a union, the more agile it can become in its general activities. A decline in one sector can be recouped with gains in another. It provides an added strength to a union's overall organization. As John Hughes argued in a 1973 Ruskin College Trade Union Research Unit paper:

A structure of narrowly conceived industrial or occupational unionism may be a dead hand on union development. This form

table 1.8 Proportion of United Kingdom trade union membership in larger and smaller unions

Year Number	1960			1970			1974			1977		
	Number of unions	Number of members (1,000s)	% of total membership	Number of unions	Number of members (1,000s)	% of total membership	Number of unions	Number of members (1,000s)	% of total membership	Number of unions	Number of members (1,000s)	% of total membership
Unions with 100,000 members or more	17	6,590	67.0	23	8,343	74.7	25	9,259	77.5	26	10,166	80.0
Unions with 50,000 members or more	38	7,995	81.3	40	9,545	85.4	40	10,304	86.2	41	11,181	88.0
Unions with 10,000 members or more	93	9,097	92.5	109	10,582	94.7	88	11,424	95.6	82	12,202	96.1
Unions with less than 10,000 members	571	737	7.5	443	593	5.3	400	526	4.4	398	504	4.0
Unions with less than 1,000 members	362	91	0.9	291	76	0.7	258	74	0.6	263	73	0.6

(Bullock Report on Industrial Democracy, 1977; *Department of Employment Gazette*, January 1979)

of unionism does not use its strength and organisational capacity in sector A to build or strengthen unionism in sector B. It closes its recruitment area and what happens beyond is the affair of some other union.

The unions who grow are those most pliable and open in recruitment. The very existence of a few zealous unions who want to grow in the labour market can stimulate union growth elsewhere. ASTMS acted as a catalyst for expansion in the white-collar field.

The growing intensity in the search for new members has led to an increase in inter-union rivalry. The TUC affiliated unions are supposed to be bound by the 1939 Bridlington rules. Dispute committee hearings in Congress House seek to resolve conflicts between competitors, not always with conspicuous success. Still, the need for the protection of Bridlington was a major reason why the Society of Civil Servants swallowed its scruples and joined the TUC in 1974, because of the real fear that ASTMS might make inroads into the disgruntled executive grade of the civil service. One thing is certain. The massive growth of the unions since the mid-1960s owed very little to any preconceived planning. There was no grand design.

A serious time-lag exists between the membership expansion and the internal union reforms necessary to make the unions fully equipped to meet the challenge. Union critics like to portray the unions as overmighty subjects, highly disciplined monoliths. Nothing could be further from the truth. In manpower and financial resources, the British unions are ill prepared to provide their members with an adequate back-up service. Behind the often impressive façade of union head office, there is often little more than an empty shell. The number of full-time union professionals remains severely limited in Britain. No British union carries a top-heavy bureaucracy of highly paid functionaries. A 1976 TUC survey found the majority of unions had fewer than 50 full-time officers each. On average, unions employ one full-timer for every 3,300 workers. Around 2,800 people work as trade union officers. The 1970 survey carried out for the TUC by the Warwick University Industrial Relations Unit provides some useful information on

table 1.9 The work of the full-time official

Activity	Weighted index of time consumption (maximum = 100)	'Very tc' (ie a day a week or more on average)	'Fairly tc' (ie 2 hours a week or more on average)	'Consumes little time'	'Not part of job'
Routine office work and correspondence	82	72	23	3	1
Conducting negotiations with managers at the workplace	80	70	24	3	2
Preparing material for negotiation	62	42	45	11	2
Supervising and guiding the work of shop stewards or other workshop representatives, and communicating with them	53	30	48	18	3
Attending branch meetings	50	25	50	24	1
Recruitment	44	24	30	42	4
Attending meetings of joint negotiating or consultative bodies at district or regional level	41	18	38	37	7
Handling legal matters, such as cases of industrial injury, unemployment insurance claims, redundancy payment claims, etc	37	14	38	40	9
Attending meetings of union district, regional or national committees or conferences	35	12	29	58	2

Activity	Weighted index of time consumption (maximum = 100)	'Very tc' (ie a day a week or more on average)	'Fairly tc' (ie 2 hours a week or more on average)	'Consumes little time'	'Not part of job'
Finding suitable candidates for vacancies as shop stewards or other workshop representatives	27	8	21	53	18
Supervising branch administration/finance	26	10	19	42	29
Conducting trade union training and education	25	5	24	50	21
Attending meetings of joint negotiating or consultative bodies at national level	24	9	17	43	31
Acting as branch secretary	18	10	7	28	54
Sitting on government planning and economic and social agencies, including hospital management committees, school boards, etc	15	3	12	37	48
Sitting on industrial tribunals or other social insurance appeal tribunals	11	0	12	33	55
Trades council work	11	11	5	41	53
Membership of local authorities, Labour Party committees, etc	10	0	5	41	54

(*British Journal of Industrial Relations* November 1973. Vol XI No 3, William Brown and Margaret Lawson – 'The Training of Trade Union Officers')

who the full-timers are. The average age of their selection to full-time office is surprisingly young at 37.5 years, with white-collar unions recruiting even younger officers (34 years) than the manual unions (37.9 years). As many as 69 per cent of those officers left school before they reached the age of 16 with only 24 per cent of officers in manual unions going to either a grammar or technical school and half the officers in white-collar unions. By contrast, the McCarthy-Parker study for Donovan estimated that 46 per cent of full-time officers had some part-time adult education.

Workplace experience was very widespread. As many as 80 per cent of all officers had held posts as workplace representatives with half of them having been convenors or senior stewards and slightly fewer than a half serving as branch secretaries. The 1970 study found recently recruited officers enjoyed 'a greater depth of experience in lay posts than their predecessors' for the proportion of officers who had been senior stewards went up from nine in twenty for those recruited more than five years ago to thirteen in twenty for those recruited in the last two years. The previous experience as a bargainer and persuader is crucial to the full-time officer, far more so than any known aptitude to be a good administrator. Fewer white-collar officers had held a responsible union lay post at the workplace, but this was understandable and the majority had been branch secretaries. There were marked industrial contrasts. As William Brown and Margaret Lawson wrote: 'New officers appear to be short of experience in negotiations in transport, public utilities and local authority work, whereas in engineering, metals, chemicals and rail they were exceptionally strong.'

How do the full-time union officers divide up their working time? Table 1.9 illustrates the results of the 1970 survey. It highlighted two different types of full-time union officer. The first is the 'organizer', most evident in distribution, agriculture and the white-collar sector of private industry. As Brown and Lawson describe him:

The activities that distinguish him are those of recruiting, finding candidates for the post of shop stewards, acting as branch secretary, attending branch meetings and guiding shop stewards. Negotiation and the preparation for it are below average importance to his work. He has a smaller constituency, but a larger number of branches than average.

By contrast, there is the full-timer who is the 'negotiator', most prominent in the engineering, metal and chemical industries and to a lesser extent local authority services. His work consists

table 1.10 The British trade union bureaucracy, September 1976

Union	Officials
Transport and General Workers'	483
General and Municipal Workers'	282
National and Local Government Officers' Association	191
Amalgamated Union of Engineering Workers (Eng Section)	187
Electrical, Electronics, Telecommunications and Plumbing Union	150
Union of Shop, Distributive and Allied Workers	133
National Union of Public Employees	122
Union of Construction and Allied Trades (UCATT)	170
Association of Scientific, Technical and Managerial Staffs	72
Civil and Public Services' Association	21
Union of Post Office Workers	12
Iron and Steel Trades Confederation	31
National Union of Railwaymen	22
Tailor and Garment Workers	45

chiefly of 'preparing for and conducting negotiations, attending joint committees at both local and national level and (again) supervising shop stewards'. The workload of full-time officers is a constant source of complaint, for the job is not just a nine to five chore. The full-timers do not resent the long hours they devote to the work, but feel they have not enough time to carry out an effective job for the members. The 1970 survey suggested the officers have to react more to events and lack the time to keep in mind the wider implications of the work they are doing.

The growing emphasis on shopfloor bargaining has altered the job of the full-timers. Local trade union officers are now expected to have extra skills in dealing with sophisticated productivity deals, job evaluation, work study and written collective agreements. Moreover, full-time officers in clothing, food, distribution and public utilities suggested in the 1970 survey that the members now expected more and had become far more aware of their rights.

The amount of formal training given to Britain's full-time officers is not very adequate. The 1970 survey discovered that at the time of their appointment, 55 per cent of all officers had had a week's training, but the overall figures mask the wide difference between the white-collar and manual unions. Only 40 per cent of full-time officers of a manual union had received a week's training before appointment, compared with 70 per cent of the white-collar, but since the early 1960s the standard and extent of union education for full-time officers has improved. Table 1.10 underlines just how few full-time officials the unions have to administer their needs.

Britain's trade unionists enjoy their membership on the cheap. Subscriptions remain painfully low. During the 1970s they failed to keep pace with the rate of inflation. On the basis of the returns to the TUC for 1977, the average membership contribution amounted to £11.56 per member, just over 22 pence a week which was less than the cost of half a pint of bitter in the pub.

A total of 81 TUC affiliates participated in the 1977 survey, representing 91 per cent of the entire membership. The total membership contributions totalled £127,718,736, providing 89.8 per cent of total income. This made up most of the £142,139,014 worth of income those unions raised during the year. The total income derived from investment was only £12,012,682 or £1.09 per member. Most of this money derived from fixed interest stocks in central and local government. What equity investment there was tended to be in private companies with a small holding in unit trusts. Few unions derive much income from the stock market. A few like the National Union of Railwaymen and the Electricians (EETPU) are less held back by high-minded dogma.

As many as 83.2 per cent of all union members paid less than

40 pence a week in subscription fees during 1977. Forty-one unions (with just over 5,000,000 members) made provision in their rules for the payment of an admission fee. For the most part, this is little more than a nominal sum. In 1977 the subscription to the union amounted to a mere 0.29 per cent of the average weekly male wage of £76.80.

The total assets of British unions in 1978 amounted to more

table 1.11 The wealth of the TUC's top unions in 1976

	Income (£)	Expenditure (£)	Investments (£)	Assets (£)
Transport and General Workers' Union	18,804,000	15,493,000	22,428,000	32,676,000
Amalgamated Union of Engineering Workers (Engineering section)	13,272,000	10,439,000	6,020,000	18,030,000
General and Municipal Workers'	10,710,000	9,342,000	5,046,000	16,063,000
National and Local Government Officers' Association	9,807,000	6,939,000	4,832,000	10,684,000
National Union of Public Employees	5,435,000	3,734,000	4,524,000	6,749,000
Association of Scientific, Technical and Managerial Staffs	3,683,000	3,830,000	94,000	2,033,000
Union of Construction, Allied Trades and Technicians	3,363,000	3,130,000	1,371,000	2,528,000
Union of Shop, Distributive and Allied Workers	3,606,000	3,262,000	2,239,000	3,681,000
National Union of Mineworkers	6,963,000	5,475,000	12,290,000	17,597,000
National Union of Railwaymen	3,917,000	2,811,000	12,022,000	13,368,000

(The Certification Officer's Report, 1977)

than £263.8 million (of which £56.8 million were in fixed assets and £157.3 million in investments), but very little of that money is in liquid form. Clive Jenkins of ASTMS reckons the unions are lucky if they could raise more than £15 million between them in cash at head office level. There are some very rich unions, most notably those who have been well established for generations and prodigal in their spending habits such as the Dyers and Bleachers, the Boot and Shoe Operatives and the Iron and Steel Trades Confederation. While the average per capita assets in the unions stood at £14.51 in 1970, a number enjoyed figures far above that average. The National Graphical

Association, with its élite membership of skilled printing workers, is particularly well-off with £2,512,000 in income of which nearly a quarter comes from investments.

Unions which hold undisputed sway over a single industry where the employer operates a check-off system (union dues deducted by the employer from the pay packet for the union) also tend to be relatively prosperous, even when their membership has been falling over recent years.

The Railwaymen (NUR) have total assets of over £13,368,000 and a healthy annual surplus of income over expenditure. Under Sir Sidney Greene's leadership in the 1960s, the NUR was willing to diversify its investments into private firms like Imperial Tobacco and Imperial Continental Gas as well as the traditional union investment areas of government and municipal securities. The Trade Union Unit Trust under the chairmanship of Lord Hirschfield, founded in 1961, has enjoyed a modest success in attracting unions into the world of private investment, but old hostility to the bankers and capitalism prevents the kind of uninhibited entrepreneurial trade unionism so typical in West Germany.

Many of the older, craft unions derive almost half their income from investment, but this does not apply to the white-collar unions, who usually have a more fragile base for their activities. They lack deep roots, generations of financial accumulation; and they have to compete with each other in a highly competitive area of the labour market, where if affiliation fees are too high workers are discouraged from joining. White-collar staff are unwilling to pay realistic subscriptions. The financial problem is a major obstacle for the Banking, Insurance and Finance Union in their long campaign to win support from bank staff belonging to the staff associations. That union's annual subscription went up in 1974 to a mere £9 maximum for the over-25s and £4.50 for the younger staff. Those are desperately low levels of subscription for any union that wants to provide adequate back-up services for its members.

Clive Jenkins's ASTMS is in a similar position, with as much as 95 per cent of its income coming from subscriptions. It is true the union has experienced substantial growth through mergers and recruitment drives. In 1961 when Jenkins became general secretary his union had 18,000 members and the money available at head office totalled no more than about £65,000. In 1973 ASTMS had around 300,000 members and a disposable income of over £2,000,000. Yet the assets of ASTMS were still no more than £570,000 and the special reserve fund no higher than £93,000. By 1976 ASTMS enjoyed an annual income of over £4 million.

Britain's unions suffer from an intractable dilemma. The more members they recruit, the more difficult it is to raise the subscription rates. Open, general unions have to operate in difficult circumstances. The main obstacle to the introduction of realistic affiliation fees is union competition for members. No union wants to sacrifice its numerical size to become a highly professional and effective pressure group for its members. The relative poverty of our unions stems from their very haphazard structure and organization.

What do unions spend their money on? The annual returns to the TUC for 1977 provide some good indicators. In that year total expenditure on administration and benefits among the unions who filled in the TUC questionnaire amounted to £112,381,149 or £10.17 per member. The king-size portion of the money spent was on administration (£95,707,386 or £8.66 per member). Dispute benefit proved to be the most widely provided benefit with 60 unions covering 10,032,256 members paying it out to striking members. A total of 41 of those unions spent £4,130,514 on dispute benefit, which averaged out at 44 pence a member. A total of 34 unions, representing over 4,731,701 members, provided members with unemployment benefit. The majority of them paid out in the range of £1 to £3 a week. Members who suffer accidents at work or who are ill can also expect a small benefit from their union. In 1977, 27 unions (representing just under 7,872,786 members) made such provision. As many as 72 unions spent £12,543,249 between them on benefits, other than disputes, averaging £1.18 a member.

A major outlay for the unions is the provision of legal services for individual members. Geoff Latta and Roy Lewis carried out a survey of TUC affiliates in January 1972 with a membership of more than 20,000. The forty-seven unions cov-

ered made up 96 per cent of the total TUC membership. Unions
provide representation for members at local appeal tribunals
and medical appeal tribunals in cases of industrial injury. In
thirty-one out of the forty-seven unions surveyed, an area or
divisional full-time union officer attended the appeals. Other
unions relied on branch officers, but in the case of the Post
Office Engineering Union, a head office official was called in.
Latta and Lewis calculated that unions supported around
10,000 appeal cases every year. They argued:

The value of union representation can scarcely be over-emphasized.
There is evidence that active workplace unionism leads to many
accidents being registered with the Department of Health and
Social Security which would not otherwise lead to claims for
benefit and also to a higher success rate for appeals. Union
representation may well be an important explanatory factor in the
relatively high success rate of local tribunal appeals in the
industrial injuries scheme.

In 1971 unions negotiated around 50,000 successful common-
law claims for employers' liability on behalf of their members,
which produced damages totalling £20 million with between 2
and 3 per cent of those cases being determined by a court decision. Yet this is only a fraction of cases of industrial accident
in a year. Latta and Lewis reckoned there were around half a
million union members suffering accidents during any one year,
but the unions only managed to gain common-law damages in
about 10 per cent of those cases. Only about one in five of all
accidents are actually reported to a union. The print unions,
notably SOGAT and NATSOPA, have an outstanding record
in helping members with even small claims. Some unions are
willing to give their members insurance coverage. As many as
thirty-one out of the forty-nine in the Latta-Lewis survey extended protection for accidents involving members on their way
to and from their workplace, but the larger unions do not
cover general road accident cases. The TUC carried out a survey
among affiliate unions in the compilation of its evidence for the
royal commission on legal services, which was published in
1977. Just under half the unions (55) representing around 80
per cent of the TUC membership joined in the exercise, which
began in October 1976.

Less than half the union respondents said they had either a separate legal department or specific legal officers. As many as 19 of the smaller unions actually left such matters to their general secretary or assistant general secretary, while a further 15 had the administration and provision of legal services carried out by full-time union officers as part of their general functions. The TUC survey revealed that only five union legal departments had at least one person with some formal legal qualifications.

A major area of activity lies in dealing with industrial accident claims from union members. The TUC survey found that in the case of unions covering industries where health and safety hazards are high, ten unions each received between 1,000 and 5,000 claims for assistance in 1974, representing one claim for every 50 members. More than 70 per cent of all accident claims were pursued by the unions, but at least 80 per cent were settled outside court. In 1974, 37 unions representing 35 per cent of all trade unionists in Britain recovered £33 million between them for about 35,000 members and about 50,000 accident forms were forwarded as potential claims.

The majority of workers who appeal to tribunals on social security questions are not represented by unions, but where they are they stand a good chance of winning their case. The annual reports of the Supplementary Benefits Commission reveal that trade unions and similar representatives have a highly successful record when they act for claimants in supplementary benefits appeals.

With the arrival of the new labour laws (1974–6), and new rights for workers and trade unionists, the volume of cases being heard by industrial tribunals is mounting rapidly. But union involvement remains sketchy. In 1975, 15 unions, according to the TUC survey, with 1,568,000 members between them provided advice about industrial tribunal applications in 887 cases, but 1 union alone acounted for nearly half that number. A mere 9 unions run a formal legal advice centre for members, while a further 6 said they gave advice on an informal basis totalling around 1,000 cases a year on average.

The TUC survey estimated that a total of 30 unions paid out solicitors' fees of £1,164,787, but this is an underestimate of the costs, because they fail to take into account the proportion of wages and other expenses of full-time officers and their staff attributable to the time spent on legal work. The spending by the unions on legal services in some cases amounts to only 4 to 6 per cent of their total expenditure.

For the most part, unions have proved reluctant to invest their money in anything but local or central government stock. Suspicion of the ways of the City of London and the capitalist system have prevented unions from maximizing their assets. There is a fear of what is known as business unionism, that somehow the British trade union movement would lose its moral ideals, if it began to speculate with the money of the workers on the Stock Exchange or indulged in profit-sharing schemes. Moreover, despite the demands made by union leaders on private investors to devote more funds to the regeneration of manufacturing industry, no union has seemed willing to take the risk and step into the breach. In Sweden in 1976 the union (LO) movement's chief policy-maker, Rudolf Meidner, came up with the revolutionary idea that the unions should buy their way into the ownership of Swedish industry through the collective purchase of company shares. Such a proposal would find no supporters here.

By keeping subscriptions absurdly low and refusing to increase the wealth of their assets through Stock Exchange speculation or industrial investment, our unions have failed to maximize their potential influence on the capitalist system. This is not to argue that they should be transformed into willing partners with capital in the mixed economy at the expense of their members. But a holier-than-thou refusal to accept any involvement in the wealth-producing centres of our society makes it much more difficult for the unions to exercise any power and influence over company decision-making. They must be expected to do so, if or when Britain achieves any meaningful measure of industrial democracy.

2 The Trades Union Congress – carthorse of Great Russell Street

What Are We Here For? (George Woodcock, TUC 1962)

The TUC has arrived. It is an estate of the realm, as real, as potent, as essentially part of the fabric of our national life, as any of the historic estates. (Harold Wilson, June 1968)

The Trades Union Congress (TUC) is now a mighty influence in the land. No government of whatever persuasion can afford to ignore its demands or spurn its advice. TUC bosses are a familiar sight going in and out of Downing Street and Whitehall departments and cabinet ministers are now visitors to Congress House, TUC headquarters in London's Great Russell Street, not far from the British Museum. No state body or Royal Commission is complete nowadays without some TUC worthy sitting on it. Its top leaders sit round the table with ministers and employers at monthly meetings of the National Economic Development Council, working out the industrial strategy which is supposed to bring the revival in Britain's ailing manufacturing fortunes. On an ever-widening range of topics – from unemployment to public expenditure cuts, from football train hooliganism to race relations, from child benefits to the issue of early retirement – the TUC has a collective voice, which cannot go entirely unheeded in Whitehall ministries.

But the TUC is allowed to exercise only influence, not power. Its affiliated unions have been slow to accept the merits of providing the TUC with any more authority and control than it already possesses. The TUC remains what it always has been – a loose confederation, not a centralized monolith. 'I don't think pulling power to the centre is compatible with our democracy,' says Len Murray, the TUC general secretary. As the TUC explained in the 1970 interim report on its structure and development:

The TUC is primarily concerned with developing policy rather than acting as an executive body. It produces a means through which unions can collectively achieve objectives which they cannot achieve, or which it could be difficult for them to achieve separately. It identifies things which unions should be doing, but which for one reason or another they are not doing, and stimulates them to take the necessary action. It reminds individual unions or groups of unions of their duty to take into account the interests of other unions, and the broader interests of trade unions as a whole. It thus establishes standards of good union practice.

All this implies a slow, prudent, reactive approach, but the TUC cannot really adopt any other course of action without endangering its unity. Its sole authority stems from a 'willingness by unions and by their members to abide by decisions to which they are parties'. However the need to move at the pace of the slowest makes it very difficult for the TUC to become an innovator.

In essence, the TUC has scarcely changed since the early 1920s, when Walter Citrine (general secretary 1926–46) tried to update the TUC to meet modern circumstances. As Citrine wrote in his memoirs, the perennial problem of TUC reform comes down to one of power 'to act on policy issues in a cohesive manner'. He recalled:

This could be done only by a central body representing all the unions. People who thought like myself had for years been talking about a general staff of labour. 'All power to the General Council' they declared. Such slogans seemed not only eminently desirable but just plain common sense. We didn't realise how conservative a force the trade union movement could be in relation to its own affairs.

As long ago as 1924 the TUC launched a full-scale inquiry into the merits of industrial unionism and how to speed up mergers and amalgamations. After three years it came to the sadly realistic conclusion that it was 'impossible' for a body like the TUC, made up of every kind of union, 'to reach agreement on any specific form of organization'. Under the impetus of the Second World War, the TUC launched yet another attempt at internal reform. Once more the sober result was a recognition that nothing could be done. 'It is one thing to plan an entirely new structure on unoccupied ground; it is another to plan and

rebuild where so many institutions already exist. Basic structural changes are impracticable,' intoned the 1947 report. The
hopes and idealism, born in the war crisis, soon vanished once
victory was achieved. In the words of the 1947 report: 'Practical experience shows that the obstacle to greater cohesion is
the tendency to struggle for the union or the theory of organization, in which members have an interest or a loyalty, rather
than the trade union movement as a whole.' There seemed
only one practical answer. 'Unions themselves must strive for
closer unity and resolutely pursue that end, probably making
some sacrifices on the way.' The report warned: 'The trade
union movement in a changing world cannot retain its pre-war
conception of organization if it is to prosper and efficiently fulfil its ideological and practical functions.'

Another attempt at reforming the TUC was made at the
1962 Congress. Ron Smith of the Post Office Workers moved a
motion instructing the General Council to examine the TUC's
structure and the trade union movement 'with a view to making
it better fitted to meet modern industrial conditions'. Other
union leaders gave the proposal their uncritical blessing. The
new TUC general secretary, George Woodcock, replied in
laconic vein: 'The general council do not as a rule welcome
motions on the Congress agenda. Our general attitude to motions is that if they tell us to do what we already intend to do
they are redundant; and if they try to tell us what we do not
intend to do they are offensive.' This was hardly a clarion call
for action. 'Structure, particularly in the trade union movement, is a function of purpose,' he went on. 'We expect that we
shall first of all in our inquiries, inquire into trade union purpose and policy, and ask ourselves, "What are we here for?"
When we know what we are here for, then we can talk about
the kind of structure that will enable us to do what we are here
for.' Woodcock warned that it would take two years for the
TUC to complete its task and he concluded: 'There could be
one of two things done with a motion of this kind: it could
be smothered, or it could be the beginning of a tremendous
undertaking.'

Woodcock was as good as his word. Nothing emerged in
time for the 1963 Congress, where he took the opportunity to
theorize in pessimistic mood:

So far as the TUC is concerned all unions are equal. All are of equal merit; all of equal value. The problem for the TUC is how to hold together unions free, sovereign, and independent in themselves and at the same time make some common step forward, make some common development. Diversity of structure is a characteristic of British trade unionism and always will be. We see no real alternative to a continuation for a long time, I would say as far as this Congress is concerned, for ever, of a great degree of diversity.

By September 1964 the whole reform drive had ground to a halt. The problem of planned change looked insuperable, just as it had been for Citrine in the 1920s and Sir Vincent Tewson in the 1940s. Woodcock pronounced the idea of industrial unionism (one union for each industry on the West German model) to be 'neither practicable nor desirable'. 'We have temporarily abandoned the idea that trade unions can be directed as to their structure from the top,' he added. 'We can generalize until we're blue in the face, but when we come to practise, when we come to the hard, solid, current coin of the realm, we must have time to do the job, and I am optimistic that we shall still do it. It is still to me a great adventure.'

Such words failed to please the reformers. The Clerical and Administrative Workers (now APEX) moved a motion criticizing the General Council for lack of progress. A short, sharp debate followed, where the big general unions made it crystal clear why no advance had been made. Frank Cousins, the tetchy general secretary of the Transport and General Workers, suggested that the present TUC structure was a 'good' one. As for talk of mergers and amalgamations, he thought his union provided the best model of all possible. The motion went down to an inglorious defeat.

Whatever happened to the Woodcock 'reform programme', launched with such hope and good intentions? We can now see that he lost a great opportunity. In retirement, Woodcock admitted to me that he was never able to devote enough of his time to the subject. Moreover, instead of trying to find out what the unions were here for, he rushed too quickly into ideas of structural change. The first year was a complete waste. It was not until the winter of 1963–4 that the Congress House secretariat got down to the job of drawing up blueprints. More

seriously, the reformers were sidetracked into yet another look
at industrial unionism and no serious debate was ever launched
on how the TUC itself could be modernized during those years.

A memorandum on structure, written by the TUC Organization Department under Woodcock's direction, was finally
presented to the TUC Finance and General Purposes Committee on 10 February 1964. This laid down areas of possible
merger and amalgamation in various industrial sectors, but on
Woodcock's insistence paragraph 37 was added to the document which made it clear the big general unions would have to
break up to achieve industrial unionism.

The very idea of a disintegration of the big giants and their
submergence in one body of miscellaneous groups was far too
much for Frank Cousins of the TGWU and Jack Cooper of the
GMWU to swallow. Woodcock addressed innumerable trade
group conferences during 1964, where he argued the case for
mergers, but it proved a painstaking, thankless task. Between
March 1964 and September 1966 as many as twenty-four conferences were held on union reform. In 1962 there had been
182 affiliates in the TUC; by 1966 the number had fallen to 170
– a reduction of only 12. 'Many unions are dissatisfied with the
present position. No common thread, either of criticism or suggestion, emerged,' intoned the TUC report in 1966. Nor had
there been any big increase in the numbers of unionized workers in the TUC. In 1962 there were 8,315,332 affiliates; by
1966 the number had risen to 8,787,282. This represented only
a 2 per cent increase in four years, hardly much better than
during the do-nothing years of Tewson in the 1950s.

The creation of a Royal Commission on the unions and employer associations under Lord Donovan in April 1965 was
seen by Woodcock as an excellent forum to try and revive his
ideas of union reform. If the TUC General Council was incapable of providing the energy, then the outside stimulus
might provide the necessary catalyst for change. But three
years of Donovan proved a great disappointment for Woodcock as well. Though a member, he failed to get his colleagues
interested in the problems of structure and function. Most of
the time was devoted to whether unions should be brought
within a framework of revised labour law. Woodcock admitted
in retirement that the Commission's members were too tired by

the end to give such questions any close attention. Moreover, from the early months of 1969 the TUC was forced to devote a good deal of energy, expertise and its limited finances to the defence of its position, as successive governments tried to bring the trade union movement within a codified framework of law. Vic Feather spent most of his first year as TUC general secretary battling with Labour's short proposed Bill to tackle strikes through penal clauses. That particular struggle ended in a TUC victory. Harold Wilson was forced to sound the retreat after a number of long, wearisome Downing Street sessions between the TUC and ministers. The 'solemn, binding agreement' reached by the TUC and the Cabinet pushed the TUC into a more interventionist role in industrial relations. In his memoir of the period, Harold Wilson – with characteristic hyperbole – suggested the TUC had 'moved forward forty years in a month'.

For a year, Feather found himself as the trouble-shooter, with a placatory finger in every industrial dispute. Feather was a jolly Yorkshireman from Bradford with a love for compromise and conciliation. What he lacked in Woodcock's brains, he made up for with limitless energy. He liked nothing better than to fudge up settlements round the negotiating table. There were many in the trade union world who believed Feather overstretched the TUC's functions by his interference – not just in disputes between unions, but in those where employers and workers were at loggerheads. Feather disagreed and he reckoned that by July 1970 the TUC conciliation service had saved the country 3,000,000 lost working days and £10,000,000 in lost production. It needs to be remembered that Feather's coaxing and cajoling took place at a time when price and wage inflation was starting to climb and there were signs of growing militancy among lower-paid workers in the public sector. By sheer force of personality, Feather made a modest success of the 'solemn, binding agreement', even though he lacked sanction powers.

The interesting experiment that took the TUC right into the fray of the industrial relations system proved short-lived. After three months of Conservative rule, the 'steady flow' of Department of Employment notifications of disputes to the TUC, in Feather's words, came to 'a dead-stop'. It is questionable

whether the fault for the breakdown of relations between the
TUC and the in-coming Conservative Government lay entirely
at the door of Edward Heath and his Cabinet colleagues, but
the Conservatives made it quite clear from the start they intended to legislate on industrial relations as soon as possible in
a manner that would not please the unions. Initially, it did not
seem as though the TUC would succeed in resisting the Industrial Relations Bill, although one of the biggest mass demonstrations in the history of the Labour movement was held by
the TUC in London on 21 February 1971. Predictably Heath
got his massive and complicated measure on to the statute
book, but it proved virtually impossible to enforce. This was
mainly because the TUC was able to mobilize most of its members into line behind a boycott of the Act's machinery. The
crucial point was registration. Under the new law, every union
had to stay on the register of friendly societies if it wanted to
enjoy the rights and privileges of the Act. Ever since Donovan,
Congress House had been suspicious of any attempt to make
unions submit to registration. Ken Graham, the wily head of
the TUC Organization Department, was quick to see the dangers of such a step. He said it would have eclipsed the traditional rights of trade unions, in the case of the 1969 Labour
proposal. What the Conservatives had promised was even
worse. Feather and his staff hammered home the point to
doubting colleagues that the very fact of registration would
fail to protect them from the rigours of the law, unless they
were ready to knuckle down to a drastic change in the whole
way in which they conducted their affairs. In Feather's opinion,
trade unions under the 1971 Act would have become 'like centralized, corporate business enterprises with authority resting
at the top'. Nevertheless the TUC's eventual victory was a very
close-run one. Both the General and Municipal Workers and
the Electricians hesitated about the wisdom of not registering.
The crucial factor was the narrow decision at the 1971 Congress – forced by the Engineers – by 5,625,000 to 4,500,000
votes which 'instructed' unions not to register. As many as
twenty unions were eventually expelled from the TUC, because
they refused to go along with the TUC policy of non-cooperation. Surprisingly, the government did not try to make the
nationalized industries work the Act in its entirety. Almost all

major private employers preferred to keep away from its provisions, and thus avoid damaging their existing industrial relations procedures with the unions.

Under threat, the TUC displayed a cohesion and sense of collective self-discipline that it usually finds hard to match in taking any positive initiative. But its behaviour between 1974 and 1977 in its relations with the Labour Government suggests the TUC is not as moribund an organization as its critics like to maintain. Edward Heath may have been right to doubt the TUC's capacity to deliver its side of a bargain at the time of the 1974 national coal strike. Yet his Cabinet did not respond to the TUC initiative, which suggested other unions would accept the miners as a special case and not press wage demands that would break through the pay norms of his Stage Three incomes policy.

The TUC general secretary has an unenviable, ill-defined job. Rule 10 of the TUC constitution merely states he is elected by Congress and sits in an *ex officio* capacity (without a vote) on the General Council. He symbolizes the TUC, acting as its collective spokesman to the outside world, but what power and influence the general secretary can exercise over his independent colleagues depends on personality and diplomatic skills as well as the circumstances of the time. Len Murray, the holder of the post at the time of writing, has spent almost his entire working life in the backrooms of the TUC, since he joined the Economic Department in 1947. He is a Shropshire man, born in Wellington in 1922. He attended the local grammar school, and spent a year reading English at London University, before leaving in disgust at the course's emphasis on Anglo-Saxon. Murray saw active service in the war in the King's Shropshire Light Infantry, where he rose to the rank of lieutenant. He was wounded just after the 1944 Normandy landings. Following a short spell as an English teacher, he gained a place at New College, Oxford, where he read politics, philosophy and economics and graduated with a second class honours degree. Murray went up to Liverpool to train 'as a superior sort of a waiter', but also applied for a post in the TUC. He was interviewed by Woodcock and impressed his future boss with the cynical observation that unions could bargain best with private business monopolies who controlled prices.

In 1954 Murray was appointed head of the TUC Economic Department. He worked closely with Woodcock through the 1960s, when the TUC secretariat was becoming involved in economic policy-making. Murray became Feather's deputy in 1969, where he was the main coordinator of the anti-Industrial Relations Act strategy. Left of centre, he is more willing to ally closely with Labour in power than some of his predecessors at Congress House. Married with two boys and two girls, he commutes from a semi-detached in Essex. Murray likes reading economics in his spare time. His favourite leisure activity is going to watch Orient playing football. When he came to the top job in the TUC, Murray was regarded as something of a radical. After years of internal stagnation, it was hoped by many TUC staff that he would innovate. 'I want trade union activists to realize the TUC's potential,' he told me in August 1973. 'We must be the generalizer of good labour practices – the pusher out and puller in of ideas and information. The TUC is not just a platform of people who meet once a year by the seaside nor is it merely a name at the top of official headed notepaper.' His stated aim was to give everybody 'a share in the action'. But Murray's heart attack in the summer of 1976 has slowed him down. Although he does not have to retire until he is 65, some union leaders fear that he may wear himself out too quickly. His first years imposed a crippling burden and there were many frustrations. In the spring of 1975 Murray and his full-time advisers grew impatient with the inability or refusal of the unions to reduce their wage demands. The flimsy promises of the Social Contract Mark One were simply not carried out, and Murray's efforts to tighten up the guidelines found no favour on the General Council.

Murray must tread carefully. He has no big battalions to mobilize in his own support. His primary task is to retain the confidence of the General Council. It would be foolish to get out of step with the thinking of the big union bosses. Through persuasion and reason, Murray must hope to win the arguments. Unlike his colleagues, he has no muscle to buttress his position. Yet it would be wrong to overstress the limitations of the office. To the media, Murray is Mr TUC. He remains the collective expression of the trade union movement, its senior mandarin. And over the years – like Citrine, Woodcock and

Feather – he can be expected to impose his own earnest personality on the TUC. If his health does not deteriorate any further, Murray should stay at Congress House until the middle of the 1980s. This gives him plenty of time to carry through longer-term reforms. Or does it? The problem is whether the new generation of union leaders, coming to the fore in the next few years, will really be ready to let Murray and the TUC grow stronger at their own expense which would be the inevitable result of a serious modernization.

After all the sound and fury of the past ten years it is hard to see signs of any fundamental change in the TUC. This remains particularly true of the composition of the forty-one-strong General Council, where tradition and practice, not reason, determine who sits on it. All the unions vote on who should sit for each trade group, providing a chance to play power politics.

The composition of the TUC General Council is raised intermittently as an issue of controversy at Congress. In 1971 at Blackpool, Bill Kendall, then general secretary of the 200,000-strong Civil and Public Services' Association (CPSA) and not a General Council member, moved a resolution calling for a General Council to be created where there was at least one member from every union in the TUC with over 150,000 members. Alternatively the CPSA motion suggested that some General Council members should be chosen from groups whose numbers totalled together the minimum figure of 150,000. Kendall pointed out that in 1945 there were only thirteen unions with more than 100,000 members, two of which had no seats on the General Council. By 1971 there were twenty-three such unions, of whom no fewer than five did not sit on the General Council. Clive Jenkins of the giant Association of Scientific, Technical and Managerial Staffs (ASTMS), not elected on to the General Council himself until September 1974, contributed a pungent speech to the brief debate. 'The present groupings are a reflection of a ghostly membership of long-dead trade unionists. What we have is a muddle which is based on ancient patterns of nineteenth-century trade and organization, a pattern of industrial archaeology.' No delegate was prepared to defend the status quo.

As the 1975 TUC General Council report intoned:

The guiding principle in elections to the General Council should be the need to preserve a fair balance of different interests and experience, and this should take precedence over the simpler approach of distributing seats on a purely arithmetical basis.

In the opinion of the 1975 report the General Council's structure has 'stood the test of time remarkably well'.

The impetus for any structural change of the way the General Council is elected suffered a setback in the late 1970s that suggests the forces of conservatism remain as strong as ever. The last bid to change the TUC came in 1975 when John Lyons, general secretary of the small but powerful Electrical Power Engineers' Association (EPEA), demanded that Congress should hold a full-scale review of TUC structure. What especially annoyed Lyons on that occasion was that the inner group of the 38-strong General Council had just bargained on behalf of the whole movement for a £6 a week flat rate incomes policy. Lyons went on to instance two other examples of non-consultation affecting his members by the TUC. Congress House submitted evidence to the Plowden Committee on the electricity supply industry which recommended 50 per cent trade union representation on the board, though the TUC had not bothered to find out the views of the unions in the industry. In Lyons' view the TUC had also made statements in their evidence to the Royal Commission on the Distribution of Income and Wealth that were 'immensely damaging in their implications to the management structures and therefore the efficiency of national industries'. Lyons' suggestion to the 1975 Congress was simple enough – make the TUC 'practise what it preaches – management by consent'. Partly as a result of the Lyons motion the TUC carried out an inquiry into its own structure. There was hardly much enthusiasm among affiliate unions for the idea of TUC reform. The replies to a circular asking for comments and views on the work of the TUC were so few that a second circular had to be sent out in August 1976. Eventually 40 unions representing 8,500,000 members responded. In March 1977, the TUC General Council issued a booklet to the unions on consultative arrangements within the TUC. This was the main discussion document at a special conference held on 28 April that year.

table 2.1 The General Council of the TUC, autumn 1978

	Trade group	Unions	Representatives	Numbers	Fees £
1	Mining and quarrying	3	Lawrence Daly (NUM) Joe Gormley (NUM)	295,187	50,181.79
2	Railways	3	Ray Buckton (ASLEF) Sid Weighell (NUR)	280,449	47,676.33
3	Transport (other than railways)	6	Jim Slater (NUS) Walter Greendale (TGWU) Stan Pemberton (TGWU) Moss Evans (TGWU) Harry Urwin (TGWU)	2,141,927	364,127.59
4	Shipbuilding	1	John Chalmers (Boilermakers)	129,956	22,092.52
5	Engineering, founding and vehicle building	10	Reg Birch (AUEW) John Boyd (AUEW) Terry Duffy (AUEW) George Guy (Sheet Metal Workers)	1,389,411	236,199.87
6	Technical engineering and scientific	4	Ken Gill (TASS) Clive Jenkins (ASTMS)	679,758	115,558.86
7	Electricity	1	Frank Chapple (EETPU)	420,000	71,400.00
8	Iron and steel and minor metal trades	9	Bill Sirs (ISTC)	146,745	24,946.65
9	Building, woodworking and furnishing	4	Glyn Lloyd (UCATT) Les Wood (UCATT)	390,148	66,325.16
10	Printing and paper	6	Bill Keys (SOGAT)	420,939	71,559.63
11	Textiles	15	Fred Dyson (Dyers and Bleachers)	125,617	21,354.89

	Trade group	Unions	Representatives	Numbers	Fees £
12	Clothing, leather and boot and shoe	6	Jack Macgougan (Tailors and Garment Workers)	267,679	45,505.43
13	Glass, ceramics, chemicals, food, drink, tobacco, brushmaking, distribution	10	Lord Allen (USDAW) Charles Grieve (Tobacco Workers)	596,782	101,452.94
14	Agriculture	1	Jack Boddy (NUAAW)	85,000	14,450.00
15	Public employees	11	Terry Parry (Fire Brigade union) Geoffrey Drain (NALGO) Alan Fisher (NUPE) Albert Spanswick (COHSE) Fred Jarvis (NUT)	2,197,175	369,609.92
16	Civil servants and Post Office	12	Anthony Christopher (Inland Revenue) Tom Jackson (UPW) Ken Thomas (CPSA)	949,073	160,637.17
17	Professional, clerical and entertainment	10	John Morton (Musicians) Alan Sapper (ACTT)	404,220	68,717.40
18	General workers	1	David Basnett (GMWU) Ken Baker (GMWU) Jack Eccles (GMWU)		
	Women		Marie Patterson (TGWU) Audrey Maddocks (NALGO)	945,324	160,705.08
	General secretary		Len Murray (no vote)		

(TUC Statistical Statement 1978)

A report on the inquiry was presented to the 1977 Congress. It is clear from the introduction that the voices demanding change in the TUC were few in number. As the report argued : 'The replies to the TUC's circulars and the views expressed at the consultative conferences did not reveal any widespread dissatisfaction with what the TUC was doing or how it was doing it.' The only main cause for criticism lay in the methods of representation on the General Council itself and the arrangements for the annual Congress.

The reformers, most notably the General and Municipal Workers' Union, favoured the principle of automatic representation for unions over a certain size to ensure their general secretaries were members of the General Council by right. The most radical variant of this suggestion would have involved the disbanding of the trade group structure (including the women's group), and its replacement by automatic representation. Unions with over 1.5 million would have five seats, unions with between 1 million and 1.5 million, four and so on down to unions of over 100,000 having one seat each. The TUC report summed up the arguments for and against the proposed change in an even handed way.

The case for doing nothing was clearly put in the 1977 Congress Report. 'It has been argued in favour of the existing system that it produces a General Council which is responsible and answerable collectively to the whole of Congress and ensures that the special interests of all industries or groups of similar industries are reflected in the composition of the General Council.' The existing system was also 'tried and tested', providing 'a reasonable balance between unions and sectors', to avoid the over-dominance of any one union.

The arguments for change were based on the principle that 'every union of a certain size ought to be represented on the General Council by right and should not be excluded simply because of the vagaries of the trade group system'. It was alleged that the introduction of industrial committees in the TUC removed whatever value the trade group system of election had. A slight increase in the total size of the General Council (maybe from 41 to around 47) would prove beneficial because it would help to ease some of the burden of committee work from existing members. But such a change would also mean the end of the separate women's group. The majority of replies to the TUC questionnaire favoured that drastic step.

No decision was taken by the 1977 Congress on the issue of reforming the General Council, but it was decided to discuss the matter further. In March 1978, the General Council considered proposals from the Finance and General Purposes Committee which would give automatic representation for unions with more than 150,000 members. This would have meant 28 places being filled without any election. The smaller unions would have had 14 seats allocated to them, making a 42-strong General Council with the exclusion of the two women. Four different methods for electing the smaller union representatives were floated before the General Council. Firstly, the voting could be restricted to the smaller unions themselves; secondly, voting within groups; thirdly, by all the TUC affiliates voting for them; and fourthly by restricting voting to within groups but allocating all unions to groups, irrespective of size.

After a long debate the General Council turned down the proposals; but this particular move to reform the TUC's ruling body was finally given the *coup de grâce* by the giant unions and their allies at the 1978 Congress after a debate, where only those seeking change spoke from the floor. The important development in 1977–78 was that the General and Municipal Workers took up the reform cause, although the union stood to gain no obvious benefit from any change. Over the years other unions like the Post Office Engineering Union, the Civil and Public Services' Association and ASTMS had championed the cause, but all of them spoke as injured parties, being kept off the General Council due to the voting system, and the slowness of the TUC to reorganize the trade groups to accurately mirror social and occupational changes in the TUC. Jack Eccles of the GMWU spoke with persuasive reason in favour of automatic representation.

Eccles maintained that the existing structure hit the medium-sized unions particularly severely. He mentioned a number that had been kept off the General Council because of the voting system, notably SOGAT and the CPSA in the past and the POEU and APEX in recent years. He denied that the GMWU reform proposals would mean the end of small union representation, but pointed out that the present system had meant the growth of 'a client relationship' between the big and the small. Eccles claimed that the proposal, which involved the retention of the women's section, would require a 43-strong General Council, a net increase of only 4, with automatic representation for unions of over 100,000 members and seats for the smaller ones through election from among themselves.

A procession of speakers went to the rostrum to voice their approval for what was being proposed. Roy Grantham of APEX, who was thrown off the General Council in 1975, upset the big union bosses by revealing some of the reality behind the abstraction. As he pointed out:

If we said that the citizens of Glasgow should have their members of Parliament elected by the rest of the United Kingdom we would have a revolution. But that is what we basically do in the case of the General Council. Indeed, we do worse than that. We restrict the people who actually vote to a small élite. Although we have abolished aldermen in local authorities, in the elections to the General Council it is half a dozen members of this union and half a dozen members of that union who decide how the votes are cast and who is going to be on the General Council. It is election by a small coterie of a small coterie behind me.

Grantham commented that Arthur Horner of the Miners had been kept off because he was a Communist, and others like Clive Jenkins, Jack Peel of the Dyers and Bleachers, Cyril Plant of the Inland Revenue Staff Federation and Tom Jackson of the Post Office Workers had suffered from unsettling attacks through the bloc vote system of election. Grantham did not mention his own ejection for taking moderate lines in the past. His public revelations suggest that he will find it very difficult to win back a seat on the General Council. Grantham spoke scathingly of the patronage vote on that august body. 'I have seen members of the General Council who have had to wait to see how some other member would come to vote before they could raise their hand on an issue. Do not blame them. People who have to rely on the goodwill of others cannot be blamed for trimming their sails.'

Eccles said he was tempted to waive his right of reply, because no opposition had been heard from the floor of Congress to criticize his suggested reform, but when it came to the vote the motion was narrowly defeated by 6,529,000 to 5,215,000 – thanks mainly to the opposition of the Transport and General Workers and the Engineers with their allies.

Such negativism about TUC internal democracy by the unions suggests that conservative attitudes die hard, even when many claim to wish for an extension of industrial democracy in industry. But most large unions with muscle are naturally reluctant to give up their patronage powers for the greater good of the TUC.

The TUC has tried to involve far more unions in the work of the movement, who do not sit on the General Council, through the industrial committees system. At present, there are nine of them in business, bringing together unions in the same areas of activity (construction; fuel and power; health services; hotel and catering; local government; printing industries; steel; textile, clothing and footwear; and transport). The aim is to pool information, swap ideas and in a number of cases formulate policy. The committees meet in Congress House and they are serviced by the TUC secretariat. They have arrived, not via a TUC blueprint, but through a revamping of already existing advisory bodies or to meet a genuine need. The committees have brought together blue- and white-collar unions and given them a chance to reach common ground on problems of mutual interest and provide some cohesion to their practical work. They could provide the catalyst for a speed-up in union mergers and amalgamations by breaking down old suspicions that hamper inter-union cooperation.

So far, the actual performance of the industrial committees has been rather patchy, but they retain great potential. The most long-lasting and successful has been the Steel Committee, set up in 1967 when the industry was re-nationalized. Under the chairmanship of Bill Sirs of the Iron and Steel Trades Confederation (ISTC), it has widened its task from merely gathering facts or sending delegations to lobby ministers. The TUC Steel Committee was the forum used by the unions in the industry to battle against the British Steel Corporation's plans to introduce plant closures and redundancies as part of its strategic development plan to the 1980s. The committee is a recognized body in collective agreements in the steel industry, responsible for wage bargaining for the workers.

The Construction Committee under the chairmanship of George Smith of UCATT devoted much of its time to the vexed issue of the 'lump' and the need to de-casualize the industry. The Fuel and Power Committee under Frank Chapple of the Electricians has been in constant touch with the Department of Energy. The Printing Industries Committee under Bill Keys of SOGAT was the main union vehicle for the talks on Fleet Street new technology in 1975-7. A disputes liaison procedure was agreed on by the print unions on the committee, which has involved itself in resolving disputes in the newspaper industry. The TUC industrial committees appoint the trade union members to the little NEDDIES in their particular areas. The General Council keeps in close touch with their work and a sprinkling of General Council members are on each of them.

But even in the provision of basic services for its affiliates, the TUC has a long way to go. There is no widespread dissemination among all members of committee minutes and background papers. No union off the General Council ever gets that body's agenda and minutes. The TUC still fails to issue any systematic data on economic trends for affiliates. Unions must rely on their own over-stretched research departments or subscribe to outside bodies like the highly effective Ruskin College Trade Union Research Unit or Incomes Data Ltd. No flow of information from the TUC tells unions about new wage agreements. A Collective Bargaining Committee was formed in 1970, but had died by 1974. There has been the idea of creating a TUC Research Bureau, but it remains just talk. There is no TUC legal service for affiliates. The TUC Centenary Institute of Occupational Health – opened in 1968 at the University of London – remains under-used by the unions. After the resignation of Dr Robert Murray early in 1975, the TUC was for two years without any resident occupational health expert.

In response to the TUC's growing involvement in national economic policy-making, the Congress House secretariat has developed a greater expertise. Since 1968 the Economic Department has produced an annual economic review, now published in the early spring before the budget. This has rapidly become a key document in the trade union world. Not only does the review provide a detailed critique of the economy's overall performance over the preceding period, it also lays down the TUC's own counter-proposals to prevailing government orthodoxy. Under the direction of Bill Callaghan, head of the Economic Department, the TUC is in close day-to-day contact with Whitehall and NEDC (some say too close). Some union leaders believe the TUC Economic Department is too willing to mouth Treasury assumptions about the economy. A close understanding existed between Congress House and the Chancellor's senior advisers in 1975 and 1976. But the TUC has been a source of ideas on economic affairs since the early 1960s. The secretariat provided the arguments and the data for the TUC demands for import controls, an investment reserve fund to revive British manufacturing industry, and the programme of subsidies as part of the Social Contract between government and the unions.

The TUC economic policy alternatives are usually left-of-centre with a sharp cutting edge, but they are meant to be an agenda for serious negotiation, not a public relations exercise. Callaghan has twelve assistants to help him in the Economic Department. This is a very small staff to really take on the formidable Treasury, but the TUC is forced to operate on a shoe-string. Murray is untroubled by the need for leanness. 'Living a bit hand to mouth makes you think of how to use your resources best', is his view. Lack of both finance and power limit the ability of the TUC to transform itself into a more formidable organization. There is far too much penny-pinching and frustration in Congress House. Traditional union dislike of bureaucracy ensures that the TUC operates on an intolerably short shoe-string. The tiny secretariat of no more than forty administrators has to service the General Council, the various committees and Murray, as well as argue with senior civil servants and keep affiliated unions in touch with what is going on at the centre. The bulk of the bureaucracy is made up of young university graduates, with a strong commitment to the trade union movement, but most soon advance into university posts or the research departments of the unions themselves. In September 1978 the General Council agreed to a report from a joint review committee on TUC staff salaries, which will raise staff pay to levels comparable to similar posts in industry, the civil service and the City by the early 1980s. Yet the TUC represents no more than 1.5 per cent of total union annual income. You only have to scrutinize the TUC's annual financial statement to appreciate just how puny its resources still are. The annual affiliation fee per member only went up from 17 pence to 20 pence on 1 January 1978.

In 1977 the TUC's total income from union affiliation fees amounted to £2,016,809.68. Office expenses totalled just over £596,220. This included salaries and insurance (£482,008), postage and telephones (£32,550), advertising, legal and professional (£27,109). The Tolpuddle Martyrs Memorial Trust got £1,515.16 and the private Manor House Hospital in Golders Green £378.79. Affiliation fees to international union organizations swallow up a large slice of the TUC budget. In 1977 those to the International Confederation of Free Trade Unions (ICFTU) totalled £420,000 and the European Trade Union Confederation a further £105,000. Union contributions have simply failed to keep up with rocketing price inflation.

The TUC's internal structure has hardly changed since the days of Walter Citrine between the wars. Indeed, his legacy remains the most effective part of Congress House, notably the central filing system and the tradition of providing comprehensive, detailed Congress reports, which often contain many of the supposedly confidential conversations between the TUC and government ministers. There are seven main departments in the TUC. *Organization and Industrial Relations*, headed by John Monks, covers union structure and industrial relations as well as race relations, inter-union disputes, women's issues, trades councils, regional organization and labour law. *Economic*, under Bill Callaghan, services the TUC economic affairs as well as industrial policy and company law. *Social Insurance and Industrial Welfare*, under Peter Jacques, covers pensions, factory legislation, accidents and pollution as well as social security. *Education*, under the control of Roy Jackson, speaks for itself and so does *International*, headed by Alan Hargreaves. There is also a *Finance* Department dealing with affiliation fees and investments, and *Press and Publicity*.

TUC business is administered by a committee system, made

up of General Council members and serviced by the full-time secretariat. This is where the main work of the TUC is carried out. The Finance and General Purposes Committee is the key body. There are eight main committees at present, which report back regularly to the TUC General Council. Who sits on what committee is determined after each Congress in the autumn, by an inner coterie of senior union bosses, known as the Committee on Committees. Committees like Economic and International rank high up the pecking order, while others such as Education and Social Insurance carry much less weight. Despite a general dislike of bureaucracy, those who take their TUC duties seriously soon find themselves spending more and more time on TUC committee work and less on the affairs of their own unions. It is very difficult for the TUC to modernize itself. For the most part, it moves along recognizable lines, spurning change. Until very recently the TUC displayed no interest in providing the unions with a comprehensive education service. Education in the unions has usually been regarded as an expensive waste, an excuse for the occasional residential junket, not a central part of a strategy to improve the living standards and working conditions of the rank and file. In most unions, stewards and full-time officials have to rely on self-help, on their own intuition and common sense, in dealing with management. Anti-intellectualism retains deep roots in the trade union movement, which has kept education in a subordinate role.

The education provided in the past – notably by the Workers' Educational Association and the National Council of Labour Colleges until its unhappy merger with the TUC training college in 1964 – concentrated on purely academic subjects and its contents were often of no practical value to the life of the shopfloor. Frugally minded unions did not see why they should pour out large sums from their tight budgets for a service which produced no immediate and obvious return. By the standards of other Western industrialized nations, Britain provides the worst education services of any trade union movement. In 1975 the TUC conducted a wide-ranging survey on the subject. Forty-six unions responded, representing 72.2 per cent of all TUC affiliates (7,240,037 members). On the basis of their replies, the TUC estimated that there were just over

400,000 voluntary union officers to cover the entire movement, made up of 291,000 stewards, 2,800 full-time officials and 112,500 lay branch officers. Their basic training need was for 80,000 a year. But the 1975 provision fell far short of that – in particular for stewards responsible for bargaining. In 1975 there were only facilities for half a day for every union office-holder every year, or two-and-a-half days for every hundred trade unionists. Between September 1975 and June 1976, 693 students attended forty-nine courses held at Congress House. Of those a total of 391 were full-time officers on five- or three-day courses on subjects like safety and health at work, industrial law, and bargaining information. Only 302 were lay activists. Out in the regions, where the TUC works closely with the Workers' Educational Association and around 140 educational establishments such as polytechnics, extra-mural departments of the universities and technical colleges, the picture is better. In 1977 more than 27,000 students were involved in 2,008 separate day-release courses. This is a far more cost-effective method for the TUC in teaching basic union skills than holding weekend residential schools, especially if the companies pay their stewards for attending the courses. But a 1976 TUC survey found that only 12 per cent of tutors in colleges of further education were actually contributing to TUC courses. Under section 57 of the 1975 Employment Protection Act, union lay officials are entitled to time off from work on full pay to attend trade union courses recognized by the TUC. There will have to be a substantial growth during the 1980s, if the British unions are going to match the educational provision of their colleagues abroad. In West Germany day and weekend schools are organized in 250 local offices. Nothing so ambitious can be tried here, for the primitive character of the TUC regional structure makes that impossible.

Until 1975 the TUC had been very reluctant to press for state aid in the financing of union education. There was an understandable fear that this might only be obtainable if the government itself decided what form the courses should take. The unions have always tried to make sure that they do not lose control over the content of the education and the teaching methods. In 1975 the TUC education committee approached the Department of Education and Science. It proposed that the

government should refund course fees on day-release courses
and provide £40 bursaries per place for union residential
courses with the funds channelled through the TUC. The TUC
survey related union educational provision to the total number
of voluntary office-holders. It calculated that the ratio of
student days provided by the unions for their official (lay and
full-time) was 0.31 a year or three days per office-holder every
ten years. It is scratching at the surface of the problem. The
Danish unions, with a tenth of the British membership, provided twice as many courses for their shop stewards as we did.

The 1973 report by the Commission on Industrial Relations

table 2.2 TUC spending (in £'s)

	Affiliation fees	Rates	Education
1968	195,151	51,463	156,934
1969	140,547	55,847	163,494
1970	207,028	63,964	185,108
1971	185,583	75,448	218,339
1972	214,333	85,872	212,893
1973	245,367	121,013	207,826
1974	334,657	157,315	238,337
1975	376,545	223,249	275,990
1976	564,388	195,643	308,912
1977	544,000	198,483	254,242

(General Council reports)

discovered that employers were responsible for training 68 per
cent of stewards in industry. Unions dislike such interference,
but they did little themselves to provide an alternative. In
1973–4 the unions spent only £1,200,000 between them on
education on 125,000 student days. By contrast, the TUC devoted around £200,000 to education (that figure included the
salaries of its five full-time staff at the TUC training college, a
few backrooms at Congress House). As the figures in table 2.2
show, this amount compares unfavourably with the sums spent
on affiliation fees to international organizations and the rate
bill for the TUC site.

In July 1976 the government agreed to provide £400,000 during the 1976–7 financial year to meet union education costs,

and the TUC wants £3 million a year from the state in the 1980s for this. State funding of union education is commonplace in Sweden and Ireland, and it was started in 1975 in Australia. Government finance for union education was one of the proposals in the abortive 1969 *In Place of Strife* White Paper. In the financial year ending 31 March 1978 grant-aid of up to £650,000 (a 62.5 per cent rise on the previous year) was provided by the state to the TUC for education purposes. In 1978–9 that figure rose to £1 million.

Until recently the TUC postal courses were the main concern of Congress House. In the year ending 30 June 1978 as many as 3,179 students enrolled on courses and 1,664 completed them. The Trade Union Studies Project, in cooperation with the BBC Further Education Department and the Workers' Educational Association, got under way in 1975 with around 700 trade union members enrolled on the basic trade unionism course. Yet all this is a belated recognition by the TUC that the training of the shopfloor in the expertise and skills of collective bargaining is the essential need of an effective trade union movement. The mass of legislation put on to the statute book over the period since February 1974 has transformed the needs of the unions. It gives them the potential power to extend their influence on decision-making across the industrial relations system, if they can learn and are willing to use it.

Efforts by the TUC to establish a presence in the regions have not proved very successful. Ever since the days of Walter Citrine, the TUC has tried to give regional reorganization a top priority. The 1970 TUC interim report on structure suggested the trend towards government decentralization required an urgent review of TUC regional facilities. The string of TUC regional advisory committees were set up during the Second World War to perform liaison work between government and industry but, as the 1973 TUC report argued, they had become 'little more than talking shops for union officials'. Their part-time officials could not afford to devote their energies to work on the regional economic planning councils or carry out investigations 'into matters of concern to trade unionists within the area'. Starved of finance, the nominated committees made next to no impact on regional life. The 1973 TUC study recommended the abolition of the advisory committees and their replacement by TUC regional councils for each of the eight planning areas of England and Wales. The councils would be made up of representatives from the main unions in an area in proportion to the number of members they had there. It was also at first suggested that full-time regional secretaries should be created, but the TUC General Council turned down that idea for the time being on the ground of cost. A major reform in the trades council system was also proposed in the 1973 report to bring them into line with the reorganization of local government through merger and amalgamation. A quarter of the representatives on each TUC regional council were to be drawn from the trades councils in the area. The regional changes went through virtually undebated, but there was serious reluctance among union leaders to put any finance into the new TUC structure. When the question of providing financial assistance for the creation of full-time regional secretaries was discussed again in November 1975, it was felt spending as much as £90,000 a year was too great. As the 1976 TUC report states: 'It was considered that having full-time secretaries would necessitate an increase in affiliation fees which unions would be unwilling to pay.'

All unions in the region are entitled to nominate officials (either full-time or voluntary) while the county associations of trades councils appoint a quarter of the members of the regional councils. These bodies meet four times a year and they elect executive committees made up of 12 members – nine from the unions and three from the CATCs. A conference of regional union delegates in 1977 suggested the reforms had been reasonably successful, especially in giving a local focus to the work of the TUC in developments with local CBIs, the economic planning councils, district manpower committees and the like. The 1977 TUC structure report suggested: 'The changes for the first time enabled the trade union movement to be taken seriously in the regions.' But delegates expressed doubts whether the regional TUCs could develop much further on a part-time basis, because the sheer burden of work was starting to impose an intolerable burden on the secretaries who had full-time jobs to do in their own individual unions. But the General Council still believed the cost of having permanent full-timers in the regional posts would prove too expensive (over £10,000 a year in each region), though there was more sympathy for the need for more clerical help. In 1978 the General Council finally agreed to provide financial assistance for some regions to help clerical expenses.

TUC regional secretaries have an increasingly heavy workload. 'The extent of trade union representation is a reflection of our ability to get the right people for the job,' said David Perris, TUC regional secretary in the West Midlands and secretary of Birmingham Trades Council. As the TUC presence in England's industrial heartland, one of his primary tasks is to nominate local union worthies for jobs on the bench, industrial tribunals and hospital boards. Every year he throws out a 'wide trawl' with application forms to union branches for nominations to his panels of potential candidates for public office. Yet Perris is unable to provide local union organizations with any assistance in their work. The TUC regional offices are worked on a shoe-string, often from private homes. There is no back-up service, nor are there any research facilities. 'We have not really grown out of being vehicles of protest,' said Perris. 'We deal with matters in an empirical way with next to no financial help.' The creation of regional secretariats, TUC centres of power outside Congress House, looks far away. Such a development would be viewed suspiciously by the larger unions, who do not want to see the TUC develop a momentum at regional level, even though it makes real sense by ensuring most unions do not overlap in the services they provide. Medium- and smaller-sized unions would benefit from a more dynamic and effective TUC presence in the regions. But this looks unlikely to happen for the moment.

In the foreseeable future the affiliated unions will not allow the TUC to widen its powers and grow into a highly centralized and professional trade union organization like the DGB in West Germany or the Swedish LO. The logic of events might dictate such a development, but the powerful forces of tradition and conservatism in the TUC are unlikely to tolerate it. The Congress House secretariat will have to go on making a virtue out of necessity. Low's cartoon image of the TUC was of a carthorse – cautious, plodding, suspicious. Despite the pressures and changes of the past fifteen years it is far too early to suggest the animal has been metamorphosed.

3 The politics of the unions

The TUC is not a party political organization, but we are not aloof from politics. We are in politics. (Len Murray, TUC, 1978)

Labour is nothing without the trade unions but the trade unions can survive without the Labour Party. (Eric Heffer, MP, 1973)

Labour

For good or ill, the trade union movement is enmeshed in the British party political system. The personal loyalties and formal ties of most active trade unionists lie overwhelmingly with Labour. The party's tentative beginning as the Labour Representation Committee at London's Memorial Hall, Farringdon St, on 27 February 1900 was the direct result of a TUC decision to establish a pressure group in Parliament at the 1899 Congress. Like Siamese twins, Labour and the unions are indissolubly linked together. The connection is both emotional and pragmatic, the product of history and common self-interest. During the formative years the unions provided the financial and numerical muscle which helped to turn Labour into a mass national party. They remain vital to Labour's strength.

In the opinion of Ross McKibbin, at least until the formation of the first minority Labour Government in 1924, 'the local party organization was utterly dependent upon the unions as institutions and upon their officers and members as individuals' (*The Evolution of the Labour Party*, Oxford, 1974). Apparently, 'for the most part, the unions and their officials made up the deficiency of individual members. They provided the volunteer workers, the local party officers, and the money. Local parties with strong trade union branches were usually well organized; those with a union-sponsored candidate were well financed too.' McKibbin's view is that the relationship between Labour and the unions was unequal. 'The Labour Party always needed the unions; the unions did not always need the Labour Party.'

Has the relationship really changed in any basic way since the 1920s? In its evidence to the 1968 Donovan Commission the TUC stressed differences rather than similarities:

At the turn of the century there was no party in Parliament prepared to look after the interests of working people, so one had to be established. The creation of the Labour Party as the political arm of the trade union movement is clearly of immense historical significance; its roots in the community find their strength, in common with those of the trade union movement, in the experience of working people, and this common approach to practical problems means that the Labour movement does not get out of touch with the realities of everyday life. Trade unions and political parties do, however, perform quite distinct functions and their preoccupations can often be quite different. The growth of the Labour Party to the point where it became the Government of the country has entailed a significant divergence of function. The existence of common roots yet distinct functions is therefore the most important feature of the relationship between trade unions and the Labour Party.

In the TUC's view the strength of the alliance lay 'paradoxically in the looseness of the ties'. Both the unions and the party have recognized the need for the other and most of the time they have shared mutual ideals and practical policy objectives, but very often a certain lack of trust has scarred the deeper loyalties of tradition. Critics of the uneasy alliance between the party and the unions suggest that the relationship is constructed on flimsy, contradictory foundations. David Farnham, in an article in *Parliamentary Affairs* (January 1975), has argued it is 'a relationship of convenience, not of conviction. As they are currently organized, professionalized business unionism and re-formist parliamentary politics are institutionally incompatible. The Labour alliance is formally a reality, but its unity is a myth.' Many on the far left believe the Social Contract forged between Labour and the unions in the early 1970s has paralysed the will for radical change. Break the stifling cords that bind the partners together in the flabby dogmas of Labourism and the unions could go on to generate a fiery working-class consciousness. Such is the logic of David Coates's tirade – *The*

Labour Party and the Struggle for Socialism (Cambridge, 1975). Theorizing may intoxicate the militants, but it remains an unreal strategy, a leap into fantasy born of economic decline and political failure.

On the other hand, there are those who think Labour needs to disentangle itself from the powerful grip of the unions. Free of the restrictions imposed by being tied to one of the most conservative and insular trade union movements in the world, Labour could then become a truly social democratic party, dedicated to the defence of the mixed economy and the Western way of life. That prospect should not be treated scornfully. It is undoubtedly true that the majority of public opinion dislikes Labour's close links with the unions, though this does not seem

table 3.1 Labour's big union allies (Conference 1978)

	Affiliated unions
Transport and General Workers' (TGWU)	1,200,000
AUEW Engineering Section (AUEW)	877,000
General and Municipal Workers' (GMWU)	650,000
National Union of Public Employees (NUPE)	500,000
Union of Shop, Distributive and Allied Workers (USDAW)	383,000
Electrical, Electronic, Telecommunications and Plumbing Union (EETPU)	260,000
National Union of Mineworkers (NUM)	253,000
Union of Construction, Allied Trades and Technicians (UCATT)	200,000
Union of Post Office Workers (UPW)	192,000
National Union of Railwaymen (NUR)	180,000
Association of Scientific, Technical and Managerial Staffs (ASTMS)	147,000
Association of Professional, Executive, Clerical and Computer Staffs (APEX)	102,000

to harm the party very much when it comes to a general election. David Butler and Donald Stokes found only 17 per cent of their 1970 sample of voters thought there should be a close tie-up between Labour and the unions and as many as 72 per cent thought the unions should 'stay clear of politics', whatever that might mean. As many as 51 per cent of the sample survey

taken for the 1976 Houghton Committee on Financial Aid to
Political Parties thought it was 'bad' that the Labour party
should get finance from the unions. Opposition to a formal link
between the unions and Labour is even strong among workers
who are traditionally staunch Labour voters. Stephen Hill, in
his study of London dockers, discovered that 60 per cent were
hostile to the connection. In October 1974, 66 per cent of trade
unionists polled by Crewe, Alt and Servlik disapproved of the
union link with Labour (*Erosion of Partisanship*, 1976). Yet a
separation of Labour from the unions is an unreal option, unless we introduced state financial aid to the political parties.

Today the unions are more firmly entrenched and more
necessary than ever for the financial health of the party, and
the only real counterweight to combat the negative extremism
of the constituency rank and file. In 1978 only 52 out of the 113
TUC unions were actually affiliated to the party, and they accounted for 5,913,159 of the party's total membership of
6,616,271. Around 90 per cent of the votes cast at Labour's
annual conference come from the unions. (In 1978 out of
6,751,000 votes at the conference, as many as 6,061,000 were
union block votes and 633,000 from the constituencies.) As the
figures in table 3.1 illustrate, the top five constitute over half the
union bloc voting strength.

Labour's National Executive Committee is dominated by the
unions. There are twelve members, all from the union ranks.
Most come from the second layer of union leaders. After the
Blackpool conference of 1978 they were:

Tom Bradley MP   (Transport Salaried Staffs' Association)
John Chalmers   (Boilermakers)
Doug Hoyle   (ASTMS)
Harold Hickling   (General and Municipal Workers)
Gerry Russell   (AUEW)
Alex Kitson   (Transport and General Workers)
Sam McCluskie   (Seamen)
Fred Mulley MP   (APEX)
Walter Padley MP   (USDAW)
John Golding   (POEU)
Russell Tuck   (Railwaymen)
Emlyn Williams   (Mineworkers)

The union bloc votes are also involved in the election of the five
women members of the national executive and the Young
Socialist member. The party treasurer is also a virtual trade
union appointment. Since 1937 the local parties alone have
elected the NEC members for the constituency section.

The union presence in the Parliamentary Labour Party remains fairly strong, even if the social composition of that body
has changed over the past fifty years. In May 1979 as many
as 48 per cent of all Labour MPs were sponsored by a union
(133). This is actually one of the highest proportions since the
1935 intake (51 per cent of the PLP or 78) and far above the
figure for 1945 when only 31 per cent of the PLP were sponsored trade union MPs (see table 3.2). The Mineworkers still

table 3.2 Sponsored trade unionists in the Parliamentary Labour Party
1945–79

	1945	1950	1951	1955	1959	1964	1966	1970	(Feb) 1974	(Oct) 1974	1979
Total	120	111	108	95	92	120	132	114	127	127	131
% of PLP	31	35	37	34	36	38	37	40	42	40	48

have a substantial contingent, led by the redoubtable Denis
Skinner, MP for Bolsover. The NUM has precise rules on
sponsorship. Selection is left to the areas, who may sponsor a
candidate for every 5,000 members up to 15,000 members and
one additional candidate for each 10,000 members after that.
A successful NUM candidate must be a paid-up member of
the constituency party, a miner for at least five years and enjoy
the NUM executive's blessing. The miners have proved a stolid
bulwark in the PLP. If few have risen to high office, they were
a force for stability. As Ellis and Johnson have written:

They were, after all, men of strong regional and local loyalties
who had often spent their whole lives in small, isolated semi-rural
communities. Their expertise in the affairs of their union and of
the coal industry was seldom matched by any wider political
knowledge or even interest. They were infrequently men of
ministerial age or calibre and Labour leaders, eager to have some
representation from this major section of the Labour movement,

were prone to give them dead-end jobs in the Whips' Office – where their bearing, authority and experience of face-to-face bargaining stood them in good stead. (*Members from the Unions*, Fabian Society, 1974)

Nevertheless the NUM had two members of Mr Callaghan's Cabinet in the spring of 1979 – Roy Mason, Secretary of State for Northern Ireland, and Eric Varley, the Industry Minister.

The NUM provides substantial finance to many local constituency parties. In the two general elections of 1974 as much as £35,975.90 was paid out to twenty-two separate constituencies, while a further £37,836.45 went to the Labour Party centrally in the form of fees. The seven Yorkshire NUM MPs were provided with £866.68 between them by their union with a maximum of £200.

The large general unions have strong contingents in the Parliamentary Labour Party as well. In the Transport and General Workers' Union general discretion on the magnitude of the sponsorship system rests with the General Executive Council. As Ellis and Johnson explain:

The process is initiated by discussions at branch level of a particular candidate being put forward for TGWU sponsorship. If the candidate is unknown to the local membership the branch may exercise its right to interview him before passing on a recommendation to the union's regional committee. This committee gives further consideration to the proposed nomination and may interview the nominee themselves. If the committee is unfavourable to the nomination, it has the power to 'kill' it. Only in the case of a favourable recommendation is the nomination forwarded for consideration by the GEC – which in turn may interview and reject or accept the candidate for sponsorship.

Around half the twenty-two TGWU sponsored MPs in the 1974 Parliament were said to be from middle-class/professional backgrounds, but the decline in the numbers of rank and file trade unionists in the TGWU list has been halted. Jack Jones never disguised his determination to see more working-class MPs sent back to Westminster. In the General and Municipal Workers the rank and file sponsored MPs remain in a small minority. This is in line with the union's declared aim of sponsoring able people from outside the GMU's own ranks. In the 1974 Parliament there were 14 MPs on the union's official parliamentary panel, with a further seven from the unofficial panel who included Jim Callaghan, Bill Rodgers and Harold Wilson. There is no encouragement for the GMWU's able officials to take the parliamentary road, but the union has made it clear that it wants to make an effective mark in Parliament through a judicious selection of energetic MPs. As Ellis and Johnson have commented:

In one sense, then, the GMWU is the most parliamentarist of all the major unions. It has clearly revised and operated its candidate selection procedures with an eye to the skills and qualifications increasingly in demand at Westminster. As a result it has succeeded in increasing its representation and in developing prestigious and powerful connections in the House.

The Amalgamated Union of Engineering Workers has sponsored younger members of the rank and file in recent years for parliamentary seats. A recent selection procedure has been established in the AUEW to ensure its parliamentary panel members are suitable and well-qualified for the rigours of being an MP. The union's National Committee keeps a firm hold on the selection process. Through this method the AUEW has managed to ensure its representation at Westminster is highly effective but also remains based on working-class rank and file membership. As Ellis and Johnson concluded:

The union has shown it is possible to satisfy parliamentarist criteria without surrendering the principle of actual representation. Though meritocratic selection of candidates means the AUEW is losing talent to Parliament, the union appears to accept the price without qualms or any serious detriment to its industrial activity.

The union sponsored MPs seldom act as a cohesive force in the PLP. The only recent occasion when they flexed their muscles was in resistance to the *In Place of Strife* White Paper in 1969. The trade union group plays an essentially passive role. Well stocked with middle-of-the-roaders, many of its members are also scattered throughout the Tribune and Manifesto groups.

The finances of the Labour Party by the end of the 1970s were in an appalling condition. In 1977 Labour created a deficit of £61,403 and the party anticipated a further deficit of around £100,000 for 1978, despite the increase in affiliation fees to 24 pence a member. A further rise to 28 pence a member in 1979 and 32 pence in 1980 is likely to do no more than keep the size of Labour's deficit within reasonable proportions.

table 3.3   The Unions: Labour's paymasters 1970–77

	Total £	Trade Unions £	Labour Parties £	Societies £	Parliamentary Labour Party £
1970	443,625	401,792	40,083	1,750	2,348
1971	483,269	422,865	58,798	1,606	—
1972	613,484	550,520	58,510	4,454	—
1973	753,208	670,488	77,568	5,152	—
1974	828,319	738,142	82,152	6,094	1,931
1975	1,246,978	1,117,515	119,467	6,530	3,466
1976	1,366,895	1,221,291	130,084	8,895	6,501 (plus 124 from overseas members)
1977	1,420,364	1,267,796	135,811	9,637	6,972 (plus 148 from overseas members)
1978	1,667,740	1,501,413	143,175	15,620	7,204 (plus 328 from overseas members)

(Labour Party Conference Reports)

The big unions were anxious to remedy the problem. In January 1978, the National Executive agreed to establish a party organization inquiry committee with the specific task of considering ways of 'establishing closer liaison with trade unionists and trade unions at all levels' as well as looking at ways of raising and more efficiently using party finance and launching joint action to combat racialism and the National Front. Four senior union leaders agreed to serve on the committee – David Basnett, John Boyd, Moss Evans and Alan Fisher.

But the committee produced no fundamental recommendations for the 1978 party conference, suggesting that 'the national officers and national committees of affiliated trade unions be asked to give a lead in encouraging support and activity on behalf of the party' and full-time officials be released from their union duties to help Labour in marginal constituencies during general election campaigns. It was also proposed to create 'better liaison at organizational level with the trade unions' through the establishment of a committee of senior party and union officials. John Edmonds of the GMWU criticized the lack of real progress towards a thorough re-examination of party structure on the committee, which had been established mainly at the behest of the GMWU.

'The constitution of this party has always been based on a delicate balance between the constituency parties and the trade unions,' argued Edmonds:

But the fact is – and perhaps conference will think the sorry fact is – that each year the balance is tipping further and further away from the constituency parties towards the unions ...

We may have an organization that assumes we have a mass party, but we do not at the moment seem to be very effective at retaining a mass membership. Power is shifting in the party and trade union votes are becoming more and more dominant on the floor of conference. Party finances have gone exactly the same way. Over 80 per cent of the party's central funds comes from the trade unions. Even at local level the trade unions contribute heavily to constituency party funds. What should worry us is that each year the balance shifts further. At each election the party seeks more money from the trade unions, and the trade unions strain to provide that money. But the party must recognize that union funds are limited. We nearly exhausted them in the two elections of 1974, and a political party that relies to this extent on trade union finance is extremely vulnerable and some would say unhealthy at its very heart.

As the figures in table 3.4 indicate the individual membership of the party has shrunk at an alarming rate during the past twenty years, while the dominance of the unions has grown correspondingly greater. The constituency membership figure is also a fiction. All local parties must affiliate at 1,000 members each, but in many cases membership is far lower than this. The number of individual party members is believed to be as low as 200,000. If this dismal trend continues through the 1980s it will ensure that Labour is far more a trade union party than at any time since its origins. Without union money, personnel and influence Labour is in grave danger of becoming a mere sect, not a mass political party. The decline in individual participation in democratic politics is one of the most serious problems facing Labour. As Jim Callaghan told the 1978 party conference:

One of the new phenomena of modern politics has been the rapid growth of what I call single-issue pressure groups, usually formed by concerned people, deeply devoted to a cause which they press vigorously. The devotion and effort that they expend reveals clearly to me that there is a source of democratic strength that we have not yet fully tapped, and to which we should respond.

The sad fact is that beyond the politicians themselves, journalists and a dwindling band of party activists, few people in Britain take any active interest in politics. The political party has become little more than an election machine. Young men and women of idealism turn to admirable pressure groups like Shelter, the Child Poverty Action Group, the National Council for Civil Liberties, the Anti Nazi League, Amnesty International and Mind to articulate their hopes and fears in practical, remedial action. The time is long overdue when the Labour Party itself began to make a wider appeal which would channel those causes through its own organization at all levels.

But for the foreseeable future the union presence will grow more vital and necessary than ever to Labour's financial health and the only real counterweight to the negativism and unreality of so many constituency rank and file members. Yet at the same time, the number of trade unionists affiliated to the Labour Party is going to dwindle in the 1980s.

The overwhelming bulk of the political finance accumulated by the unions from their members does not derive from a rank and file that are enthusiastic members of the Labour Party. In February 1974, for example, only 48 per cent of trade unionists actually voted Labour, although 58.3 per cent of union families did so, while 66 per cent of trade unionists in October 1974 disliked the close union links with Labour. A trade union fund for use in pursuing political objectives was authorized under the 1913 Trade Union Act. This law reversed the controversial judgment made by the House of Lords in the case of Osborne v. the Amalgamated Society of Railway Servants, which had made it null and void for a registered union to have a rule allowing the collection and administration of political funds for the purpose of parliamentary representation. The 1913 Act enabled trade unionists to contract out of paying the levy to their union's political fund, if they expressed a clear wish to do so. In the bitter aftermath of the General Strike, the Baldwin government pushed through the 1927 Trade Disputes and Trade Unions Act that required, among other things, for trade unionists to contract in to pay the political levy. The onus was placed on union enthusiasts to make the effort and provide their affiliation fee to the political fund. As a result, the Labour Party membership figures slumped dramatically by nearly a million, but in 1946 the Attlee Labour Government reversed the principle by legislation to contracting out. Immediately the trade union membership of the party jumped from 2,635,346 in 1946 to 4,386,074 a year later. In 1978 around 80 per cent of trade unionists in unions affiliated to Labour were estimated to be paying the levy.

Michael Moran in his study of the Union of Post Office Workers in 1975 found that while 95 per cent of his small sample paid the levy, only 51 per cent realized they did so and only 21 per cent thought their union should be affiliated to Labour. Similar rank and file ignorance about the political levy was discovered by Goldthorpe and his colleagues in their study of Vauxhall car workers in Luton in the middle 1960s. In four out of the five occupational groups interviewed as many as 70 per cent paid the levy, though a third to a half (excepting the craftsmen) did not know that they did. Of those who were aware of the levy, a sizeable number did not think their union should be affiliated to Labour. Nearly a third of the craftsmen and setters at Vauxhall had contracted out of the levy. This adds strength to the view that trade unionists value their union purely as a means of improving and safeguarding their pay and conditions and not as a way of achieving a wider involvement in party politics.

Statistics contained in the annual trade union returns to the Certification Office suggest a growing number of trade unionists are contracting out of payment of the political levy, particularly in the white-collar area, despite those very close national ties between the union leaders and the party establishment forged in the 1970s. Clive Jenkins' ASTMS had only 147,000 (33.3 per

table 3.4 The unions and Labour

	Constituency parties	Total individual membership		Trade unions		Socialist and Co-operative societies, etc		Total membership
	Number	Men	Women	Number	Membership	Number	Membership	
1945	649	291,435	195,612	69	2,510,369	6	41,281	3,038,697
1946	649	384,023	261,322	70	2,635,346	6	41,667	3,322,358
1947	649	361,643	246,844	73	4,386,074	6	45,738	5,040,299
1948	656	375,861	253,164	80	4,751,030	6	42,382	5,422,437
1949	660	439,591	290,033	80	4,946,207	5	41,116	5,716,947
1950	661	543,434	364,727	83	4,971,911	5	40,100	5,920,172
1951	667	512,751	363,524	82	4,937,427	5	35,300	5,849,002
1952	667	594,663	419,861	84	5,071,935	5	21,200	6,107,659
1953	667	584,626	420,059	84	5,056,912	5	34,425	6,096,022
1954	667	544,042	389,615	84	5,529,760	5	34,610	6,498,027
1955	667	488,687	354,669	87	5,605,988	5	34,650	6,483,994
1956	667	489,735	355,394	88	5,658,249	5	33,850	6,537,228
1957	667	527,787	385,200	87	5,664,012	5	25,550	6,582,549
1958	667	515,298	373,657	87	5,627,690	5	25,541	6,542,186
1959	667	492,213	355,313	87	5,564,010	5	25,450	6,436,986
1960	667	459,584	330,608	86	5,512,688	5	25,450	6,328,330
1961	667	434,511	316,054	86	5,549,592	5	25,450	6,325,607
1962	667	444,576	322,883	86	5,502,773	5	25,475	6,295,707

Year								
1963	667	480,639	349,707	83	5,507,232	6	20,858	6,358,436
1964	667	478,910	351,206	81	5,502,001	6	21,200	6,353,317
1965	659	475,164	341,601	79	5,601,982	6	21,146	6,439,893
1966	658	454,722	320,971	79	5,538,744	6	21,175	6,335,612
1967	657	427,495	306,437	75	5,539,562	6	21,120	6,294,614
1968	656	401,499	299,357	68	5,364,484	6	21,285	6,086,625
1969	656	387,856	292,800	68	5,461,721	6	21,505	6,163,882
1970	656	394,290	295,901	67	5,518,520	6	23,869	6,222,580
1971	659	699,522		67	5,559,371	6	25,360	6,284,253
1972	659	703,030		62	5,425,327	9	40,415	6,168,772
1973	651	665,379		60	5,364,904	9	42,913	6,073,196
1974	623	691,889		63	5,787,467	9	39,101	6,518,457
1975	623	674,905		61	5,750,039	9	43,930	6,468,874
1976	623	659,058		59	5,800,069	9	48,120	6,459,127
1977	623	659,737		59	5,913,159	9	43,375	6,616,271
1978	623	675,946		59	6,259,595	9	54,623	6,990,164

(Labour Party Report, 1978)

cent) out of his 441,000 members paying the levy in 1977. In the Communist dominated TASS section of the AUEW, Ken Gill leads a union where over half the members do not pay the levy to Labour (97,756 out of 183,492 in 1977).

Many trade unionists in craft unions also choose not to fund Labour's coffers. As many as 48,246 out of the 129,956 members in the Boilermakers' contracted out in 1977 (37.1 per cent). So did 60,714 of the 109,438-strong print union, the National Graphical Association (55.5 per cent). Only 49,203 members of the Society of Graphical and Allied Trades (SOGAT) affiliated to the political levy out of its 198,182 members in 1977 (75.1 per cent). The large white-collar unions with often militant attitudes and radical policies stay clear of Labour altogether by not affiliating at all. The most prominent in that position are the National and Local Government Officers' Association (NALGO), the National Union of Teachers and the Civil and Public Services' Association (CPSA). The last sizeable union to reaffiliate to Labour was the Post Office Engineering Union in 1964 and nearly a third of its members do not pay the levy.

This means that it is still the general manual and industrial unions who form the basis of Labour's strength in the trade union movement. The Mineworkers remain one of the most loyalist of unions, with only around 14,000 members out of the 258,695 members contracting out and the vast majority of them hailing from the clerical section (COSA). Only a handful of the members of the National Union of Railwaymen contract out (7,766 out of 171,825 in 1977) just 4.5 per cent. With a long non-party political tradition in the Engineers' during the period before the Second World War, it is perhaps not so surprising that as many as 297,686 of the 1,173,000 members of the engineering section of the AUEW did not pay the levy in 1977 (25.4 per cent). In the Transport and General Workers', on the other hand, only 60,123 contracted out in 1977 from a membership of 2,022,738, while 19,214 (2.0 per cent) out of 945,324 did so in the General and Municipal Workers' and 67,747 (15.6 per cent) out of 432,628 members in the EETPU. The National Union of Public Employees had a mere 10,280 (1.5 per cent) out of 693,097 members contracting out in 1977. NUPE has now replaced the former giants of coal and the railways as one of Labour's major trade union supports.

The dependence of Labour on the unions for its very existence in the 1980s cannot be exaggerated. The unions remain very much the paymasters, who keep the party afloat, weak though their total help may seem when placed against need. Annual returns to the Certification Office for 1977 reveal that the total income of the political funds held by the unions amounted to £3,400,000 and as much as £2,500,000 of that sum was spent. At the end of 1977 there were 79 unions who actually maintained political funds, totalling 9,700,000 members, with 81 per cent of them (7,900,000) contributing to those funds.

There is a widespread, passive acceptance by most trade unionists of the existence of the political levy and a willingness to tolerate the political activities of the minority in the unions who participate fully in their affairs. As Martin Harrison wrote in 1960: 'No one who has worked among trade unionists could fail to be aware of how often affiliation with Labour is taken as a natural and undiscussed part of union life' (*Trade Unions and the Labour Party Since 1945*, London, 1964). Despite the setbacks of the years since those remarks were made the position has hardly changed at all.

Yet the vital link between the unions and Labour is not very popular, even with the party voters. Nearly a third of the people interviewed in a random sample of 2,000 people from 105 constituencies for the 1976 Houghton Committee on party finance believed the unions were a 'bad' source of income for the Labour Party. Of those who did so, two thirds thought the unions exercised far too much influence over the party's activities as a result. Certainly the unions played a substantial role in the Labour Party's election effort in May 1979 through a separate organization known as Trade Unionists for a Labour Victory under the chairmanship of David Basnett of the GMWU. The unions contributed around £1 million to the Labour campaign and also spent more on their own sponsored MPs. They produced posters and leaflets for distribution on the shopfloor in key marginal constituencies.

As the unions were mainly responsible for the industrial unrest of the previous winter, some observers believed their close identification with Labour's campaign helped to lose the party the election. But the moribund state of the party organization made the infusion of union officials into marginal constituency campaigns a virtual necessity. If Labour is ever to reassess its ties with the unions, state funding of party work will be vital, but there are no signs of this coming in the immediate future.

Conservatives and the unions

The very much closer ties forged between the TUC and Labour in the early 1970s would have failed to please earlier TUC general secretaries. When the Conservatives took office in 1951 the General Council issued a statement which said: 'We shall continue to examine every question solely in the light of its industrial and economic implications.' The desire to retain freedom of manoeuvre from party political pressures was central to the TUC's strategy of influence. Woodcock would not have approved of the work of the Labour/TUC Liaison Committee. 'It is making formal what has been *ad hoc* for a long time,' said Murray, but only just over half the TUC unions are affiliated to Labour and most of the white-collar unions have kept well clear of any overt party commitment. This is the paradox. The TUC has grown more influential in the Labour 'movement', at the very time when it has broadened its membership base. The cold war atmosphere of the early 1970s when Edward Heath and the TUC were scarcely on speaking terms is one explanation for what happened, but not the whole story. The strains of economic decline pushed party and TUC much closer together than they were in the 1960s. For Labour leaders there seemed no sensible alternative. It was their answer to the confrontation politics of 1970–4. Yet an estimated 40 per cent of all trade unionists voted Conservative at the 1979 general election. During Labour's dismal by-election record from 1966 to 1970 thousands of working-class voters deserted Labour's ranks for the Conservatives, and again after 1974. There is now considerable research evidence that very few workers see either the unions or Labour as anything more than 'defence organizations required to insure the working class obtain their "fair share" '. As McKenzie and Silver argue: 'Only a very few see these organizations as means whereby to transform or radically alter present social and economic arrangements' (*Angels in Marble*, London, 1968.)

To a surprising extent, the economic views of most trade
unionists are closer to those of the Conservatives than the
Labour Party. A survey carried out for the Confederation of
British Industry in the autumn of 1976 found that the belief in
private enterprise, profit and incentive was not confined just to
company boardrooms and white-collar staff. Down on the shopfloor the majority of manual workers support the capitalist
system too. As many as 82 per cent of the trade union manual
workers in a 1975 NOP disagreed with the proposition that
profit was a dirty word, while 78 per cent said company profits
were not immoral. A total of 89 per cent believed it was fair for
a company to pay dividends to its shareholders, while a similar
proportion thought it was fair for a firm to pay interest on the
money it borrowed from a bank. As many as 86 per cent of
those trade union manual workers said it was important for
them to live in a free enterprise society. The survey found there
was widespread support for the idea of worker profit-sharing.

Nevertheless the Conservatives find it difficult to establish
working contacts with union leaders. The sorry tale of the Industrial Relations Act soured relations. There was a widespread
belief that the Conservative Party could no longer govern, because of the refusal of the powerful unions to allow it to do so.
This did not reflect the views of the TUC general secretary. 'The
Tories are entitled to ask for our help if they are an elected
government. The TUC should cooperate with them, as far as
its members will permit, to get things done,' said Len Murray.
'I would utterly oppose the idea we never talk to Tories.' The
problem for the Conservatives derives from the need to both
win the confidence of senior union leaders and mobilize the
support of trade union voters. Either objective is not always
compatible with the other. Many Conservatives on the right
wing of their party would like to see legislation to outlaw the
closed shop and the introduction of compulsory ballots in
union elections. Senior Conservatives acknowledge such political action would destroy any tentative understanding between
a Conservative government and the TUC. After the trauma of
February 1974 there is little relish to return to self-destructive
confrontation. Jim Prior, the Conservative spokesman on industrial relations, emphasized in a speech at Manchester in
February 1976 that a future Conservative government would

not introduce any major legislation to reform trade union law. The lesson of 1971 has been learnt.

The main failure has been in the Conservative inability to encourage working-class and trade union involvement in the organs of their party. As *The Times* wrote on 18 April 1883: 'In the inarticulate mass of the English populace, Disraeli discerned the Conservative workingman as the sculptor perceives the angel prisoned in a block of marble.' Yet at no time in their history have Conservative leaders made a deliberate and sustained effort to provide an active role for trade unionists in their ranks. Before the rise of Labour many respectable Protestant working men in Lancashire and London were voting Tory at elections, and the cotton spinning unions were particularly susceptible to Conservative Party influence. Archibald Salvidge in Liverpool and Joe Chamberlain in Birmingham both mobilized working-class support into a formidable election machine, but for most of their history the Conservatives have kept at a distance from trade union participation in their affairs.

In 1918 the party formed a National Trade Union Committee, but it was not until after the 1945 election defeat that the Conservatives gave priority to the creation of an organization that would make a direct appeal in the ranks of organized labour. A trade union department was established at Central Office under the direction of the chairman of the party, Lord Woolton, as part of R. A. Butler's industrial charter and in 1950 George Beck, a worker with London Transport, was made its national organizer. Industrial officers were appointed in every area office, with a further 50 part-time organizers spread across the country. In the early 1950s Edward Brown, a trade unionist from Walthamstow, was promoted by Woolton as an archetypal Conservative trade unionist. He eventually became MP for Bath. But during the 1960s the trade union organization in the party went into decay, becoming a major victim of economy cutbacks. By the autumn of 1974 there were only two CTU national organizers left. After the appointment of Michael Wolff as director-general at Conservative Central Office, Andrew Rowe was made Youth and Community Affairs officer and the remaining CTU officials were dismissed. But with the election of Margaret Thatcher as party leader in February 1975 and the sacking of Wolff there was a major re-appraisal of the trade union activities of the Conservatives. Under the influence of the new party chairman Lord Thorney-croft, the CTU was given a new lease of life. John Bowis was appointed national organizer, a shrewd observer of the trade union scene with none of the anti-union instincts of so many party stalwarts. Between 1975 and 1979 the CTU has become a sizeable and occasionally influential force in the party. By the spring of 1979 there were 280 separate trade union branches at constituency level and a small full-time staff of half a dozen to coordinate work. The CTU national committee was made more representative of trade unionists, with fewer deferential Tories in its ranks. A number of specialist groups for local government workers, teachers, workers in transport and members of ASTMS were established and the annual conference of the CTU became an important fixture on the party calendar, where the leader made a key-note speech. Before 1976 the CTU met for usually half a day in London and hardly more than a handful attended. By the time of the 1978 Bradford conference the CTU claimed to have nearly 1,000 delegates and they debated trade union issues. But both right and left wing Conservatives are less enthusiastic about the idea of a separately organized trade union group within the party, arguing that this is divisive, while the main emphasis should be on unifying the party. The CTU was generally a sensible, moderating force on the leadership between 1975 and 1979. It took a hostile view to George Ward of Grunwick, although he was put on to the candidates' list, a badge of approval from Central Office. Jim Prior, as employment shadow spokesman from 1974 to 1979, took a keen interest in the work of the CTU, although their views were not always listened to by Mrs Thatcher and her colleagues. For instance, the CTU argued against the withdrawal of state benefits from strikers' families, a view which was not shared by the majority of the shadow cabinet.

After 1975 the leadership sought to emphasize that many trade unionists vote Conservative (almost 40 per cent did so in May 1979) and it tried to encourage greater participation by Conservative trade unionists in their union's affairs. As Mrs Thatcher told the 1975 party conference:

When the next Conservative government comes to power many
trade unionists will have put it there. Millions of them vote for us
at every election. I want to say to them and to all our supporters
in industry: go out and join in the work of your union; go to their
meetings and stay to the end, and learn the union rules as well as
the far left knows them. Remember that if parliamentary
democracy dies, free trade unions die with it.

In the policy statement – *The Right Approach* – which won
the approval of the 1976 party conference Mrs Thatcher and
her colleagues presented a more conciliatory face towards the
unions. 'On our return to office we do not intend to introduce
a major round of new industrial relations legislation,' they asserted. But the document made it clear that the unions would
not continue to enjoy a special influence with a Conservative
government in power. 'We believe that a strong and responsible
trade union movement has an important role in a free society,'
it explained. 'It should be widely consulted and its interests
acknowledged and understood. But the trade unions are not the
government of the country. It is Parliament, and no other body,
which is elected to run the affairs of this country in the best
interests of all the people.' *The Right Approach* expressed support for the use of public money to encourage postal ballots for
union elections when requested, the encouragement of firms to
provide time and facilities for the conduct of union meetings;
safeguards to protect individual rights in the closed shop,
including the right to appeal to an 'independent tribunal to
safeguard the right of an individual whose livelihood is endangered by arbitrary exclusion or expulsion from a trade union'.
The Conservatives turned down the idea of a social contract,
because it meant entering arrangements with the unions which
might damage the national interest by committing the government to unwise policies as part of a bargain for pay restraint.
The document praised the 'concerted action' approach of West
Germany; but it conceded it would take 'time, and patient and
painful adjustment to economic reality' to bring about such an
arrangement in Britain.

The most definitive view of Conservative industrial relations
policy came in October 1977 with the publication of *The Right
Approach to the Economy*, a symposium of views embracing
Jim Prior, Sir Keith Joseph, Sir Geoffrey Howe and David

Howell and edited by Angus Maude. This maintained: 'Our
strength lies in the fact that we have never forged a narrow
relationship with any minority group or sought to shuffle off
on to union leaders responsibilities which properly belong to
government.'

The Conservative aim was to let the unions 'deal at arm's
length with a government which knows both its place and theirs'.
The October 1977 statement made it clear the Conservatives
would resist, 'firmly and decisively', any 'direct political challenge' to their authority when in power from 'within the ranks
or organized labour'.

The Conservatives were anxious in the years of opposition
from 1974–9 to reassure the doubters that their party was not
intent on any showdown or confrontation with the unions on
their return to office. 'To suggest that the Conservative Party
would seek to be in conflict with trade unions is to suggest
that we are in favour of cutting off one of our own limbs,' said
Prior in a speech at Clapham on 20 July 1978. 'Without
the support of several million trade union members, we never
could form a government. We are part of the trade union
movement and they are part of us.' He welcomed the code of
practice on time off for union activities, 'since it helps fulfil our
pledge to allow union elections and meetings to take place on
the firm's premises and in the firm's time'.

But by the early winter of 1978–9, and the deterioration in
the industrial climate with the six-week strike at Ford and clear
evidence of a massive push against the Government's flimsy 5
per cent pay guidelines, the tone and content of Conservative
Party speeches became more shrill. Speaking in Paddington on
18 December 1978, Mrs Thatcher declared: 'Today union
power is feared, sometimes even by union members. There is
grave public distrust about their willingness to bargain responsibly. It is as much in the interests of the unions themselves as of
the public that a start should be made towards finding a remedy
for these problems which are daily becoming more pressing.
We intend to make that start.' In her view 'power and responsibility' no longer marched together in the unions and the 'balance of power in normal wage bargaining' had been 'tipped
dramatically away from management towards the unions',
while the country has one of the worst records in industrial

production in the Western world. 'We shall not bash the unions,' promised Mrs Thatcher. 'Neither shall we bow to them. Higher wages – real wages, not just paper money – must come not from holding the country to ransom but from raising productivity and reducing restrictive practices. In the long run, unions can only prosper when the nation prospers – and vice versa. As the song about love and marriage pointed out: This I tell you, Brother, you can't have one without the other.' In her opinion, once convinced 'of this simple truth' the unions could 'regain the confidence and trust of the public'.

The onset of the damaging road haulage drivers' national strike in January 1979 brought the call from Mrs Thatcher on television for 'a rational debate about the question of trade union power'. In a speech at Huddersfield on 12 January 1979, Prior also took a critical attitude about the use of the strike weapon as the first resort, the tearing up of agreements, and the aggressive tactics of flying pickets. 'The country is now reaping the full effects of those damaging aspects of industrial relations law which were introduced by Mr Michael Foot between 1974 and 1976,' he argued. 'Thanks to him, the closed shop has become a fearful instrument for union discipline, forcing some people out of work without any compensation: and thanks to him blacking and blockading have become ready tools in all too many industrial disputes.' Prior said that the Conservatives wanted to give 'the moderate majority' in the unions 'a bigger say' by helping to make the trade unions more representative of the views of the membership. Here, he repeated Conservative arguments for the wider use of the secret ballot in the election of union officials and encouragement to firms to allow union meetings to be held on company premises. By this stage the Conservatives were favourable to the idea of trying to establish voluntarily secret ballots of union members before the calling of strikes, not just for the election of their officials. Prior suggested there was 'justified and widespread public anxiety' about the payment of supplementary benefits to strikers, although admitting there was 'some exaggeration' about the effect of benefit payments on the prolonging of strikes. He went on to propose a 'non-aggression pact' in 'key areas of national life' where people gave up their right to strike in return for a guarantee about their pay position. Prior called for a 'sensible code of conduct' on picketing. He also proposed a code of practice for the establishment of closed shops to ensure they were only introduced 'if a massive majority voted in favour' and existing workers were exempt from its provisions along with others who objected to joining a union 'on reasonable grounds of conscience'. Prior warned that while the Conservatives hoped to reach agreement with the TUC through consultation on the closed shops issue, they would legislate if necessary. The party was already pledged to allow workers, who were dismissed from their job because they had been expelled or excluded from a union, to seek compensation in damages from a court of law.

The events of the winter of 1978–9 undoubtedly helped to toughen up the Conservative proposals on industrial relations reform but, mainly thanks to the patience and tact of Prior, the shadow cabinet was not swept along by the irrational anti-union hysteria of the moment into any rash commitment about the use of the law as a weapon to humble the unions or even weaken them significantly. 'None of these proposals is as important as the patient and long-term attempt to improve collective bargaining,' he declared in his Huddersfield speech. The often hostile Conservative rhetoric against the unions co-existed with a fairly modest series of proposals to change the existing labour law.

The Conservative general election manifesto in April 1979 trod carefully in this potentially explosive area, but there was a renewed note of impatience in its language about the unions. Under the heading – 'restoring the balance', the document described the 1974–6 labour laws as a 'militants' charter'. It went on: 'Labour claim that industrial relations in Britain cannot be improved by changing the law. We disagree. If the law can be used to confer privileges, it can and should also be used to establish obligations.' There were clear proposals to bring in immediate legislation to limit picketing to the premises of the company where the workers were in dispute; the right of appeal to a court of law to employees losing their jobs in a closed shop and much tighter conditions for the acceptance of closed shop agreements with wider conscience clauses for those who did not wish to join a union; the introduction of state aid for postal ballots for union elections and 'other important issues'. As a concession to anti-union feelings, the Conservatives also decided to review the issue of state benefits for strikers' families. 'We shall ensure that unions bear the fair share of the cost of supporting those of their members who are on strike', argued the manifesto.

The Conservatives pledged themselves to restore 'responsible' pay bargaining, leaving it to employers and workers in the private sector to agree on what their companies could afford to pay out in wage increases, while making it quite clear 'there can be no question of subsidizing excessive pay deals'. In the public sector, cash limits would apply and pay bargaining would 'take place within the limits of what the taxpayer and ratepayer can afford'.

During the general election campaign, Mrs Thatcher made the issue of trade union 'power' a major one for the Conservatives. As she told her adoption meeting in Finchley, 'What we want to see drawn are certain legal boundary lines, within which the trade union movement can fulfil its proper role – of ensuring a fair return for the work of its members. We shall not wait until there is another industrial crisis on our hands to bring about the changes that everyone knows are needed.'

Communism in the unions

If Conservatives find it difficult nowadays to reach a *modus vivendi* with the unions, the same cannot be said of the Communists. The Red menace is a familiar bogey of popular journalism. Political extremists are often seen as being behind industrial disputes.

Should we take the Communist presence in industry seriously at all? In the past, the party has proved a useful scapegoat for the country's economic troubles. Harold Wilson pinned the blame on Communists during the seamen's strike of 1966, when the economy was 'blown off course' into a sterling crisis and deflation. On that famous occasion the Prime Minister talked about the 'tightly knit group of politically motivated men' within the National Union of Seamen, whom he claimed were responsible for pushing a hitherto moderate union into an unseemly act of militancy. Wilson told the House of Commons that the Communists had at their disposal 'an efficient and disciplined industrial apparatus controlled by headquarters. No major strike occurs anywhere in this country in any sector of industry in which the apparatus does not concern itself.' In the winter of 1973–4 Edward Heath came to the conclusion that the Communists were trying to sabotage his government. At the December 1973 Common Market Summit in Copenhagen, he informed other heads of state that the Reds were behind the industrial unrest.

As a well-established political party, the Communists espouse the parliamentary road to socialism with conspicuous lack of success. Acceptance of the inevitability of gradualness has done the party no good at all. At elections, the Communists suffer constant humiliation. In May 1979 all 29 Communist candidates lost their deposits. In October 1974 they polled 17,426 votes or 601 each. This was the lowest vote the party had achieved since the 1931 election. No Communist has sat in the House of Commons for over a quarter of a century. The party's local election performance is little better. There are no more than a smattering of Communist councillors, almost all of them on Clydeside, in the Fife coalfield or the valleys of South Wales. The party's individual membership is also in a bad way.

At the end of 1978 there were 25,000 party members and the Communist daily newspaper – the *Morning Star* – probably sells more copies in the monopoly markets of Eastern Europe than it does in Britain.

Such a recent dismal record does not appear to worry the Communist Party, at least outwardly. 'It is superficial to judge a party by the numbers in it,' said Bert Ramelson, former national industrial organizer, in 1974. 'We have more influence now on the Labour movement than at any time in the life of our party.' But influence is not the same as control. Party leaders might like to play at conspiracy, but they are no longer able to do so. The atmosphere of the Stalin era has passed away and right-wing authoritarian leaders in the unions are also less obvious. Twenty years ago tough bosses like Arthur Deakin of the Transport and General Workers and Bill Carron of the Engineers could mobilize their big battalions against the Communist 'menace' in industry. In their turn, the Communists could exploit genuine rank and file discontents with the ways of the bosses, notably among dockers. London busmen and engineering workers (particularly in Manchester and on Clydeside). In those days, Communist militants looked to the party's then industrial organizer, Peter Kerrigan. Orders and directives flowed out of King Street and they were invariably obeyed without question.

This became more difficult by the late 1950s. In the Electrical Trades' Union, the Communists were compelled to resort to ballot-rigging to keep their iron grip until 1963. By then, the monolith was cracking. The traumas of 1956 with Khruschev's exposure of the evils of Stalinism to the 20th Soviet Party Congress, followed by the Red Army's brutal suppression of the Hungarian revolution, undermined the party in Britain. As many as 7,000 members tore up their party cards.

But in the middle of 1970s it was still possible to find plenty of comrades in the ranks of the trade union movement. Estimates suggest that 10 per cent of officials in the unions are Communists. There are six of the twenty-seven members of the NUM Executive in the party. There are said to be four Communists on the Executives of the NUR and UPW respectively. A sprinkling of party members are to be found among the civil service unions. The construction workers' union – UCATT – has four Communists on its Executive. In 1968 the TGWU lifted its old ban on party members holding office in the union. It is claimed ten out of the thirty-six-strong Executive Council are Communists. The Electricians are the only union who forbid Communists holding any official post. An attempt to change that rule at the 1973 Rules Revision Conference was heavily defeated.

Communists are particularly numerous in the AUEW. After Hugh Scanlon reached the presidency in 1967 with CP backing, some of the restraints on shopfloor activity were lifted, but in recent years the Communists have suffered losses with the arrival of the postal ballot in union elections. The defection of Jimmy Reid, the hero of the 1971 Upper Clyde work-in, from the party in the spring of 1976 was only the most prominent of a number, which weakened the direct influence of the Communists on Britain's second biggest union. Reg Birch used to be a party member, but he left in 1968 to become a Maoist in the Communist Party of Britain (Marxist-Leninist). He sat on the AUEW Executive Council until 1979. The Communists can usually reckon to have fifteen members on the fifty-two-strong National Committee of the union – the supreme policy-making body. It is reckoned that around 1,000 of the 30,000 stewards in the AUEW belong to the Communists. 'Where the struggle is, there are Communists also,' said Ken Gill, the tough and able general secretary of the Technical and Supervisory section of the AUEW. Gill was not elected to his top post but appointed by the TASS Executive. He became a Communist in 1950 in disgust at the record of the Attlee Government. George Guy, general secretary of the Sheet Metal Workers, is a Communist, elected to the General Council in 1977.

A check-list of card-holding members in the unions is perhaps a futile exercise. The party leadership is no longer that concerned with making sure of maximizing their support. Communists acknowledge there is no future in self-isolation as a pure disciplined cadre of élite troops. The emphasis since the mid-1950s has been on the need for unity on the left. Party members say their relations with the Labour left have never been better. The TUC agreed in 1973 that the old prohibition on Communists attending the annual conference of trades councils as delegates should be lifted. Transport House's famous list of banned Communist front organizations has been torn up.

The industrial climate of the early 1970s helped to blur the distinction between the Communists and the Labour left. 'The party can float an idea early in the year and it can become official Labour policy by the autumn,' said Ramelson. 'A few years ago we were on our own but not now.' Ramelson claimed that it was the Communists who led the fight in the unions to oppose any kind of incomes policy. The party also pioneered opposition to any industrial relations legislation through the Liaison Committee for the Defence of Trade Unions, set up to oppose Labour's prices and incomes strategy in 1967. In Ramelson's opinion, that *ad hoc* rank and file organization of convenors and shop stewards had more impact than the party's Minority Movement between the wars ever achieved. It reached its peak in 1971 with strike action against the Industrial Relations Act, at first in defiance of TUC policy.

Communists claim – with some justice – that it was their members who forced the Heath Government drastically to reverse its lame-duck policy towards industry in 1971. Communist shop stewards at Upper Clyde Shipbuilders decided to stage a work-in by the 8,000 workers to save the four shipyards on the Clyde threatened with complete closure. The action – led by Jimmy Reid and another Communist convenor, Jimmy Airlie – was revolutionary in one sense because it challenged existing property rights; but the far left have argued that the Communists in UCS were too respectful in trying to seek a broad consensus of support for the UCS cause. There was no sit-in or similar action. As the party's own chroniclers of that event wrote: 'The work-in was not an attempt to establish "workers' control" on a permanent basis. Such a conception would lack all credibilty.' This view was supported by the findings of Professor Ken Alexander of Strathclyde University. The Communists dislike the idea of factory sit-ins and talk dispairingly of syndicalism. The party feels such behaviour could isolate the Communists and bring disaster to the whole trade union movement. The party decried the breakaway tactics of the Trotskyists during the Pilkington Glass strike of 1970 and the long-drawn-out efforts of the ultra-left at the Fine Tubes dispute in Plymouth.

The party opposes shopfloor action as an end in itself. Communists believe militant behaviour is a way of bringing pressure to bear on established union leaders and making them pursue policies that reflect the mood of the rank and file. Herein lies the paradox of modern British communism. As its outright control and manipulation has slackened, the party's wider influence has grown. But it becomes a problem to know who is really absorbing whom in the Labour movement as a result. In practice, the party is unwilling to throw away its gains through impetuous, ill-conceived adventurism. They believe the far left put all leadership in question and this only attracts immature young people who like shouting revolutionary slogans. The party has learnt from bitter experience. It realizes it is impossible to act without popular support, not just in leading men out of work in a strike but taking them back intact after the battle is over.

Yet the party can still flex its industrial muscles if it feels the need to do so. When the Yorkshire miners contacted the party's Birmingham offices for help during the 1972 national coal strike, it was forthcoming. The Communists were at the forefront of the picketing of the Saltley coal depot when 10,000 Birmingham engineering workers turned up outside the gates to stop the movement of supplies in solidarity with the miners. But such action was limited and conditional. If Communists ever tried to go beyond the immediate, they would have the shaky ground cut from under their feet. Party shopfloor workers accept there is a wide gulf between economic issues and political ideology. Despite the fiery rhetoric, Communist Party workers are grounded in a harsh realism, based on long experience. British communism has predicted too many false dawns.

The greater openness and tolerance within the Labour movement during the 1970s breathed some fresh life into a withering party, at a time when raging price inflation and wage controls, industrial relations legislation and divisive social policies should have brought the Communists rich dividends. What influence the party carried in the TUC and the Labour Party reflected the abdication and bankruptcy of the moderates in the Labour movement. Yet Communists admitted their left policies were not really socialist. Influence is an uncertain intangible, but with the collapse of the old disciplines and the decline in the control of industrial events, perhaps that is what the party will have to settle for in future, even if such a strategy of permeation makes the whole point of a separate Marxist party seem rather pointless.

The political groups on the far left – notably the Socialist Workers' Party – were unable to exploit the recession with much success in their recruitment drives. The Right to Work campaign (mainly organized by SWP) aroused some publicity at various TUCs, but it has so far failed to grow into a mass movement of the unemployed on the scale of the National Unemployed Workmen's Movement between the wars. However, the SWP have numerous articulate and persuasive young militants in a number of white-collar unions, such as NALGO, CPSA and the NUT. The group is now running candidates in parliamentary elections and it has taken a militant, controversial stand against racialism. SWP has kept clear of the efforts of other Trotskyite groups to infiltrate the Labour Party, but its concentration on building up shopfloor support through factory branches looks like an uphill struggle. Whether the present severe crisis and drastic fall in living standards among workers will generate a more militant kind of politics in the unions or merely produce a sullen, bewildered response, the next few years will tell. The prospects for revolutionaries look bleak for the 1980s.

4 The unions, the Labour Party and the Social Contract 1972–9

This honourable and open alliance. (Pete Curran of the Gasworkers at the 1908 Labour Party Conference on the links between the party and the unions)

The joint understandings and programmes worked out through the Liaison Committee over the last five years have made a significant contribution to the nation's economic recovery. (*Into the Eighties: An Agreement*, July 1978)

During most of the 1970s the Labour Party and the trade union movement worked closely together in the revived alliance known as the Social Contract. Despite the severe economic troubles which Labour was compelled to grapple with after taking office unexpectedly in the dark days of March 1974 – rampant inflation, the return of mass unemployment, a weak and unstable currency, balance of payments deficits, low growth and stagnant production, an alarming deterioration in the country's manufacturing base and the first cuts in real living standards for most people since the Second World War – the partnership between Labour and the unions displayed far more resilience than in previous periods of Labour Government.

Both wings of the Labour movement have recognized the need for the other and most of the time they claim to share mutual ideals and practical policy objectives, but very often a certain lack of trust has scarred the deeper loyalties of tradition. Ramsay MacDonald scarcely disguised his contempt for the union leaders during the period of his two minority Labour governments; though it was the emphatic stand against cuts in unemployment benefit by the TUC in August 1931 that rallied the fainthearts in the Cabinet against Treasury orthodoxy, helping to push MacDonald into his National Government.

Between 1945 and 1951 the TUC tried to cooperate wholeheartedly with the Attlee Government, and in 1948 even agreed to a voluntary restraint on pay demands until the inflationary floodgates burst open two years later. To establish a virtual wage standstill for such a length of time through the suspension of the most cherished principles of 'free' collective bargaining was quite an achievement. The main reason for this temporary success lay less in the conviction of union leaders that such a policy made economic sense, than in the close, personal and political ties of friendship that had been established between the union bosses and the Labour Cabinet.

As Gerald Dorfman has written:

There was displayed a strong feeling of identity by the General Council members with the Labour Government. It was 'their' Government. It had delivered on promises of economic and social reform. It had kept its pledge to sustain full employment, even against some very powerful arguments in favour of deflation in 1947. (*Wage Politics in Britain 1945–67*, London, 1974)

Once again, between 1964 and 1970, the TUC found itself making sacrifices for the well-being of a Labour government – much to the obvious distaste of George Woodcock – with their grudging consent for a short period even with a statutory pay policy. But during the Wilson years union sourness set in early. By 1967 Labour was having to govern with only the 'reluctant acquiescence' of the TUC. The pay explosion of 1969–72 was partly caused by the three years of severe control over the level of wage rises. Trade unionists were, in fact, among the main sufferers from Labour's incomes policy. In the words of Leo Panitch, 'In four out of the six half yearly periods between Labour's 1966 election victory and the summer of 1969, workers experienced declining real incomes before tax' (*Social Democracy and Industrial Militancy*, Cambridge, 1976). H. A. Turner and Frank Wilkinson calculated that the net real income of an average male manual worker, married with two children, rose by a mere 0.5 per cent a year during Labour's term of office, despite the achievement of an annual rate of growth of 3 per cent (*Do Trade Unions Cause Inflation?*, Cambridge, 1975). The pressure on the living standards of trade unionists was made even more burdensome by the onward march of direct taxation, in making up what union leaders like to call the 'social wage' or government spending on transfer payments and public services. In 1960 a manual worker's social insurance contributions and tax amounted to no more than 8 per cent of his total gross earnings; by 1970–71 that proportion had risen to 20 per cent and by the late 1970s it had climbed as high as a third. The alliance between Labour and the unions has failed to produce obvious material benefits for trade unionists in the post-war period. Indeed, the best time for the growth in real incomes for manual workers has been when the Conservatives were in power – during the golden days of Butskellism between 1952 and 1955 and in Heath's lame-duck period from June 1970 to the pay freeze of November 1972. No wonder Turner and Wilkinson have written: 'It almost appears as if the objective economic-historical role of the Labour Party is to do (no doubt despite itself) those things to the workers that Conservative governments are unable to do.'

After Labour's election defeat in June 1970, relations between the unions and the Labour Party were unhappy and strained. The memories of the months of self-destructive struggle over the ill-fated January 1969 White Paper – *In Place of Strife* – and the 'short, sharp' Bill to deal with unofficial strikers had done much to damage the foundations of the old alliance. At the last minute Harold Wilson and his Employment minister Barbara Castle had been forced to back down from a showdown with the TUC in the face of a Cabinet split, a sizeable revolt in the Parliamentary Labour Party and the well-nigh unanimous hostility of the TUC under general secretary elect Vic Feather. The 'solemn and binding' agreement of 18 June 1969 was both a belated recognition by the government of the dangers of a break-up of the Labour movement and an acceptance that union reform by law with sanctions was impossible to impose on the trade union movement.

But the wounds were hard to heal quickly. At the 1970 Labour Party Conference Jack Jones launched a bitter attack on the politicians and the 'sham democracy' of Britain. 'For too many Members of Parliament the constituency Labour Party is a bit of a nuisance, a device for giving him a free hand as the mood takes him. And when we are in power, the relationship with ministers is sometimes even more remote,' complained Jones. 'Representative conferences should be set up, through which Members of Parliament are required continually to consult with community representatives. And maybe we shall eventually get round to the idea of shop stewards in the streets.'

But in the early 1970s there was a fresh attempt to establish a close, working partnership between the unions and the party. At the 1970 Labour Party Conference both Jack Cooper of the GMWU and Alf Allen of USDAW supported the idea and Thomas Balogh in an influential Fabian pamphlet – *Labour and Inflation* – also pointed in that direction. But it was in 1971 that the real initiative for the Social Contract was taken by Jack Jones. He told the conference:

There is no reason at all why a joint policy cannot be worked out. But let us have the closest possible liaison. This is not just a matter of brainstorming in the back rooms of Congress House and Transport House just before the next election. In the past we have not had the dialogue necessary. The unions and the party leadership perhaps have both been unsure of their own ground but we can make this policy into a great campaign to open up the approach to genuine industrial democracy based on the unions.

In the unlikely venue of a Fabian meeting at the 1971 conferance, Jones emphasized the value of such an approach.

Union leaders and the Labour shadow cabinet had found a new cohesion in their opposition to Edward Heath's Industrial Relations Bill and it was decided in the autumn of 1971 to establish a committee on a more permanent basis. The TUC–Labour Party Liaison Committee met for the first time on 23 January 1972, at Transport House, made up of six members of the shadow cabinet led by Harold Wilson, six from the National Executive Committee and six from the TUC led by Vic Feather. It was agreed they should meet on the first Monday of every month alternating their meeting place between Transport House, the House of Commons and Congress House – with a rotating chairman and serviced jointly by the Labour Party research department and the TUC. Within six months a joint statement was issued by the Liaison Committee on industrial relations policy which called for the repeal of the Industrial Relations Act and the creation of a Conciliation and Arbitration Service, independent of government and made up of employer and union representatives and 'other persons with industrial relations experience'. It also called for an extension of worker rights over being able to belong to a trade union, unfair dismissals, shorter qualifying periods for minimum notice and longer periods of notice from employers. Trade unions were to be able to take employers refusing them recognition or information for collective bargaining purposes before an arbitration committee, which would have the power to make an award that became binding on employers in individual contracts of employment. Trade union representatives were also to be provided with statutory rights on safety and health at work.

By the summer of 1972 the Liaison Committee decided to expand the range of its work into economic policy, looking at the obstacles to growth such as inflation and the balance of payments. On top of this, it was agreed they should examine industrial democracy and regional policy as well as new strategies to deal with unemployment.

The next policy document from the Liaison Committee emerged early in 1973 when Harold Wilson and Vic Feather unveiled *Economic Policy and the Cost of Living*. This amounted to a virtual shopping list of proposals for the next Labour government. It called for a control of basic food prices through subsidies, the subsidization of public transport fares, the public ownership of land for building purposes, a 'large scale' redistribution of income and wealth, the phasing out of social service charges, and an 'immediate commitment' to old age pension increases – to £10 a week for single pensioners and £16 for couples. The statement added: 'The first task of a new Labour government would be to conclude with the TUC a wide ranging agreement on the policies to be pursued in all these aspects of our economic life and to discuss with them the order of priorities for their fulfilment.' A further statement emerged from the Liaison Committee on the EEC's common agricultural policy in July 1973, which was extremely critical of its operation. Although the controversial *Labour Programme*, 1973, provided the basis for the party manifesto in the February 1974 general election, it was clear the Liaison Committee was to play a key role in future party policy-making.

Indeed, when Labour took office again in March 1974, a decision was reached to keep the Liaison Committee in existence, meeting every month with the Prime Minister and senior Cabinet ministers in attendance. By the winter of 1975–6 it was to the Liaison Committee that the Cabinet looked for support rather than to the left-dominated national executive.

Between March and September 1974 the minority Labour Government's domestic programme met with general TUC approval. This is hardly very surprising. In a TUC statement to the 1974 Congress, *Collective Bargaining and the Social Contract*, a check list was drawn up of what the Government had achieved during its short spell in office and it amounted to a virtual item by item implementation of the February 1973 Liaison Committee statement on economic policy. The old age pension increase in Denis Healey's first budget gave single people £10 a week and married couples £16. The income tax changes to help the less well-off through increased allowances plus higher tax rates for those with large incomes were also in tune with TUC priorities. There was the promise of the early introduction of a wealth tax and a gifts tax. An extra £550 million was provided for food subsidies, aimed at cutting the rise in food prices and the retail price index. A freeze was imposed on all public and private sector rents. Not everything pleased the TUC in the 1974 budget, especially the increases in the prices of coal, electricity, postal services and rail fares. Nor were the defence cuts as large as the TUC would have liked. But the TUC was well satisfied by the repeal of the Industrial Relations Act, which was the first priority of the new Government. Within a few days of Labour taking office the TUC had dispatched a detailed draft repealing Bill to Michael Foot, the Employment minister. The measure was primarily drawn up by Bill Wedderburn, professor of labour law at the LSE, and it contained proposals for the new Conciliation and Arbitration Service as well as provision for unfair dismissal clauses. Foot persuaded impatient union leaders that not all their recommendations could be introduced at once, because the government lacked an overall majority in the House of Commons. Nevertheless the General Council pressed the government hard for changes in the picketing laws to be included in the proposed Bill, which would allow pickets to stop vehicles and peacefully persuade drivers not to cross picket lines. But again union leaders recognized such a controversial reform would not win the approval of the House of Commons. The Trade Union and Labour Relation Act, passed in the brief 1974 parliamentary session, repealed the Conservative measure, but also ensured that unions did not lose any of their old legal immunities by restating the previous legislation. The TUC expressed its opposition to the government suggestion that 'conscientious objectors' should be protected from dismissal if they refused to join a union in closed shops. In the event, the opposition parties and the House of Lords amended the Bill to weaken the protection of the unions under the law in industrial disputes and closed shops. Nonetheless the General Council expressed their 'appreciation' of government efforts to secure the successful passage of the Act on to the statute book by late July 1974. One other piece of legislation of direct interest to the TUC was also passed by the minority Labour Government. This was the Health and Safety at Work Act, which had previously been introduced by the Conservative administration. The TUC played a major part in crucial changes in the new safety law to tighten up and codify existing legislation and to make enforcement more effective. The unions managed to achieve the provision of trade union safety representatives and safety committees in the Bill, though these did not come into legal existence until October 1978 and, despite TUC protests, the government failed to give the health and safety at work issue a high priority in the provision of financial assistance for training.

On the whole, with the important exception of the picketing law and the rise in nationalized industry prices, the TUC and the minority Labour Government worked harmoniously together up to the October 1974 general election. In the words of the TUC statement to Congress that autumn, 'since taking office, the government have demonstrated their commitment to implementing the general approach' (of the Social Contract statement of February 1973). Jim Callaghan, as fraternal delegate from the party, addressed the 1974 Congress in ebullient mood.

But there were already strains beginning to appear in the alliance in the vexatious area of pay bargaining. Through all its deliberations in opposition, the Liaison Committee had kept well away from any discussions over a future incomes policy. After Callaghan had tactlessly raised the issue at the 1970 Party Conference and suffered root and branch denunciation from Jones and Hugh Scanlon for doing so, the party leadership had let the matter drop. Heath's statutory incomes policy was allowed to continue until July 1974, but thereafter it was to be left to the unions themselves to conduct their own bargaining without any interference from government. As Callaghan told the 1974 TUC: 'Rigid wage controls, statutory controls, interference with free collective bargaining have all finished, whistled down the wind, a complete failure.'

In its advice to affiliates the TUC warned, 'over the coming years negotiators generally should recognize that the scope for real increases in consumption are limited and a central negotiating objective in this period will be to ensure that real incomes are maintained', but a low pay target of £25 a week minimum was laid down, there was to be a 12 month interval between wage settlements, and better fringe benefits. In November 1974 the General Council agreed to send out a circular to affiliates pointing out that it would be 'far better to get prices rising more slowly, with money wages correspondingly not going up so fast, than to have prices and wages equating with each other at a higher and higher level which would inevitably be self-defeating'. Very few negotiators appeared to take much notice during the winter of 1974–5 when pay rises began to rise over 25 per cent. Union leaders urged the Chancellor to boost public spending by £975 million in the spring of 1975 in his budget; but Healey moved in the opposite direction with cuts totalling £1,000 million in government expenditure and a reduction in demand of £350 million. Healey confessed to union leaders that his measures would not prevent an increase in the number of unemployed over the million figure by the end of the year. The General Council and the Liaison Committee expressed their disappointment at this change of policy at the Treasury but it was agreed that there must be continued 'co-operation in order to prevent unnecessary misunderstandings and divisions'.

By this stage even the TUC was worried at the growth in the rate of inflation, with the big push on pay rises. In the spring of 1975 the TUC admitted that 'there have been undesirable gaps in the observance of the guidelines' and it recognized that 'if settlements in the next round of negotiations were pitched at the level of some of those negotiated towards the middle of the year, or if new settlements were made before the due date, the prospect of reducing inflation towards the end of the year and during next year would be seriously threatened'. In fact, the country was heading towards a major economic crisis with the pound under severe pressure on foreign exchange markets and inflation rising rapidly. Union leaders like Jack Jones recognized catastrophe was staring them in the face. With the real threat of a government imposed wage ceiling, the majority of the General Council (the vote was 19 to 16) endorsed a pay policy of their own with a £6 a week rise for everybody except those earning over £8,500 a year who got nothing beyond increments. The government agreed to accept the TUC's own approach, but in July the Remuneration, Charges and Grants Act was passed, which gave ministers the powers to act should voluntary restraint fail. In the summer of 1975 the TUC was forced to swallow some unpalatable truths about the state of the British economy. The alternatives were either an agreed and effective pay policy, massive borrowing from the International Monetary Fund or savage deflation. 'Not a free for all but a fair for all – that is our policy,' argued Jones at the TUC, where the £6 policy was approved by 6,945,000 votes to 3,375,000. But as the 1975 TUC statement – *The Development of the Social Contract* – made clear, the pay policy was only supposed to be part of a wider programme of action by the government to protect the less well-off from the full impact of the economic crisis. The unions said they wanted to see much more rigorous control of price rises, the continuation of food subsidies to help low income families, the maintenance of rent subsidies, improvements in the 'social wage', manpower planning and industrial investment. Murray told the Congress bluntly: 'Some people, for a time, are going to have some reduction in their living standards. We are a low wage country. That is because our country's industrial performance has been low, below that of our competitors; because investment has been too low and too often in the wrong places and because in turn productivity has been too low. We cannot put that right in real terms merely by paying ourselves more money.'

In the event, the government found itself in no position to meet its side of the social contract. Healey was compelled to introduce two emergency packages in September and December 1975 to try and 'take the worst out of the expected winter increase in unemployment'. Further Treasury action followed in February 1976 to try and ease the jobless crisis and boost investment. The *TUC Economic Review* in the spring of that year called on the Government to set itself a target of 600,000 unemployed by 1978. It also supported the introduction of a wealth tax and demanded that old age pensions should be 33 per cent of average earnings of a full-time male worker and 50 per cent for a couple. The total TUC budget demand was for a £1,900 million boost in public spending, 1.9 per cent of gross domestic product. But Healey's spring 1976 budget was a broadly neutral affair. The Chancellor proposed a trade-off between income tax cuts and a further round of voluntary wage restraint. He suggested that if agreement was reached on pay increases 'in the area of 3 per cent' then there could be an increase in personal allowances and thresholds. The cost of those conditional allowances amounted to £920 million. The General Council told Healey that it wanted to see 'progress on a wide range of issues such as prices, unemployment, import controls and investment', and argued the overall level of wage rises would have to be higher than 3 per cent. After many painful meetings the TUC Economic Committee inner six agreed with ministers on a new pay policy from August 1976 to August 1977 with a £4 a week increase as the ceiling and £2.50 a week as the floor, but it was clear that the government had not been able to swallow the wide range of TUC demands as a precondition for pay restraint. The only apparent concession to TUC pressure came in the decision not to put up the price of school meals by 5 pence, planned for that autumn, at a cost of £35 million. As Scanlon bluntly told the special TUC Congress, called to endorse the pay policy: 'We did not achieve what we wanted. We managed to push the wage level up to what it is now and we managed to get assurances that there would be no diminution of the tax concessions.' A second year of pay restraint with the likelihood of a widening gap between the level of price rises and wage increases involved a real cut in living standards, but as Scanlon told Congress, what alternative faced the union leaders? 'We honestly believed then – and still do – that no agreement would have meant a catastrophic run on the pound that would have made what has recently happened look like chicken feed.' The unions were faced with the unwelcome prospect of the downfall of the Labour Government in the midst of an economic crisis. Congress therefore endorsed the second year of a tighter pay policy by a massive vote of 20 to 1 proportions (9,262,000 to 531,000).

Unfortunately TUC backing for more wage restraint failed to stabilize sterling. Jim Callaghan, then Prime Minister, and Denis Healey told senior union leaders on 14 July that the Government would have to take the painful step of cutting back its public sector borrowing requirement if it was to restore overseas confidence in the British economy by £1,000 million in the 1977-8 financial year. The TUC was informed that 'the main contribution would have to come from public expenditure since tax changes on this scale would be an intolerable burden on the pay policy'. At a special meeting on 16 July the TUC Economic Committee said to Healey that it did consider there was a good economic case to make such cuts in public expenditure, because present plans would entail a massive switch away from the public sector up to 1980.

Union leaders also suggested that industry would have more than adequate finance for the coming recovery, so that the only outcome of cutting back public spending would be to increase the dole queues. They urged Healey to consider import controls as an alternative, making the point that there was no guarantee at all that a further round of cuts would secure foreign confidence in the pound, but it would damage confidence among 'working people' in the government's policies. But union leaders faced the desperate truth. Healey told them bluntly: 'Early action is needed to prevent a run on sterling, which could force the UK to borrow from the IMF and force down the value of sterling to a level requiring even more severe public expenditure cuts. These could threaten the Government's existence.'

The Chancellor agreed to set up a joint government–TUC working party to look at the problem of the sterling balances, but he did not bow to TUC pressures to think again. On 22 July he announced planned public spending cuts of £1,012 million for 1977-8, while at the same time he raised employers' national insurance contributions by 2 per cent, which would bring in an estimated £910 million over the same year. The total effect of those measures was to reduce the PSBR by around £1,500 million to £9,000 million. It was a damaging blow to hopes of industrial recovery. There was a relaxation in the price code, an acceleration in the phasing out of food subsidies, cuts in defence, house-building and road construction programmes, and the school meal charges were put up by 10 pence from the autumn of 1977. The TUC Economic Committee – despite its distaste for the whole business – swallowed the inevitable. It issued a statement saying: 'It is vital to continue the social contract policies and we will continue to press for the implementation of these policies against the background of a desire to maintain a Labour government in office.'

But at the September 1976 Congress the first steps were taken to end the policy of voluntary pay restraint. A motion was moved by Lord Alf Allen of USDAW and seconded by Harry Urwin of the TGWU which called for a 'planned return to free collective bargaining' during 1977. It recognized the need to avoid a 'wages free-for-all', but called for the restoration of wage differentials, action on low pay, consolidation of the pay policy supplements in basic rates for overtime and shift pay calculations, and encouragement of incentive schemes.

As Murray explained to delegates: 'We cannot go on ignoring for ever the cumulative pressures that we know are always built up by the operation of such restraints.' But there was no mistaking the general feeling among even the most loyalist of union leaders that a permanent system of pay restraint on voluntary lines was no longer feasible beyond the summer of 1977. The only safeguard the majority of the TUC was prepared to concede, to lessen the dangers of a pay explosion, was the adherence to a 12 month rule between pay settlements, something that had been contained in the 1974–5 TUC pay guidelines. Yet at the time ministers clearly believed that when the time came for serious talking on pay policy another deal could be cobbled together. Certainly there was precious little optimism about in the government in September 1976 that the country was pulling out of its economic troubles. Quite the opposite.

At the 1976 Labour Party Conference, Callaghan spoke in a mood of blunt realism about the perilous condition of the British economy, even if most of the delegates preferred not to heed his words. 'Britain has lived for too long on borrowed time, borrowed money, borrowed ideas. We live in too troubled a world to be able to promise that in a matter of months, or even a couple of years, that we shall enter the promised land.' And he went on:

For too long, perhaps ever since the war, we postponed facing up to fundamental choices and changes in our society and in our economy ... governments of both parties have failed to ignite the fires of industrial growth in the ways that countries with very different political and economic philosophies have done.

Callaghan then turned with prophetic words to the expression of public scepticism of how governments had tried to spend their way out of trouble in the past. 'The cosy world we were told would go on for ever, where full employment would be guaranteed by a stroke of the Chancellor's pen, cutting taxes, deficit spending, that cosy world is gone.' In Callaghan's view the problem was caused by the process of free collective bargaining.

Each time we did this the twin evils of unemployment and inflation have hit hardest those least able to stand them. Not those with the strongest bargaining power, no, it has not hit those. It has hit the poor, the old, and the sick. We have struggled as a party to try to maintain their standards, and indeed to improve them, against the strength of free collective bargaining power that we have seen exerted as some people have tried to maintain their standards against this economic policy.

The mood of the Blackpool conference was unsympathetic to such unpleasant truths and Denis Healey, hot foot from London airport having decided at the last minute to stay in Britain because of the run on sterling rather than leave for an IMF conference in the Philippines, received an angry reception from delegates who did not want to hear his characteristically brutal frankness. The Cabinet had now decided to seek a loan from the International Monetary Fund. Healey was under immense pressure by the speed of events in the real world. He launched an attack on the supporters of massive import controls and the introduction of a siege economy.

The TUC Economic Committee urged Callaghan to resist any attempts by the IMF to hold back growth prospects in Britain in return for the loan and it asked him to think again about phasing out food subsidies, and not bringing in import restrictions. But Callaghan warned that any move towards protectionism was out of the question. He said the IMF loan was essentially a bridging loan until the economy returned to balance and that the size of the PSBR would have to be adjusted 'even if no agreement on the IMF loan was reached'.

The terms of the IMF loan were announced by Healey on 15 December. They involved cuts in the PSBR of £1,000 million in 1977–8 and £1,500 million in 1978–9. This meant further reduced spending on roads, house building, hospitals and schools. In return, Britain received a loan of £2,300 million. The regional employment premium was abolished – to the obvious distress of the TUC. Food subsidies were virtually brought to an end. Government holdings in British Petroleum were reduced to 51 per cent and a new selective investment scheme was introduced. The TUC did not like what was happening; but union leaders did not break with the government. Indeed, they appeared to take the view that there was no other sensible choice open to ministers but acceptance of the IMF loan, with its attendant cutbacks in public spending. The Economic Committee issued a statement on 16 December that said: 'It has to be accepted that there was no real alternative to seeking financial support abroad if the pound was to be protected against continuing downward pressure, the consequence of which would have been even more difficulties on the balance of payments and even more unemployment.'

The 1977 *TUC Economic Review* expressed strong criticism of the 'shift in emphasis towards monetary economics and an over-reliance in monetary targets' and called for a budget boost to the economy of £2,400 million, with £1,500 million of that figure coming from cuts in direct taxation. In fact, Healey's spring 1977 budget amounted to a boost of £1,300 million in a full year, with the promise of a further £1,000 million in tax cuts, conditional on reaching agreement on another year of voluntary pay restraint round a guideline figure. But talks in the spring and early summer failed to produce a new agreed formula on pay. The union leaders could only promise to uphold the 12 month interval between wage settlements. Consequently the government decided to push on alone with pay guidelines. On 15 July Healey told the Commons that the government had a responsibility to try and get the rate of inflation down into single percentage figures so as to ensure that the national earnings amounted to no more than 10 per cent in the period from August 1977 to August 1978.

Limits on dividends of 10 per cent were to stay for another year and the pay sanctions contained in the 1975 Remuneration Charges and Grants Act were to remain in force. Healey said that the aim was to take action so that people had confidence their living standards were being safeguarded. The petrol duty was reduced, while tax allowances were raised and income tax was cut by one pence in the pound from 35 to 34 pence. Child benefit rates were to be increased, while the milk subsidy was to be put up to keep the price of milk unchanged until the end of the year. The total cost of Healey's July measures was £1,250 million in 1977–8 rising to £1,500 million in 1978–9 though it would only add a net increase of £100 million to the PSBR.

To try and restore a sense of greater unity between the unions and the government, the Liaison Committee drew up a broad policy statement – *The Next Three Years and Into the Eighties* – that put events into the optimistic prospectus of a future Britain with self-sufficiency in its energy needs from North Sea oil. It spoke of an 'end of a period of falling living standards'. 'Our task is to ensure that the sacrifices of recent years have not been in vain,' it argued. 'We can now look forward to the time when the IMF arrangement will no longer be necessary.' The 1977 Congress found the majority of unions emphatically backing the return to free collective bargaining. 'Collective bargaining is what we are formed to do,' said Murray. 'It is one reason – to some people the main reason – for the existence of unions.' But he went on to warn that 'bigger pay packets all round are not going to buy us out of our personal troubles if inflation snatches back the gains that we make; and we know it'. In Murray's view, 'the brutal fact is that living standards are bound to be undermined if the economy sinks into a run-down condition, which is what is happening. These problems cannot just be swept away on a big tide of wage increases. They will be with us until we have made our industries more efficient by investment in the right places and more productive by better methods.' And Murray added: 'The motto of "Every man for himself" was taken down from the wall when the first trade union was formed and it does not become an acceptable motto if we change it to "every union for itself".'

The new mood was not one of confrontation. On 26 October 1977, Healey announced measures to boost economic growth amounting to £1,000 million in 1977–8 and over £2,000 million in 1978–9. Help was provided to the depressed construction industry and a tax-free Christmas bonus given to the old age pensioners. By patience, flexibility and some luck the wage round of 1977–8 was weathered. The firemen's strike put the position of the General Council under enormous strain and at its December meeting there was a very close vote (21 to 19) against the TUC giving positive support to the Fire Brigade Union and launching an all-out campaign against the 10 per cent guidelines. The unions did not go out of their way to wreck the policy, though groups like the Ford car workers, the lorry drivers, and the miners enjoyed increases outside the 10 per cent figure and blacklist sanctions were deployed against some firms who decided to ignore government guidance. The average increase in earnings from August 1977 to August 1978 came out around 14 to 15 per cent, more than the government would have liked to see, but much better than most observers of the union scene believed possible.

The 1978 *TUC Economic Review* took a realistically sober view of prospects. It spoke of the 'daunting' magnitude of the unemployment problem. The TUC's budget proposals were for a £3,575 million net boost, half coming in direct tax cuts, with particular help to the low paid through higher child benefits and personal allowances. Despite some criticisms, Healey's 1978 spring budget was much more to the TUC's liking than any for four years, with a reflation of £2,500 million. There were increases in child benefits and personal allowances as well as old age pensions. But by the summer of 1978 the old tensions between the economic and political wings of the Labour movement were once more becoming apparent.

Union after union rejected any further incomes policy and came out in favour of free collective bargaining at their delegate conferences. Even Labour loyalists like John Boyd of the AUEW no longer believed it was possible to ensure another year of wage restraint or an understanding between the TUC

and the government over a specific pay norm. Despite all the
warning signs, Jim Callaghan pressed ahead with plans for a
further year of incomes policy with a figure, and nobody in his
Cabinet (not even Tony Benn) demurred at its necessity. Indeed, the Labour Government was convinced, by the hard experience of the 1974–7 period, that the British economy could
not hope to survive without an annual consensus on wage
determination.

As the White Paper – *Winning the Battle Against Inflation* –
published in July 1978 explained, 'The country should aim at a
long-term approach in which collective bargaining is based each
year on a broad agreement between government, unions and
employers about the maximum level of earnings which is compatible with keeping inflation under control in the following 12
months.' There was a further acknowledgement of such a sensible outlook in the Liaison Committee document – *Into The
Eighties* – which was endorsed by both the TUC in September
1978 and the Labour Party Conference. This spoke of the need
for a 'thorough discussion with the trade union movement
each year so that there is a broad understanding in this as in the
other areas of our national economic life'.

But the Cabinet's decision that the overall pay increase
figure for the next wage round should be no more than 5 per
cent flew in the face of practical reality. Perhaps if the TUC had
been prepared to bargain in a serious mood about pay, the
figure might have been pitched much higher or even dropped
altogether in return for agreement to keep pay settlements within single percentage figures. The concession to help the low paid
– by allowing higher percentage rises as long as the result for
earnings did not exceed £44.50 for a normal full-time week –
was not seen as generous enough by the unions with low paid
members.

Murray told the 1978 Congress: 'There must be sufficient
flexibility if unions and employers are to sort out difficult
problems and anomalies and to take account of profitability,
without splash headlines about defeats or surrenders or nonsense of that sort.' He believed that the government had underestimated the 'deep and cautionary effects' of the inflation of
1974 and 1975 in influencing the outlook of union negotiators.
The motion opposing any form of pay restraint was moved by

Lawrence Daly of the Mineworkers and seconded by a triumphant Ken Gill of TASS. 'I hope this motion heralds the end of a period which has unfortunately transformed Britain into a low wage country and slashed differentials, turning skilled friends into disillusioned enemies,' argued Gill. A motion moved by NALGO for a structured pay policy on the lines of the West German concerted action approach went down to heavy defeat.

The union leaders were, however, anxious not to upset Labour's election chances. There was a widespread assumption that Callaghan would appeal to the country for a fresh mandate in October 1978 and the TUC did not wish to harm Labour's hopes with a public blood-letting over pay restraint. The TUC pledged its support for the return of a Labour government. Despite the setbacks and disappointments union leaders appeared to be in no mood to repeat the self-destruction of the 1968–70 period. The Liaison Committee document – *Into The Eighties: An Agreement* – passed with little opposition at Congress, lay down the outlines of a programme for the next decade. But before the end of Congress – to the obvious surprise and indignation of most union leaders – Callaghan went on television to announce that he intended to soldier on through another parliamentary session and not call a general election.

Private poll forecasts suggested Labour would lose an early appeal to the country, even though inflation was down to 8 per cent and real living standards rising rapidly. Consequently Callaghan pulled back at the last moment from taking the plunge. He was to live to regret his decision within a matter of months. The dénouement came at the 1978 Labour Party Conference. Now Callaghan did not intend to call the expected autumn general election, union leaders were determined to make it clear that the government's 5 per cent pay policy was impossible. The crucial motion was drawn up by the constituency's Labour Party in Liverpool Wavertree, a middle-class stronghold at all times. The key passages said: 'Conference demands that the government immediately cease intervening in wage negotiations and recognize the right of trade unions to negotiate freely on behalf of their members. Conference further declares that it will only support the planning of wages when prices, profits and investment are planned within the framework of a socialist planned economy.' In other words, this side of Utopia, pay policy was out. Amazingly, the major unions decided to throw their considerable weight behind this shrill resolution that went on to call for a campaign against pay restraint. Joe Gormley, president of the Miners, told Callaghan, 'For God's sake trust us', while the usually moderate Gavin Laird of the AUEW engineering section announced, to loud applause, that 'the Cabinet have not the sole prerogative of intelligence in economic thinking'. He went on: 'We have accepted social contracts and, comrade Callaghan, we are not prepared to accept any more and certainly not a 5 per cent norm.'

The only forceful dissenting voice from the unions at the conference came from Sid Weighell of the NUR. In characteristically pungent mood, he tore aside the façade of 'responsible' voluntarism. Weighell denounced the Wavertree motion as 'an emotional spasm, based upon nothing' and the huge pay claims being drawn up as 'the philosophy of the pig trough – those with the biggest snout get the biggest share'. But the Wavertree resolution was passed by a crushing 4,017,000 votes to 1,924,000, despite an emotional appeal from Michael Foot for a remittance of the motion. On the following morning Callaghan addressed the conference in a firm but avuncular mood and he did not dodge the implications of what the party had done.

As a seasoned union negotiator himself, Callaghan proceeded to think aloud about the intractable tensions in pay bargaining that have bedevilled British industrial relations for most of the post-war period.

How are we going to help the low paid workers and prevent them from feeding all the way through the wages structure and at the same time keep inflation down to single figures? Help me to do it. We must find a better way to resolve the issue of pay levels.
The power of the organized worker in society today demands that we do. We heard them yesterday – Sid Weighell promising that Joe can dig the coal, but he will not move it. Oxygen workers, who are the next on the list, will be able to take out much of Britain's industry over a matter of weeks. The power workers can shut off our lights. The sewage workers can stop work, too, with all the consequences. Yes, society today is so organized that every

individual group almost has the power to disrupt it. How is their power to be channelled into constructive channels? That is the question for the government, but it is a question for the trade union movement too and I hope we can begin to talk about it.

Immediately after the conference an effort was made by the senior Cabinet ministers and TUC Economic Committee to try and hammer out some general economic understanding. But this failed to win the approval of the General Council. By 17 votes to 17 the TUC could not agree to back two documents drawn up after long discussions with the Government that would have fleshed out the meaning of 'responsible' collective bargaining. The Ford strike paved the way to the demolition of the government's unilateral efforts to impose a voluntary pay policy on unwilling workers. The House of Commons voted down the sanction powers of the government in December and ministers were left defenceless before the onrush of pay claims. The lorry drivers' strike of January 1979 brought huge 21 per cent rises for those workers; but the government tried to hold the line at around 10 per cent, while conceding more to public sector workers with muscle like the miners, water workers and electricity supply workers. On 23 February 1979 Callaghan and Murray presented a joint government–TUC statement – *The Economy, the Government and Trade Union Responsibilities*. This so-called 'concordat' was an essentially political document, a belated attempt to patch up the differences between the unions and the government after a winter of bitter industria strife. Efforts to convince senior union leaders of the need for a more structured approach to pay bargaining were not altogether successful, but the two sides committed themselves to bring down the rate of inflation to 5 per cent by 1982. The efforts of ministers to insist that the document should become the basis for all further bargaining in the existing annual pay round was not accepted by union leaders, but it was agreed to hold annual economic assessments every spring.

More important than the vague and rather turgid economic sections of the 'concordat' were the TUC ground rules for trade union negotiators sent out to all affiliate unions. These attempted to remove some, if not all, of the popular odium against the trade unionists for their aggressive picketing tactics used both in the lorry drivers' strike and the action of the low paid public service workers. Guide one stated that there should be orderly industrial relations 'without interruptions' through adherence to collective agreements arrived at, and close scrutiny by union officials to see if unofficial industrial action could be avoided; where it occurred unions should take 'energetic steps' to get a return to normal working. The TUC laid down model rules for a disputes procedure. On top of this, the TUC told its affiliates that striking should only be used as 'a measure of the last resort' and 'one that should be used responsibly'.

The TUC guide even suggested unions might introduce ballots before or during strikes to ascertain the views of the membership involved and attention was drawn to the legal restrictions on picketing.

The 'concordat' became Labour's demonstration of the continuity of the old alliance with the unions; but the events of the winter 1978-9 did much to destroy the government's boast that it could work in harmony with the trade union movement for the good of the country.

The creation of the new Standing Pay Commission on Comparability in the public sector under Professor Hugh Clegg of Warwick University was a belated attempt to construct an institution with independence that could find a way through the thorny issue of public/private sector pay comparisons. The Pay Research Unit, introduced for the civil service in 1955, works on the broad basis of this philosophy, that the rates of pay for people doing broadly similar work in the public sector should be the same as those employed by 'good' employers in private industry. The Clegg commission was given the claims of the local government manual workers, the ancillary hospital workers and the nurses to look at by 1 August 1979. The Labour Government agreed to honour the commission's binding awards in stages, and it gave £1 in down-payment to the public service workers and £2.50 to the nurses on top of the 9 per cent general increase eventually reached. There is little doubt that Labour ministers hoped the standing commission would develop a wider influence with time; but the Conservatives took a more cautious and sceptical view of its value, worrying about the impact of high comparability awards on public sector spending and cash limits.

In the Labour Party manifesto for the May 1979 general election Callaghan placed a special emphasis on the renewed alliance between Labour and the unions, even if the over-done phrase – 'social contract' – was no longer in evidence. He expressed a hope that unions, employers and Government could have an annual assessment on the best way forward for the country's economy. As Callaghan wrote himself in the manifesto: 'Germany's Social Democratic Government under Willy Brandt and Helmut Schmidt has proved this is a good way to reach agreement on how to expand output, incomes and living standards.'

Under the umbrella of Trade Unionists for a Labour Victory senior union leaders like David Basnett and Moss Evans played a leading role in the 1979 general election, emphasizing their wish to work with a Labour government. Unprecedented sums of union money were poured into Labour's penny-farthing election machine.

A sense of common purpose survived intact, even if the tensions over pay bargaining were as strong as ever. Yet the events since 1974 suggest that the unions and a Labour government find it very difficult to work together for very long in harmony, particularly in an economy subject to problems as severe as Britain's. Robert Currie in his important study – *Industrial Politics* (Oxford, 1979) – has traced the dominance of *laissez faire* ideas in the unions ever since their origins in the middle of the nineteenth century. Despite the general commitment of union activists to the ideas of collectivism in economic and social policy, there is a firm belief in trade union sectionalism, of a freedom from outside interference in pay bargaining. Liberal, individualist instincts remain as strong as ever in the trade union movement, as we saw with the TUC's repudiation of an incomes policy, no matter how voluntary, in 1977 and 1978.

The dominance of the pursuit of money as the main objective for good trade unionism rules supreme. This continues to influence the nature of the Labour Party, despite its espousal of a socialist faith. H. M. Drucker in his *Doctrine and Ethos in The Labour Party* (1979) has described the union–Labour *entente* of the 1970s as 'corporate socialism'. And he writes: 'It has no goal, but possesses an astute and sensitive awareness of what it wants to protect: the economic standards of employed working-class men. It is really very similar to the position taken up by the party leadership before 1914.' Ideas of equality and social justice are not central to this pragmatic vision.

In this respect, the British Labour movement has not much in common with the social democracy of most of Western Europe, where unions and party have established a much more fruitful collaboration that has brought substantial increases in real living standards as well as a general acceptance of solidaristic ideas between workers. This is particularly true of Sweden and Norway, less so of West Germany. The sad truth is that despite being in power for 11 out of the 15 years between 1964 and 1979 Labour failed to overcome the individualistic ideas, the certainties of moral Victorianism that continue to dominate the outlook of organized workers. Most left-wing union leaders combine their demands for 'more' money for their members at all costs in a free market with an insistence on the creation of a more planned society. The Social Contract managed to protect the old age pensioners from inflation and it was responsible for the introduction of child benefits in 1977, but in retrospect its tangible achievements were few.

Once more (as in 1964–70), Labour's alliance with the unions brought a standstill to the growth of living standards during the worst recession the country has suffered since the early 1930s. But no other way forward was really possible. Thanks to a Labour government, the unions cooperated in pulling Britain back from the brink of catastrophe in the summer of 1975. Hyperinflation was avoided, but only just. A harsh price had to be paid with higher unemployment, cutbacks in the public services, a lowering of expectations of what governments can promise as well as achieve. As we shall see in the next chapter, the influence of the unions on Labour in the 1970s was much exaggerated. While Labour is more than ever the trade union party, in power it remains susceptible to greater pressures from other interests beyond its own sectionalist power base.

5 The influence of the unions

We see trade unions not simply as fruit machines in which workers put tanners to get the jackpot; we see trade unionists as agents of social change. (Bernard Dix, National Union of Public Employees, 1974 TUC)

We have got to know what we can do well. Our people are at their best on what they know about. (Len Murray, *Observer*, 5 September 1976)

The unions are often portrayed by their critics as nothing more than sectionalist pressure groups who demand rights and privileges from employers and the state, but refuse to shoulder any burdens of responsibility themselves. 'Our movement is clannish, inbred,' said George Woodcock in an interview with me. 'It prefers to stick to itself and avoid outside influences. It is a bit afraid of entanglements.' The unions remain, for the most part, obstinate and proud, complacent and suspicious of change. But their home-spun conservatism no longer makes the unions the immutable force they used to be. Since the early 1960s, and more particularly after the return of the Labour Government in February 1974, they have become more innovatory and socially responsive. Old fears of involvement with government have begun to disappear and for the first time, outside the pressures of war, the unions have started exercising power and influence over areas well outside collective bargaining (see figure 5.1).

The TUC presence is now regarded as vital on boards of public corporations and state agencies that cover a variety of functions. 'We have always been very good at stopping what we don't like, but not at starting anything,' said Murray. 'Our influence has been largely saying "no" up until now but this is changing.'

As long ago as 1946, Citrine in his farewell address to the

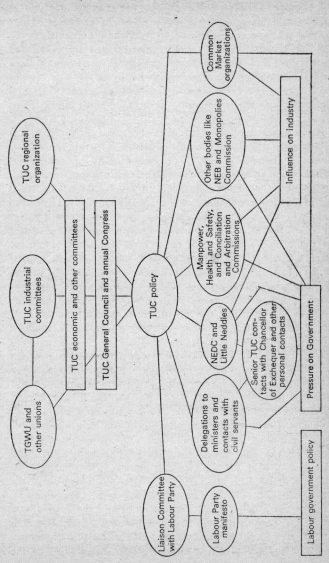

figure 5.1 The web of influence (*Financial Times*, 29 August 1975)

TUC spoke of the movement entering the 'era of responsibility', but the move from mass demonstrations in Trafalgar Square to behind-the-scenes pressure in Whitehall departments did not take place without years of agonized debate and indecision. Nor is there any certainty that the era of the Social Contract will ensure an irreversible transformation in the way the unions behave. The corporate state – where unions bargain with governments outside Parliament – could well have only a short life.

It is instructive to realize that the union presence in the citadels of state power is a new departure. Up until the Second World War the TUC was hardly consulted by governments at all, let alone given any responsibilities. Citrine's aim was always to broaden the TUC's influence – to win for it what he called 'power to act on policy issues in a cohesive manner'. Central to that vision was acceptance by governments of all parties that the TUC was an indispensable estate of the realm to be listened to and heeded on issues well beyond just collective bargaining. Such consultation is believed to have started with the request to the TUC in 1932 by Ramsay MacDonald's National Government to send observers to the Ottawa conference, which introduced Imperial preference. But it was not developed in a systematic way during the rest of the 1930s. By 1939 the TUC only nominated trade unionists to twelve government-appointed committees. Union delegations were not yet a commonplace feature of Whitehall life. The submissive deference and coolness of the get-togethers between Baldwin, his senior Cabinet ministers and the TUC inner circle during the run-up and aftermath of the 1926 General Strike was the familiar style. The days of beer and sandwiches at Number 10 were far away.

The war changed those strained, often difficult relations between TUC and Government. Thanks to Citrine and above all Ernest Bevin, who became Minister of Labour in Churchill's coalition of May 1940, the trade union movement was brought fully into the decision-making processes. You can sense the new mood of self-confidence and realism in the unions by reading the TUC General Council reports of the early 1940s. Beveridge consulted the TUC over his social insurance plan and Keynes found common ground with the TUC in the economic strategy for post-war reconstruction, exemplified in the famous bipartisan 1944 White Paper with its commitment to full employment. By 1948 TUC nominees sat as of right on as many as sixty governmental committees, from advisory bodies on economic and employment questions to agricultural marketing boards and consumer councils for the nationalized industries. The TUC had established the right to be heard on what Citrine regarded as 'those questions of general policy which were of common interest'. But in reality the practice never matched the ideal. Most public jobs held by trade union worthies have been no better than sinecures for the 'blue-eyed' boys, a way for politicians to settle old debts or reward personal friendships. In the uncertain, ill-defined relations between unions and government the pork barrel is an essential lubricant, like the honours system. The Americans have invented a useful word to describe these public jobs – QUANGO – or Quasi Autonomous Non-Governmental Organizations. In 1976 the Civil Service Department reckoned there were just under 5,000 paid jobs in the patronage of government ministers. As many as 3,300 of them are paid a fee on a sliding scale. Only 1,600 receive an annual salary and this is rarely more than a nominal £1,000 a year plus expenses. In 1977 the 39 members of the TUC General Council had 180 state appointments between them.

'Seniority, union muscle, competence. You need one of those assets to get a job and in that order,' said George Woodcock. Buggins's turn is the bane of the trade union movement. There is a strong, often misplaced respect for long service on the TUC General Council. The longer you last there, the better chance of picking up some juicy jobs. Woodcock recalls the unseemly lobbying by senior union bosses, who wanted to gather up QUANGO posts as perks. Until recently most of those public posts were treated as sources of extra income rather than opportunities for hard work in the trade union interest. Sir John Hare, when Conservative Minister of Agriculture in the 1950s, actually complained to the TUC about the lack of effort being put in by union nominees serving at that time on the marketing boards. 'It is true. There was no reporting back. We never knew what they were doing. In fact, they did damn all,' said Woodcock. Vincent Tewson served on the National Economic Planning Board for the TUC, but he did not even tell Woodcock what was happening on that august, long-forgotten body. Such behaviour reflected badly on TUC competence.

Yet until 1962 the TUC was in no mood to reform the QUANGO system. The sudden conversion of the Conservatives under Harold Macmillan in that year to the virtues of economic planning provided the TUC with an opportunity to play a more effective role. The General Council's agreement to participate in the National Economic Development Council (NEDDY for short) proved a watershed and a triumph for Woodcock. He spoke out forcefully for TUC involvement at the 1962 Congress:

We must not as a trade union movement give the impression that we are claiming absolute, unfettered, unqualified freedom to do what we like and to hell with the rest. That is not trade unionism, never has been. The whole point and purpose of trade unionism is for people to get together and collectively come to a common policy. That is what NEDC is for in intention.

NEDDY was seen as the instrument that would break down the defensive attitudes of the unions, and make them more ready to take what Woodcock called 'a completely impartial, coldly analytical view of all our problems'. The Macmillan Government made a number of important concessions to the TUC over the powers and composition of NEDDY. These allowed the unions to take part in its deliberations alongside Cabinet ministers and employer representatives. At the outset, Woodcock insisted that the TUC should pick its own six-man team for the NEDC and not leave it to the Chancellor of the Exchequer, Selwyn Lloyd. This was made a condition for TUC involvement. Moreover, the TUC nominees were to sit as a collective entity not as individuals, reporting back formally to the TUC Economic Committee and the General Council. 'The idea was that they should go as ambassadors of the movement,' said Woodcock. For the first time, there was precise and sustained accountability for trade union nominees sitting on a public body. This remains the practice on NEDDY and it has shaped that organization's erratic development.

The TUC's NEDDY six are the inner group of senior union bosses. In the autumn of 1978 they were Len Murray, Lord Alf

Allen (USDAW), David Basnett (GMWU), Moss Evans
(TGWU), Geoffrey Drain (NALGO) and Terry Duffy (AUEW).
At no time have the NEDDY six become mere placemen. In
fact, the part-time members of NEDDY do not get paid any
fee for their efforts. They meet with senior Cabinet ministers,
a chosen six from the Confederation of British Industry, a
couple of 'independents', and two leaders from the nationalized
industries once a month (every first Wednesday morning) at
NEDDY headquarters at Millbank Tower close to the River
Thames, not far from Whitehall and Westminster. The TUC
has never pulled out of NEDDY, not even when its relations
with the Heath Government were virtually non-existent between June 1970 and the early summer of 1972. 'Nobody cuts
a meeting, unless they have gone abroad on business,' said Sir
Ronald McIntosh, director-general of NEDDY, in an interview
with me in March 1976. 'When you realize the commitments
of the people round the table that is astonishing.' The TUC are
the main group on NEDDY who believe in the virtues of planning and economic growth, but the unions have never been very
enthusiastic about discussing incomes policy or any matters of
collective bargaining. McIntosh called NEDDY 'an island of
consensus in an increasingly divided country' during a lecture
at Oxford University in November 1974. It was the forum that
the TUC used to launch a peace initiative at the height of the
Heath Government's conflict with the miners. After 1975
NEDDY was given the urgent task of preparing sector reports
for the government's industrial strategy. It provided the tripartite umbrella for the Chequers conference between government, TUC and employers in November 1975. Employers on
NEDDY believe the voluntary organization has the merit of
providing a point of contact with the union leaders and provides everyone with a wider perspective on Britain's economic
problems. The CBI thinks it is a useful place where the TUC
can be educated in the painful realities of company life. The
necessity for private profit and the cash flow troubles of industry are thought to be better appreciated by the unions as a
result of their close involvement in NEDDY.

In many ways NEDDY, with its unfashionable commitment
to the middle way and consensus, exemplifies most of the
strengths and weaknesses of the TUC itself. The willingness is

there to argue amicably round the council table, but also there is a refusal to limit freedom of action and reach decisions that are binding and effective. NEDDY is something of a talking shop. Over the years it has been in and out of favour with successive governments. In October 1974 the new Labour Government ripped out NEDDY's planning heart by transferring all its planners to the new Department of Economic Affairs, where they drew up the ill-fated 1965 National Plan. The whole growth obsession fell apart in the July 1966 sterling crisis and NEDDY disappeared into the shadows. It became little more than a productivity agency for individual sectors. The Conservatives thought seriously of closing down NEDDY on their return to power in June 1970. It was saved but only after a detailed reappraisal, and the outcome was touch-and-go to the end. In the spring of 1972 Edward Heath used NEDDY to try and draw the unions back into closer contact with Government. His U-turns breathed fresh life into Millbank Tower. During the talks over the second stage of the incomes policy in the early summer of 1976, the TUC leaders who bargained with the Chancellor of the Exchequer were the NEDDY six.

The union presence is not limited to the top council. All the little NEDDIES, covering the major industrial sectors of the economy, are bodies where union leaders or their second-rung colleagues sit and discuss problems of mutual interest with employer representatives and civil servants. In some areas where trade unionism has been traditionally weak, such as hotels and catering, distribution and construction, the NEDDIES have enjoyed success through the benefit of practical union involvement. The wool textile NEDDY, under the chairmanship of Peter Parker, now head of British Rail, is a good example of the impact of NEDDY on policy-making. Its ideas about state financial help for the industry were transmuted into a government scheme under the 1972 Industry Act. The report on the reasons why skilled workers leave the engineering industry, published in the winter of 1976, illustrates the important work that NEDDY carries out, of immense help to the unions. Nevertheless many unions are still unwilling to allow their habits and customs to come under the critical scrutiny of outside bodies, even the little NEDDIES. Criticisms of overmanning and the poor utilization of labour in the industrial sector reports published in 1976 were always couched in generalized terms so as to offend nobody. For their part the civil servants remain unwilling to share their thoughts on economic forecasting with NEDDY. 'I wanted a body that would commit the parties to common action for common ends,' recalled Woodcock. Nobody was really ready for such a purpose in 1962; perhaps few are even today.

'Useful, not earth-shattering; it's not very sexy' is one TUC view, but over the years it has enabled many trade unionists to acquire an expertise and knowledge about the industries they cover. And a more informed trade union movement is better than one whose views are based merely on ignorance and prejudice. NEDDY has provided the best example of the new, responsible role for the unions, if they are willing to seize the opportunities.

But what influence did the unions really have on the industrial strategy between 1975 and 1979? The answer is – not very much. The General and Municipal Workers' Union, in a conference in January 1977, criticized the lack of trade union impact on the sector working parties (SWPs). As a background paper to the conference argued:

One of the difficulties of the industrial strategy so far has been the inadequacy and lack of coordination of the trade union effort. The TUC office attempt to attend and brief on most SWPs, but a complete service to trade union members is beyond the TUC's resources. The numbers of trade union members on the SWPs and the frequency of other pressures on their time has tended to mean also that SWPs are dominated by employers and this is reflected in the drawing up of the reports.

This was particularly noticeable in the widespread demand for cuts in taxation for companies as well as relaxation of the Price Code and a lack of priority being given to manpower issues. The GMWU background paper instanced the 'enormous reluctance' by management representatives on the SWPs to talk about their investment plans. It went on:

Where new industry schemes for expenditure under the 1972 Industry Act are proposed, there is resistance from both government and employers to trade union involvement in the deployment of these funds or to the attachment of a code of practice in relation to manpower consequences – if this resistance continues it makes a nonsense of the tripartite structure of SWPs as soon as recommendations are put into operation.

The GMWU believed a major drawback to the success of the industrial strategy lay in the inability to spread a knowledge of either its objectives or existence to the shopfloor and management in individual enterprises. The report went on, 'The GMWU have acquired copies of most SWP reports for distribution, but numbers are severely limited and clearly very little is getting down the line.'

A special TUC conference on the trade union role in industrial policy, held at Congress House on 31 October 1977, reflected even more union concern at the lack of progress. Jack Jones made a particularly bitter speech about the industrial strategy. As he argued:

An industrial strategy which relies only on the deliberations of sector working parties, on polite talks with industrialists and trade associations – and do not forget the degree of influence they have been using in the sector working parties – is not a strategy at all but an excuse for one. The present industrial strategy without action at the company level seems more likely to provide yet another collection of industry studies for use by the universities, another academic national plan rather than the industrial regeneration that we need in this country.

In truth, the TUC influence on Labour's industrial policies was not substantial. The TUC was closely involved in the preparation of the 1974 White Paper – *The Regeneration of British Industry* – which outlined the proposed legislation for the creation of a state holding company, the National Enterprise Board (NEB) and the introduction of planning agreements, jointly worked-out plans for the future of a company between management and unions. In talks with Tony Benn, then Industry minister, the TUC agreed to the idea of a joint planning committee with union representation to carry out the preparatory work for the NEB's creation. But in the face of stiff opposition from the CBI, the Cabinet began to waver. Harold Wilson had earlier stepped in to ensure there was an explicit and enthusiastic endorsement of the mixed economy in the

White Paper, for the government had no intention of creating any massive new public body that would frighten business confidence. The TUC welcomed the Industry Bill and its proposal to establish the NEB with an initial fund of £700 million, voluntary (not compulsory) planning agreements and the provision of much more information about the plans of manufacturing industry to both government and the unions. There were protracted talks between the Prime Minister and the TUC over the NEB guidelines. While Wilson wanted to keep a tight control on the NEB's acquisition of holdings in private sector companies, the unions urged more freedom for the NEB to work out its own strategy. In June 1975, the Prime Minister insisted that disclosure of company information should not be made compulsory. By the time the draft guidelines on acquisition appeared in March 1976, the government had moved closer to the TUC's position on the NEB's powers of acquisition, but the new Industry Act was far less radical and far-reaching than the TUC had wished for, mainly due to successful pressure from the CBI, the civil service and from within government itself where Bennery was seen as public enemy number one. The biggest failure was over planning agreements, whereby all strategic decisions of large companies should be a matter of joint control. The TUC regarded these instruments for planning as vital in the spread of union influence at company level through participation in corporate programmes covering hitherto untouched areas like investment policy, exports and imports, pricing strategies. With the exception of a planning agreement with Chrysler, which was quickly proved worthless as a result of the Peugeot deal in 1978, none emerged in the late 1970s, despite the demands of the TUC. As early as August 1975, when the Department of Industry produced a discussion paper, union leaders were complaining about 'a slackening of commitment by the government'. Eric Varley, who took over from Benn as Industry minister in a crucial post-EEC referendum Cabinet shuffle by Wilson, assured the TUC the government intended to have talks about planning agreements with a range of industries, notably petrochemicals, motors, process plant, food and drink. The General Council eventually agreed that it was 'unwise' to insist that planning agreements should be made compulsory, despite concern that their voluntary character would make them less likely to influence private companies.

The 1976 *TUC Economic Review* said the TUC was 'disturbed at the slow progress' towards planning agreements and demanded that they should be introduced for the top 100 firms by 1978. Nothing happened. As the 1977 *TUC Economic Review* grumbled: 'No planning agreements have yet been concluded, even with the nationalized industries or with companies heavily dependent on state financial support; this does not indicate that the government have given planning agreements any priority.' Nor did the TUC manage to persuade the government to provide extra financial resources for the NEB. The 1975 Act provided £1,000 million for five years, whereas the TUC had wanted £1,000 million a year. There was some improvement in the state funding of the NEB after 1978. The TUC was pleased about the nationalization of the shipbuilding and aerospace industries and the establishment of the British National Oil Corporation, but none of these measures were undertaken simply on union insistence. The government refused to respond to persistent TUC demands for the creation of a new agency – an investment reserve fund – to help finance industry. In July 1976, the Liaison Committee statement even took up the cry. 'Our aim is to ensure that the financial system acts in the public interest and is genuinely responsive to the needs of manufacturing industry.' All the Government did was to set up Sir Harold Wilson's committee to review financial institutions.

Lack of union influence in the industrial strategy shows NEDDY tripartitism is more a façade than a working reality. But NEDDY is now only one of a multitude of QUANGOs created over recent years where TUC nominees sit down and help to administer the system. Of course, there remains a serious danger of too much collaboration between the trade union movement and the government of the day in the emergence of what is called the corporate state.

But greater union involvement in the actual administration of the state does provide the opportunity for organized labour to make a profound impact on the social and economic life of the country. In Austria and Sweden, in particular, where Social Democrat governments have had close historic ties with their union movements, such participation has been vital to the success of social democracy. Workers in those countries as well as West Germany and Belgium elect hundreds of representatives to bodies involved in medical insurance, pensions, unemployment and accident insurance. The first, tentative steps towards similar union incorporation in Britain have aroused criticism. The new QUANGO bodies are innumerable. The Advisory, Conciliation and Arbitration Service (ACAS) was set up in 1974 under the chairmanship of a former union official, Jim Mortimer of the draughtsmen's union DATA (now TASS section of the Engineers), with three TUC nominees. TUC nominees have been chosen by ACAS to serve as arbitrators. The Manpower Services Commission also has a 3 man contingent from the TUC – Ken Graham, TUC assistant general secretary, Bill Keys of SOGAT and Harry Urwin, former assistant general secretary of the TGWU. Trade unionists are being brought into active work on the district manpower committees established under the MSC. Although the new agency to deal with labour market policy has a long way to go before it achieves the scope and sophistication of the Swedish and West German boards, the TUC presence suggests that the unions will begin to play a progressive role in the formulation of policy in a potentially sensitive area.

The Health and Safety Executive is headed by a former trade union general secretary – Bill Simpson of the Foundry Workers with three TUC nominees. The Equal Opportunities Commission appointed three TUC nominees early in 1976. 'Good legislation is no longer enough for us. It must be worked flexibly and sympathetically,' said Ken Graham. The recruitment of full-time Congress House staff is a new departure. David Lea, an assistant TUC general secretary, served on the Bullock Committee on industrial democracy and he was on the Royal Commission looking into the distribution of wealth and income. Ther are three TUC nominees on the National Enterprise Board.

Harry Urwin, former assistant general secretary of the Transport and General Workers, was a key behind-the-scenes trade union figure. Sitting on the National Enterprise Board, the Manpower Services Commission and the National Freight Corporation, he had experience of work on public bodies in the trade union interest. 'Personally I much prefer straightforward union work, negotiating and organizing, but in this business one thing leads on to another,' he said in an interview with me. 'For years we have talked about the need for an effective manpower policy for Britain in the TUC. I was one of those who condemned the old antiquated system. I don't really have the time to spare, but I wanted to see those changes through. You get frustrated if you just pass resolutions at Congress and do not bother to see them implemented and working.' The TUC presence on the Manpower Services Commission enables the unions to press ideas of how to reduce the level of unemployment. Schemes like job creation and the temporary employment subsidy owed much of their origin to TUC thinking.

Urwin took a special interest in the making of industrial policy. In 1972 he was nominated by the TUC to sit on the Industrial Development Advisory Board, set up under the Conservatives' Industry Act to give advice on whether ailing firms deserved state financial support. Urwin was pleased by the performance of that body, which was mainly composed of industrialists and financiers. Without the board's existence he is sure the Meriden motorcycle cooperative would never have got off the ground in 1975. He was also a member of Lord Ryder's team, which examined British Leyland and came up with the £1,400 million eight-year rescue plan for the ailing car giant.

A significant breakthrough in QUANGO appointments came in 1975 when Hugh Scanlon was made chairman of the Engineering Industry Training Board. This was the first time any union boss had been put in charge of an ITB. It was quickly followed by the appointment of union officials to head the training board for the construction industry, to take charge of the Distribution Training Board and chair the ITB for paper and paper products. Ever since the creation of the training boards began in 1963, the unions have played an important role in their development. Much of the old union craft resistance to government training in skills has now gone.

A minister normally makes informal soundings to the TUC before appointing a trade unionist to a public post, but this is not always so. In 1966 an exchange of letters between Harold Wilson and George Woodcock attempted to clarify the procedure with a distinction being drawn between salaried and unsalaried appointments. It was suggested the former posts were entirely at the minister's discretion. The attempt at clarification arose from the unrest caused by the elevation of Ron Smith of the Post Office Workers to a full-time directorship with British Steel – a decision which the TUC knew nothing about. In fact, the government picked the wrong man. They had Charles Smith of the Post Office Engineers in mind for the job. He was later rewarded with a peerage, perhaps as compensation for the mistake.

The pork-barrel system upset Woodcock's sensitivities and there was a clear change of attitude by the TUC to the whole question of trade unionists sitting on boards when it presented its evidence to the Donovan Commission. It involved a more flexible, modified view of worker participation. As the TUC argued in 1966:

There is now a growing recognition that at least in industries under public ownership provision should be made at each level in the management structure for trade union representatives of the workpeople employed in these industries to participate in the formulation of policy and in the day to day operation of those industries.

There was an admission too, in the TUC evidence, that old policy had been based on 'an uncharacteristically theoretical argument rather than on what was actually happening at the place of work'. The TUC floated the idea of industrial democracy, but Donovan paid no attention and the TUC failed to pursue the matter with much enthusiasm at that stage.

In 1968 the TUC did suggest that the unions should appoint workers in the industry to serve on the new passenger transport authorities, but the proposal failed to convince Barbara Castle, who turned it down. There was hope of union involvement in Labour's plan to nationalize Britain's ports in 1970, and at Congress that year a resolution was passed which called on the government to provide for trade union representatives to sit on the management boards of all nationalized industries. At the 1971 Congress of the TUC a motion was passed that called on active support for the development of the principle of 'direct participation by public service workers'. During the following year the TUC Transport Committee sought direct union representation on the new Civil Aviation Authority and on the new regional health and water authorities, but the Heath Government showed no interest in the suggestion. As the 1974 TUC White Paper on industrial democracy proclaimed:

The representative approach has not so far sought to change the attitude of the government in principle. These *ad hoc* policy decisions taken together represent a major shift in TUC policy. In no case yet has the government indicated its agreement with the TUC approach.

Union leaders are becoming much keener on the idea of direct worker representation on public boards. By tradition the TGWU has a seat on the Mersey Docks and Harbour Board. In 1975 the union decided to throw open that job, not to a nominee, but to a shop steward elected by the workers who faces recall every two years.

Up until 1977 only the nationalized steel industry had introduced worker directors. This happened when the industry was brought back into public ownership in 1967, under the chairmanship of Lord Melchett. There are fourteen worker directors now, nominated by the powerful TUC Steel Committee and appointed by the BSC chairman. But in a company of 220,000 workers a handful of worker directors can hardly expect to make any dramatic impact. What they have done is humanize company policy and soften the sharper edges of management behaviour. At present, British Steel has kept its worker directors on a tight rein. As Peter Brannen and his Warwick University colleagues argued in their study of the experiment at British Steel:

The worker directors had no effect on the decision-making process because the board was not really the place where it occurred; even if it had been things would have changed little; managemena has a monopoly of knowledge, of language, and of authority; the worker directors were individuals with no sanctions and no power. (*The Worker Directors*, London, 1976)

The British Steel scheme fell far short of what the TUC proposed in its 1974 plan for industrial democracy. This called for fifty-fifty representation for trade union nominees on the boards of private and publicly owned companies, who would be elected through recognized trade union machinery. Len Murray made it clear in his address on the subject to the 1974 TUC that what was suggested was 'a logical development of what we have established by collective bargaining'. In July 1975 a committee of inquiry was set up to look into industrial democracy under the chairmanship of Alan Bullock, the Oxford historian, with members from both sides of industry and the academic world. Its terms of reference said that the TUC's parity proposals should be specifically taken into account when drawing up recommendations.

As industrial democracy got closer to reality, differences began to emerge among the unions. Jack Jones of the TGWU had been the champion of the idea, ever since he chaired a Labour Party working party on the subject in 1967. In a host of evidence presented to the Law Committee on industrial democracy in the nationalized industries, Jones gave parity representation for workers top priority. The document on worker participation in transport pointed out that the National Dock Labour Board had operated with fifty-fifty union-management representation since it was founded in 1946 to regulate the supply of the labour market in dockland. It was critical of the appointment of union worthies to QUANGO posts. 'We do not consider that the present arrangement in the nationalized sector, whereby national trade union officials are appointed to boards, secures any significant representation of the workers to their unions,' intoned the TGWU document.

What Jones favoured was the election of stewards to carry on the function of worker representatives on the boards. 'This is in the interests of Britain,' said Jones at a press conference in August 1976. 'Worker democracy is an urgent necessity.' He put his faith in what he called 'the common sense of the shop floor'. 'There is no reason why managers and workers cannot act jointly together,' he argued. 'Trust the workers and they will respond. In the public sector it means a move from bureaucracy to democracy.' The TGWU policy documents made it clear that the worker directors would have a 'fairly free and full report-back to their trade unions and their constituents'. A procedure for recall and re-election was envisaged. Day-to-day management and wage negotiations would remain in the hands of the senior managers. Confidentiality was not seen as an intractable problem. The stewards on the board would carry on with their jobs on the shopfloor and continue to hold union positions outside the industry.

Jones refused to accept the unions would lose any of their precious autonomy as defenders of the interests of their members, if industrial democracy on his lines was introduced by law into British industry. He suggested it would 'carry collective bargaining on to a more sophisticated stage'. In Jones's view, the proposed system would 'add to the efficiency of management and the satisfaction of workers'. What Jones had in mind were not jobs for the blue-eyed boys with lavish salaries and perks. The stewards would have to make do with their usual weekly wages for the effort they put in. The conception of how industrial democracy would work arose from Jones's own experiences with shopfloor bargaining, but the degree of self-reliance needed, and the refusal to acknowledge that workers would require some rewards for carrying on the difficult work of helping to run the industry, cast doubts on its practicality.

Root and branch opposition to the idea of worker directors on the TUC model came from the Electrical, Electronic, Telecommunications and Plumbing Union (EETPU). In its evidence to the Bullock Committee in 1976 the EETPU argued it was quite impossible to separate boardroom consultation from negotiating with an employer. The EETPU spoke of the creation of 'irreconcilable split loyalties' among worker directors themselves. The union threw its backing behind the idea of 'greater consultation and involvement' by workers in areas which were 'previously subject to managerial prerogatives'. The Plowden Report that investigated the electricity supply industry reported early in 1976 with severe criticism of the TUC industrial democracy proposals:

We fear, that if the TUC proposals were carried out the Board would be merely the forum for endless negotiations between two groups of representatives. . . . In our view, employee participation will only work if a substantial number of workers want to make it work and are ready to accept their share of responsibility for the industry. Schemes for participation can be imposed from outside but the moral commitments which alone can make them worthwhile must come from within. . . . We believe that employee representation must therefore be built up from the bottom within the industry.

The General and Municipal Workers also voiced its reservations about what the TUC proposed. That union told Bullock it wanted to see a new law to require all employers to negotiate on strategic issues like corporate planning, closures and mergers as well as mass redundancies. What the GMWU opposed was the passage of any mandatory legislation which would lay down an inflexible procedure and machinery for the achievement of industrial democracy. Where it was jointly agreed to create seats on a supervisory board for trade unionists, then it should be introduced, but the maximum flexibility was essential. The Amalgamated Union of Engineering Workers appeared to turn down the whole idea of worker representation on the boards of private companies. It preferred to push 'the unrestricted extension of collective bargaining'. The 1971 agreement in the engineering industry with its inclusion of a *status quo* clause which prevented management from unilaterally introducing changes and the exclusion of the management's right to manage seemed to the AUEW to provide the climate for the new possibilities of improved bargaining. In the case of nationalized industries the AUEW came out in favour of 51 per cent worker representation on the boards.

The Bullock Committee produced a divided report in January 1977. The majority came down in favour of equal representation for trade union and shareholders on the boards of Britain's top 735 companies with over 2,000 workers on their pay-rolls. They also favoured a small group of coopted directors from outside the company, mutually agreed upon by the rest, to constitute no more than a third of the entire board. This was called the 2X + Y formula which, if it had reached the statute book, would give Britain a more radical system of worker control in private industry than even Sweden and Denmark. The minority report, signed by the three employers on the committee, denounced the whole idea of worker directors on the top board. It was alleged that they had been unduly influenced by pressures from the Confederation of British Industry. With the promise of a self-destructive conflict between capital and labour, the government responded cautiously to the Bullock proposals, but the very trenchant language used by the majority of the committee suggests industrial democracy in some form, which will provide the unions with the opportunity to exercise new powers and influence, is going to reach British industry during the early 1980s.

In Bullock's view, the debate about industrial democracy is not over whether it is a good idea, but rather the pace at which it will be introduced into Britain and in what form. The overwhelmingly hostile attitude of employers to what was being proposed revealed an odd reversal of roles. Until very recently the unions have always believed in an adversary, them/us strategy in their relations with employers, while employers have always liked to stress the common interest between themselves and their workforce. Now many (but not all) unions favour a partnership between capital and labour in industry; and it is the employers who reject such a radical proposal.

The majority report admitted its ideas involve a new role for the unions. It recognized between 6,000 and 11,000 employee representatives on company boards would need initial training in residential colleges for three to four weeks at a cost of £3 million in the first three years. It may well be wondered whether our unions are really equipped at present to provide such a service, even with the generous help of state funds. The joint representation committee of shop stewards in the firm is seen by the Bullock majority as the key institution below board level for the workforce. It is the JRC – not the shopfloor – that they recommend should choose their representatives on the board, not as delegates with mandates but with the power of recall. Those employee representatives would be paid no fee for onerous duties and it is likely to prove difficult to attract able part-timers from the shopfloor to carry out such work.

Only in 1977 did the debate over union influence at company level through industrial democracy cease to be remote and academic. Workers on the board was seen by Bullock and his majority as 'a decision which will have to be taken, whatever government is in power'.

During the spring and early summer of 1977 it soon became

clear that the champions of the Bullock Report had a fight on their hands. The well-nigh universal denunciation by employers and other political parties of what was being proposed, coupled with the clear divisions within the TUC on the subject, made it difficult for the Cabinet to reach agreement. Eventually the government's White Paper emerged on 23 May 1978, fifteen months after the publication of the Bullock majority report.

The Prime Minister Jim Callaghan introduced it to Parliament. The document revealed the philosophy behind the arid technicalities that had bogged down a Cabinet Committee for over half a year. 'The objective is positive partnership between management and workers, rather than defensive coexistence,' it argued. The White Paper made it clear that the government favoured a voluntary, agreed approach to industrial democracy, with only statutory back-up rights if this failed.

The often tedious saga of industrial democracy never really sparked off a serious 'great debate'. The issue failed to find much enthusiasm among the unions: it was a complete bore. With Jack Jones's retirement in February 1978, life seemed to go out of the subject. Yet it is unlikely to die away completely. During the 1980s we can expect to see some kind of legislation on the statute book, even though it will be at best a pale version of the Bullock majority report. But before we reach that stage, it is to be hoped that the unions will re-examine the wisdom of the whole concept of workers on the board. The employer resistance was highly predictable. The negative hostility of the revolutionary left was also to be expected. More damaging to the cause of industrial democracy have been the criticisms of more responsible and experienced figures respected by the trade union movement, like Professor Hugh Clegg and the distinguished labour law academic Professor Otto Kahn-Freund.

John Edmonds, the able industrial officer of the General and Municipal Workers' Union, speaking in a personal capacity to a conference on Bullock at Leicester University in April 1977, put his finger on the crucial question to which the enthusiasts of industrial democracy have failed so far to address themselves. As he argued:

Should a trade union regard itself as being in permanent opposition to management or should it become more and more involved in management decision-making and take more and more responsibility on a joint basis for the corporate decisions made by the company? Should a union remain independent or should it participate?

Edmonds placed these issues in a practical context.

If a company is in trouble or if a company is declining, should a union stand back and wait for management to make the decision to close a plant or should it join in discussions with management, and take some role in deciding which plant to close? On the other hand, when members in the plant say they do not like the situation, they do not like redundancies, the union can come in like the American cavalry, with banners waving, saying it will support them. On the other hand, the unions can take part in the decision. The union must then describe to the members the background and the economic realities and justify the particular closure to those members worst affected.

Edmonds quoted from the 1949 TUC report on the nationalized industries:

The trade union movement should retain its complete independence of the executive and employing authority of a nationalized industry. Only thus can unions exert their power of independent criticism and perform without divided loyalties their primary functions of maintaining and advancing the working conditions of work people.

In his view, it is impossible to do what Bullock recommended – 'to graft a little bit of involvement on to a union structure devoted to independence and collective bargaining'. Edmonds suggested that the report had failed to make up its mind between participation and independence for unions and thereby reached 'the worst of all worlds'. He went on to point out another under-emphasized weakness of Bullock: by relying on lay worker directors the proposals cut off industrial democracy from formal trade union structures and full-time union officials, with resulting confusion. As he argued:

Under the Bullock Report's proposals we will have two groups of union representatives. The negotiators are going to be part of the union structure: they will control the union system; they will be mandated by the members; they will be independent of detailed involvement in day to day management decisions; they will be free to support members where they wish. The worker directors will be outside the union structure at two removes from the members. They are going to be enmeshed in a web of commitments that arise out of the discussion in the boardroom. The worker directors will look very much like natural scapegoats when anything goes wrong.

The members of the Bullock Committee and union leaders should have taken more notice of the research papers, produced for their investigation into industrial democracy by Eric Batstone and P. L. Davies. Batstone produced a particularly impressive and scathing critique of industrial democracy, as practised in Western Europe. As he argued,

A consideration of the European experience of worker representation at board level suggests that, to be even marginally effective as a meaningful form of industrial democracy, workers require parity representation on a meaningful board, a formal recognition of their links with trade unions and a less restricted notion of board secrecy. Without such conditions worker directors are trivial in democratic terms. Even with such conditions the European experience suggests that conventional business interests will not be endangered. Collective bargaining, extended in scope and with broader rights for unions to receive information, would appear to be a more adequate method of pursuing workers' interests in the context of our present society.

Batstone found that worker directors, even in West Germany, had made a 'minimal impact'. As he explained: 'They have neither brought great rewards of a substantive or symbolic nature to workers nor have they endangered business efficiency or the interests of shareholders.' Similar doubts were expressed in Davies's examination of worker representation on the boards of European companies. Even if the parity approach was accepted, employee representatives would be 'unable to stand out against the prevailing ideology of the shareholder/management representatives, if they themselves are not firmly grounded in the constituency whose interests they are there to promote'. Moreover, Davies maintained, 'None of the systems studied had made much headway in making sense of the notion of the company as an institution or in tackling the real, but perhaps often overestimated, problems of confidentiality except by adopting a notion of confidentiality which made communication between representatives and the constituency extremely difficult.'

As this book argues – elsewhere – unions should become more aggressive bargainers, pressing for a much greater say on all the major decisions made at boardroom level that affect their members. But the dangers of a blurring of function cannot be dismissed as lightly as the Bullock Report chose to do. Industrial democracy has become a trendy, imprecise catch-word that means different things to different people. If we take the Bullock definition – of workers on the board in equal numbers with shareholder representatives – then it is open to very serious criticism.

Perhaps a watered down system of worker representation in the boardrooms of Britain would ensure an 'economic miracle', and a new age of industrial peace. It seems most unlikely, despite the rhetoric. On the contrary, such a development could bring with it far more conflict within union structures, as well as between management and workers. Not only would this be a serious blow to the well-being of the enterprise, but it could set back the hopes of radical trade unionism. 'All power short of the boardroom' looks a much more attractive proposition, and this is now partly recognized by the TUC as a sensible way forward. The sterile debate over whether workers should be represented through unions and the JRC or by a workplace ballot needs to be terminated. After all, we may lose sight of the purpose of industrial democracy by an over-concentration on its mechanics. Worker rights remain few in Britain, despite the new labour laws. If unions intend to exercise a greater influence over industry, they must build up their strength but without bartering their own independence.

The undoubted growth in trade union influence in our society should not be exaggerated. Far more decisive power rests with the senior civil servants in Whitehall, the financial houses of the City of London, in the boardrooms of the big companies, not in the headquarters of the various unions or even Congress House. In the words of the late Allan Flanders, 'trade unions cannot determine a greater part of the experience to which their members react'. The new state agencies or QUANGOs and the advent of some kind of industrial democracy may improve the position, but it would be naïve to suppose any real progress will come about without a struggle or a compromise by the unions with their cherished belief in the dogmas of voluntarism. The

British unions – far more than any others – remain very much prisoners of their chequered past, victims of custom and tradition. George Woodcock used to lament the emasculation of his grand ideas as he sat in seclusion at the top of Congress House. 'I would float a proposal. It would be chewed over in committee, then on the General Council, finally at Congress by which time it was unrecognizable.'

What remained was, in Woodcock's memorable words, 'a shoddy, shabby compromise'. In comparison with Sweden, Austria or West Germany, our unions have so far failed to make any major constructive impact on the development of post-war British society, but the little-known, *ad hoc* developments traced in this chapter suggest that the old traditional union desire to keep clear of outside entanglements may be slowly disappearing. At national level union leaders are not feudal barons but social partners, who are being made answerable for their actions. Making unions more collectively responsible by participation and persuasion rather than through the rigours of a penal code should be the primary aim. The ultimate success will rest on how the new labour laws and QUANGO bodies make an impact – not in union head offices, but on the shopfloor and in the offices. The degree of incorporation by the unions into the administration of the state will be decided by the rank and file in the last resort, not the leadership. As long as the new responsibilities are seen to be used for the good of the membership, they will be acceptable, but only so long as they neither compromise nor divert attention away from the primary role of the unions as bargainers and protectors of their members' well-being.

6 How democratic are the unions?

To many people, unions seem to be no more than overbearing bullies run by autocrats, contemptuous of the 'national interest' and public opinion. There is a widespread belief that those who control the unions at national or local level fail to reflect accurately the true voice of the supposedly moderate rank and file. Apparently a militant few – motivated by extreme political dogma – manipulate and distort the real wishes of the apathetic majority. The cartoon of the tyrant union boss is a familiar one. Jack Jones of the TGWU was dubbed 'Emperor' Jones in a particularly savage onslaught on the unions by Paul Johnson in the *New Statesman* in September 1976. It is argued that union leaders display arrogance and ruthless power in the pursuit of political objectives. Orders and directives pour out of the union headquarters to be instantly and unquestioningly obeyed by the serried ranks of unthinking members. The unions are portrayed as regiments of labour fighting the class war and seeking unconditional surrender from their enemies. The hysteria generated over the closed-shop issue suggests that this is no caricature of what a large number choose to believe about the unions. Once the champions of the underdog in the fight for social justice and equality, the unions are seen as the new barony, the masters now. Consequently they have become the scapegoats for Britain's economic decline since the mid-1950s. A poll carried out for Granada Television's *World in Action* by Market and Opinion Research International in the summer of 1976 found as many as 23 per cent of their sample blamed the unions for high unemployment, while a mere 5 per cent blamed employers, 3 per cent investors and 11 per cent the international situation.

The demand to make unions more 'democratic' has grown fiercer since the early 1970s. As the Conservative statement of aims – *The Right Approach* – argued in October 1976:

The main drive for improvement in the democratic procedures of trade unions must come from union members themselves. But we are ready to help. Public money should be made available for the conduct of postal ballots for union elections where these are requested. Firms should also be encouraged to provide time and facilities for the conduct of union meetings; this should lead to greater participation in union affairs.

The criticism of the lack of union democracy is not confined to the right of British politics. The ultra-left are equally hostile, seeing union leaders as timid bureaucrats out of touch with the militant moods of the shopfloor. In the words of Tony Cliff, guru of the Socialist Workers' Party:

One thing that terrifies the trade union bureaucrats more than anything else is the independent action of workers. Nothing is better calculated to cut down their importance, their status, their prestige. And nothing is more likely to strengthen their attachment to the status quo. That attachment is not straightforward. The trade union bureaucrat is not a capitalist, but he's not a worker either. He lives off class struggle, but he can't let it go beyond the point of mediation, or negotiation. His basic rule is to keep the contestants alive and able to fight – gently.

At a time of severe economic crisis, it is understandable that unions should face such hostility, however contradictory or ill-informed it might be. It is important to know whether individual trade unions do accurately reflect the views of those they claim to represent. Nor is it merely a question of accountability to satisfy an academic interest. Industrial democracy is now near the top of the political agenda. Whatever shape the British proposals for worker 'participation' take, one thing remains certain: the trade unions are virtually sure to dictate the ultimate character of industrial democracy. But this new power will be hard to justify if it is exercised through undemocratic union structures, which fail to give all the members the opportunity to take decisions. A familiar accusation is that unions are nothing more than hollow façades run by dedicated minorities, where the idealism of the public rhetoric masks oligarchic rule.

Unfortunately no subject arouses more inadequate generalization than that of union democracy. The sheer diversity of custom and practice among the British unions makes it hazardous to formulate iron-clad judgements. What little empirical evidence we do possess suggests that few unions have yet managed to resolve the genuine dilemma posed for them by Sidney and Beatrice Webb over seventy years ago in their now-forgotten classic, *Industrial Democracy*: 'How to combine administrative efficiency with popular control.'

There is broad agreement that only minorities play an active part in the formal running of their unions, from the local branch right up to the annual or biennial conference of the unions and the national leadership. John Goldthorpe and his colleagues discovered that as many as 60 per cent of their sample of Vauxhall car workers in Luton during the mid-1960s 'never' attended branch meetings of their union. The number of those who turned up was particularly low among workers with semi-skilled jobs like process, assembly and mechanical production where a mere 2 per cent bothered to attend union branch meetings and another 11 per cent did so only 'occasionally'. Another picture of rank and file apathy with union branch meetings can be found in Denis Brooks's study of London Transport workers (Oxford, 1975). He found only 4 per cent of the busmen in his representative sample went to those union get-togethers, 10 per cent of those working on what is known as the permanent way on the London Underground system, and 3 per cent of the station staff. As many as 96 per cent of the busmen had never held any union office at all and neither had 80 per cent of the station staff. Yet this lack of interest in the union (TGWU mainly, as well as NUR) took place among a section of the labour force which had a militant rank and file movement in the 1930s, when the busmen were a thorn in the flesh of Ernest Bevin, TGWU boss. Bob Fryer and colleagues in the sociology department at Warwick University found in their 1975 internal survey of the National Union of Public Employees (NUPE) that 67 per cent of union branches reported that no more than 5 per cent of their members ever went to meetings of the union. In his study of the Colchester branch of the Union of Post Office Workers, Michael Moran showed that 60 per cent of uniformed staff never went to branch meetings or only went occasionally.

Not all recent surveys support the gloomy picture of low membership involvement in union branch meetings. The

National and Local Government Officers' Association (NALGO) enjoys a fairly respectable level of branch membership participation. An internal survey in 1975 found that as many as 46.5 per cent of NALGO male members and 26.6 per cent of women members attended their branch general meetings, which average around three a year. Among those who did not attend, the main reasons given for not turning up to the meeting were 'inconvenient time' or 'inconvenient place' and domestic responsibilities. Only 14.7 per cent of the women and 22.1 per cent of the men said they were simply 'not interested in attending'. As many as 90.2 per cent of those get-togethers took place after office working hours. Attendance at branch meetings in the National Union of Teachers (usually held on school premises after hours) is reasonable with an average of a quarter turning out to every one.

These specific findings in individual unions remain in broad line with the more general ones arrived at some time ago. In 1948 Political and Economic Planning (PEP) reckoned no more than between 15 and 20 per cent of trade unionists went to branch meetings, while Professor B. C. Roberts put the figure as low as between 4 and 7 per cent in the mid-1950s. Joseph Goldstein, in his seminal work on the Transport and General Workers' Union, estimated that rank and file attendance never rose much above 15 per cent in the branches of that union. There is no reason to suppose that this depressing state of affairs has improved for the better over the past twenty years. In fact, quite the reverse may well have happened. Most union rulebooks place a particular stress on the crucial role the branch is supposed to play in the union structure. The Webbs spoke of the branch as 'the local centre of the union's intellectual life'. Such an elevated view was probably mythical even at the time the Webbs wrote those words. It is now certainly dead and buried. Most union branch meetings are dominated by tedious, administrative chores, which attract the dedicated bureaucrat, or political debates that usually bring in the dogmatic zealot. 'It is terribly difficult to get the younger men to take an active interest in union work. No more than a handful turn up to branch meetings,' a TGWU branch secretary told me in Birmingham in March 1975. 'We meet in a pub on Sunday mornings near the works, but the business is very dull and routine. Most of our

active members will have retired in another ten years. Few are
coming on to replace them. It is a tragedy for the trade union
movement, like falling church attendances are for organized
religion.' A similar apathy even grips other parts of the union's
local structure. Once the annual election for officers is complete, attendance starts to dwindle on the Birmingham engineering group's district committee. Ultimately less than half turn
out to preside over the union's affairs.

There is no reason to suppose the TGWU is any worse than
others. Union activists I have talked to believe lack of participation comes down to a problem of generations. 'We were
reared in hard times. The union meant something to us in the
1930s in the fight against unemployment and for social justice,'
a Birmingham TGWU shop steward told me. 'Now the members who are married with kids and live miles away from the
works do not see the point any more of giving up their leisure
time to come to meetings.' In trade unions where the branch is
based on the geographical area and not the place of work, it is
hard to breathe any life into the fossilized local union structure.

In the Amalgamated Union of Engineering Workers branches
exist with members from as many as twenty-five to thirty different factories who can attend. At other plants with 2,000
members, it is not unusual to find thirty-five separate branches.
No wonder these bodies seem meaningless to most trade unionists. Years ago the branch – particularly in craft-dominated
unions – was the focus of social life. It remained the source for
many local friendly society benefits and the place where the
union subscriptions were paid in. The spread of the check-off
system (whereby the subs are detached from the worker's pay
packet by the employer) has accentuated the attendance problem. As the branch serves no practical value to most members,
its *raison d'être* is far weaker. There has been a growing trend
since the late 1960s to try and rejuvenate the union branch by
building it up at the workplace level, not in the district, but
such a process faces serious difficulties. Many workers work in
very small units, scattered over a district. It is therefore hard to
organize branch life around one workplace. Moreover there is
always the danger of members retaining a sectionalist outlook.
In a large, general union the structure needs to try and bring

together members from different trades and occupations, otherwise fragmentation and breakaway threaten, because many members will fail to appreciate the wider interests of the union beyond the narrow limits of their own occupations. As we shall see in a later chapter, more and more of the collective bargaining functions of the union are going to the place of work and closer to the individual member. This is helping to reduce the value of the old branches. Unions are now having to try and link the informal, spontaneous structure that has grown up to meet the needs of the workers with the older system that they developed long ago.

Elections in the unions also pose a difficulty. Levels of voting do not often rise particularly high. Very few of the full-time union officials have to face contests, let alone the uncertainty of re-election. In most white-collar unions it is customary for all of them to be appointed by an elected lay executive committee. Those general and craft manual unions where elections for full-time jobs do take place rarely have big turnouts, though it can happen. Jack Jones (whose power was strengthened by the fact that he was the only elected full-time official in the TGWU) became general secretary in November 1968 on an impressive rank and file poll with 334,125 votes against nine opponents who only gathered in 195,026 votes between them. There was a turnout at the branch meetings of just over 50 per cent in a union with 1,100,000 members at the time. To get the disparate and varied sections of the TGWU to vote in that number was quite an achievement, whatever the critics might argue.

The National Union of Mineworkers has a long tradition of high polling at national officer election time. Both Joe Gormley, the president, and Lawrence Daly, the secretary, were elected on turnouts of over 75 per cent of the members at pithead ballots. Hugh Scanlon, on the other hand, triumphed in the 1967 election for the presidency of the Engineers with no more than 7 out of the 11 per cent of members who voted doing so for him at branch meetings in the run-off with his closest rival, John Boyd. All the 180 or so officials of the AUEW engineering section must face election and re-election – in the first instance for three years and thereafter every five years until the incumbent reaches the age of 60 at which age he is allowed to see through his last five years of union service unchallenged.

The practice of the Engineers is enshrined in the ultra-democratic nineteenth-century craft traditions. But until 1972 all the voting at these regular elections was done at the branches of the union. This ensured a very low turnout of no more than 5 to 7 per cent on average. In 1972 the union's National Committee voted narrowly to change the electoral system from branch voting to postal ballot. Now members can vote in the solitude of their own homes after work and send in their ballot paper to head office, though election addresses still go to the branches, so members often don't know who they are voting for. As a result, the numbers taking part in the union elections rose to an average of 33 per cent, though it costs around £150,000 a year to operate, compared with £65,000 under the old method. The greater membership involvement has helped the 'moderates' in the union.

Voting by post is also a major reinsurance in the Electricians' union (EETPU) to combat the methods of corruption used by the Communists in the late 1950s to hang on to their national power. Since 1965 the EETPU rule-book has laid down a careful and detailed procedure for elections to the national full-time Executive Council. The Electoral Reform Society – an independent body – is responsible for the administration of all elections in the union. That independent organization, which also looks after the elections of a number of other unions, issues the ballot papers to members listed by the union and it carries out the count. Participation levels in the EETPU tend to fall around the 20 per cent mark: not as high as one might expect, though the tight qualifications for getting on to the union's electoral register are formidable. Probably a better safeguard against 'extremist' takeover is the rule that Communist Party members cannot hold full-time office in the union. Frank Chapple won a huge victory in the general secretary election in the spring of 1977. Thanks to the independent electoral system not even his many bitter enemies could suggest he won by manipulation and fraud – once the favoured weapons of the Communists in the EETPU.

Postal ballots are not a panacea, even if they do tend to favour the 'moderates' against the 'extremists'. In 1974 and 1975 some popular newspapers – notably the *Sun* and the *Daily Express* – openly championed certain candidates in elections, first in the AUEW, later in the EETPU and construction workers' union (UCATT), where voting is by show of hands at the branch. For the most part, those press campaigns hurt left-wing candidates like Bob Wright in the AUEW, who fell from being Boyd's chief opponent in the 1975 election for the general secretaryship and a leading left-winger on the Executive Council to an ordinary rank and file member in less than two years. In the autumn of 1976 Wright made a surprise comeback to win the post of assistant general secretary on a second ballot and run for the presidency in 1977. But he was decisively defeated by Terry Duffy in the 1978 presidential election on the second ballot. A strong argument against the postal ballot is not its cost (which can be considerable) but the external pressures that can influence a trade unionist outside work on how he or she should vote. The left attack the distortions of the mass media as the reason for their failure to combat the drift to the right in the trade union movement in the mid-1970s. Such an argument would carry less plausibility if all elections were held at the workplace under independent supervision. The outcome is unlikely to prove any different, and the turnout might actually be even higher than a postal ballot.

Small minorities voting at the branches for full-time union leaders is not always a hindrance for the victory of 'moderation'. The indefensible bloc vote system is used in some unions, notably by the General and Municipal Workers, the Shopworkers (USDAW) and the National Union of Railwaymen. Under this scheme those who actually turn up at the branch to vote in the election can also use the votes of those who do not. As a result, the whole branch vote is thrown behind one candidate irrespective of the minority support for others. What looked like very impressive turnouts for the election of David Basnett to the general secretaryship of the GMWU and Sid Weighell of the Railwaymen were very misleading as a consequence. In Basnett's case, he won on a minority vote with probably no more than 15 per cent of those voting in the poll.

With the exception of the AUEW and EETPU, once union leaders have been elected into office, they do not have to face the members again through the ballot box. The only grounds for their dismissal is if they lose the confidence of their lay executive. This rarely happens. The elections all unions hold

for their Executive Committees are also rarely occasions for
mass democratic participation. Bob Fryer and his colleagues
found few members bothered to vote in Executive Council elections in NUPE. A quarter of the branches did not take part at
all in the contests in 1973, while only just over a half said they
always voted in Executive Council elections. As the Warwick
team observed:

Even in those branches which did not vote last time, their choice
of candidate depended more on inertia than close evaluation. One
third supported a candidate because he or she came from a nearby
branch, and a similar number because the candidate was well
known; almost as many supported candidates because they were
already executive councillors and only 18 per cent voted on the
basis of knowing and agreeing with the candidate's views. Indeed
over two thirds of branches said they had insufficient information
upon which to base their choice.

The electoral process is more widely used in NALGO, according to the union's internal 1975 survey. As many as 63.7
per cent of men and 51.8 per cent of women voted in the previous year's National Executive Council elections. Some unions
have their executives elected each year by their annual conferences, notably the Civil and Public Services' Association, the
Post Office Workers and the Post Office Engineering Union.
Most are ruled by executives or lay activists, who are elected
biennially or annually through the branch system. The National
Union of Railwaymen makes a special effort to ensure the
executive members do not lose touch with the membership. Its
Executive Committee, made up of twenty-four members, is
elected by a single transferable vote at the branch for periods of
three years. Eight members retire each year from the committee and eight new ones are elected. The rules forbid an executive incumbent to stand again for three years when his term of
office comes to an end. This ensures all the executive members
have to go back to their old jobs on the railways after a full-
time stint on the executive. All executive members must provide
regular report-backs to the NUR district councils in their areas,
attend branch meetings and keep in touch with the rank and
file. The executive members are closely involved in negotiating
and their aim is to determine day-to-day policy.

How 'democratic' are union conferences, usually held every year – though in some cases biennially? (The TGWU, EETPU and UCATT among the larger unions follow the latter practice.) There are some wide variations in the way delegates are elected. In the TGWU the biennial delegate conference is made up of delegates nominated from the branches. Election is by ballot vote of the regional trade groups of the union on a membership basis. The Engineering section of the AUEW is governed by a fifty-two-strong National Committee, which meets annually. It is made up of two representatives from each union division who must have been a member of one of the qualifying sections for seven years. Those delegates are elected every year at the first session of the divisional committee, which follows the annual election of its own branch officers and delegates in November. In the General and Municipal Workers, supreme authority lies with annual Congress. One delegate is elected in each region of the union for every complete 2,000 financial members, as stated on the previous September's quarterly balance sheet. Each branch in a GMWU region can nominate a delegate to represent the region at Congress. In the GMWU the full-time officials play a powerful role at Congress. All the national officers and regional secretaries attend Congress. So do a third of the organizers and a third of the branch administrative officers. They have the right to speak at Congress, but they are not allowed to vote.

In the National Union of Railwaymen the supreme government is the seventy-seven-strong annual general meeting, which meets for a fortnight each July. Its members are elected by ballot on the single transferable vote system by the bloc vote of branches which are bunched together in each locality. Nobody can be a delegate unless he has been a member of the union for five consecutive years. Every branch has the right to nominate one candidate for election by the electoral area to which it belongs. The area elects a delegate from those nominated each year, but nobody is allowed to attend more than three consecutive annual meetings.

Balloting members on specific issues is still not widely used by unions, though there is an increasing tendency to seek rank and file approval before the ratification of wage agreements. But some unions do favour this ultra-democratic procedure.

The National Union of Mineworkers regularly uses a ballot of the entire membership to decide union policy. It has virtually eclipsed the annual conference in recent years as the ultimate arbiter of NUM strategy. Such a system carries risks and it can limit the room for manoeuvre. The need to consult members goes back to the origins of the Miners' Federation. It was first introduced in 1911, when no national strike could be called without a two-thirds majority of the miners backing such action. The ballot was used for the first time in 1912 when the vast majority of miners voted for a strike. After a month's stoppage of work, the Federation balloted again on the coal owners' offer and that failed to get the necessary two-thirds majority to persist with the strike. In both 1919 and 1920 ballots were again held on the coalfields, leading to strike action. There was no need for one in 1926 for the long, nine-month struggle that year was caused by a lock-out of the miners by the owners, who wanted to cut wages drastically. It was not until 1970 that the NUM called another ballot on strike action. As many as 55 per cent voted in favour of stoppage in pursuit of higher pay, but this fell short of the required two-thirds majority. But the following year the required majority to make a ballot decision binding was brought down to 55 per cent. Without that important rules revision the NUM executive would have been unable to call a national strike in 1972, for on that occasion only 58.8 per cent voted for a strike.

The Seamen held a ballot on industrial action in September 1976. The 1971 Industrial Relations Act procedure was used by the government to enforce a strike ballot on the three railway unions in the spring of 1972 over a wage claim. That particular step rebounded on the Cabinet, when the railway workers backed up their union executives in an impressive display of solidarity. In the AUEW it is the Executive Council which sanctions national stoppages and gives the stamp of approval to local strikes, backed by district committees. In the TGWU a strike can be called among the members on a mere show of hands at a mass meeting. In the General and Municipal Workers the procedure is far tighter. A branch committee can call for a strike, if two-thirds of those voting in the branch decide to support this, although it then requires the sanction of the regional committee of the union. That body can give its blessing to a particular strike as long as no more than 300 workers are involved. If there are more workers in dispute, the question must be referred to the Executive Council. This meets once a month in practice, and the general secretary has the power to support or veto a strike between executive meetings.

Most unions leave the final word to the national full-time officials, on whether to give official backing to a local strike or not. As most such disputes fail to last more than a few days, this usually takes the form of *post facto* support for members' action. A major problem about all union strike ballots is that they tend to harden existing attitudes and make it difficult to reach compromise settlements. The NUM's long-drawn-out ballot procedure is a model of union democracy, but it can help to cut the ground from under the feet of union conciliators. The complexity of bargaining and a spirit of give and take are usually necessary for any successful outcome of an industrial dispute and ballots can often stop that from happening.

The obstacles to union democracy are considerable, but they tend to be overlooked in most public discussions. The most serious is labour turnover. Unions are not static organizations with stable memberships. Many find it difficult to stand still, for they have to recruit substantial numbers of new members all the time to compensate for the losses they suffer. In NUPE this is a major problem. Fryer and his colleagues found that in one large branch in the last quarter of 1973 it was necessary to recruit 9 per cent new members to record a 1.5 per cent net increase in branch membership. The bulk of NUPE's members are part-time women workers (around 81 per cent of the female members are in local government and half those working in the National Health Service). The shopworkers' union (USDAW) has a similar difficulty with high membership turnover. That union estimates it loses as many as a third of its members every year. In 1973 USDAW recruited 123,525 members, but only made a net gain of 1,436. The loss of members also hits the big general unions as well, if not so badly. There is around a 16 per cent turnover in membership in the GMWU and the figure is believed to be slightly higher in both the TGWU and the Engineers.

With around 5,000,000 workers with their employer for less than a year, it is very difficult for any trade union to keep a close eye on who is a member and who is not. In the print unions where turnover is less severe and members control the entry flow, turnouts are much higher. NATSOPA, SOGAT and the NGA insist on compulsory attendance at all chapel meetings under pain of a fine if you fail to turn up. Clearly a perpetual ebb and flow makes it very difficult for many unions to have up-to-date electoral registers. Moreover most unions insist on a period of membership before somebody can enjoy voting rights in elections. In the TGWU and NUPE you have to be a member for thirteen weeks or more to qualify, while in USDAW and the AUEW the period is as long as a year.

The arrears problem is also a serious handicap for achieving a reliable list of members able to vote in union elections. The growth of the check-off system, whereby the employer deducts union dues from the workers' pay packet for the union, has eased that difficulty, but during the early 1970s the AUEW, in particular, had a large number of members who had failed to pay their union dues on time. By doing so, they lost their right to vote at election time.

Elections pose another problem. They can lead to the promotion of incompetents into posts where administrative ability is the paramount need. In a few unions, notably the Iron and Steel Trades Confederation and the National Union of Railwaymen, potential candidates for union office must face fairly stiff tests before they can even stand for a high post, but most unions appear to believe internal recruitment through the ballot box remains an unsatisfactory method of turning a trade union into an effective force. The trend is now towards the appointment of all the full-time officials, who are responsible to the general secretary, an elected executive of lay activists and an annual conference, which is usually the supreme governing body in the union. The growth in the career trade union officer is a fairly recent development as unionization has spread far more into the white-collar and public service sector, but it is a trend that has come to stay. Men like Clive Jenkins of ASTMS and Alan Fisher of NUPE have enhanced the status of their respective unions through a fluent, persuasive advocacy of the cause of their members. Neither was elected by the rank and file. On the other hand, it would prove fatal for them if they behaved like unbending autocrats. This would upset the lay activists among the membership to whom they are answerable in the last resort for their actions. Union full-timers lack the means of coercing the membership into policies they do not want to follow. John Lyons, the highly respected general secretary of the Electrical Power Engineers' Association since 1973, is a new-style professional in the trade union movement. He moved to the EPEA after a spell as assistant secretary of the civil service union – the Institution of Professional Civil Servants (IPCS). Such inter-union career patterns still remain unusual, though Mark Young, general secretary of the airline pilots' union BALPA, used to be a full-time officer with the EETPU, and Laurie Sapper of the Association of University Teachers was formerly a senior union official for the Post Office Engineering Union. Simon Petch, now deputy general secretary of the EPEA, used to be chief of research at UCATT.

To a remarkable degree, the British unions rely on the voluntary help of an activist minority to survive. To try and narrow the gap – both physical and psychological – that separates the formal union organization from the life of the shopfloor and the office, the unions are trying to involve those activists more and more in decision-making, but it is a difficult problem to solve easily. An increase in the number of union participators would help.

The level of membership involvement in trade union affairs is partly determined by who sits on the various committees at local, regional and national level as part-time lay activists. Figures compiled in 1976 do not suggest that women play the kind of role in union machinery that their numerical strength in the rank and file would justify. The paucity of female representation in the unions is a source of acute embarrassment at the TUC. The figures in table 6.1 were compiled by the Equal Pay and Opportunity Campaign at the 1976 Trades Union Congress.

The reasons for low female membership involvement in union life are not hard to understand. For most women, the working day does not end when they leave their employer's premises. More than half the women workers in Britain are married and they have domestic responsibilities to look after. This reduces the amount of time they have available to become active trade

table 6.1 The sex breakdown in the unions, where women dominate, 1976

	% of members women	NEC male	female	full-time officials male	female	TUC delegates male	female
Tailor and Garment Workers	88	10	5	34	6	11	5
National Union of Teachers	75	41	7	24	2	30	1
Hosiery and Knitwear Workers	73	23	2	29	2	11	1
COHSE	70	27	1	35	5	8	—
CPSA	68	18	8	24	4	22	8
NUPE	65	20	6	120	2	29	4
Tobacco Workers	65	18	1	6	3	4	1
USDAW	59	16	1	129	4	21	5
Inland Revenue Staff Federation	58	25	3	6	1	9	—
APEX	55	11	4	5	1	10	3
Ceramic and Allied Trades	53	16	2	6	—	7	2
Footwear, Leather and Allied Trades	48	15	1	46	2	13	—
Bank Employees	46	21	3	28	3	13	—

(*Low Pay Unit Bulletin*, Number 14, April 1977)

unionists. There is also still undoubtedly widespread male prejudice against the appointment of women as full-time union officers or as delegates to the union conference.

The assumption that abortion, equal pay and sex discrimination are 'female' issues is shared by many male trade unionists. On Tuesday morning at Trades Union Congress there is always a rapid drift to the bars when those topics come up for debate. If expressions of male chauvinism are heard less often at the rostrum of union conferences, it does not mean that the new anti-sex discrimination laws have swept away instinctive prejudices. As we shall see in a later chapter, few unions have made any vigorous effort to use the Equal Pay and Sex Discrimination Acts militantly on behalf of their women members.

The most formidable of the few active women trade union leaders is Marie Patterson of the TGWU. As president of the TUC in 1975, she told delegates: 'It is not lack of interest or lack of ability that causes women to be under-represented in this Congress and in union executive committees and as full-time officers. Trade unions are representative bodies by definition. They are not thoroughly representative when nearly three members in every ten are women but there have never been more than eighty-four women among the thousand delegates to Congress and among the full-time officers the men outnumber the women by thirty-two to one.' And she concluded: 'The better the example we set in our own movement the better the chances will be for women to find their rightful place in every other walk of life.'

Another group who are under-represented in the decision-making processes of the unions are black workers. Nobody knows how many black shop stewards now exist in British industry, but there is widespread agreement that the number has risen sharply since the early 1970s, particularly on night shift-work, where black workers tend to predominate. At the 1976 TUC a passionate debate on the evils of racialism underlined the opposition of union leaders to any discrimination on the shopfloor or in the office, but expressions of moral indignation mask a sorry record of apathy and inactivity since the early 1960s.

As long ago as 1955 the TUC passed a resolution condemning racial discrimination. It stated:

This congress condemns all manifestations of racial discrimination or colour prejudices whether by governments, employers or workers. It urges the General Council to lose no opportunity to make the trade union attitude on this issue perfectly clear and to give special attention to the problems emerging in this country from the influx of fellow workers of other races with a view to removing causes of friction and preventing exploitation.

But as David Smith found out in 1974 (*Racial Disadvantage in Employment*, London, PEP) the ideal and reality remain far apart. 'It's the same with this as with so many other union matters – the bullshit beats the brains every time,' a prominent union boss told him. Actual opposition from a union to an employer who takes on black workers was very rare, but on the other hand, there was little contact between employers and unions on race relations questions. No more than a handful of complaints are ever made to the Commission on Racial Equality about discrimination at the workplace, but this does not mean that it does not go on. A 1974 Commons Select Committee criticized the TUC's attitude. Like the CBI it had declared opposition to racial discrimination, but 'taken wholly inadequate steps to ensure that their members work effectively to eradicate it'.

At national level the unions have been unwilling to make race relations a vital issue. Full-time black union officials are a rarity. Bill Morris, the TGWU district secretary in Northampton, is a Jamaican who spent nineteen years as a lay official (first a steward, later a convenor) at Hardy Spicer's in Birmingham, as well as being elected to the National Executive Council of the union. In 1972 he was appointed to a union post in the Nottingham office, and in 1976 he moved to Northampton. The print union SOGAT has a black area organizer in east London and the nurses' union, COHSE, has also appointed some black members to full-time jobs. The bakers' union has an Asian regional organizer. 'Not enough black workers have yet got sufficient experience to be made union officials,' said Bernard Dix of NUPE, which has many black members among local government manual workers. This is a plausible argument, but PEP found in 1974 that the big unions are reluctant to take any kind of definite action to integrate black workers into their organizations. As Smith wrote: 'Most of the unions were concerned to avoid anything that might be interpreted as specific action, because they feared that white members might think that the minorities were being given special treatment.'

The lack of black worker involvement in the unions was symbolized by the way Dr Ray of the Medical Practitioners section of ASTMS was treated at the 1974 Congress. On arriving at the conference centre to get his credentials as a delegate, he was directed by a helpful steward to the foreign visitors' gallery. This indifference was dented in October 1975 with the creation of a TUC Equal Rights Committee. Early in 1976 it was agreed to set up a Race Relations Advisory Committee to help the parent committee in its work. This might go some way to transform attitudes, but it will be a slow process. Since the early 1970s the TUC has recommended the inclusion of equal opportunity clauses in union agreements with employers. In March 1976 the General Council recommended how such a clause should be worded: 'The parties to this agreement are committed to the development of positive policies to promote equal opportunity in employment regardless of workers' sex, marital status, creed, colour, race or ethnic origins. This principle will apply in respect of all conditions of work including pay, hours of work, holiday entitlement, overtime and shiftwork, work allocation, sick pay' and other fringe benefits as well as training, promotion and redundancy. But how far are those declared good intentions going to be translated into action on the shopfloor? The TUC crossed paths with the Race Relations Board on two occasions. In April 1976 the Board asked the TUC whether it would be allowed to circularize TUC affiliates about the need to avoid discrimination in redundancy situations, but the TUC objected. There was also strong resistance to a proposed amendment to the 1976 Race Relations Act, which would make shop stewards legally liable in taking up cases of discrimination put to them by black workers. The TUC lobbied the Home Office to stop such a development on the ground that this was reintroducing the principle of legal sanctions into industrial relations, something the whole TUC had opposed rigorously between 1969 and 1974.

Not nearly enough has been done by the unions in race relations. But under the conflicting pressures of black militancy, black unionization and the growth in the activities of the National Front with its blatantly racialist appeal, attitudes are changing. 'Until workers themselves start fighting against an injustice, it will fail to have any attention. Once the process grows, then all that is best and healthy in the union movement will act.' That comment in June 1976 by an observer of the race relations problem in industry may sound too optimistic, but the developments since the race strikes of 1974 suggest the TUC and its major affiliates are in a more responsive mood. It is a belated recognition that race at work can no longer be allowed to suffer 'benign neglect'. As Miles and Phizacklea have argued: 'The change in TUC policy since 1974 is both significant and substantial. The explicit concern is no longer with "integration" and immigration but with racial discrimination and to a lesser extent with disadvantage and the possibility of the growth of a neo-fascist political organization feeding upon working-class racism' (*British Journal of Industrial Relations*, July 1978).

Whether women or black workers begin to play a more active role in the unions will depend on how ready union leaders are to accommodate their needs within existing structures. Union rule-books are very hard to change. Deeply rooted vested interests remain formidable obstacles to either union amalgamations or internal modernization. What a growing number of unions are trying to do is establish a new layer of organization, which bypasses the static, geographical structure and links up with the realities of workplace life. The industrial conference idea has now gained wide acceptance in many general unions, whose members are scattered through a variety of different occupational groups and find it hard to cohere at local or regional level. The shopworkers – USDAW – pioneered the idea in the early 1950s through trade conferences. These covered groupings such as the multiple meat trade, multiple grocery and the cooperative retail trade. Meetings of these sections were held at divisional as well as national level. John Hughes argued in his second background paper to Donovan:

As the arrangements fall into an accepted and expected pattern they can be seen as the development of a largely unwritten constitution of considerable significance in the formation of the union's industrial policies. Through these channels the industrial interests of active members are developed, their views are coordinated and at the same time the participants can be given a wider view of the union's concerns and a sense of its principles and strategy can emerge.

The logic of industrial conferences stems from their connection with collective bargaining. It is a democratic method of making sure a growing number of activists (particularly the stewards) are drawn into the wider decision-making processes of the union. Calling lay delegates together in a particular industry to hammer out a pay claim and choose its negotiating team is a significant development in many unions. The need to ratify an agreement through a recalled industrial conference is also happening more often. The ETU introduced industrial conferences in 1965. They now have annual area conferences of stewards in electrical contracting, supply, shipbuilding and ship repair, engineering and 'such other industries as the Executive Council may determine'. Between its biennial conferences, the EETPU holds national industrial conferences for the same industries. Yet the leadership keeps a careful control of the process. It is the Executive Council which determines the method of representation and 'all questions relating to the composition, agenda and procedure'. This is as it should be. There is always a danger industrial conferences may become centres of breakaway attitudes and weaken the centralizing forces in a general union. In public sector unions like NALGO and the CPSA sectional interests are catered for through the organization. In NALGO, group annual meetings are held for members in local government, the public utilities and the universities as an integral part of the annual summer conference. A similar process is used by the CPSA and POEU among others.

The major unions are involved in a serious attempt to readjust their structures to the industrial reality of their memberships. This is not always possible without internal friction. The need to reconcile the wider interests of the union with the specific needs of individual groups of workers is urgent, but few trade union activists are willing to spare the time and energy to connect the different layers of the union together in a meaningful whole. The emphasis of present union reform is moving in the direction of greater responsibilities being placed on the broad shoulders of the unpaid activists at the workplace, with the full-time staff acting as a kind of civil service, who provide expertise when needed and subtle guidance. But there remains a wide gap between the full-time leaders and the rank and file. As the Webbs wrote over eighty years ago in their *Industrial Democracy*:

Directly the working man representative becomes properly equipped for one half of his duties, he ceases to be specially qualified for the other. If he remains essentially a manual worker, he fails to cope with the brain-working officials; if he takes on the character of the brain-worker, he is apt to get out of touch with the constituents whose desires he has to interpret.

The difficulty is compounded by the lack of a coherent political perspective among most of the rank and file outside the activist minority. In an *ad hoc*, hand-to-mouth way the unions are re-shaping themselves to accommodate the pressures for change, though this amounts to nothing very dramatic. Those who seek to generate outside pressure through legislation may find themselves in conflict with entrenched, suspicious union leaders.

Yet does the question of union democracy really matter anyway? For the most part, members give a passive compliance to what unions do in their name. They only stir at moments of crisis, and this is natural. Nobody denounces those thousands of shareholders who fail to turn up in droves to the annual general meeting of the company they have a stake in. What little research has been done suggests that trade unionists do not see their organization as a way towards democratic self-government. Most do not share the wider social, political and cultural goals of the activist minority who run the unions at all levels. Members tend to regard their union membership card as a kind of commodity, which they pay for in order to gain tangible rewards in better pay and conditions. In the words of John Goldthorpe they practise 'instrumental collectivism – the achievement of individual private goals outside the workplace'. As long as unions appear to be delivering the goods, members will tolerate the activities of the minority who administer the unions. But if a union fails lamentably to fulfil its primary function, members will eventually respond by leaving it. There is nothing like a stagnant or falling membership to stir the need for internal reform. The General and Municipal Workers provides a good example of this process in the early 1970s. The extension of the closed shop and the existence of the TUC Bridlington agreements to prevent inter-union recruitment and poaching are not implacable barriers to membership preference, though there is always a danger that they may become so in the future. Of course, the pursuit of purely materialistic ends can breed chaos in a union. Many officials find themselves constantly fighting to persuade hot-headed members not to settle locally in breach of a national agreement.

There is a mutual conspiracy between union leaders and government – aided and abetted by the media – to convince the public that unions can deliver their side of a national bargain on pay or anything else. It is not so. The pressure from the rank and file can upset even the most complacent and self-righteous of union bosses. At a crunch they lack leverage, the means of coercion to compel acceptance of something the members refuse to stomach. Far from helping the cause of 'moderation', the compulsory existence of postal ballots in all union elections could undermine the full-time activists in their struggle to retain cohesion and stability in the organization.

This does not mean that 'what is, is best'. The lamentable ineffectiveness of unions is far more apparent in our society than their supposed muscle power and greed. Through the shop steward system, Britain has developed a unique layer of democratic trade unionism, which needs to be nurtured and stimulated by every possible means, as long as it does not fragment trade union unity and stimulate sectionalism. Perhaps the Michels law of oligarchy does apply to many unions in the way they conduct their business, though this suggests a static picture, which is inaccurate. All unions are capable of dynamic change, even if the economic and social forces that compel this do not always lead to progressive reform.

In the debate over union democracy, an effort must be made to establish a balance between the full-time professionals with expertise at the centre and a self-confident, militant workplace organization. Unions can never afford to lose sight of what they are here for. 'Moderation' should not mean wage restraint, feeble bargaining, obedience to a mythical 'national' interest, which is part of the ritual language of British politics. The danger is not that unions will become instruments for 'extremist action'. Once even the ablest of stewards tries to act as well as talk of the 'revolution', he can expect to be repudiated by his colleagues. More serious, unions could lose their independence by finding themselves enmeshed in the machinery of the state as a partner, even a policeman, of government. The voluntary wages policy of 1975-7 was an infringement of the freedom of unions to bargain on behalf of their members, however 'necessary' it was at the time. Those who want unions to be more democratic than they already are would be upset if those fragile, defensive organizations faced too many buffetings at the hands of the fickle rank and file, whose mood can change drastically from day to day. Too much union democracy could wreck the attempt to establish an alliance between the TUC and the government of the day on a more permanent basis.

The advocates of more postal ballots are the fair-weather friends of collective bargaining, who assume that more voting will lessen militancy. But if union leaders are ever to acquire a wider perspective, they must have the opportunity to provide a democratic leadership. Argument and persuasion are the only real weapons that unions can use to convince their invariably apathetic, but often restive, members of what they believe to be the sensible course of action. Constant electioneering would politicize the unions even more and undermine the stability that union officials need to establish any kind of moral authority over their rank and file. The ultimate test for a union's failure or success must lie in its ability to improve and safeguard the living standards of its members. The exercise in democratic self-government is only a byproduct, a safeguard against an entrenched oligarchy ignoring rank and file opinion. This may not please the postal vote champions, but that is life. Legislation to enforce postal ballots would do nothing but harm, for it neglects the ultimate purpose of what trade unionism is all about.

General guidelines are therefore very difficult to construct. We need to be guided by specific examples and circumstances.

Making the unions more representative of the views of the rank and file is a vital necessity if we intend to take the wider issue of industrial democracy at all seriously in the 1980s, but we should not suppose postal ballots are only nor even necessarily the best way to achieve this admirable objective.

7 The challenge from below

When the public at large think about us they often have in mind the general secretary. But to the members in your shop the image which the union will conjure up will certainly be you. Make sure you are a good advertisement. The way to do this is to carry out efficiently your job as a shop steward. It is the only way. (*Shop Steward's Handbook*, Transport and General Workers' Union, 1974, p 4)

Unions are not highly centralized, tightly disciplined monoliths where hard-faced bosses bark out orders to a passive and obedient rank and file. This has always been a caricature, even if many people choose to believe it. To an alarming degree, the very opposite is the sad truth. Unions at the centre have too little power, rather than too much. Down on the shopfloor or in the office the wise or foolish words of a trade union general secretary do not enjoy a lasting impact on the course of industrial relations. The gulf between the settled world of the union leader sitting in head office (usually down in London suburbia a long way from Britain's industrial heartland) and the fluid, informal routine of union life in industry remains enormous.

A good example of the troubles of a full-time union boss (no matter what his national prestige) is what happened when Jack Jones of the TGWU tried to restrain the wages explosion that occurred in the winter of 1974–5, starting in the West Central region of Scotland. In November, at Motherwell, Jones made a speech that urged restraint and responsibility, but thousands of his members in the area ignored his pleas. The rash of unofficial strikes that broke out among Scottish lorry drivers, bus drivers and sewage men in West Central Scotland tore a gaping hole through the flimsy Social Contract Mark One. Over 23,000 workers were on strike by early November. Officials from the TGWU headquarters in London tried to calm down the militancy, but they got nowhere. The TGWU's trade group officer for transport told me the workers refused to compromise: 'They plucked a round sum of money out of the air that they wanted and kept on saying they would not stop the strike until they got it.' Union officials are unfamiliar with that kind of unyielding attitude, for they thrive as bargainers. 'It was the first time in all my years of negotiating that I have gone into talks with the employers and got everything,' admitted the official.

To a very large and still growing extent, it is the shop stewards and staff representatives who are the direct union presence in the workplace. They are now the unpaid subalterns of the trade union movement. What cohesion and order still exists in workplace bargaining is a result of their efforts. To many critics, the stewards are portrayed as bloody-minded militants, trouble-makers, who are ready to issue strike notices at the drop of a cloth cap. Fred Kite, played by Peter Sellers in *I'm All Right Jack,* is the stereotype steward of popular imagination – bone-headed, sanctimonious, humourless, a stickler for the blessed rule-book and a formidable obstacle to industrial progress. Nothing could be further removed from the truth. It is about time the accumulated empirical evidence of academic research began to dispel the popular widespread misconceptions about shop stewards.

The latest (1975) TUC estimates suggest there are 291,000 workplace representatives in Britain. This works out at about one for every sixty-five trade unionists. The 1972 Commission on Industrial Relations inquiry estimated around 350,000 people were workplace representatives, but that figure covered manual and non-manual, accredited and non-accredited, union and non-union. Nearly half the shop stewards in the CIR survey belonged to the big three trade unions. (The Transport and General Workers, the General and Municipal Workers, and the Amalgamated Union of Engineering Workers; see table 7.1.) William Brown and colleagues at Warwick University estimated that in 1976 there were 5,000 full-time shop stewards covering manual workers in 3,000 manufacturing plants. Ten years before there had been no more than 1,000 (*British Journal of Industrial Relations,* November 1978).

The Donovan Commission concluded in 1968 that stewards were 'rarely agitators pushing workers towards unconstitutional

table 7.1 Shop stewards

Union	Manual shop stewards	Non-manual shop stewards	TOTAL number	%
AUEW (excluding TASS)	34,700	900	35,500	19
TGWU (including ACTSS)	28,900	3,100	32,000	17
GMWU	13,300	600	13,900	7
ASTMS	200	8,800	9,000	5
EETU/TPU	7,600	100	7,700	4
USDAW	3,100	3,500	6,600	4
DATE (now AUEW/TASS)	100	6,200	6,300	3
CAWU (now APEX)	100	5,900	6,000	3
NALGO	300	4,100	4,500	2
NUR	3,700	800	4,400	2
SOGAT	2,700	200	2,800	2
NGA	2,200	*	2,200	1
NUPE	1,800	400	2,200	1
ASW (now part of UCATT)	1,900	*	2,000	1
NUTGW	1,900	*	1,900	1
NUVB (now part of TGWU)	1,800	0	1,800	1
CPSA	*	1,700	1,700	1
TSSA	100	1,500	1,600	1
COHSE	1,200	400	1,600	1
ASBSBSW	1,300	*	1,300	1
AUBTW (now part of UCATT)	800	0	800	—
Other Unions	19,800	7,900	27,700	15
Unspecified	10,600	2,000	12,500	7
TOTAL All unions	138,000	48,000	186,000	100
Base numbers	20,031	6,859	26,890	

* denotes less than 50 shop stewards
(CIR Study 2, *Industrial Relations at Establishment Level*, HMSO, 1973)

action'. And it added : 'In some instances they may be the mere mouthpieces of their work groups. But quite commonly they are supporters of order, exercising a restraining influence on their members in conditions which promote disorder.' In the words of

Stanley Parker and Bill McCarthy: 'For the most part the steward is viewed by others, and views himself, as an accepted, reasonable and even moderating influence; more of a lubricant than an irritant.' Follow-up surveys on workplace industrial relations in 1972 and 1973 support those earlier observations. Far from being wreckers or extremists, stewards are conciliators, men and women of reason who help to ensure that industry functions smoothly. In the 1973 Parker survey as many as 79 per cent of senior managers in the sample actually thought their stewards were 'helping' them solve their industrial relations problems, while 27 per cent even admitted stewards helped management quite a lot or in a minor way with the solution of production troubles. For their part, 87 per cent of the stewards agreed that they did help the management.

Nor was it automatically assumed by respondents to the surveys that shop stewards simply take the workers' view of an issue. A total of 54 per cent of workers thought their stewards had a balanced fifty-fifty attitude on any specific point of conflict. As many as 36 per cent of senior management believed the stewards did so too; while 93 per cent of senior managers believed the stewards were reasonable to deal with, and 82 per cent of the stewards thought that managers did a lot to, or made some effort to, establish good relations with them. Management prefers to work with the stewards rather than full-time union officials from outside the workplace.

Who are the stewards? Their average age is around 42–3, while senior stewards are around 48 years old. On average, they have represented their workplace unit for five years and have been continuously employed by the same company for eleven years. Just over a quarter of all shop stewards hold another office in their trade union, mostly at branch level. The vast majority – as many as three quarters – became stewards without having had to stand for election by their workmates. A total of 14 per cent became stewards in elections after the previous steward had resigned from the job, but a mere 7 per cent were elected stewards by actually defeating the previous incumbent. On average, stewards spend seven hours a week on their shopfloor responsibilities, while senior stewards put in twice as much. Stewards appear to be popular figures, having close day-to-day contact with the workers they represent. In the 1973 Parker survey 44 per cent of workers said their personal earnings had at some time been increased as a result of the efforts of their steward, though this was far more pronounced in the two-tier wage system of engineering (61 per cent) than in the nationalized industries (33 per cent). A total of 69 per cent of stewards claimed that they had increased the earnings of their work colleagues as a result of their own efforts. As many as 89 per cent of stewards were either 'very' or 'fairly' satisfied with the opportunities to contact their members, though around a third of those in metal manufacture and engineering thought that the facilities for holding meetings were inadequate.

In the 1973 survey, 69 per cent of senior managers said they had joint committees or councils in the workplace, where worker representatives met management jointly to discuss and settle problems. In metal manufacture and mechanical engineering, as many as 86 per cent and 78 per cent respectively said this was the organizational system they worked with. Stewards appear to enjoy easy access to the management. While 83 per cent of the 1972 survey made contact with the foremen to discuss issues (as many as 42 per cent in an 'always informal' way), a total of 78 per cent of the stewards often raised matters directly with senior management. Almost all stewards were allowed personal contact with the top of the company when they felt that the situation required it and 68 per cent of stewards could go direct. Written national and local agreements were in force in most workplaces, but the formalism of such procedures was not allowed to create inflexibilities. In the 1973 survey 56 per cent of senior managers said they had unwritten workplace agreements for settling disputes and claims. Custom and practice was particularly widespread in the chemical and textile industries as well as the distributive trades. As many as 59 per cent of senior managers said they liked to reach agreement at workplace level with a total of 71 per cent and 70 per cent respectively saying so in metal manufacture and mechanical engineering.

Neither the CIR nor the Parker/McCarthy survey material suggests that stewards are tyrants, who can push their rank and file into any kind of militant action. A total of 73 per cent of the workers sampled said that it was the majority of the trade union members who decided what to do over any grievance or claim. Only 13 per cent suggested it was the steward who made the decision on his or her own. While 15 per cent of stewards claimed that they could always get their members to see their way and get them to do what they thought was right when a dispute broke out, 47 per cent agreed they could 'usually' do that, while 31 per cent said only 'sometimes'. The 1972 survey found that two-thirds of the foremen questioned thought that stewards acted more as the mouthpieces of their members and only 31 per cent that they acted more as leaders. Nor are stewards the only people who raise issues; as many as 79 per cent of foremen represented workers' views to management and 42 per cent of senior managers said that representations were made to them on behalf of a workgroup other than through stewards.

Sweet reason dominates most of British manufacturing industry. Research carried out in the Department of Employment revealed in 1976 that as many as 98 per cent of all plants in manufacturing industry – representing 80 per cent of all employment – are strike-free during any one year. Disputes are unpopular among stewards and workers, just as much as they are in the boardroom. As many as 71 per cent of workers in the 1973 Parker survey suggested they would get more satisfactory results over a problem from the management by going through the recognized disputes procedure than by striking or taking some other form of militant action. A third of the stewards believed quicker and better results would arise from exerting pressure than exhausting recognized procedures with as many as 55 per cent believing this in the engineering industry, a note of criticism at the long-established and slow-moving procedures covering that sector. Parker's 1973 survey found that the preference for strike action is much stronger among professional and technical staff, and more likely in the ranks of skilled than unskilled manual labour.

The trend to workplace bargaining has grown strongly since the early 1970s, despite the existence of various forms of national incomes policy. W. W. Daniel, in his important 1976 PEP study *Wage Determination in Industry*, found an astonishing 90 per cent of the union negotiators in the manufacturing sector were predominantly part-timers. As he wrote:

In only about half of the cases was a full-time officer of the union, at any level, spontaneously cited as having been involved in preparing the claim. And in only a quarter of the cases where a full-time officer had been involved was he identified as having had the most influence in the preparation of the case.

Thus, although wage negotiations often involved consideration of complex financial, statistical and technical issues, they were very frequently conducted, on the union side, by lay officers with little or no training and without any expert or professional support or advisory services.

Daniel found that the representative body of workers was involved in 74 per cent of the claims submitted to management. As many as 55 per cent of the firms covered in the PEP survey said that the most important level of formal bargaining over wage rates was at the plant or establishment, with 71 per cent saying so in engineering and 73 per cent in the metal-working industry. This compared with only 37 per cent in chemicals and 33 per cent in food and distribution.

The survey discovered considerable opposition to any national incomes policy among the shopfloor negotiators, particularly those from the Amalgamated Union of Engineering Workers. As Daniel concluded: 'For plant union officers generally, formal incomes policy is at best acceptable only as an emergency measure in special circumstances. Very few (21 per cent) looked favourably upon the idea of incomes policy as a permanent feature.' In his view the position has now been reached in vast tracts of private manufacturing industry where 'trade union representatives operate at the works level, largely independent of their national or even regional organizations'.

The extent of fragmentation suggests that national union leaders can only exercise a very limited influence on wage determination, but it would be wrong to exaggerate the loss of central control. The survey referred to in the last few paragraphs was heavily biased towards engineering and metal manufacture where the two-tier system of bargaining has a hallowed history, going back beyond the 1890s. Many other sectors of the British economy remain where national pay agreements reached in London lay down wage rates that do not fall very far short of what workers make in gross weekly earnings. This is particularly true of the public service sector and the nationalized industries – local and central government, and public utilities like gas, water and electricity, and education, as well as coal mining and iron and steel. But even in private sectors like electrical contracting, paper-making, retail cooperatives, road haulage and chemicals, the basic pay covered by national agreements is very close to the standard weekly earnings of workers in those sectors, according to Earnings Survey data.

Self-reliant stewards often appear to operate outside the confines of their own union's national policy. And unlike the leaders who sit at the TUC or in national headquarters, most stewards lack any party political perspective. The 1968 Parker and McCarthy survey found that only 17 per cent of stewards belonged to a political party. In the General and Municipal Workers, a mere 54 per cent of stewards paid the political levy. This suggests that stewards are unlikely to swallow readily the wider considerations that shape national union policy, such as the Social Contract between Labour and the unions.

Despite this, the survey evidence reveals most full-time union officials have no grumbles about how the British industrial relations system works. In the 1973 Parker survey, in as many as 78 per cent of establishments the full-time officers believed they enjoyed enough influence over the activities of the stewards. Only 15 per cent said they would like to play a more important role in domestic collective bargaining. On the other hand, just under a third of the stewards in the sample said they wanted to see their full-time officials playing a more important role in local negotiations.

It is not surprising that many stewards find their work stressful. Nigel Nicholson, in a survey of stewards at an engineering firm, found plenty of evidence to support the view that many are under considerable strain. The feeling that stewards had too much to do was echoed by three-quarters of those he spoke to. 'You sometimes feel at the end of the day as if your brain's addled – it just couldn't function any more,' one told him. Nicholson observed that 'role ambiguity' was a major cause of distress to stewards. 'A high proportion said they frequently felt at a loss to decide the right course of action, or that they often experienced more general feelings of not knowing what was expected of them.' To many stewards the stress was welcome as part of the job, but the anxiety and impact on the steward's health even in a plant where industrial relations were essentially amicable suggests the burden on the steward can be a test of human endurance.

To what extent are stewards left to their own devices, once their union has recognized their credentials? The 1972 CIR report reckoned that no more than 15 per cent of stewards received some industrial relations training during 1970, with the average length of time on a course being around three-and-a-half days. The report suggested between 8 and 10 per cent of manual worker stewards also attended courses held outside working hours. This comes to about forty to fifty thousand out of the two hundred thousand stewards the CIR estimated to be serving in British industry. The unions have always disliked the employer providing any training for the steward in his or her job, but in practice companies are responsible for around half the shop stewards' courses. As we have seen in the discussion of the TUC education programme, considerable strides were made between 1974 and 1977 to improve both the extent and quality of shop steward training. The 1975 Employment Protection Act lays down specific rights for union representatives to have paid time off work to go on training courses. The provision of massive state aid may go some way to rectify the problem, but it seems unlikely that this will be nearly enough.

The more the workplace becomes the centre of industrial relations, the more difficult it is to maintain order and cohesion. This poses problems for the stewards in larger multi-plant combines like Leyland or Ford, where it often proves hard to reach agreement across the company between the different plants and grades. Joint combine committees are the usual answer and some, notably those at Joseph Lucas, Vickers and Ford, are fairly effective. Nevertheless stewards find it hard to reconcile the need to represent the particular views of their own small constituency with the strategy of the workplace company-wide. The Commission on Industrial Relations in a 1974 study suggested the spread of the informal system of collective bargaining was one way management could retain the initiative. As it explained:

Management do not wish, in the majority of cases, to have more formal relations with the full-time officers of the unions. It seems that, generally in plant-bargaining companies, they have built up the authority of senior stewards as part of a deliberate policy of retaining the control of industrial relations matters generally within the organization.

There is a serious danger that individual stewards can be effectively isolated and divided from each other as a result. Moreover, by an overemphasis on the workplace, the range of bargaining issues can be severely limited. As the 1974 study argued:

Plant issues are generally looked at in isolation from matters which affect a number of plants. This means that union organization is often much less effective once it is faced by matters which reach beyond the plant. As a result, in the majority of companies where one-level plant bargaining exists, collective bargaining is typically centred on a limited range of issues. It rarely produces redundancy agreements or an adequate company pension scheme, features which owe as much to management's centralization of decision-making on such matters as to the limited view taken at plant level about the range of collective bargaining issues.

The existence of more than one union in a workplace no longer provokes the kind of inter-union conflict that it used to do. To a very large extent, it is the stewards who mend fences and prevent conflict between unions wrecking the harmony of the workplace. In Parker's 1973 survey it was found that in 58 per cent of the workplaces where there was more than one union representing workers, 46 per cent of the stewards said they sometimes acted on behalf of another union's members as well as their own.

The pressure on lay activists to play a more vital role in collective bargaining grew during the 1970s, but the growth in trade union membership was not paralleled by a rapid expansion in the number of full-time union officials. Hugh Clegg and his colleagues at Warwick University reckoned in their study of the local relationships of unions (*Workplace and Union*, London, 1974) that full-time lay officials (convenors, senior stewards, branch secretaries and the like paid by their employers most or all of their time to do union business) outnumber full-time officials of the unions.

In the TGWU many large plants never see any full-time union officers from one year to the next. Joe Bond is senior TGWU steward and branch secretary of a large Birmingham brewery with 2,200 union members. Along with twenty-four other stewards, he is responsible for collective bargaining in the company. The full-time officer in the district office leaves them well alone to get on with their jobs, though once a year he turns up to lead the negotiating team. 'We could do without him, mind: but it is a kind of tradition that he does it,' said Bond, when I talked to him in February 1975. 'But don't get the impression that the union is remote. We can get somebody down from district office straightaway on the telephone but we rarely need to do that.' The brewery is well organized, with self-confident and articulate shopfloor enthusiasts. The men were earning an average of £4,000 a year in 1974 – thanks to hard plant-bargaining – and there have been no strikes for over eighteen years. The union branch that covers the whole plant is extremely well-off. It donates large sums of money to local charities and good union causes like the Upper Clyde shipbuilding workers in 1971 and the miners when they were on strike. The branch has not always been like that. It was Harry Urwin (assistant general secretary) who brought the TGWU into the poorly organized and badly paid Birmingham brewery industry in the late 1950s. This is the ideal – union stimulus for the organization of effective plant-bargaining and then an encouragement of self-reliance.

When Jack Jones became general secretary of the TGWU in 1969 he arrived at Transport House with a clearly thought out philosophy of industrial relations. 'All power to the stewards' became the rallying cry. As Jones told a conference of the Institute of Personnel Management in October 1969: 'We have got to get our agreements down to the point where the workers themselves are involved in the negotiations – and want to keep the agreements because they have had a decisive hand in making them and therefore understand them.' In Jones's view the full-time union official is very much 'the coordinator, the encourager, the man to call in when a problem cannot be resolved or when it gets a wider significance. He is the man, to be honest, who should be (increasingly) working where trade unionism is weak, where it needs to be built up. Where it is

strong he should not be required so much.' And Jones added:
'I am working for a system where not a few trade union officials
control the situation but a dedicated, well-trained and intelligent body of trades union members is represented by hundreds
of thousands of lay representatives – every one of whom is
capable of helping to resolve industrial problems and assisting
in collective bargaining and the conclusion of agreements.' The
TGWU has made a determined effort to upgrade the stewards
and make them an essential key in shopfloor relations.

A special shop stewards' handbook has been produced by
the TGWU to help its lay activists with their work. Under Rule
11 of the union, stewards are elected wherever possible by the
membership in organized factories, garages and depots, on
wharves and on building sites. Like Mao's *Little Red Book*,
the TGWU shop stewards' guide is full of sound common sense.
In the section on relations with the management it is clear
Transport House does not envisage the steward as a firebrand.

Don't try to jump over the foreman. Settle your grievances with
him wherever possible ... never boast about victories over
management or about having the foreman under your thumb.
This kind of conduct needlessly asks for trouble.... The workers
themselves should themselves show the courtesy to the
management which they expect to receive. Courtesy applies not
only to the manner of speaking; it applies to punctuality and to
general bearing as well.

The TGWU handbook takes the steward through the various
duties he must perform if he is to become effective. This
involves familiarity with wages systems, contracts of employment legislation, redundancy payments, the law on unfair dismissals, safety, health and welfare, action to be taken over
industrial accidents, organizing members and recruiting. Jones's
strong emphasis on shopfloor bargaining meant a wide degree
of self-reliance, for the union's stewards. The handbook warns
stewards against becoming mere messengers. 'So far as possible
only major issues or matters of principle should be referred to
the district officer.' On the other hand, it also opposes any
break with the union outside the plant.

[There is a danger of] relying so much on yourself that, in
effect, you run your own union and proceed without any regard

for the importance of working as a team. Sooner or later, however, even the strongest workshop group needs help from fellow workers outside. It is, therefore, a matter of self-interest not to undermine the unity of the working class which is expressed in the trade union movement.

But the attempt to marry the informal system that has grown up in industry to the more rigid structure of trade union organization often proves difficult. In the past, the stewards have often been seen by union bosses as serious threats to their own authority. But union hierarchies have often found it very difficult to establish any control over their stewards, because their rule-books do not provide any clear-cut function for the stewards to perform within the union organization. Stewards grew up to meet a real need by filling the vacuum of the union presence on the shopfloor and in offices. The rule-book of the EETPU has clear regulations to cover the work of the stewards (Rule 15). It states that they are under the 'jurisdiction of the area full-time official' and must 'obey the directions of the Executive Council'. Since the mid-1960s the union has attempted to integrate the stewards into the procedures of the EETPU through the introduction of industrial conferences, made up of lay activists who meet regularly to discuss the bargaining issues. A similiar development has occurred in the General and Municipal Workers since 1969, where stewards are brought together in industrial conferences for particular sectors to discuss pay and conditions. Under Rule 41 of the GMWU the union's estimated 22,000 stewards have their credentials supplied by the regional secretary. The actual appointment of a steward must be approved first of all by the branch, followed by regional office. The GMWU shop stewards' handbook emphasizes the need for the steward to keep in close touch with the life of the branch. Particular attention is paid to ensuring the stewards are not left too much on their own. Under Rule 27 no steward can enjoy the power of sanctioning strike action. This must be done through the regional committee (which has the power to approve an official strike where up to 300 members are involved) or the National Executive Committee, if the numbers involved are larger.

In the Amalgamated Union of Engineering Workers the stewards are under the firm control of the district committee.

No steward can operate in the AUEW until he has won the approval of that all-important body. The powers and duties of the stewards are closely laid down by the district committees. The stewards must report once every three months to the district committee 'on all matters in the shop affecting trade'. Rule 13 states that the AUEW steward's primary function is to keep a close eye on the contribution cards of all members in his workplace, to make sure the workers there belong to the union, and that they are getting the approved rates of pay. Stewards sit as of right on the district committee on the basis of one for every 5,000 members in the district. The district committees have to convene quarterly meetings of stewards. The shop steward system is more widely developed in the AUEW than in other unions. This derives primarily from tradition and the two-tier system of bargaining in the engineering industry.

The complexities of shopfloor bargaining in engineering are well illustrated by Arthur Marsh's survey of 432 firms in the powerful Engineering Employers' Federation in the early part of 1969. The sample suggested 77 per cent of the labour force was unionized at that time (41 per cent of them in the Engineers), with as many as forty different unions having members in some of the companies. There were estimated to be 9,000 shop stewards, which came out at one for every thirty-two trade unionists. In the Engineers the proportion was lower than average at one for every thirty. Marsh and his colleagues reckoned there were 40,000 stewards in engineering that year. Like Parker and McCarthy, they found that the overwhelming majority of firms believed they enjoyed good relations with their manual and white-collar unions (89 per cent in the case of the former and 67 per cent for the latter). A total of 80 per cent of managers thought that the stewards were helpful and only 9 per cent believed them to be obstructive. Despite the reality of multi-unionism on the shopfloor, a mere 9 per cent of managers said they had suffered from a conflict between unions in their plant over membership and 7 per cent mentioned inter-union disputes over union policy.

None the less, Marsh and his colleagues did find that as many as 74 per cent of engineering managers believed work organization in their establishments could be bettered, if they had more power ·to move workers from one job to another round the plant. It was on such sensitive matters as the manning of machines, general labour mobility and job demarcation (not seniority or apprenticeship restrictions) which really worried management. And it was the unions who were regarded as the main obstacle to change in the eyes of employers. Interestingly enough, employers pinned the blame on outside union interference for the opposition, not on the shop stewards themselves. Moreover 80 per cent thought it was at district committee level where the resistance lay, not at the headquarters of the unions. A 1974 CIR study of industrial relations in multi-plant firms even found instances where AUEW stewards failed to persuade a district committee to accept their negotiating policy.

The 1968 McCarthy/Parker survey for Donovan provided further interesting data on union differences. The best educated and qualified stewards were those belonging to the EETPU, with as many as 60 per cent of that union's stewards having had part-time further education. This compared with only one-third of stewards generally. A quarter of stewards served out a full industrial apprenticeship with as many as 53 per cent in the EETPU doing so and 46 per cent in the AEU. While only 17 per cent belonged to a political party, in the National Union of Railwaymen the proportion was as high as 51 per cent; and it was lowest in the General and Municipal Workers, with 13 per cent. As many as 70 per cent of stewards said they paid the political levy, but a large minority in the GMWU (46 per cent) contracted out. Twenty-three per cent of the McCarthy/Parker sample said they held another office in their present union. Just over half (55 per cent) of stewards said they were not interested in promotion, but 28 per cent did admit they were interested in becoming foremen. Keenness for moving up the hierarchy of the firm was strongest among EETPU stewards (56 per cent) and least evident in the NUR (26 per cent). It was the young stewards who were most interested in promotion, those having less than ten years' service with their present firm. The NUR had the most enthusiastic stewards, with as many as 52 per cent saying they volunteered to do the job. Only 32 per cent of stewards giving ten or more hours a week to the job needed to be persuaded to take it on.

This contrasted with 48 per cent of those giving four hours or less. In the General and Municipal Workers (81 per cent) and the EETPU (79 per cent), stewards are far more likely to get their posts without an election. In the NUR well over half the stewards faced competition for the job. In the EETPU 91 per cent of steward elections were by show of hands at the workplace. By contrast ballots were most common in the NUR (73 per cent) and the TGWU (41 per cent). Annual elections were most frequent in the AEU and the EETPU, but in the NUR stewards serve from two to four years.

NUR stewards were more likely to have experienced some kind of training or instruction for their jobs than those of other unions. As many as 67 per cent of that union's stewards had received some training, compared with 22 per cent of those in the GMWU and 29 per cent in the EETPU.

The National Union of Public Employees, with its main interests in local government and hospital ancillary manual work, did not introduce the idea of shop stewards until the 1960s. It was only in January 1969 that union stewards were given official recognition by employers in local government and 1971 before they won similar acceptance in the national health service. The steward system spread rapidly through NUPE. In 1970, 38 per cent of the union's branches had no stewards at all, while 21 per cent had five or more. By 1974 only 11 per cent of branches said they had no union stewards and the proportion with five or more had grown to nearly half. More than half the stewards in NUPE negotiate with management on errors of pay, while 40 per cent bargain about working hours. A third negotiate on questions of bonus and a third meet management about the safety of their members' working conditions. Global figures disguise a patchy picture. As Bob Fryer and his colleagues discovered, 40 per cent of branches had only three union stewards and 12 per cent had 100 or more members for every steward in the branch. Although women made up 63 per cent of NUPE members, only 28 per cent of the stewards were women. As many as 70 per cent of stewards had never been on any training course and 56 per cent told the Warwick University investigators that they had received no form whatsoever of education or training connected with their duties as stewards. Only £8,713 was spent by head office on education and training in 1974. Facilities for NUPE stewards remain rudimentary. In 1974 two-thirds of the stewards had a notice board and half had access to a telephone, but just over two-thirds had no use of a room for meetings. Little over a third had no agreement with the employer to carry out steward's duties during working hours.

'All power to the shop stewards' sounds an attractive slogan, but it can often lead to a serious division of opinion at a workplace, if driven to its logical conclusion. For the most part, the workers see the steward as their representative in the union, but there is a serious danger that in the years ahead far too many onerous duties will be imposed on the shoulders of the lay activists, which they will only be able to perform indifferently. The Bullock Report recommended equal control for employee representatives (stewards) with those of shareholders on the boards of the top companies with over 2,000 workers. The ultimate responsibility will rest with the hard-pressed, overworked steward, who (as this chapter has shown) is expected by his or her union to make bricks out of straw with the minimum of back-up services. The majority of the Bullock Committee asserted:

The trade unions have harnessed the desire of employees both to be protected and to have a voice in decision-making and have strengthened the position of employees in many large companies by expressing their hopes and fears collectively. The extension of trade unions' influence on the economy and on industry has been one of the most marked changes in the last decade, and it is through the trade unions that a large measure of employee participation has already been achieved.

Bullock goes on to claim:

Trade unions are no longer concentrating exclusively on questions of pay and conditions, but are pressing for an extension of collective bargaining to cover decisions which were traditionally the prerogative of management. In its evidence to us, the TUC identified a number of areas apart from wages where some unions are already in substantive negotiations with management. These areas include provision of facilities for lay trade union representatives, such as office services and time off for union duties; manpower planning; job and income security; and disclosure of information. This gradual, albeit uneven, extension of the scope of collective bargaining is evidence of the shopfloor pressures for greater industrial democracy.

Maybe, but all this looks more real in academic textbooks than in the messy processes of shopfloor industrial relations. There is a danger the stewards will be overwhelmed by the magnitude of their diversity of unpaid tasks and cut off from the aspirations of the shopfloor. The diffusion of effort in the face of a highly professional management is more likely to weaken than strengthen trade unionism where it matters most. There is a real danger in assuming that the trade union activist at the shopfloor can be a kind of Renaissance man, with the ability to grasp and resolve all problems confronting him. As Bullock argued unconvincingly:

In the long run we believe that the value of the contribution
which employee representatives will make on the board will depend
less on their mastery of the tools used in the professional practice
of management than on their personal qualities of judgment and
leadership and their ability to interpret and represent views of
their constituents.

This looks like industrial democracy on the cheap. It is expecting a great deal from the stewards to make an effective response to such a challenge without a major reform and expansion of the full-time union machines.

Over the next decade shop steward 'power' is likely to become an even more unstable, unpredictable element in our mixed, interdependent economy, which the unions are going to find hard to control or even influence. The main initiative for reform is likely to arise from employers, intent on legitimizing and therefore buttressing the position of the stewards. This will add to the pressures on the often difficult relations between full-time union officials and the lay activists. A return to centralized union authority looks difficult to achieve, but the exact balance of power between the divergent interests within the union is hard to predict. What is not in doubt is the persistence of the 'challenge from below' with unforeseen consequences for the future of the trade union movement.

8 Workers of the world unite

If we can only remain a nation as a socialist nation without the bankers and the capitalists, then let us be a British socialist nation and we can show the world once again what we are really made of. (Richard Briginshaw, general secretary of NATSOPA, TUC 1971)

We want to see a more peaceful world, a more equal world, where economic progress can be made by working people everywhere. Solidarity, understanding and friendship are the trade union answer to international tension. (Jack Jones, general secretary of the TGWU, TUC 1975)

Foreign affairs fail to enjoy a very high priority on the TUC agenda nowadays. Perhaps it is just as well, for no other issue seems to arouse quite the same mixture of humbug and unreality in the British trade union movement as international relations.

During the 1930s the TUC played an important and honourable part in the campaign against the Chamberlain Government's appeasement of the fascist dictators. Under the strong leadership of Walter Citrine, the TUC spoke with a powerful, eloquent voice on foreign affairs and it put some badly needed backbone into the Labour Party, where pacifist sentiments were widespread. The TUC's support for rearmament and coolness towards the supposed virtues of Stalinist Russia was a welcome sign of realism when many in the Labour movement chose to believe that all wars were a result of the capitalist system and Stalin was a benign Fabian socialist at heart. Even during the war years the TUC under Citrine never harboured any doubts about the cruel nature of the Soviet regime. Hatred of Russian communism was intense and deep-rooted. Consequently the TUC always turned its face against the assiduous attempts of the Soviet Union to undermine and wreck free trade unionism. Indeed, the British unions were at the forefront of the struggle against Stalin's efforts to transform the international trade union organization – the World Federation of Trade Unions – into a propaganda weapon for the furtherance of Russia's national interests. The TUC played host to a conference in London in December 1949 which created the rival anti-communist body – the International Confederation of Free Trade Unions (ICFTU). In the early 1950s most big union bosses were the implacable opponents of the Labour left, many even being ready to swallow the need for German rearmament. During the Labour Party's internal conflict over unilateral nuclear disarmament between 1959 and 1961 the unions were more evenly divided, but in the last resort most rallied behind the need to preserve the Western alliance.

How different the picture looked in the mid-1970s. At a dinner given by the American trade union organization, the AFL/CIO, in the summer of 1975, Alexander Solzhenitsyn poured bitter scorn on the TUC's complicity with the Soviet bloc. The spirit of *détente* and Helsinki has gone a long way on the General Council, and the old caution and suspicion have evaporated. In place of the once sober realism, there is now an increasing willingness among many TUC leaders to turn a blind eye to the odious behaviour of the Soviet Union and its satellites in Eastern Europe. The visit in April 1975 to Britain of the ex-Soviet secret police chief, Alexander Shelepin, then head of the Soviet trade union movement, as a guest of the TUC, revealed to the outside world just how far East–West union camaraderie had advanced.

Such a willingness to act as host for junkets involving communist trade union delegates from countries where 'free' collective bargaining is a criminal offence does not mean that the TUC has lost all sense of morality in its attitude to foreign affairs. It still remains customary for the General Council's spokesman to go on an oratorical tour of denunciation around the more obviously repressive regimes in the world at the start of what now amounts to little more than an annual perfunctory debate. Here is a splendid and painless opportunity to put the boot into Pinochet's Chile, Argentina or South Africa. Over those countries the TUC can demonstrate its internationalist zeal. But when it comes to the communist tyrannies east of the River Elbe where independent trade unions do not exist, where strikes are not tolerated, and where dissenting workers are thrown into jail, all the TUC does is remain silent or indulge in mealy-mouthed platitudes. If the regimes of Eastern Europe were moving in an obviously more liberal and tolerant direction such an attitude might have its excuses, but there is no reliable evidence that any such development is taking place at all.

The double standards of the TUC in its attitude to the Communist regimes of the world were seen at the 1978 Congress in Brighton, when Frank Chapple (EETPU) moved a motion which reaffirmed the 1973 TUC policy on human rights and said that 'acts of repression against workers and trade unionists by totalitarian regimes have continued and indeed become worse since that time'. He suggested that the unwillingness of the TUC to 'criticize the abuses of freedom and the penal and savage sentences handed out in the Soviet Union and the Communist bloc countries' was 'devaluing the currency of our criticism in the field of civil rights over the rest of the world'. Chapple recalled the proud history of the TUC in championing freedom from the time of the American civil war and Garibaldi's fight for the liberation of Italy in the 1860s. 'It seems to have escaped the notice of the General Council that the repressive apparatus created by Stalin has never been dismantled. The concentration camps as well as the penal sentences are still there,' argued Chapple. Geoffrey Drain of NALGO wondered whether, 'after 62 years of the regime there must surely be room now for some flexibility and a greater measure of free expression. In the history of our movement we have had to adapt often to changing circumstances. They [the Russians] seem incapable of adaptation.' An innocuously phrased peaceful coexistence motion was moved by the Inland Revenue Staff Federation, seconded by the Transport Salaried Staffs' Association, which took a pro-Soviet view of the problem and this was carried with little dissent. Chapple sought to add the phrase – 'and other features of the Stalin era' after the reference to 'the current revival of cold war propaganda' in the motion, arguing that the movers of the motion used different criteria when they talked of the Soviet Union and its allies as opposed to Western countries. Jack Jones, retiring as chairman of the International Committee, attacked Chapple's position, as 'not helpful' but 'irrelevant'. As he argued: 'If you look in the past and talk and think about the cold war, is not the name of Churchill there? Was not Richard Nixon a bit of an advocate of the cold war? Let us have none of that.' Jones said he was against double standards. 'I fight for peace, I fight for working people, and what we are getting is cold war propaganda,' he declared.

Chapple was elected to the TUC International Committee in September 1978, but the TUC overtures to the Communist tyrannies of Eastern Europe have continued without abatement. The TUC played host to the leaders of the Czech trade union movement in April 1979, even though Karel Hoffman, its genereal secretary, was one of the anti-Dubcek Communists who welcomed the Warsaw pact armies into his country in 1968. There is no evidence whatsoever that TUC officials raised the cases of workers dismissed in Czechoslovakia for signing Charter 77 in favour of the human rights supposedly guaranteed in the Helsinki Accords. Even the ILO has condemned the Czech government for its behaviour.

In fact, the whole tone and content of Chapple's strictures flew in the face of the whole TUC *détente* policy, which did so much to upset other Western European trade union movements in the early 1970s. The Soviet invasion of Czechoslovakia in 1968 held up the process, but not for very long. In 1971 the TUC passed a resolution which called for fraternal relations between the Prague-based World Federation of Trade Unions and the ICFTU. Two years later there was a call for the creation of an international liaison committee to bring Communist and non-Communist unions together. Over the early 1970s the TUC sent numerous delegations to Eastern Europe. In July 1973 there was an East–West conference in Vienna. This was followed by a meeting in Geneva in January 1974 under the umbrella of the International Labour Organization. The pace of cooperation was studiously slow. As the General Council representative said at that consultative meeting in Geneva: 'A careful and cautious approach to more fruitful relationships was necessary in view of limitations arising out of differences of circumstances and politics – though there was no need to stress differences or to be unduly hesitant.' It was agreed to have a further East–West jamboree in Geneva during the following January. Forty-four national union organizations met at that conference at the end of February 1975 to discuss the working environment and the use of toxic substances in industry.

The closer links between Communist and non-Communist trade union movements was also demonstrated by the decision in 1974 to allow the Italian trade union movement – the CGIL – to join the European Trade Union Confederation, a body which brings together free trade union organizations from the countries of Western Europe, set up in January 1973 with its headquarters in Brussels. There were also moves afoot to extend entry to the French Communist CGT. There is no shred of evidence that the Soviet Union has ever been ready to make even verbal concessions to any idea of *détente* in their dealings with the TUC. Shelepin made it perfectly clear (when Soviet trade union boss) that what went on in his country was no concern of Western unions. On the other hand, the crisis of the capitalist system is very much of interest to the Soviet unions and no reluctance has been displayed by their propaganda machine in exploiting the worldwide recession for political ends. The only topic where there seems to be any mutual talk between unions is on health and safety, though even on those issues the communist trade unionists from the Eastern bloc like to suggest the problems of 'alienation' in the workplace and industrial accidents have been solved in the so-called socialist democracies. Perhaps it is about time other questions were placed on the agenda for East–West debate. There is no legal right to strike in the Soviet Union. Why not? Under a Soviet government order of 5 May 1961 those responsible for 'unauthorized interruption of work' are deported and subject to forced labour for two to five years.

As Chris Harman showed, in his excellent chronicle of Soviet post-war repression of working-class revolt in Eastern Europe, trade unionists have been among the primary victims of Soviet tyranny. In East Germany in 1953, in Hungary in 1956, in Czechoslovakia in 1968, in the Polish shipyards in 1970 and 1976, it was the workers who led the struggle against despotism. After every uprising thousands were tried, many were shot and the rest imprisoned or purged. Is it now bad form to suggest that those who claim to be democratic trade unionists should question such methods and the principles that govern those regimes where such behaviour goes on? The Soviet trade unions bear no resemblance at all to those in Britain. The leaders are not recruited from the rank and file through a democratic process. In Eastern Europe it is hard-liners with a reputation for disciplinarian attitudes who are appointed to the top union jobs. Unions in the Soviet bloc are not independent bargaining agencies. They have no powers to stop an autocratic management, who can behave in an arbitrary manner, taking away bonuses, deducting from a worker's pay packet for neglect, transferring a man for no good reason to a lower-paid job. Such practices are now commonplace in Eastern Europe, where an increasing number of American-owned multinational companies find they have a compliant, cowed labour force ripe for exploitation.

No doubt a summer holiday in a Black Sea resort is a pleasant prospect for a hard-working British union boss, and the Soviet regime is always generous with its hospitality for the gullible and greedy. But instead of making so many journeys to the fleshpots of the East, the TUC needs to spend far more of its time sending out delegations to the poorer countries of the Third World in Africa and Asia, where genuine trade unionism needs all the help and moral support it can find to survive. In 1974 only six delegations went from the TUC to visit Commonwealth countries, and most of those were to old white dominions. The record has been little better since then.

The lack of direct TUC contact with most of the underdeveloped world may help to explain the unthinking parochialism that besets the British unions. 'Import controls' is a ruling orthodoxy among the economic thinkers of the TUC. The vision of Britain alone (1940-style) remains an endearing one for many union leaders. Certainly a strong case can be made out for selective import restrictions to help Britain's hard-hit textiles and footwear industries, even certain areas of the electronics industry, but this should not be taken as a *carte blanche* for general import controls. There is nothing particularly internationalist or socialist about the call for autarchy. Some union leaders have always advocated a total control on capital investment overseas no matter where it is taking place. At no point has any union leader raised the question of what effect import restrictions would have on the prospects for working people in other countries. Unemployment in Hong Kong or Calcutta, Rio de Janeiro or Lagos, Toledo or Lisbon is apparently of no concern to a British trade unionist. The threat of retaliation has always been underestimated by the union protectionists, while the number of jobs saved by such drastic action has been exaggerated. The dangers of a world trade war are underplayed and our obligations to GATT and OECD conveniently forgotten on the grounds that other foreigners discriminate so why shouldn't we? Yet the need to maintain close trading links with the new Commonwealth (not just as a source of cheap food and raw materials for Britain) was deployed as a major argument in the TUC's implacable hostility to Britain's membership of the European Economic Community.

Between 1974 and 1979 the TUC pressed the Labour Government to introduce selective import controls as a way of protecting the country's vulnerable manufacturing industry. The 1974 *TUC Economic Review* proposed the immediate introduction of an import deposit scheme. It argued that such a remedy was 'only a holding operation to allow time for measures to promote changes in the structure and performance of UK industry to improve its long-term competitiveness in domestic and world markets'. A similar demand was also made in the 1975 *TUC Economic Review* with no effect. Union leaders argued that action against imports through quotas and other forms of restriction would not result in any damaging retaliation and international treaty obligations to GATT and OECD did not rule out the use of such controls to help industries facing particularly difficult structural problems as a result of the inflow of foreign imports in excessive quantities. But Harold Wilson and later Jim Callaghan were reluctant to follow TUC advice on trade policy. Even as late as the May 1979 election manifesto the commitment to import controls was couched in imprecise language. The textile, clothing and footwear industries were aided by quota restrictions after 1978 under the Multi-Fibre Agreement. Yet the government remained unimpressed by the TUC's general arguments.

Until the early 1970s the TUC took a generally sympathetic attitude to the prospect of Britain as a Common Market member, but such feelings did not long outlast the return of a Conservative government. The TUC came off the fence in oposition to the entry terms (before they had even been announced) in September 1971. A motion hostile to British membership was passed by a massive majority. In 1972 the TUC went one better and passed a resolution which opposed the very principles of the EEC and urged immediate withdrawal. This went through by 4,892,000 votes to 3,516,000. The TUC decided to boycott all the institutions of the Common Market in the following year by a narrow majority of 400,000. This meant TUC nominees were absent from such bodies as the Economic and Social Committee and the Standing Committee on Employment in Brussels – a fact that incensed many Western European union leaders, who found themselves out-voted because the Confederation of British Industry filled its quota on those bodies as soon as Britain became a Common Market member. In 1975 the TUC campaigned vigorously against continuing membership in the referendum campaign and the overwhelming verdict of the voters for staying in was met with ill grace by some union leaders, notably Jack Jones of the TGWU, one of the most impassioned opponents of British involvement in the Common Market. Many of the anti-Market arguments were soundly based on economic doubts, but underneath the whole debate in the TUC lay chauvinistic attitudes. TUC contacts with the unions of Western Europe have always been perfunctory, although it was the TUC who helped to create the West German trade union movement during the late 1940s. The Swedish experience has had a profound influence on many progressive trade union leaders ever since the early 1930s, but fraternal links with the mainland of Europe remained virtually non-existent until very recently. Some of the reasons for that detachment are understandable. Continental trade unionism has been fractured by deep divisions on political, religious and class lines. There were few comparable large bodies like the TUC with which to fraternize. This is in marked contrast with the historic ties of the British TUC with the American labour movement. Ever since the 1894 Congress a delegate from the American Federation of Labor (since 1954 the AFL/CIO) has attended the TUC every year and a TUC delegate has been to the labour convention in the USA held biennially. A similar reciprocity has occurred with the Trades and Labor Congress of Canada since 1913. In recent years some American delegates in the hawkish style of AFL/CIO president George Meany have been given a rough reception by Congress delegates for their tough talk about *détente*. Yet in the coming years we can expect to see closer ties with some Western European trade unions, notably those in the West German DGB. At present fraternal greetings arrive for the TUC from Communist countries in Eastern Europe and Communist ambassadors are now a familiar sight at Congress, but it is to be hoped the practical day-to-day involvement with the European Economic Community will turn the TUC away from its senseless and corrupting *entente* with the East.

The TUC is not entirely negative now in its attitude to Western Europe. In February 1973 it agreed to join the newly formed European Trade Union Confederation (ETUC) and Vic Feather became its first president. After considerable argument it was agreed that the word 'free' should not be included in the title of the new body – a decision opposed by the West German DGB. It was accepted that membership should be open to all the European members of the ICFTU as well as any other union organizations. But in practice the ETUC's main work has centred on the European Economic Community from the beginning. Until the end of the TUC boycott of the institutions of the Common Market in the autumn of 1975, the British participants found themselves in the absurd position of having to keep out of discussions about EEC issues when they were raised in the European Trade Union Confederation.

There has been an understandable exasperation with the Common Market among British union leaders. Membership of the EEC was blamed for the country's economic crisis at the 1976 Special Congress on incomes policy, and such an accusation raised loud applause. The terms of trade between Britain and her EEC partners deteriorated sharply after 1972, but it is too simplistic to assume the deeply rooted ills of modern Britain would either be cured or made worse by closer involvement with the continent of Europe.

The insular outlook of many union leaders suggests the residue of nineteenth-century-style nationalism has found its resting place on the left of the Labour movement. At the 1973

Congress Bob Wright of the AUEW declared: 'The economic miracle is a capitalist miracle, not one for the people of this country.' During the Common Market debate at the 1972 TUC Ken Gill, Communist general secretary of the TASS section of the AUEW, informed delegates: 'If we allow the old rulers of Britain to replace their imperial past by taking us into this shabby second-rate empire, we are betraying the traditional principles of trade unionism.' Jack Jones on one occasion attacked the dreadful EEC on the grounds that his members who worked for the Imperial War Graves Commission had to be paid a lot more because of the higher cost of living in France.

Chauvinism is a strong emotional force among many British trade unionists, who scorn the peculiar habits of their continental colleagues and look with deep distrust at other Western trade union movements.

Clive Jenkins (who admires what the Swedes do) regaled the July 1971 Special Conference of the Labour Party on EEC entry with a picture of Western Europe as 'a hot-bed of reaction and instability'. He pointed out that France had been near to civil war only three years earlier (a reference to the events of May 1968, which brought workers and students together in impressive solidarity), Italy was apparently in a state of near-anarchy and menaced by the prospect of a right-wing *coup d'état*. Why should Britain imperil its tradition by joining countries like those? Besides the Common Market was capitalist, so it must be bad. 'We can look after ourselves,' asserted Clive Jenkins. There was no need to be ruled by faceless Brussels bureaucrats.

Behind the platitudes of brotherly internationalism, a deep gulf still divides British workers and unions from their counterparts in the rest of the industrialized world. As Walter Kendall pointed out in his study (*The Labour movement in Europe*, London, 1975): 'The difficulties of organizing effective international inter-union solidarity would appear to lie much more in the mind of unionists than in external objective economic and social conditions.' He argues:

Although travel expenses and language difficulties remain problems to be overcome, these are clearly not on such a scale in themselves

as to inhibit close union and workplace ties. Rather it is the deeply
ingrained localist thinking of the members of the workforce and
the unions themselves. The individuals who comprise the workers
and union officials in each plant, brought up behind curtains of
national sovereignty, have been walled off from one another by
traditions with their origins in centuries of war and national
prejudice. As far as day to day experience is concerned, the
workforce of plants in other countries frequently seem as far away
as Australia or, almost, the moon.

The day of international union agreements still seems a long
way off, though there are straws in the wind. In the autumn of
1976, Ford car workers at Dagenham and Halewood claimed
wage parity with their colleagues in West German and Dutch
Ford plants. In its campaign for a shorter working life, the
National Union of Mineworkers was ready to emphasize just
how far behind other member states of the European Coal
and Steel Community Britain still was in 1976 in its treatment
of miners. NUM leaders and steel union bosses spend a growing amount of their time travelling into Europe to the institutions of the Coal and Steel Community. The TUC ended their
boycott of EEC institutions after the 1975 Congress. Now
senior union bosses are serving on various bodies in the EEC,
notably the Economic and Social Committee and the Standing
Committee on Employment. So far, the British union presence
has failed to make any difference to the ineffectiveness of those
bodies in providing a powerful and effective trade union voice
in the EEC. Rightly, Len Murray and Jack Jones in particular
have used the forum of the EEC to champion Britain's national
self-interest, especially against the absurdity of the common
agricultural policy and the lack of success in formulating a
European policy to combat high unemployment.

The stirring slogan 'Workers of the world unite' is used too
often as a windy rhetorical flourish at international union jam-
borees, but an exchange of ideas and mutual understanding of
the differing policies of trade unions in societies outside the
closed, tyrannical system of the Soviet bloc is urgently needed.
The day when shop stewards of multinational companies bargain together across national frontiers against their mighty
bosses still seems a long way off although economic and
political logic point in that direction.

Certainly the unions have had to face the fact that foreign-owned multinational firms have been growing apace in Britain since the early 1960s. Figures for 1973 revealed that 10 per cent of the country's top 500 companies are foreign-owned and they account for 14 per cent of the manufacturing sector. Up to 80 per cent of the pharmaceutical business is now in foreign hands. So is well over half British car production and 50 per cent of electronics. In 1969 there were 1,600 separate American-owned subsidiaries in Britain, half of them in South-East England. By 1973 it was reckoned the 124 American companies based in Scotland had brought 82,000 extra jobs to that region. As long ago as 1967, the TUC surveyed its affiliate members to find out about their experience with foreign multinationals. The results showed they were no better nor worse than home-grown firms. But there has been some company resistance to unionization. The most notorious example was the American firm of Roberts Arundel, which took over a Stockport textile business and then withdrew recognition from the Engineering union in the factory. It took a year-long bitter strike for the union to recover its lost rights. The company decided eventually to shut down its production and go back to the USA. A few important American companies still refuse to recognize British unions, including IBM, Mars, Texas Instruments and Michelin for staff. Caterpillar Tractors relented eventually to union pressure and accepted recognition. This does not mean firms that resisted unions were appalling employers. It is often the reverse. In his researches, Dr John Gennard of the London School of Economics found it was those multinationals resisting trade unions who were far more ready to buy off trouble with higher pay, greater job security and more generous fringe benefits.

For the most part, foreign multinationals have not tried to bulldoze their way through the minefield of British industrial relations. Most remain content to allow local management to run their subsidiaries unhindered by any central directives from abroad. Research by David Forsyth in Scotland found American firms had a worse strike record between 1960 and 1969 than others, but in Gennard's view 'multinationals have made few challenges to the voluntary system of collective bargaining'. They have chosen compromise rather than confrontation. Yet many have proved pace-setters in the introduction of new

industrial relations management techniques, which have won
the active support of the unions. The most famous example is
the 1960 Esso productivity agreement. Ford, Vauxhall and
Chrysler demonstrated how to escape the chaos of the piecework wages system with union consent, albeit reluctant. They
introduced what is known as measured day work, the system
where the worker is paid over a time period fixed to an understanding that the employee will keep up a specified level of performance. His pay does not go up and down week to week with
the actual output he achieves. A number of American-owned
firms have insisted on bargaining on a company-wide basis as
they do at home. Foreign firms have also demonstrated ways
of reducing unofficial stoppages through offering incentives to
workers. In 1969 Ford tied lay-off pay and the holiday fund
together with the promise of no industrial conflict. Any
militancy and lost production would affect the rewards. It is the
foreign-owned firms which have also championed the fixed-
term contract with workers and attempted to reduce the number of unions they have to bargain with. Japanese firms like
Sony and NSK insisted on only having one union in the plant.
This was a virtual condition for building up production plants
in the UK. It was not the existence of unions that worried them,
but the effects of having a multiplicity of them fighting for
membership on the shopfloor. The Dutch-owned Philips company managed to establish a joint council with the seven unions
in the firm in 1973. This has proved a successful attempt to
close the gulf between white-collar and manual unions. Union
officials from the TGWU and GMWU sit round the table with
the Engineers, the EETPU and clerical unions such as APEX
and ASTMS.

The hard-nosed bargaining between John 'flamethrower'
Riccardo, Chrysler's boss, and the British Cabinet in late 1975
demonstrates that multinationals are perfectly capable of ruthless arm-twisting to get their way with governments or anybody
else. A similar neglect of the unions was displayed by Chrysler
in 1978 when the company decided to sell its European operations to Peugeot-Citroën. For the most part, British unions and
foreign-owned companies have established a surprisingly co-
operative relationship. The major problem is familiar: an inability or reluctance by our unions to invest money and recruit

personnel who can master the sophisticated techniques of financial control and management that the multinationals use in their individual operations. Unions must become more professional in their dealings with foreign firms, but there is a long way to go before we will achieve that ideal. The Ford pay claims (drawn up by Ruskin College Trade Union Research Unit in conjunction with the TGWU research department) are a promising start. It has not yet been followed up in a wider and more systematic way.

The days of multinational trade unionism lie far in the future, but this is no reason why the British unions should be slow in devising a coherent strategy for dealing with the multinational giants. This should not be a negative, hostile opposition to their very existence. The answer lies in the creation of a workable balance, between the furtherance of better pay and conditions for workers in the mighty foreign companies, and a willingness to accept more efficient methods of labour productivity. Gaining an effective union voice in multinational operations must not go so far that it frightens them away altogether.

9 How effective are the unions?

For the union makes us strong. (From the American union song 'Solidarity for Ever')

Don't let us trouble ourselves about foreign thought; we shall invent the whole thing for ourselves as we go along. (Matthew Arnold, *National Review*, November 1864)

Pay bargaining

To many people, the unions are the main cause of inflation. Through the pursuit of 'irresponsible' wage claims, it is argued, they push up labour costs without any improvement in levels of productivity. The employer is unable to meet the demands of his workers without increasing his prices and thereby contributing to another bout of inflation. The Confederation of British Industry in its 1976 study *The Road to Recovery* described the process:

The balance of power has been distorted overwhelmingly in favour of many groups of employees, so that collective bargaining has ceased to be a process whereby voluntary agreement on terms and conditions is sought to the satisfaction of both sides and consistent with economic needs. It has been effectively replaced by the imposition of uneconomic settlements thought reasonable by one side only.

This is seen as the irreversible trend of the years since the Second World War and not merely confined to Britain. Professor Phelps Brown concluded a pessimistic OECD conference in Paris in July 1973 with the opinion that wage determination had reached a state of 'anarchy' where rates of pay were 'less guided ... by custom and consensus than by the general acceptance of common norms'. The bargaining process (in his view) had degenerated into what he saw as 'a war of all against all'.

The commitment of successive British governments to 'full' employment was regarded as a primary cause of wage push inflation from the unions. The old harsh dictates of the labour market were eased by the civilized opinion that nobody should go without work. This strengthened the power of organized labour to dictate its own terms. The very belief in economic growth fuelled wage inflation. Aubrey Jones, former chairman of the Prices and Incomes Board, sketched out the process in his book on inflation in 1972:

A 'leading' sector grants wage increases which set the pace for other sectors to follow. Let us suppose that this leading sector is the one in which the growth in productivity is fastest; then if similar wage increases follow in the sectors in which productivity is growing more slowly, wages in those will be rising faster than productivity, and prices will accordingly need to be raised if the rate of profit is to remain unchanged. Thus the leading sector could be an important force in the inflationary process, particularly if it is a fast-growing sector.

No group of workers feels it should fall behind what has become the optimum going wage rate for the annual round, no matter how well the firm is doing that the worker is employed by. In Jones's opinion, the causes of modern inflation lie in political and social changes far more than in immutable economic laws.

What Britain lacks is any firm consensus on wage distribution, and the unions by themselves have failed to achieve the kind of collective solidarity that would ensure the success of a permanent, voluntary incomes policy. This is, in part, due to the complexities of the wages system itself. Figures for the April to November 1973 period reveal that there were 1,096 agreements at the time covering enterprises with over 1,000 workers on their payroll, compared with 6,000 for firms from 100 to 999 strong and between 50,000 and 80,000 agreements affecting fewer than 100 workers. While 40.6 per cent of manual male workers are covered in their pay by national agreements alone (62.2 per cent in the public sector and 31.5 per cent in the private sector), as many as 32.2 per cent can top up their national agreements with extra money negotiated at the workplace (25.2 per cent in the public sector and 33.8 per cent in the private sector). 10.4 per cent are covered by a company, district or local agreement only and 16.8 per cent (22.6 per cent in the private sector and 6.7 per cent in the public) are covered by no formal agreements at all. There is a marked difference between white-collar male workers in the public and private sectors, for while 72.9 per cent of the former are covered only by national agreements a mere 15.5 per cent of the latter are in the same position, with 57.6 per cent of them covered by no agreements at all. The clear trend among both manual and non-manual workers is to more company, district and local agreements.

But around 30 per cent of the workforce have jobs in the public sector (seven million workers) and their rates of pay are not always related to the play of competitive market forces. In general, public sector pay improved relative to private during the 1970s. Between 1970 and 1977 there was a 16.2 per cent annual increase in the public sector earnings of manual males, compared with 14.7 per cent for the private, while there was a 14.7 per cent on average annual rise for the public sector white-collar male, compared with 13.9 per cent for the private. Only since 1977 have the private sector earnings pulled away from the public. In the 1976–7 wage round public sector manual male earnings rose by 8.2 per cent, but by 10.4 per cent in the private, while in 1977–8 it was 10.6 per cent for public sector male manuals, compared with 14 per cent in the private. A big explosion in public sector pay took place in 1974–5, when for manual males the increases averaged 36.1 per cent and manuals in private industry and services had a 24.6 per cent increase. Yet despite this the level of average earnings remained higher for manual workers in the public sector (£72.70 in April 1977 and £81.20 in 1978) compared with manuals in private employment (£71 in 1977 and £80.50 in 1978). The overall picture was also broadly similar in the public sector for white-collar males, where in April 1978 average earnings were £101.30 but only £100.30 in the private sector.

Despite these figures, unions in the public sector argued their members' pay rates fell far behind private industry between 1977 and 1979 because they had been held back by government pay restraint policies. The explosion in early 1979 reflected deep frustration and anger at stagnating living standards and a genuine sense of grievance about low pay and high taxation on personal incomes for those on the bottom rates of earnings.

During the early years of the 1974–9 Labour Government real living standards of working people declined by more and for longer than at any time since the 1930s. But from the beginning of 1977 real living standards began to climb again. The graph below shows the ups and downs of real weekly net income (gross earnings less income tax and national insurance contributions but plus family allowances and child benefits) from 1970 to September 1978 at October 1978 prices. By September 1978, net weekly income was slightly above the level when Labour first took over from the Conservatives in March 1974 (see table 9.1).

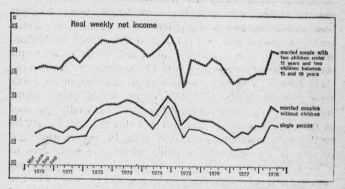

figure 9.1 Britain's living standards 1970–78 (*Hansard Commons*, 4 April 1979)

In Labour's first year earnings rose on average by 27.6 per cent and prices by 21.7 per cent; tax increases brought the actual increase in real earnings to no more than 1 per cent. With the combination of the flat rate £6 incomes policy of 1975–6 and the £2.50/£4 a week policy of 1976–7 real living standards fell by between 6 to 8 per cent on average. This was a deliberate attempt by the government in alliance with the unions to reduce Britain's level of inflation, which reached

table 9.1   Real incomes in 1970s

A married man with two children under 11

Average earnings	Earnings	Tax £	National Insurance contributions £	Net income £	Real net income at August 1978 prices £
1973–4	£2,330	378	136	1,862	3,848
1974–5	2,821	520	166	2,182	3,827
1975–6	3,448	750	190	2,586	3,639
1976–7	3,910	824	225	2,939	3,589
1977–8	4,358	862	251	3,375	3,614
1978–9 (August)	4,852	968	315	3,807	3,807

Average earnings: real weekly take home pay for worker on average industrial earnings (at February 1979 prices)

	£
1970–1	56.00
1971–2	57.30
1972–3	62.40
1973–4	64.10
1974–5	63.00
1975–6	59.70
1976–7	58.10
1977–8	58.40
1978–9	61.60

The rise in direct taxation: proportion of income liable to tax

	per cent
1970–1	34.4
1971–2	33.7
1972–3	31.8
1973–4	48.6
1974–5	50.8
1975–6	57.0
1976–7	55.0
1977–8	52.3
1978–9	57.6

(*Hansard Commons*, 4 April 1979)

frightening heights in the spring and summer of 1975, through wage restraint, public expenditure cuts and a high level of direct taxation. Tax cuts and a reduction in the rate of inflation brought some recovery in living standards after early 1977. During 1978 they rose on average by 6 per cent.

A major problem in Britain's wages system lies in the multiplicity of bargaining dates which cover wage agreements in Britain. All through the year somewhere in the country, pay is being bargained. The wage round is a crazy leap-frogger's calendar, where early on a group of workers with muscle attempt to establish a high settlement that then becomes the going rate, the virility symbol, for those who follow. The following gives an indication of the annual wage scramble.

August
Public sector: 5,500 BBC weekly paid staff; 26,000 staff in British Steel.
Private sector: 15,000 bacon-curing workers; 12,000 flour-milling workers; 40,000 workers in the heating, ventilating and domestic engineering industries; 33,000 plumbers in England and Wales; 8,000 Kodak workers.

September
Public sector: 116,000 policemen; 30,000 dockers.
Private sector: 60,000 workers covered by national agreement in clothing manufacture; 18,000 workers in the timber trade; 18,000 in wire and the wire rope industry; 12,000 workers in the glass container industry; 5,000 manual workers at the British Sugar Corporation; 3,200 manual workers in British Oxygen (gases division); 4,500 brewery workers.

October
Public sector: 20,000 BBC monthly paid staff; 35,000 university teachers and 17,500 university technicians; 4,500 manual workers in the UK Atomic Energy Authority.
Private sector: 55,000 manual workers and 14,500 staff at Ford Motor Company; 12,000 manual workers at Metal Box; 5,600 manual workers at British Nuclear Fuels; 5,600 white-collar Prudential staff.

November

Public sector: 1,063,000 local government manual and craft workers in England and Wales; 30,000 firemen; 22,000 manual workers and craftsmen in British Road Services; from November 1979 all 100,000 Leyland workers; 80,000 workers in British Shipbuilders.

Private sector: 8,000 retail staff at Burton Jackson group; 122,000 workers covered by the national agreement for the retail multiple groceries.

December

Public sector: 238,000 ancillary workers in the National Health Service; 39,000 manual and craft workers in the water services; 5,500 white-collar staff in British Road Services.

January

Public sector: 220,000 Post Office manual workers; 118,500 British Steel manual workers; 50,000 British Airways manual workers; 43,000 gas manual workers; 10,000 maintenance workers in the health service; 24,000 busmen.

Private sector: 257,000 agricultural workers; 38,000 merchant seamen; 40,000 electrical contract workers; 46,000 workers in the biscuit industry; 60,000 rubber manual workers; manual workers at Dunlop, Shell UK.

February

Public sector: 30,000 electricity supply technical staff.

Private sector: 50,000 workers in the retail meat trade; 48,000 workers in paper-making.

March

Public sector: 230,000 miners; 105,000 manual workers in electricity supply.

Private sector: 2,700 workers at Findus Foods and 1,200 workers at General Foods.

April

Public sector: 500,000 civil servants; 65,000 Post Office clerical and executive staff; 568,000 teachers; 420,000 nurses and midwives; 180,000 British Rail workers; 30,000 London Transport workers.

Private sector: 183,000 printing workers; 27,000 Vauxhall car workers; 20,000 vehicle (car) building workers; 55,000 ceramic industry workers.

May
Public sector: 50,000 electricity supply staff.
Private sector: 1,500,000 workers covered by the national engineering industry agreement; 146,000 retail distribution workers; 48,000 chemical and allied workers; 66,000 cotton textile workers; 2,000 Esso workers; Imperial Tobacco workers; 8,000 staff at General Accident; 15,000 workers in the drug and fine chemicals industry.

June
Private sector: 600,000 building workers; 175,00 civil engineers; 60,000 food manufacturing workers; 367,000 workers in the vehicle retail and repair industry; 90,000 ICI manual and white-collar workers; 12,000 Pilkington workers; 7,900 staff at Commercial Union.

July
Public sector: 320,000 local government staff; 50,000 staff in gas supply; 24,000 staff in the water services; 176,00 industrial civil servants.
Private sector: 6,500 manual workers at Cadbury Schweppes; 3,800 Singer workers; 25,000 Chrysler car workers

Every year the depressing pay cycle continues with no end in sight. It would be sensible to move towards synchro-pay in the public sector where groups negotiate at the same time annually either at the start of the calendar year or around budget time in the spring, which would allow a trade-off between tax changes and pay expectations. At the very least there might be moves in the early 1980s to a contraction in the length of the bargaining season. This would be a sensible move towards greater pay stability, reducing the pressure on inter-union competition. The introduction of a common pay structure at British Leyland and British Shipbuilders during 1978 and 1979 is a step in the right direction.

But the pay system in Britain is dangerously anarchic. The different starting and finishing dates of agreements enable workers to leap-frog over each other up the earnings table and thereby add to the inflationary pressures by increasing unit labour costs. More and more deals are being struck at company and plant level not industry-wide or nationally. Consequently this adds an unpredictability during a period of so-called 'free' collective bargaining. There are simply too many unions in too many industries. The whole apparatus of national bargaining is in danger of falling to pieces, because it often makes no economic sense. The logic points to company bargaining in the large enterprises, so informal new structures will have to be cobbled together on the union side at the workplace level, which straddle traditional union lines of demarcation. Combine committees are undermining the *raison d'être* of union separateness at the point of production. Yet unions are held back by the inertia of their own organizations so they are failing to respond effectively to this new challenge. In the world of big companies, the unions need to maximize, not diffuse, their collective strength.

A PEP survey in December 1976 by W. W. Daniel discovered that the big wage earners among skilled manual workers as well as managers and professional people did not belong to unions at all. Those who were members of unions tended to enjoy neither very high nor very low pay, but something in between. As he argued :

Overall trade unions have a protective and levelling effect on pay. They insulate members from the very low earnings that they might experience were these subject to pure market forces. But they tend not to operate to maximize pay in the most favourable market circumstances.

Moreover the PEP research suggested that both the threat and use of strikes and other forms of industrial action by union negotiators is a consequence of below-average offers from employers rather than a cause of above-average settlements. Daniel explained :

We found the median increase in negotiations where there had been no threat of any form of industrial action was 15 per cent, while in cases where there had been threats of action or some sanction deployed, the final settlement was only 13 per cent.

These findings belie the commonly held belief that unions lie at the front of wage push in the British economy, as greedy thrusters who jeopardize industrial peace by making unreasonable demands. Research by Richard Layard and colleagues at the London School of Economics qualifies these findings. With the use of the General Household Survey they discovered that there is a 25 per cent wage differential between male manual workers who are covered by collective agreements negotiated by trade unions and those that are not covered at all (*British Journal of Industrial Relations*, November 1978). There is no apparent similar correlation between the level of earnings for white-collar workers and unionization. Indeed, the less collective bargaining in that area of the labour market, the higher the earnings tended to be. For women, the greater trade union coverage, the more they are paid by their employer, and the association is the greater for non-manual women. As the Royal Commission on the distribution of income and wealth (report number six on lower incomes) explained:

The ratio of the earnings of those 'covered' by collective agreements to the earnings of those not 'covered' appears to have increased since the 1960s. The studies showed that the increase was particularly sharp between 1968 and 1972; and industries with a higher level of collective bargaining coverage tended to have a smaller spread of earnings than others, while prior to 1972, the differences between earnings in such industries and others had increased. From 1972 to 1974, during incomes policies, the latter trend was reversed.

The Royal Commission report concluded that while the statistical evidence on the effects of trade unionism on earnings distribution was inconclusive, it was consistent with the TUC view that the lack of collective bargaining was in general an important reason for low pay among certain groups of workers (May 1978).

Much of the very deeply rooted opposition in the British unions to the idea of a statutory incomes policy gains emotional force from a dislike of legalistic interference with the processes of 'free' collective bargaining. The voluntarist philosophy that predominates in the unions is their considered, but also instinctive, response to the threat of state involvement in industrial relations. There are no stronger champions of the dogmas of *laissez-faire* in collective bargaining in British society than the unions. Self-help and independence reign supreme and carry far more weight than the countervailing pressures for collective solidarity.

No economic debate at the TUC is complete without a ritualistic reference to the virtues of voluntarism. If only trade union negotiators were allowed to get on with their job of negotiating better pay and conditions with employers without any outside interference from the state or a statutory board, all would be well. Such is the well-nigh universal public sentiment among union leaders. Even during the Second World War the TUC made it abundantly clear the threat of Nazi Germany was insufficient to let them tolerate state control of wages. The fact that for most of the post-war period there has been some kind of just such restraint on bargaining has done nothing to convince most unions that this is either necessary or desirable on a permanent basis.

Recent work by the National Institute of Economic and Social Research suggests that Britain's incomes policies during the 1960s and 1970s were less successful than appeared at the time in curbing the rate of inflation, moderating aspirations, or redistributing income between different occupational groups. S. G. B. Henry and Paul Ormerod concluded a study of incomes policy and wage inflation between 1961 and 1977 with the thought that whilst 'some incomes policies have reduced the rate of wage inflation during the period in which they operated, this reduction has only been temporary. Wage increases in the period immediately following the ending of the policies were higher than they would otherwise have been and these increases match losses incurred during the operation of the incomes policy' (*National Institute Economic Review*, August 1978, No 85).

The table below indicates the different pay policies which have been tried since the July 1966 crisis when Britain was 'blown off course'. Surprisingly, these appear to have had little impact on the differentials and relativities between workers. Andrew Dean found that even the flat rate pay policies from April 1973 to July 1974 and July 1975 to July 1977 did not narrow differentials. The compression of the differences in pay between skilled workers in manufacturing and unskilled took place over a longer time span and there was no evidence to suggest that it was government pay norms that accounted for

table 9.2 A generation of incomes policies, July 1966–December 1978

July 1966– December 1966	Freeze on pay increases, exception being made for increases in pay resulting from increased output.
January 1967– June 1967	('Severe restraint') Standstill continued, but with exceptions for increases: (a) on productivity and efficiency grounds; (b) for the lowest paid as defined by NBPI; (c) to attract and retain manpower; and (d) to eliminate anomalies in pay.
July 1967– March 1968	Prices and Incomes Acts 1967 came into effect giving the government statutory powers for a further period of seven months. Exceptions (a) to (c) of the previous policy were retained, and exception might also be made where pay for a particular group had fallen seriously out of line.
April 1968– December 1969	Statutory 3.5 per cent ceiling imposed on increases and special exceptions for pay increases: (a) to attract or retain manpower; (b) low pay; (c) productivity exception bound by general rule that some benefits to the community should be felt in the form of lower prices.
January 1970– June 1970	Government guidelines with a norm of 2.5–45. per cent for most settlements. Exceptional increases permitted after study by the NBPI for the low paid, and for efficiency arrangements. Restructuring, extreme manpower needs and moves towards equal pay for women were also grounds for exceptional increase.
June 1970– November 1972	No formal policies, but the aim was a progressive and substantial reduction in the general level of pay settlements (n minus one).
November 1972– April 1973	Statutory stage one – freeze on all pay increases.
April 1973– November 1973	Statutory stage two with £1 per week plus 4 per cent limit on increases in average pay bill per head, £250 limit on individual rises. Increases to implement equal pay for women up to one third

table 9.2 *continued*

	of the remaining differential allowable outside limit. Settlements prior to stage two allowed to be implemented in full.
November 1973– July 1974	Statutory stage three with limits of £2.25 per week or 7 per cent on increases in average pay bill per head. One per cent flexibility margin plus threshold payments. £350 a year limit on increases. Increases to implement equal pay for women up to one half remaining difference allowable outside limit. Exceptional increases allowable for new efficiency schemes, unsocial hours, London allowances, cases meeting Pay Board criteria for anomalies and in special cases receiving ministerial consent.
July 1974– July 1975	No formal policy, but TUC guidelines allowed increases to maintain real incomes. There was also a TUC low pay target of £30 a week. Elimination of pay discrimination against women.
August 1975– July 1976	Non-statutory policy with £6 limit for those earning less than £8,500 a year, and no increase for those earning more.
July 1976– July 1977	Non-statutory policy with maximum increases of £2.50 a week on earnings up to £50 a week, 5 per cent on earnings (£50–£80 a week) and £4 a week on earnings of £80 or more per week.
August 1977– July 1978	Non-statutory policy without the consent of the TUC. General level of pay settlements to ensure national earnings increase of no more than 10 per cent. 12 month interval between settlements upheld by the TUC.
August 1978– December 1978	Non-statutory policy, opposed by the TUC. Guideline of 5 per cent for increases. Special case treatment, where government approve. Higher percentage rise for lower paid where resulting earnings are no more than £44.50 a week. Productivity deals as long as self-financing.

this, compared with the more effective bargaining carried out by unions for members in unskilled and semi-skilled occupations in the private sector of manufacturing (*National Institute Economic Review*, August 1978, No 85).

For all the anarchic threat of the pay system the bargaining process provides no mechanism for changing relative rates of pay in separate negotiating units. Indeed, one of the most surprising facts is that the distribution of earnings has hardly fluctuated since 1886 when labour statistics were first published systematically.

table 9.3 Stability of pay 1886–1978:
Dispersion of weekly earnings for full-time male manual workers

Year	As percentage of the median Lower decile	Lower quartile	Median weekly earnings £	As percentage of the median Upper quartile	Highest decile
1886	68.6	82.8	1.21	121.7	143.1
1906	66.5	79.5	1.47	126.7	156.8
1938	67.7	82.1	3.40	118.5	139.9
1960	70.6	82.6	14.17	121.7	145.2
1968	67.3	81.0	22.40	122.3	147.8
1970	67.3	81.1	25.60	122.3	147.2
1972	67.6	81.3	31.30	122.3	146.6
1974	68.6	82.2	41.80	121.0	144.1
1975	69.2	82.8	53.20	121.3	144.4
1976	70.2	83.4	62.10	120.8	144.9
1977	70.6	83.1	68.20	120.3	144.4
1978	69.4	82.4	76.80	121.2	146.0

(*Department of Employment Gazette*, May 1978)

The desire for unfettered freedom is a natural one among the British unions, even if for many millions of workers that ideal is illusory in practice. At the 1974 TUC Alan Fisher of the National Union of Public Employees moved a motion which called for annual negotiations between the TUC, CBI and the government on the establishment of a national minimum wage before the start of every wage round. The targets would be laid down by the TUC in those tripartite talks on the basis of its annual economic review. Fisher explained what he wanted in a closely argued speech:

In the last six months this Labour Government at the insistence of the TUC has used legislation to help to realize the objectives of the trade union movement. It has used legislation to raise old age pensions, to freeze council house rents, to hold back price increases, and to ease taxation on the lower income groups. Are we opposed to this legislation? Of course we are not. In fact, we are demanding all the time more and more legislation. The truth is that as trade unionists we recognize that by working in cooperation with the Labour Party, which we created for just this purpose, we can secure legislative change which can speed the realization of trade union objectives and improve the position of our members.

Despite Fisher's wise, eloquent words his suggestion was turned down overwhelmingly by the Congress. While the TUC was willing to tolerate the use of the government to create a more favourable industrial climate through new labour laws to protect workers, the old prejudice against statutory involvement in wage bargaining remained as strong as ever. It is true that in 1975 and again in 1976 the Social Contract between the TUC and the Labour Government involved a severe degree of wage restraint. But this was seen as a temporary sacrifice to deal with a passing crisis and nothing more. At the 1976 TUC union leaders insisted on an 'orderly' return to free collective bargaining after July 1977. Such an attitude was far more than a recognition of the drift of so much power on wage determination to the workplace. It also derived from a deeply rooted distaste for any involvement by the state in the determination of wage levels. But the ideal of a free labour market with a balance between supply and demand is an illusion. Custom and practice, and monopoly power, as well as social attitudes, remain far more crucial.

Just how effective have the unions been in improving the wages of their members? As H. A. Turner and F. Wilkinson point out, it was much less the wage 'explosion' of the unions after 1969 which accounted for the betterment of the real earnings of manual workers than the Conservative tax concessions of Tony Barber. In fact, what workers have gained with one hand, they have been made to give away to the state with the other. Of course, union leaders are staunch supporters of what is known as the 'social wage' – public spending on social benefits, schools, hospitals and the like. Whether most of their members are quite so keen is another matter. Since the middle of the 1950s wage taxation has bitten deep into the pay packets of the average worker. In 1955 an average wage earner, married with two children, paid only 3.3 per cent of his gross income in tax and national insurance contributions; by 1975 that figure had risen to an alarming 25 per cent and two years later to 32 per cent. Even a worker with four children to support found himself having to pay 20 per cent of his income in deductions, compared with only 2.5 per cent in 1955. The tax burden of the average family has increased eightfold in only twenty years.

After 1969 many unions pushed for higher earnings for the low paid, but their efforts were always frustrated by the tax system. As the Low Pay Unit argued in their 1976 study *Trade Unions and Taxation*: 'Between 1970 and 1975 trade unions more than doubled gross pay for the male worker on the lowest decile [ie with earnings 10 per cent of the way up the income distribution]. The Inland Revenue, at the same time, more than trebled the tax bill of a worker in this position.'

It is not surprising that attacks on welfare state scroungers have been most vociferous among the low paid, some of whom would be better off for short periods on the dole than in active work. This is a low pay not a high benefit problem, but union failure to improve the wages of low paid workers (despite the flat rate incomes policies of 1975–7) makes it difficult to apply effective resistance to those who want to tax social benefits or lengthen the periods of time between their up-valuations. The unions have been far better organized in defending government attacks on public sector jobs than in crusading for those on low wages. Indeed, a major failure of the unions has been over achieving a better deal for the low paid. As the Prices and Incomes Board report of April 1971 argued:

The unions have not, by and large, been particularly effective in improving the relative position of lower-paid workers. Any attempt to increase the earnings of the low paid solely by raising general levels of pay substantially will, in the absence of greater productivity, serve merely to increase the rate of cost inflation. A concerted trade union policy towards the low paid must involve a recognition that a relative improvement of the position of some must mean a relative worsening of the position of others.

The 1971 PIB study of the pay and conditions of national health service ancillary workers was equally critical of the unions. As it explained : 'While trade unions play a full part in the central negotiating machinery, their activities at other levels on the whole are very limited. There is not much sign of unions pushing productivity locally.' The study argued that joint discussion would come with this and thus :

give the opportunity, which by and large they at present lack, to participate in decisions affecting the way the jobs which ancillary workers do are organized. Whether it proves possible to raise the pace of the introduction of schemes relating pay and efficiency will, to an important extent, depend on the willingness and ability of the unions to enlist the enthusiasm of ancillary workers for such schemes at hospital level.

The wages councils – 43 of them in 1978 – (in lieu of collective bargaining), which lay down minimum pay and conditions for nearly 3 million workers, have been the subject of severe criticism over the past ten years. The unions and the government have actively sought the abolition of wages councils, which they claimed were not providing the statutory protection that they were supposed to do. In March 1969 the TUC called a conference to examine the wages council sector. There were loud calls for its abolition. Jack Jones of the TGWU was among the champions of that cause. He told the conference the way forward was 'the replacement of the wages council system with centralized national bargaining on minimum rates, such rates becoming an implied term of contract for all workers'. In Jones's view, 'this would require a major campaign for trade union recruitment'. But the bitter atmosphere of the early 1970s, caused by the 1971 Industrial Relations Act, made the unions reluctant to envisage any legislative reform of the wages councils. Between 1971 and 1974 the Commission on Industrial Relations examined thirty of the fifty-three wages councils then in existence. The CIR recommended the abolition of ten of them and the amalgamation of another fourteen, but in the view of the Low Pay Unit the CIR underestimated the extent of the low wage problem in the ten that were scrapped. In only two of them were more than half the firms within the scope of collective bargaining. Unless the unions launched a massive recruitment campaign the low paid in those sectors were liable to suffer as a result. The Low Pay Unit asked unions in the low paid area whether they were making efforts to organize the workers. Ten unions were contacted. A mere four bothered to reply and all that did said they were making available no extra resources for the recruitment of low paid workers from wages council industries. The 1975 government survey of two-parent families in receipt of family income supplement revealed that only 26 per cent of FIS recipients belonged to unions. Only 15 per cent of them said they had been approached and asked to join a trade union. According to findings in the 1973 New Earnings Survey 35 per cent of full-time male manual workers aged 21 and over in the bottom tenth by earnings did not have their earnings affected either directly or indirectly by collective bargaining, while 32 per cent of full-time women did not, earning less than £25 a week.

The 1975 Employment Protection Act provides the legislative framework for a more concerted programme of action by the unions in spreading their influence in the wages council area, if they are willing to use the new law. As the Low Pay Unit have argued, the measure 'represents a clear commitment to the view that the only solution to the low pay problem in wages council industries lies with the extension of voluntary collective bargaining'. But its own proposals have found no favour in the TUC. What the Low Pay Unit wants is the creation of a development fund. Under this scheme, unions would all be asked to contribute the cost of recruitment among non-organized low paid workers. The government would also be asked to provide finance. The TUC General Council was asked to declare 'a year of the new unionism'. The TUC would supervise a recruitment campaign with the setting of targets for membership in industrial sectors where low paid workers are to be found.

The union problem arises from differentials and relativities. There is little point in pressing for any specific figure as a national minimum wage, if every other group of workers want to re-establish the previous earnings gap between themselves and those being helped by such statutory action. Moreover, yet

heavier direct taxation on average and above incomes is liable
to stimulate a shopfloor revolt.

W. G. Runciman, in his important study *Relative Deprivation and Social Justice* (London, 1966), argued that workers
in Britain have surprisingly small terms of reference by which
they compare themselves with others. Nearly all workers contrast themselves with those in jobs very close to or like their
own. Calls for making 'the rich squeal' fail to achieve an immediate, sympathetic response among most rank and file trade
unionists. The pressure for egalitarianism is not very strong
among organized workers, even if there is a vague commitment
to the natural justice slogan of 'a fair day's work for a fair day's
pay'.

What Runciman discovered in the early 1960s is still true today, according to PEP research carried out by W. W. Daniel.
The reference points that workers use to judge what they are
worth remain surprisingly low. What most troubles workers is
when their own earnings fall out of line with other workers
who are carrying out a similar kind of work. Neither in their
survey of 1972 nor again in 1975 did Daniel and his colleagues
find any deeply held hostility to the obviously wide inequalities
of pay between different occupational groups. As they wrote :
'Surprisingly few people in Britain felt that there was anybody
else doing better than they were.' Moreover, the lower people
were down the socio-economic hierarchy, 'the less they were to
feel that anyone else was doing better than them'. This was even
true of most union negotiators. As many as 70 per cent of them
believed no one was doing any better than their members within
the plant.

It is one of the primary functions of a trade union to widen
the perspective of its members on what they are worth. Ours
fail to do this. Union bosses use the language of the class war
in their public statements and even round the bargaining table,
but such an approach is alien to most of the members they
claim to represent. These findings tie up with the discovery during a 1976 CBI survey that workers favour profits and back
the private enterprise system. In Daniel's words : 'It is people's
position relative to others in the same social class that influences
their evaluations of their own circumstances rather than their
position compared to that of people in other classes.' And he

concluded: 'Disputes over issues of pay relativities spring more from the system of collective bargaining of which they are part than from any spontaneous or deep felt sense of injustice on the part of the workers they represent in the disputes.' The unions negotiate under the illusion that the forces of labour must wrest more of the fruits of capital. But as Phelps Brown has pointed out:

If the whole of the dividends and interest paid out by British companies in 1971 had been sequestrated and applied to raise pay, without any provision for the maintenance of those who lose retirement incomes or trust and insurance funds, average earnings would have been raised by less than 14 per cent; and this would have been once and for all. The outcome is that collective bargaining today is not between capital and labour or employees and management; for the distribution of the products of particular industries between pay and profit; but between different groups of employees for the distribution of the national product between them one with another and between them as a whole and the inactive population. Cost inflation appears basically as the process by which particular groups of employees enter and enforce claims to shares in the national product that add up to more than the total product; and the over-subscription comes out as a rise in prices. Hence today's inflation, and the anomie of pay determination. Expectations are heightened but confused; they lack norms, be it for the extent of annual betterment or the relativities between occupations and industries. Procedures that once adjusted costs to prices are pushing costs and prices up together, because institutions have changed comparatively little while the forces that operate them have changed greatly: here is the new wine in old bottles (*British Journal of Industrial Relations*, November 1973, Vol XI, No 3).

Derek Robinson made a shrewd point at the OECD July 1973 Paris conference when he argued: 'Trade unions are faced with the dilemma that their attempt to redistribute income from profits to wages is frequently merely inflationary and that if it were successful it could well lead to a reduction in investment and thus employment which would adversely affect their members.' The existence of full employment up to the early 1970s and the decline in the authority of the established order in society has intensified the 'centrifugal and fissiparous tendency' which has undermined central control. The new sectionalism (the word 'syndicalism' has been used, in my opinion incorrectly because this has a more exact meaning as a political ideology before the First World War in the European working-class movement) is hardly a revolutionary force which threatens the structure of society. The decline in the 'traditional fatalism' of organized workers in the scramble for material rewards has ensured a 'heightened expectation of annual improvement', fuelled by the acquisitive character of our society and the demands of democratic politics. In a country with our stagnant growth and low levels of productivity such an approach resembles a tread-mill, not an escalator, but the unions appear too weak to do anything about it.

Women's rights

The unions have not spurned every form of state involvement in pay determination on a permanent basis. They did not resist the 1970 Equal Pay Act, which required employers to give 'equal treatment as regards terms and conditions of employment to men and to women – employed on like work or on work rated as equivalent'. Firms were given six years to make the transition to the new system of pay equality. But progress has not proved very drastic. The 1978 earnings survey showed that full-time manual women workers earned £49.40 a week for 39.6 hours, 1.1 hours of overtime (compared with £80.70 for male manuals doing 46.0 hours). For women in full-time white-collar jobs the disparity with men remains high, with an average weekly earnings in April 1978 of £59.10 for 36.7 hours and $\frac{1}{4}$ hour of overtime, compared with £100.70 a week for white-collar males over 21 who worked 38.7 basic hours and $1\frac{1}{2}$ overtime hours. Yet the Equal Pay Act has helped to reduce the gap. In 1938 women's average hourly earnings amounted to only 52 per cent that of men's. They improved during the war years to 59 per cent, where they stayed for the next thirty years, but between 1973 and 1975 women's hourly earnings rose suddenly and sharply to reach 70.6 per cent. In 1976 it was 73.5 per cent and 73.8 per cent in 1977, falling back to 72.2 per cent in 1978. The lower paid women workers have proved the main beneficiaries of legislation. According to the register of national collective wage agreements and wage council orders relating to manual workers, the ratio of the lowest rates of pay for women to the lowest rates of pay for men rose from 76 per cent at the end of March 1970 to 96 per cent by March 1975. But ACAS also found in a survey of firms in 1975 that smaller firms have proved less diligent in meeting equal pay provisions than larger concerns.

The Equal Pay and Opportunity Campaign (EPOC) carried out a survey of TUC affiliates before the 1976 Congress to discover just how diligent they had been in campaigning for women's rights for equal pay and an end to discrimination in jobs. It concluded: 'In most cases there is little or no machinery whereby union head offices can monitor the problems of their women members at shop floor level – many do not even know whether any of their members are taking complaints to tribunals.' EPOC 'was particularly disturbed by the degree of complacency in union head offices, some representatives of which actually refused to admit there might be a problem of discrimination in the industries where they had members'.

Yet collective bargaining and industrial action remain vital weapons in the struggle for women's equality in the workplace, as the long strike of men and women at Trico (a west London firm making windscreen wipers for the car industry) proved decisively in the autumn of 1976. The Trico case tested the Equal Pay Act, and found it wanting. The employers took the matter to an industrial tribunal and won their case, but a few weeks later – after almost four months in dispute – the women won their claim for equal pay with the men. Muscle power proved more effective than the law. The Equal Opportunities Commission is condemned by many women's movement groups as a toothless, worthy body with no apparent zeal to campaign in a militant fashion for women's rights. The industrial tribunals – where union representatives and employers sit with 'independents' to adjudicate on labour law cases – were said to have a patchy record on women's rights questions.

Some unions, notably the TASS section of the Engineers, APEX and the GMWU, have made efforts to push the cause of women in their daily activities, but apathy and indifference remain widespread. The Employments Appeals Tribunal has reversed some of the more bizarre judgments. What progress we have seen so far has come more as a result of legal action, than trade union campaigning. Indeed, it is arguable just how active the unions have been in pushing women's rights at work. Around a quarter of applicants to industrial tribunals under the labour laws have had representation provided by unions, but a study carried out for the Equal Opportunities Commission in 1978 (*Equality Between the Sexes in Industry*) revealed that only a quarter of the 575 companies surveyed had written equal opportunities policies and many blamed the unions for prejudice against female workers. As the study argued: 'Shop floor and local trade union resistance to breaking down segregation is regarded by many of the companies surveyed as a substantial barrier to progress, especially in printing, chemical process and packaging work and pharmaceutical production. Some workplaces retained separate union branches by sex.' Only seven employers mentioned that they had made use of positive discrimination provisions under the Sex Discrimination Act. As the report admitted: 'The economic climate in which the survey was conducted strongly affected the reception it was given by employers. Many of the positive actions suggested by the EOC were seen as low priority compared with other business pressures. Traditional and attitudinal barriers have been part and parcel of a view that positive action on equal opportunities is unnecessary and costly,' and it added that while the majority of employers had taken formal steps to ensure the avoidance of unlawful discrimination, the 'wider issues of equal opportunities' had 'hardly been examined, indeed they might not even have been acknowledged as issues'.

Fringe benefits

Britain's unions can also be fairly criticized for not widening the scope of collective bargaining. A concentration on cash in the hand has led to a neglect of better fringe benefits for most workers. Only in 1976, under the constraint of the incomes policy, was much examination carried out of ways in which the conditions and terms of service of workers could be radically improved. The NUM call for early retirement for miners was long overdue. Suddenly it was discovered that British miners had to carry on working until they were 65, whereas in every other member of the European Coal and Steel Community the retiring age was 60 and in some cases (notably France and Belgium) 55 for face workers. Reducing the length of the working life was seen as a way to cut the high level of unemployment, but there is also a strong case of social justice for miners and other workers in physically exhausting and hazardous jobs to retire early. Finishing work at 60 is already commonplace in white-collar jobs in the civil service and local government.

But the cost to the state of enabling all men to retire at 60 would be colossal. The DHSS estimated in 1978 it would be as high as £2,500 million at present pension benefit levels. Both the TUC and the Labour Party want to ensure pensions amount to half gross average earnings for a married couple and one third for a single person. This would mean £6,000 million to lower the retirement age to 60 for men.

A substantial improvement in holiday time was gained by workers in the early 1970s. In September 1973 only 4 per cent of manual workers were entitled to a holiday of four weeks or more; by September 1975 the proportion had risen to 28 per cent, while half the manual labour force were entitled to between three and four weeks. But at the same time, most workers did not get paid average earnings when they were on holiday. The 1975 TUC survey on social tourism discovered that only 15 per cent enjoyed average earnings, while 65 per cent had to make do with the basic rate. It was suggested that unions should bargain for an extension of payment in average earnings during holiday time.

By Western European standards, British workers are badly off in this respect. Not only do they get much less pay when on holiday, but very few (even among white-collar workers) receive a holiday bonus. In France collective agreements provide twenty-four days' holiday a year and a 25 to 30 per cent additional holiday allowance for all adult wage earners, while in West Germany that bonus can rise to as much as 60 per cent extra, on top of weekly earnings. The number of public holidays is also larger in Western Europe, with eight to ten in France, ten to thirteen in West Germany, and seventeen to eighteen in Italy, compared with seven to eight in Britain.

In company pensions the difference of treatment between manual workers and the rest remains substantial. Over half the skilled and unskilled workers covered in the 1976 survey by Helen Murlis and Jill Grist for the British Institute of Management had no pension scheme at all. This is in line with the findings of the government actuary's report on occupational pensions schemes in 1972, where 81 per cent of white-collar male workers were covered by pension schemes but only 51 per cent of manual workers enjoyed the same provision.

Progress has also been slow in the introduction of sick pay schemes. The 1976 BIM survey found as many as 36 per cent of skilled workers and 40 per cent of the semi- and unskilled got no sickness benefit other than what the state provided. Nevertheless the 1976 General Household Survey revealed some improvement in remedying those particular inequalities over the previous five years.

Table 9.4 illustrates the wide disparity over sick pay between different occupational groups. The TUC's advice to negotia-

table 9.4 How sick workers are treated

	Paid when sick %	Absence rate %
Public administration and defence	97.8	4.5
Professional and scientific services	95.0	4.0
Gas, electricity and water	93.2	5.5
Insurance, banking and finance	93.0	3.3
Chemicals	88.5	4.7
Transport and communication	83.1	4.8
Distributive trades	81.9	4.4
Food, drink and tobacco	81.4	4.6
Mining and quarrying	72.3	15.8
Miscellaneous services	70.3	4.2
Agriculture, forestry, fishing	68.9	4.1
Paper, printing and publishing	62.5	3.7
Construction	57.1	5.9
Mechanical and electrical engineering, vehicles and goods	51.9	6.2
Timber, furniture	50.8	5.5
Other manufacturing industries	47.6	6.1
Bricks, pottery and glass	42.4	4.4
Metal manufacture	40.1	7.0
Textiles	33.7	8.6
Leather, clothing, footwear	28.3	5.7

(BIM Survey, 1976)

tors in 1976 was that manual workers should receive the same benefits as non-manuals, but this hardly ever occurs. None of the forty firms surveyed by the Labour Research Department in the autumn of 1976 had minimum standards for sick pay requirements that came anywhere near the TUC ideal of twenty-six weeks at or near average earnings followed by twenty-six weeks at half average earnings with no offsetting of state benefits against half pay.

But times are changing, if only slowly. The differentials between white-collar and manual status have narrowed and will go on doing so. As many as a third of the firms in the 1976 BIM study mentioned 'union pressure' as the reason for reforming their own practices.

Astonishingly, such manifest inequality at work does not appear to arouse concern among either workers or their unions. It is about time it did. What we need to see in future is a direct union assault on the ideological and market forces that perpetuate such discrimination. Manual unions must take the offensive. As Dorothy Wedderburn points out: 'Manual worker trade unions have been concerned to defend their members within management's rules rather than to question the assumptions upon which those rules are based.'

Yet this promises to be an uphill task. Britain's unions have failed to sustain their members with a sense of collective solidarity stretching beyond the individual workplace. In his comparative study (1977) of British with Swedish workers, Richard Scase found wide differences in perception. There was far less awareness or even resentment among British manual wokers at the privileges and differentials separating themselves from white-collar staff. Scase discovered that British manual workers were far more tolerant of class divisions than the Swedes, even though inequalities of income and status are much sharper in Britain. In his view, the explanation for the difference lies in the much more effective union/political challenge to inequality in Sweden, which has heightened a sense of relative deprivation among Swedish manual workers. The commitment to egalitarianism and social justice is therefore far stronger in Swedish society than it is in Britain where a more individualistic philosophy dominates. In their commitment to capitalist values, British workers are more akin to their colleagues in the USA than on the mainland of Western Europe. This is perhaps why it has proved far more difficult to establish a workable incomes policy here than in neighbouring countries. But in the last resort, no union can defy the wishes of its rank and file. Until there is far more radical and sustained pressure from below to question the rights and privileges of those who rule in industry, union leaders can hardly be expected to act any differently than they do.

Labour market policy

Despite the existence of the new labour laws which strengthen the rights of workers, the treatment of workers remains arbitrary and inhumane. A survey carried out for the Institute of Personnel Management in September 1975 found only 64.2 per cent of the sample of companies concerned themselves with the forecast of labour supply. Just over a quarter of the firms believed the benefits of manpower planning did not justify the costs. Union influence was not the major factor in getting top management involved in manpower planning. More important were local employment levels and the 1970 Equal Pay Act. The shopfloor is not consulted at all on manpower forecasting questions. As many as 64.2 per cent of the IPM respondents said they did not consult their shop stewards or union officials on the subject and 12 per cent replied they did sometimes. Only 8.1 per cent kept in touch with the unions at all times. In the words of the IPM survey:

Manpower planning is not yet seen by respondents as an area where employers and unions can contribute together to the maximum utilization of human resources. Yet in the present day climate with allegations of overmanning and the problems of growing redundancy, a greater degree of consultation and participation would seem to be essential.

It is merely one more indication that the unions are not as all-powerful as conventional wisdom likes to suggest.

The preference for the cold winds of the labour market to close planning with the unions is also visible in the 1965 Redundancy Payments Act, a measure which remains unique in the world. Under this law workers who lose their jobs through no fault of their own are entitled to a tax-free lump sum of money as compensation. The amount involved is not determined by actual need, but length of service, age and previous earnings. In 1979 redundancy payments totalled as much as £178,284,000 with 315,779 beneficiaries. The sum averaged out at £600 per person. A worker must be with an employer in the same plant for two years or more and be over 18 years of age to qualify for any redundancy payment. Gross pay must be under £80 a week, so the high-flyers cannot expect to make a killing out of it. The actual maximum payment under the law in the spring of 1979 was £3,300. It is not the unemployed who enjoy the rewards of redundancy. Bill Daniel's survey in 1974 found only 7 per cent of the jobless had ever got any compensation from their last job. A mere trickle of those losing their jobs in Upper Clyde Shipbuilders in 1971 or the AEI/GEC factory at Woolwich in 1969 got redundancy money. In fact, the manual unskilled workers come off worse yet again. As many as 88 per cent of unskilled grades either get no benefit at all (the punishment for being casual and footloose) or £100 or less from all sources (this includes pension and holiday pay). Under the 1965 Act men between the ages of 41 and 60 collect one and a half weeks' pay for each year of service. For workers between 22 and 40, the compensation by law amounts to a week's pay for every year of service. The emphasis on higher compensation for the old and loyal is an attempt to counterbalance any employer's belief that the young should be kept on the books and the elderly put out to grass. It gives statutory respect to the familiar, crude maxim of managerial policy – 'last in, first out'. The actual cost of redundancy payments is footed by employers. The obligation to make those tax-free lump sums rests with them. Half the cost is recoverable from the Redundancy Fund, which is administered by the Department of Employment. This is financed by a contribution of 0.2 per cent of the payroll up to £80 a week – payable as part of the employer's social security contributions.

The 1965 system is here to stay. Any attempt to scrap it would meet with justifiable trade union resistance. The oversubscription among Chrysler car workers at the company's Linwood plant in the winter of 1976 suggests the seduction of instant cash in hand was tempting, even in the cold of the Scottish labour market, where the level of unemployment in the West Central region had reached disaster proportions. Yet the 1965 Act is totally indiscriminate. The worker who walks straight out of his old job on the Friday afternoon to a new one next Monday morning gets his money in the same way as a worker heading for the despair of the dole queue. The acquisitive nature of the deal is a crude reflection of the shake-out mentality of the mid-1960s. During the first six years of the Act we spent as much as £381 million on redundancy payments, but a derisory £100 million on adult retraining and public employment services. It reinforces *laissez-faire* managerial assumptions about the labour market. The concession of a tax-free lump sum suggests a worker inherits some vague property right in the job he is about to lose, but the ultimate decision about who is to go and why rests solely with the all-powerful manager.

The 1975 Employment Protection Act has changed that procedure, at least in theory. As from 8 March 1976 employers have had to give prior notification of impending redundancies to both the unions involved and the Department of Employment. This is not simply a question of a *fait accompli*, either. An employer has got to give the reasons why he is having to sack workers. In case of redundancies of a hundred workers or more, a prior warning must be given within ninety days of the event; for those involving ten or more workers, at least sixty days before the first of the dismissals come into force. Whatever employers might argue against such prior warnings, it is a long overdue reform. In 1972 as many as 58 per cent of all redundancies gave four weeks' or more notice; by 1974 that figure had fallen to only 30 per cent.

In recent years some employers have introduced relatively humane redundancy and redeployment policies, which have put as much emphasis on training for a new job as on the monetary compensation. The miners and railwaymen were compensated (albeit niggardly) during the rundown of their industries in the 1960s. The British Steel Corporation has established a particularly socially responsible strategy in cooperation with the unions in the industry. Where redundancies threaten in British Steel the state manpower services are called in to assist as early as possible. Following Western European practices, a redundant steel worker receives extra cash payments from his former employer if his new job provides less than 90

per cent of previous earnings. For a worker under 55 that benefit goes on for 78 weeks, while for those in their sixties it is
extended to 130 weeks. In the steel mill closures of 1978 at
Hartlepool, East Moors and Ebbw Vale the redundancy payments were much higher, rising over £10,000 for long-serving
workers.

As we have already seen, union leaders are now playing an
active part in the new Manpower Services Commission and in
industrial training programmes. With well over a million jobless
in the middle and late 1970s the TUC might have been expected
to press even a Labour government for much more emergency
action, but senior union leaders were far less willing to take a
tough attitude about the unemployment crisis in private. To
the surprise of most people, the severe slump failed to provoke
mass demonstrations of those with no work. Public sector
unions voiced their opposition to public expenditure cuts, but
often in anticipation of future redundancies. The Chancellor's
July 1976 £1,000 million cuts hit private sector manual workers,
particularly in the badly unionized and fragmented construction industry. Very few of the estimated 170,000 jobs lost as a
result of that particular government action were from the
public sector of employment. It is probably true that the regular
provision of emergency measures like the job creation programme and the temporary employment subsidy (TES) owed
much of their implementation to TUC pressure, but most senior
union leaders accepted the government's economic policy, for
all their reservations. There was far less resistance among even
trade unionists at local level to the extension of training facilities to many workers who failed to get an apprenticeship in
earlier life. The worries about the dilution of skill seemed far
less significant by the mid-1970s, partly because traditional
preserves of the labour aristocracy such as engineering suffered
from a severe problem of turnover, with pay and conditions
as well as job insecurity driving many skilled men into more
lucrative non-manufacturing sectors of the economy. Yet
despite this the unions opposed any reduction in the apprenticeship period from four to two years, a reform proposed by the
engineering industry training board in 1978.

From the winter of 1975–6 Britain has had over a million
registered unemployed, but the unions failed to give the issue

a high priority. It was the battle to defeat inflation that dominated the Labour Government's economic policy. The unemployed have not found much sustained, direct support for their plight within the unions. Once a worker loses his job and joins the unemployed he usually ceases to be a fully paid up trade unionist. It is the fracture between people in a job and those without one which helps to explain why the TUC has been less than effective in pressing for action to cut unemployment. The mail bags of union officials have not been filled with angry or distressed letters from former members complaining of having to endure on the dole. At trade union conferences since 1975 few speakers have displayed any personal, intimate knowledge of what it is like to be unemployed. Nor have there been any well-attended demonstrations in Trafalgar Square on the issue. In 1978 the European Trade Union Confederation called for a day of protest against mass unemployment; but the British TUC was the only national centre not to follow its lead. We saw no Jarrow-style marches in the late 1970s. Stan Orme, the Social Security minister, said in 1978 that he thought it would be fair and sensible to put the 330,000 unemployed for more than a year on to long-term benefits (like the disabled) and not make them eke out an inadequate living on supplementary benefits. But he added that no pressure group had taken up the call for such a reform (the Child Poverty Action group did, though they appeared to lack much clout). The TUC did not stress the issue.

It is in this wider context of indifference towards the return of mass unemployment to Britain that we have to understand the lack of progress towards work-sharing as a way of shortening the dole queues. As long ago as 1972 the TUC committed itself to the idea of a shorter working week, mainly under the powerful inspiration of Jack Jones of the Transport and General Workers' Union. Like so many Congress resolutions it added up to little more than an attractively sounding slogan at the start. But under Jones's advocacy, the European Trade Union Confederation took up the shorter working week demand and it rapidly became the main trade union response to the slump in the industrialized Western world. The main intellectual thrust for the hours question came from John Hughes, now Principle of Ruskin College, and the college's trade union research unit, who provided the arguments for TGWU negotiators. In a TGWU pamphlet – *Target 35* – published in April 1976, Jones called for a 'normal working week of no more than 35 hours in all industries by the end of 1978'. He used the Ruskin arithmetic to argue that such a move, phased over two years, would create an extra 70,000 jobs and cut unemployment by half a million.

But during the years of severe pay restraint between 1975 and 1977 the shorter working week failed to make much headway. Unions were too preoccupied with a belated fight to save jobs from destruction to devote much attention to creating new ones through the bargaining system. The first serious claim to spell out the case for the 35 hour week came from the unions at Ford motor company in September 1977. They argued that such a change would create an extra 3,300 jobs at Ford (5.8 per cent of the hourly paid labour force) while a move to a 37½ hour week would create 1,500 jobs. The unions at Ford stressed that there would also be an improvement in efficiency as a result and shorter hours had a social advantage. But the company refused to take that part of the claim at all seriously and the unions did not press it. In fact, it was not until the spring of 1978 that the government and major employers realized that the unions were going to put the shorter working week near the top of their agendas for collective bargaining.

Ever since 1975 the TUC had been rather sceptical about the 35 hour week as an answer to unemployment. As Len Murray told the 1977 Congress: 'It is not the principal answer to economic stagnation because while the economy stays stagnant work-sharing would be of little real benefit to our members.' Congress House argued persuasively that it needed economic growth and above all coordinated international action if a shorter working week was to make practical sense. The 1978 *TUC Economic Review* conceded that the resulting increase in unit labour costs for employers of shortening hours would be 'substantial' and could not be dismissed lightly as a formidable obstacle to its introduction. The review warned that unless the move to a 35 hour week was phased and Britain's competitors went along with it too, the country's export competitiveness would suffer as a consequence. As the document explained:

The objective for unions in considering these measures is to introduce shorter working hours in a way which has the maximum impact on unemployment but which does not result in a cut in living standards for those at work either by cutting money incomes or through the mechanism of a higher rate of inflation. A prerequisite for this must be a higher rate of growth.

There has never been any suggestion that workers in jobs should take any real cut in their pay packets as a result of working fewer hours to provide more employment opportunities for those unemployed. No loss of earnings has always been an essential precondition for any move in the direction of a shorter working week. The TUC's understandable caution brought the retort from some union leaders that Congress House was deploying employer arguments and they were not in business to do so. There was a good deal of scepticism about the idea in Whitehall. Civil servants calculated that a reduction in the basic working week from 40 to 35 hours might cut unemployment by between 100,000 and 500,000 but, if weekly earnings stayed the same, it would push up the employer's labour costs by 6 to 8 per cent. This would give a fresh twist to the rate of inflation, with the result there would be fewer jobs not more. The Labour Government accepted the Whitehall arguments. The government's White Paper on pay published in July 1978 argued that any cut in working hours would not have to involve any rise in net unit costs of more than 5 per cent and whatever the amount it would have to be offset against the year's 5 per cent pay norm figure. The government appeared to believe a shorter working week might actually increase, not cut unemployment. As the White Paper argued: 'If more people were employed to produce the same output without any reduction in individual earnings, labour costs would inevitably be much higher. For example a reduction from 40 to 39, other things being equal, would result in an increase in labour costs of over 2.5 per cent. The consequent price increases would reduce sales and eventually lead to unemployment.'

Only one major group of workers achieved a breakthrough on shorter working hours in the late 1970s. These were the Post Office engineers, whose union had pressed the issue for eight years. It took protracted and widespread industrial action by the POEU to reach a $37\frac{1}{2}$ hour week. Through the more flex-ible use of working time and rotas, the Post Office deal en-sured no increase in job opportunities as a result. Nor, to be fair, was the union pressing the issue as one of work-sharing, but because it sought equality of treatment with white-collar staff in the Post Office. The National Union of Mineworkers put the four-day week (or eight-day fortnight) into its package of demands for the 1978–9 wage round, but it soon disappeared from their list of priorities. The Ford workers traded in the hours issue for more cash and this happened through the wage round for all the idealistic talk. 'The main trouble lies with

table 9.5 Workers on overtime in manufacturing industries

		Number (000s)	% of all workers	Average hours per worker
1975	January	1,785	32.1	8.3
	April	1,683	31.0	8.1
	July	1,509	28.2	8.8
	October	1,614	30.5	8.3
1976	January	1,423	27.5	7.8
	April	1,620	31.6	8.3
	July	1.649	32.0	8.6
	October	1,836	35.1	8.6
1977	January	1,720	33.0	8.3
	April	1,816	34.7	8.5
	July	1,814	34.4	8.9
	October	1,878	35.8	8.7
1978	January	1,748	33.6	8.4
	April	1,850	35.7	8.7
	July	1,812	34.8	8.8
	October	1,824	35.5	8.7
1979	January	1,631	32.0	8.2

figures after June 1976 are provisional and are subject to revision (*Department of Employment Gazette*, April 1979)

the members', a senior union leader told me. 'We ask the negotiators to press the issue, but the lads are not supporting it.' The inertia of the unions mirrored the indifference of the rank and file.

This was most graphically illustrated by the resilience of overtime working at a time of recession among manual workers. Most union leaders agree that overtime remains a social and economic evil that should be curtailed whenever possible. In the words of Ken Thomas of the CPSA at the 1977 TUC: 'We have no moral authority to go to the government and ask them to help us when thousands of our members are working overtime which, if we cancelled it and banned it, would create jobs in this country.' The GMWU argued in a policy statement in 1978: 'If we took a reduction of half in the total overtime working in manufacturing as a target, we might be expected to produce from 100,000 to 200,00 extra jobs.' Yet as the table above illustrates, overtime working for male manual workers has been remarkably constant through the recession years. The money earned from working more than the 40 hour basic week is seen as essential protection from the ravages of inflation and pay restraint policies. In April 1978 the average full-time male manual worker aged 21 and over earned £11.60 of his £80.70 a week by clocking on for an extra 6.1 hours of overtime. The money amounts to 14.3 per cent of average gross weekly earnings. As many as 57.7 per cent of male manuals worked overtime in April 1978. For them it meant an extra £20.10 for working 10.4 hours on top of their basic week. Nearly a third of male manuals actually clocked on for more than 48 hours. Figures were similar for every April in the New Earnings Survey since the start of the new recession in 1975.

The inability of the unions to act decisively on overtime was well illustrated by the serious effort made by the unions in the Confederation of Shipbuilding and Engineering Unions to try and reduce its incidence in 1977. Posters and leaflets were distributed to the members which explained the evils of overtime. The National Committee of the engineering section of the AUEW made a special effort to drive home the message, but the campaign proved to be a miserable failure. District committees, where the real power lies in that union, refused to respond. For many manual workers overtime is a necessary fact of life, a custom and practice, an added benefit in some jobs that not even the slump has managed to destroy. Employers often see overtime as a way to attract badly needed skilled labour and a sensible way to organize work. Efforts to buy it out have been singularly unsuccessful. Certainly the self-financing productivity deals of 1977-8 made no impact on reducing overtime among manual workers.

The TUC in 1977 asked the unions to try and restrict overtime to no more than 20 hours a month per worker, but even this proved beyond their powers. The railway workers, for example, averaged 53.6 hours overtime a month in 1978. In July 1978 the NUR told its local districts at every station and depot to cut excessive overtime and exert pressure on BR to fill vacancies. The NUR calculated that with a 35 hour week, BR would need 20,000 more workers. But as Sid Weighell, the NUR general secretary, questioned: 'How can we argue claims for an earlier retirement age and a 35 hour week when there are 9,000 vacancies and some staff have to work 70 hours a week just to keep the service running?'

The passive attitude of the unions to unemployment may change in the 1980s for the prospects of lengthy dole queues throughout the next decade are now real enough. In its *Review and Plan 1978*, the Manpower Services Commission said that it would not be easy to reduce unemployment by 1982 below the levels of mid-1978 (around 5.6 per cent of the workforce or roughly 1.4 million). The London Business School predicted in 1978 that unemployment would stay over a million well into the 1980s. The Treasury itself reckoned that with a rate of growth in output as ambitiously high as 3.5 per cent would still mean over a million jobless in 1981. Forecasts on the labour force for the next decade suggest that there will be a net growth of 2.4 million between 1976 and 1991 (to a total of 28.3 million) with around 1.4 million of that figure being made up of part-time women. Between 1961 and 1976 the labour force rose by 1.9 million. To get unemployment below a million Britain would need over 1.1 million extra jobs created between 1978 and 1982, according to Manpower Services Commission figures. The main victims of unemployment will be the older, male, manual workers without a skill in the severely deprived industrial regions of the north and Scotland. Many of them belong to general unions. But on top of this we face difficulties with new jobs for the school-leavers. The segmented character of the labour market carries difficult implications for the trade union movement in any concerted campaign to reduce unemployment.

Young school-leavers without qualifications are now a familiar sight in the dole queue. Youth employment is a long-term, structural problem, which is affecting all Western European countries. Some union leaders have spoken with eloquence about the plight of the young jobless, particularly Hugh Scanlon of the Engineers, but unions have failed to impress the seriousness of the crisis on to government and employers, although they are ready nowadays to relax archaic restrictive practices to enable the young to train in new skills in large numbers. As many as 300,000 youngsters left school every year from 1974 to 1977 without getting any training of any kind. A 1973 Department of Education and Science survey found that for children of 14 or more, half the schools fail to provide any career education at all. Less than half the eighty-seven schools in that survey sample even bothered to liaise with the local careers service. The state devotes large sums of public money to the provision of higher education for the bright and intelligent but it has been less forthcoming in equipping boys and girls for the harshness of the labour market. As D. N. Ashton and David Field wrote in a recent study of young workers:

The trade unions who might be expected to provide help to young people in making the transition from school to work, in fact do little for them. For those entering unskilled and semi-skilled occupations there is little incentive for the unions to do very much because of the likely instability of their membership.

What action the unions do carry out tends, therefore, to be 'of a broad and general nature', such as attempts to expand compulsory day release to all young workers, regardless of skill.

Safety at work
Another crucial area of union neglect has been health and safety at work. At least 1,400 workers are killed at work every year with another 300,000 suffering injuries bad enough to keep

them away from their job for over three days. These horrifying statistics are undoubtedly an underestimate of the problem. In non-fatal accidents it is reckoned that as many as 40 per cent of them are in general manufacturing and half those in the accident-prone construction industry are not even reported. On top of this, there are those workers who have become the victims of industrial diseases. Around 20,000 new cases of injury benefit for prescribed industrial diseases are reported every year. It is estimated at least 100,000 workers in industry have lost some of their hearing as a result of excessive noise in the plant. The 1970 Robens Report reckoned that the cost of accidents and ill-health at work amounted to between £400 and £600 million a year. Actual working days lost as a result average over 23 million a year, three times higher than the comparable strike statistics. These figures make for depressing reading, but no concerted action to combat death and injury at work has ever come from the unions. In the face of union militancy it is unlikely that insensitive, uncaring employers would have been allowed to skimp safety standards. Occasionally a major disaster like Flixborough or a pit catastrophe like Houghton Main can stimulate concern, but most accidents hit individuals, not groups. They are personal, not collective tragedies. In the opinion of the disappointing 1972 Robens Committee, which looked into safety and health at work, 'the most important single reason for accidents at work is apathy', but that body's criticisms of too much state control and not enough self-regulation did not meet with widespread approval. In the last resort, the necessity for the state to lay down standards is seen as essential. How the law is enforced or interpreted rests not merely with judges or employers, but trade unions as well.

But until the middle of the 1970s most workers in British industry, with the exception of the miners, have enjoyed fewer safety rights than many workers in other countries. As Grayson and Goodard have written: 'The main reason for this has been the insistence of employers to retain the "voluntary" approach to safety issues and the willingness of governments and until recently some sections of the trade union movement to support them' (*Industrial Safety and the Trade Union Movement*, WEA, 1976). It was not until the 1964 Congress of the TUC that a motion was passed which sought statutory safety representatives and committees at the workplace, moved by the Foundry Workers. The Labour Government between October 1964 and June 1970 made no attempt to introduce new safety at work legislation, preferring to champion the discredited voluntarist approach. Provision was not made for the creation of statutory representatives and committees until Barbara Castle's 1970 Bill, which fell with Labour's election defeat. The establishment of the Robens Committee shelved the issue for a little longer, but in 1974 legislation was finally put on the statute book. The Congress rhetoric disguises a sad story of apathy, inertia and indifference in much of the trade union movement over industrial accidents and disease. Few unions responded in a positive way to the coming of the new legislation, until recently.

The 1974 Health and Safety at Work Act has set up brandnew tripartite machinery to tackle the problem and the unions are cooperating fully in its operation. But it will take some years to assess whether the legislation will make any appreciable impact on the accident figures. One crucial step will be to expand the number of qualified factory inspectors and the number of visits they make to industrial premises. There is a promise of doubling the ranks of the inspectorate. The Robens Report found the number of safety and health inspectors in one region of West Germany came to the total strength of the entire British inspectorate. In 1974 there were just over 700 inspectors responsible for covering around 200,000 registered workplaces. No wonder it was estimated that every factory could only be checked once every four years. The 1974 Act has codified the tangle of existing safety legislation and it has brought, in theory, more emphasis on the protection of the worker, but critics have pointed to possible loopholes. The law stipulates that an employer must ensure 'the health, safety and welfare at work of all his employees', with the proviso that this should be 'so far as is reasonably practicable'. The courts decide how strong a proviso that is for the employer. Fines on negligent employers remain laughably small. In 1976 they averaged a mere £75, £35 in Scotland, though the maximum is now £1,000.

A potential change for the better is the appointment by law of safety representatives from the workforce, who consult with employers on health and safety questions. These are stewards or their equivalent. Recognized trade unions are held responsible for their appointment. Employers are obliged under the 1974 Act to provide those representatives with information on a range of safety matters, but the factory inspector can decide, on his own discretion, what information should be disclosed to the safety representatives. The representatives cannot call in experts themselves, unless their employer is agreeable. Much will depend on how the Act operates in practice, but unless unions display a hitherto unknown radical zeal, employers will find it relatively easy to maintain their traditional ways. Having safety representatives and safety committees will serve no useful purpose, unless they enjoy and use the power to ensure employers do not wreck the law.

To its credit, the TUC has been concentrating many of its limited resources on education for the unions on the new safety law. Much of the government aid will go to help train safety representatives. Yet until senior union leaders are ready to devote time and muscle power to championing the cause of health and safety at work, it will continue to rate a low priority with government and industry. Here is one crucial area that should be opened up to union influence at the workplace. Passing pious motions at Congress every September after a usually perfunctory debate is no answer. In Sweden and West Germany the trade union movement has made a substantial difference to health and safety at work laws, which provide a real and important role for the unions in their implementation. The issue is far too important to be left to employers, doctors and judges.

Productivity: the Achilles heel

Britain's unions are often criticized for their refusal to abandon restrictive practices, which hinder technological change and high levels of labour productivity. Overmanning is seen as a major symptom of the British 'disease' and it is union custom and practice far more than lack of investment in plant and machinery that gets the blame. The days of the 'who does what' dispute seem to be over. Numerous union mergers have softened though not eradicated the harshness of inter-union conflict on the shopfloor. So just how much union responsibility is there for overmanning? Plenty of *prima facie* evidence suggests it is true of the national newspaper industry. The interim report of the Royal Commission on the Press, published early in 1976, made no assessment of job evaluation, but the disclosure that as many as 21 per cent of production workers were over the age of 60 on national newspapers did not suggest efficiency. The footplatemen's union, ASLEF, insisted on a second man sitting in the cab with the driver if a train went beyond a certain distance under the 1965 Penzance agreement. Richard Pryke and John Dodgson, in their book *The Rail Problem* (London, 1976), give statistics to show just what little time railwaymen spend in productive work. On the London Midland region, it amounted to no more than $3\frac{1}{4}$ hours per driver during his 8-hours spell of duty. If shunting is excluded from the calculation, the time spent drops to a mere 2 hours per spell of duty.

In the early months of 1976 the abrasive chairman of British Steel, Sir Monty Finniston, threw down an ultimatum to the steel unions in the form of an agreement to a more flexible use of manpower, whereby old craft divisions preventing labour mobility should be put to one side and higher rates of productivity achieved with a smaller workforce. BSC claimed it took 182,000 British steel workers to get the same amount of steel produced by 146,000 French steelmen, 106,000 West Germans, 87,000 Americans and 64,000 Japanese. In 1975 BSC was producing 131 liquid steel tonnes per man-year, compared with 164 in France, 225 in West Germany, 274 in the USA and 372 in Japan.

A study carried out by Christopher Saunders between 1973 and 1975 (*Engineering in Britain, West Germany and France*, Sussex European Research Centre, 1978) looking at the relative efficiency and competitiveness of the engineering industry in Britain, found that West Germany had 50 per cent more workers employed in their engineering sector and enjoyed a level of labour productivity which was more than half again the British level and a quantum of output more than double the British. The French engineering industry employed 40 per cent fewer workers, but its level of labour productivity was similar to West Germany's and quantum of output almost the same as Britain's.

The bankrupt Port of London Authority was overmanned

by as much as a third in 1978, particularly among white-collar staff jobs. The union – NALGO – fought hard and effectively against the efforts of the management to cut the numbers by generous severance pay and natural wastage. There was more willingness to recognize the need for manpower cuts in the TGWU; but the residue of dockers employed in the Upper Docks in the East End was reluctant to accept the closure of those unprofitable, decaying berths in order to make the PLA viable once again. The 1965 Geddes Report believed demarcation lines between skilled manual jobs in the shipbuilding industry ensured the existence of overmanning on a crippling scale. This was especially true of craftsmen's mates. Although some productivity improvements were achieved at Govan Shipbuilders in 1978 through joint union–management agreement on the removal of many restrictive labour practices, the general picture of labour efficiency in the yards has not improved since Geddes reported in the late 1960s.

British Shipbuilders disclosed in March 1979, that the average production performance per worker in the yards was probably half that of Japan and some of the more efficient European builders. An internal study discovered the startling fact that three hours and five minutes of every working day were lost in production. Workers starting late and leaving early accounted for 47 minutes; idle time within the workforce's control accounted for 31 minutes; normal base to work station for 26 minutes; morning and afternoon tea breaks a further 23 minutes; and 21 minutes were lost on waiting time. On top of this 17 minutes were lost because of bad weather and 12 minutes to a correction of mistakes. Even a modest improvement in the productive day of 30 minutes would increase productivity by 10 per cent. The unions were cooperating with British Shipbuilders to try and improve efficiency in the yards; but the grim legacy of archaic labour practices and underinvestment is likely to take years to eradicate, time that the yards simply have no longer got in the midst of the worst recession for shipbuilding since the 1930s. Another example of Britain's poor relative labour productivity performance can be found in the engineering construction industry. A 1975 National Economic Development Office report states: 'A major difference between the UK and elsewhere in terms of site relations is the higher manning levels on UK sites, which are maintained for longer periods. This presents problems which neither the trade union organization or site management are adequately equipped to deal with.' The ratio of unskilled to skilled men on sites is much higher in the UK than overseas. NEDO found evidence that 'manning was higher in the UK regardless of whether or not the project was running behind schedule'. As a result much greater time must be spent by site management in ensuring 'men are adequately supervised in their work' and that 'attention is paid to their grievances and that basic amenity standards are maintained particularly when the existing standards were established with lower levels of manning in mind'. In one plant 52 per cent of the time of the workers was spent off the site during the working day and a mere 17 per cent on actual construction work. In general, British construction workers worked less time than those in Holland and the USA. The study stated: 'The shorter active period on UK sites is largely a result of more generous allowances being given for tea breaks, walking and washing time. These matters have long been determined by custom and practice and are at the discretion of the parties on site, but the observations suggested more abuse of these allowances on UK sites.'

A study also carried out by the NEDC in 1978 found that tyre manufacture was 30 per cent less efficient in Britain than among European competitors. The Central Policy Review Staff (the Think Tank) produced a study of the British car industry in 1975 that emphasized the problem of overmanning. On the basis of comparative data collected by McKinsey, the management consultants, it concluded: It takes almost twice as many man-hours to assemble similar cars using the same and comparable plant and equipment in Britain as it does on the continent. In the 1950s the British motor industry was the most productive in Europe, but by the middle 1970s its productivity was 30 per cent below France, Italy and West Germany.

'The implications for the British car industry are extremely serious,' the report maintained. 'Either twice as many men are needed to produce the same number of cars, which results in a labour cost penalty of approximately £50 per car at current wage rates, or equally manned lines are half as productive, which again raises unit costs substantially above those of the competition.' Detailed comparisons revealed that it took 50 to 60 per cent more labour in Britain than on the continent to assemble identical powertrain components like gearboxes, engines and rear axles.

The report gave an example of overmanning in the maintenance area, due to trade demarcations. 'If a multiweld machine used to weld body panels together breaks down in Britain, six maintenance men would be involved in repairing it, an electrician, jig fitter, pipe fitter, mechanical fitter, tool man and repair man. On the Continent only two men, one mechanical and the other electrical, would accomplish the job.'

A major difficulty was found to be the slow work pace. As the report argued, 'Even when manning levels are virtually identical and the capital equipment, model involved and plant layout are the same, the output of production lines in Britain is about half that of continental plants. In other words, with the same power at his elbow and doing the same job as the British worker, a continental car assembly worker normally produces twice as much as his British counterpart.'

C. F. Pratten's study of labour productivity differentials in 1976 of European firms suggested the real cause of overmanning in Britain had far less to do with lack of investment in new plant and machinery and was more to do with the organization of work. Where this country has too many workers is in what are called 'indirect' jobs such as supervision, quality control, office staff and canteen services. Lack of flexibility among workers was cited by many employers in Pratten's book. As one manager argued: 'There is a much greater tendency in this country to protect jobs and to use any changes in layout or procedure as a means of negotiating higher pay.' Elsewhere workers accept change without insisting on such demands being met. One West German company with a British plant explained to Pratten the differences in productivity performance between its workplaces as follows:

You will see that the general tone of this letter is to infer that the factors [size of plant, rate of growth, competition, product mix] you mention are not the most over-riding and of course it is impossible to prove whether that comment is right or wrong. In grossly oversimplified terms, labour productivity in our industry is lower than others because our people do not work as effectively as foreigners or we, as management, do not organize their work as well – or both.

Pratten found British unions had made 'little study of many important forces determining labour productivity', in spite of the sudden interest in productivity bargaining in the late 1960s. This is only a general observation. Many workers have co-operated fully with the reduction of manning levels in their industries. The most remarkable example is the real sacrifice made by the National Union of Mineworkers during the pit closures of the 1960s. Output per manshift rose from under 25 cwt in 1957 to 44.2 cwt in 1972 – as much as a 77.5 per cent increase. There were similar leaps in the labour productivity performance of other nationalized industries, notably in electricity supply, telecommunications and gas over the same period. A study by NEDO in 1975 of the British chemical industry concluded that our workers were more productive than their Dutch and West German counterparts.

It would be quite wrong to make the unions solely responsible for Britain's dismal productivity performance during recent years, but on the other hand there can be no denying the fact that output per head in industry lies far behind our major competitors, while our wage costs continue to rise steeply. Between 1963 and 1973 the average output per worker in British manufacturing industry only went up by 3.5 per cent a year. But from the onset of the recession it proceeded to stagnate. If output had carried on growing at the rate of the decade before 1973 it would have been as much as 15 per cent higher by the end of 1978 than in fact it was. By comparison with the other countries of the European Economic Community, Britain's industrial performance looks appalling. While this country's manufacturing output per worker went up by just over three quarters between 1955 and 1973, the average productivity in the other five major EEC countries increased by as much as one and a half times. There was a setback to growth as a result of the oil price rise and world recession in 1973–5 but in the late 1970s productivity picked up again among Britain's European competitors, but continued to splutter along at a low level here.

In truth, Britain has found it difficult to achieve what

economists call the 'virtuous circle' of high growth. As a Treasury economic progress report explained in December 1977:

Productivity is a key element. Increased productivity – briefly and in summary, a reduction in the labour cost of producing any given amount of goods – provides cheaper products; increased demand for these cheaper products increases employment and is an incentive for investment in expansion, at the same time providing the funds for this investment; expansion enables sustained higher levels of output and employment while additional investment also enables further improvements in productivity. And so the 'circle' begins again at a higher level of output and employment.

In parallel with the failure of productivity has come a rapid growth in unit labour costs and virtual stagnation in real earnings. The figures below paint a dismal picture.

table 9.6 Earnings, productivity, unit wage costs and prices 1965–77

(annual percentage rate of growth)

1965–73	USA %	Japan	France	West Germany	Italy	UK
Earnings	5.5	15.3	10.6	8.1	11.7	9.4
Output/worker	1.4	9.0	4.9	4.5	5.5	2.9
Unit wage costs	4.0	5.7	5.5	3.4	5.9	6.3
Prices	4.4	6.2	5.0	3.8	4.5	6.1
1973–7	%					
Earnings	6.8	15.4	14.4	7.5	29.5	18.4
Output/worker	0.3	2.7	2.3	3.2	−0.3	0.1
Unit wage costs	6.4	12.4	11.8	4.1	29.9	17.2
Prices	8.1	13.1	11.2	5.3	18.0	18.1

(*Economic Progress Report*, Treasury, May 1978)

As the May 1978 report from the Treasury explained: 'In the long run, increases in money earnings not matched by increases in productivity result in inflation, so that increases in money earnings are translated into real gains in living standards only to the extent that they are backed by real improvements in

productivity. Otherwise apparent gains are eroded by the resulting high rate of inflation, which at the same time is likely to
damage the confidence of those who make the consumption
and investment decisions on which activity and employment
depend.'

In fact, real earnings per head in British manufacturing industry between 1961 and 1973 only grew at an average annual
rate of 2.2 per cent, a figure which is the lowest of any western
industrialized country except the United States. In Japan the
average annual rate was as high as 8.1 per cent, in Italy 6.2 per
cent, in West Germany 4.5 per cent and in France 4.3 per cent.
And since the onset of the new recession in 1973–4 the position
has become no better – quite the opposite. There was almost
a complete standstill in living standard improvements from
1973 to 1977.

The active support of unions for productivity improvements
has been rather patchy over the past ten years. Too often so-
called productivity agreements have been spurious schemes designed to circumvent a tight pay policy, as in the case of British
Oxygen in 1977, which led to that company having a price rise
frozen by the Price Commission. But times of mass unemployment are not favourable to any union eagerness in joining with
employers in a reorganization of work to ensure higher levels
of output from fewer workers. Understandably the main purpose of unions in those harsh circumstances is to seek job
preservation for its own sake, or to help buy out jobs at a substantial price. The catalogue of specific examples in this section
cannot be shrugged off by the unions. There is abundant, in-
controvertible evidence that overmanning and restrictive practices are endemic in far too much of British industry. But the
unions cannot really take all the blame for this. Workers themselves have insisted on the defence of custom and practice and
management have gone along with their view. Many enlightened union officials and shop stewards find it hard to convince workers of the wisdom of changing their well-tried, out-
dated methods of working. There are no grounds whatsoever
to suppose the outlook would be any different, if unions did not
exist. The challenge to this stagnation must come, in the first
place, from management. There are examples of high productivity in British industry, comparable to the best in Japan and

West Germany. This has been achieved through a joint effort between employers and workers with their unions. The tragedy is that so often the improvements come too late when the firm faces bankruptcy and closure.

Unions above the law?

There is a widespread belief in this country that the trade unions are 'above the law', overmighty subjects with legal privileges that provide them with an irresponsible power to pursue their sectional interests. In the words of Lord Denning, Master of the Rolls and scourge of the unions in the Court of Appeal: 'Parliament has conferred more freedom from restraint on trade unions than ever has been known to the law before. All legal restraints have been lifted so that they can now do as they will' (BBC v. Hearn, 1977). This view is echoed by Mrs Thatcher and leading Conservatives.

But the reality is far more complicated than such rhetoric suggests. For the most part the unions remain what they always have been, insecure bodies reacting rather than initiating under the pressure of the ups and downs of the labour market and the sporadic attacks of the common law traditions of the English legal system. It is true that a plethora of detailed legislation has been put on the statue book since the repeal of the 1971 Industrial Relations Act. These are the Trade Union and Labour Relations Act, 1974 (amended in 1976); the Employment Protection Act, 1975 (amended in 1978); the Health and Safety at Work Act, 1974; the Sex Discrimination Act, 1975; and the Race Relations Act, 1976. A wide range of institutions also now exist (as we have already seen) with trade union active support – the Advisory, Conciliation and Arbitration Service (ACAS), the Central Arbitration Committee and the Employment Appeals Tribunal. A network of industrial tribunals, which first started work in 1964, provide protection for employees with grievances. There is no denying that the primary reason for all this legislation was to strengthen and safeguard collective bargaining as well as employee rights, through the statutory provision of basic minimum standards in many employment practices.

But as W. W. Daniel and Elizabeth Stilgoe discovered in a Policy Studies Institute survey published in June 1978 (*The*

Impact of Employment Protection Laws), apart from the unfair dismissal provisions (a legacy from the 1971 Industrial Relations Act) the legislation had made surprisingly little impact on medium and large enterprises with more than 50 workers. They concluded:

Many employers had developed policies and practices which were in advance of minimum standards specified in the legislation. Many others, for whom this was not the case, were able to continue much as before, presumably due to the lack of people at their workplaces with the knowledge or the inclination to draw attention to the law or invoke its requirements.

Nor, despite the hostile attitudes of employers, do the industrial tribunals appear to be forums for the triumph of greedy workers seeking cash redress from employers, backed by their unions. Linda Dickens of Warwick University Industrial Relations Unit found in a study of tribunal cases in one regional office between August and December 1976, that less than a quarter of the applicants were actually members of a trade union and their average level of settlement was a derisory £280 (*Industrial Relations Journal*, winter 1978–9, Vol 9, No 4).

There is some evidence to support the view that workers in trade unions have enjoyed more safeguards from the use of the labour laws than workers not organized. The Daniel and Stilgoe report discovered that the level of trade union organization did have the biggest single influence on the measures used by management to reduce their manpower when it became necessary. The more effective and strong the union presence in the workplace, the more likely it is that companies operate schemes of voluntary rather than enforced redundancies. As Daniel has written: 'It was clear that the voluntary strategy acted as a very effective means for accommodating conflicts as between managements, workforces and trade union representatives within workplaces in circumstances of excess labour.'

In 1968 the Office of Population, Censuses and Surveys study on the impact of the Redundancy Payments Act found only a quarter of establishments with 500 or more employees had formal written agreements with unions over redundancy, while a further quarter had informal understandings; but by 1977 Daniel discovered that as many as half of all establishments having 50 to 5,000 workers had formal agreements and a further quarter, informal ones. The PSI study says that the main explanation for this improvement derives from the growth of trade union influence, and not from the greater incidence of redundancies because of the recession. The findings of the PSI study do suggest that it is not the law by itself that determines its effectiveness in industry, but the degree to which union representatives are aware of the new worker rights and insist on making sure they enjoy them in practice. This suggests that the legal way can only work if unions remain alert and determined to insist on what they are entitled to have under the law.

Schedule 11 of the 1975 Employment Protection Act has been effectively used by the unions for the well-being of their members in bypassing government incomes policy. This provision is an extension of the old 1946 fair wages resolution that sought to safeguard the pay and conditions of workers involved in government contracts; but unlike that measure schedule 11 is not simply confined to protection for the low paid. Under the new law employers are obliged to observe terms and conditions not less favourable than those existing through collective bargaining between independent trade unions and an employers' association. Workers doing comparable work in the same area in the same industry are entitled to similar rates of pay. The thrust of the schedule is to uphold a 'general level' of pay, defined in the 1977 annual report of the Central Arbitration Committee as being 'that observed by employers for comparable workers in the trade, industry or section in which the employer is engaged, in the district in which he is engaged and whose circumstances are similar'. The definitions are left as flexible as possible to avoid over-dogmatic, too precise judgements.

The CAC is the body that unions go to in order to seek awards under schedule 11 for particular members. In 1977 as many as 742 references were referred to the CAC by unions under schedule 11, compared with only 13 for disclosure of information and 21 under the Equal Pay Act. There were 149 awards made by the CAC in this area during the year, while 48 reached report stage. The white-collar unions have been particularly adept at pressing schedule 11 cases, notably the TASS section of the Engineers, ASTMS and APEX.

It is quite true that our unions do enjoy unique legal immunities. Under section 14 of the Trade Union and Labour
Relations Act, 1974, a union cannot be sued in its own name
for most civil wrongs (torts) though it can be sued for civil
wrongs involving personal injury or the use of its property.
Just so long as the civil wrong is done 'in contemplation or
furtherance of a trades dispute' the union cannot be sued at
all (though its officials and members are not so protected in
law, even if they usually are in practice). Ward of Grunwick
showed workers have no legal rights to strike. Having broken
their contracts of employment by taking industrial action, they
dismissed themselves; and as long as the employer has none of
them back at all he is acting lawfully and the sacked workers
cannot even take their former employer to an industrial tribunal in the hope of proving unfair dismissal. The 1974 Act
simply returned the legal position to what it was under the
1906 Trades Disputes Act before the passage of the 1971 Industrial Relations Act revolutionized, albeit temporarily, the
legal framework for the unions. But under the 1976 Amendment Act unions were also protected from action if they
induced the breaking of commercial as well as employment contracts during a trade dispute. This change was made to safeguard the right to strike, which a number of cases had brought
into question during the 1960s. It enables unions to take actions
in disputes that injure third parties (the firm's customers) without facing any liability for doing so. Yet recent judgments by
Lord Denning and the Court of Appeal have severely limited
these immunities in practice, making it increasingly difficult for
unions to extend their strike actions beyond the company
directly involved.

Determined employers, who wish to thwart a union's activities, can simply apply to the courts now for an interlocutory
injunction, a speedy device that can in effect bring an industrial
stoppage to a standstill if successfully granted by the court. As
Professor Kahn-Freund, the eminent labour lawyer, has argued: 'A temporary prohibition is likely to have a permanent
effect.' Here, if anywhere, the alternative may be 'now or never'
– the preservation of the *status quo*, ie the postponement of the
action, may mean its abandonment. The plaintiff does not even

have to convince the court that the case is prima facie in his favour, just so long as it is a serious question that is to be tried. At the injunction stage all the judges need to decide is whether there is a balance of convenience or inconvenience. An attempt was made in the Employment Protection Act 1975 to prevent this formula being used in a case involving a trade dispute – by suggesting that the court must have regard to the question of whether the party against whom the injunction is aimed would be likely to succeed with the defence that his action was in contemplation or furtherance of a trade dispute.

In effect, this safeguard has been dismantled by Lord Denning and his Court of Appeal colleagues. The Association of Broadcasting Staffs lost to the BBC when it tried to refuse transmission of the 1977 FA cup final to South Africa. The court ruled that the proposed action of the ABS amounted to 'coercive interference' and not a trade dispute in the meaning of the law. In the same year when *Daily Mirror* journalists struck, Express Newspapers decided to print more copies of their paper to take advantage of the non-appearance of the *Daily Mirror*. The print union – SOGAT – tried to prevent this, but the Court of Appeal upheld Express Newspapers in the resulting injunction and ruled that the SOGAT action was not taken in furtherance of the NUJ dispute.

The case in October 1978 of Star Sea Transport Corporation of Monrovia carried even more serious implications. A bulk carrier flying the Liberian flag was about to sail from Glasgow to Antwerp. She had Greek officers and crew being paid full rates of the Greek Seamen's Union. Officials of the International Federation of Seamen's Unions took objection to the ship, the *Cammilla M*, demanding the owners should pay the crew the proper internationally agreed levels of wages. The ship was blacked, tugmen refusing to take the vessel to sea. But the Greek crew refused to sign the articles of the Federation, even though it meant they would earn more money. The court granted an interlocutory injunction to prevent the blacking. Denning judged: 'It is suggested that there was an extraneous motive in the officers of the Federation in that they disliked flags of convenience – that they had no legitimate trade object, seeing they were making demands which could not reasonably be fulfilled.'

In a case in December 1978, involving the National Union of Journalists and the Express Newspapers, the Court of Appeal again supported an injunction to quash a union instruction to Express journalists to black copy from the Press Association in pursuance of the official strike by 8,500 provincial journalists. Denning ruled that the NUJ instruction fell outside the immunities of a trade dispute. As he argued:

It is not sufficient to my mind that a trade union leader should intend to advance the trade dispute or their cause. It is not merely subjective, for there is a subjective element in it. The act seems to be such as to hold a reasonable prospect or have reasonable capability of advancing the trade dispute. This objective element was foreshadowed as long ago as 1909. Of course these words go back over 70 years now and Lord Shaw said in an earlier case: 'The conduct of a trade dispute is to have before the mind some objective event or situation.' And so it seems to me the good sense of the matter is that it is not sufficient to intend to further, help, advance or encourage one side in a trade dispute, there must be reasonable prospect or capability of advancing the cause in order for it to gain immunity. Some limit must be put on this wide immunity which is given or appears to be given by statute, otherwise the freedom of individuals to carry on their businesses in peace would go beyond all bounds and would be intruded upon beyond all reason. That is why the courts have always said, even in our latest case, that some limit must be put on the widths of this wording and the limit which should be put upon it, in the interests of the freedom of the ordinary individual, was that there must be a reasonable prospect or reasonable capability of advancing the cause which the protagonists seek to advance.

The defensiveness of the unions is also seen in their attitude towards changing the laws on picketing and conspiracy. Picketing in strikes is now a recognized form of social action. Clearly it remains in the interests of those involved in a dispute to try and dissuade other workers from taking their jobs, and the employer's customers from carrying on their business with him, while the strike persists. The obvious location for performing such peaceful persuasion is just outside the workplace. The word 'picket' was first widely used to cover industrial disputes during the 1860s. It derived from the military term for a body of outlying troops on the look-out for the approach of the enemy. But pickets are more than just watchdogs. They provide a necessary means for strikers to keep up their morale and strengthen their solidarity. Moreover, picketing is a reliable indicator of just how much popular support a particular dispute has really got. In the words of the former Conservative Home Secretary – the architect of the 1971 Industrial Relations Act, Robert Carr, 'the basic purpose of picketing – to inform and persuade in a peaceful manner – is an essential extension of the basic right to strike'.

But the problem is – does 'effective' picketing involve a breach of the existing law? The TUC believes that the law is unsatisfactory, but it failed to convince the Labour Home Secretary, Roy Jenkins, that any change was necessary. In the opinion of the TUC, the position of picketers should be strengthened by providing them with the legal right to stop vehicles and persons who intend to cross a picket line, so that they have a better opportunity to convince them not to do so. The police lobbied successfully to keep such a right out of the 1975 Employment Protection Act. Yet the TUC organized a convincing case to remedy the law. Ever since the repeal of the Combination Acts in 1825 – a measure of 'liberal' Toryism – picketing has been the source of much legal wrangling. It was not until the 1859 Molestation of Workmen Act that any safeguard for picketing was written into the statute book. The protection did not last very long. In 1867 in the case of Regina v. Druitt, the judge ruled that 'if picketing was calculated to have a deterring effect on the minds of ordinary persons, by exposing them to have their motions watched, and to encounter black looks, that would not be permitted by the law of the land'.

The 1871 Criminal Law Amendment Act gave trade unions immunity from prosecution for restraining trade, but it failed to legalize picketing and specifically disallowed 'watching and besetting' of premises. It was left to the reforming Disraeli Conservative ministry of 1874–80 to extend safeguards for pickets in the 1875 Conspiracy and Protection of Property Act. Those provisions still remain in force today. Section 7 of the measure spelt out what pickets could not do. This covered the use of any violence or intimidation against another person, or injury to his property; following anybody from place to place, hiding his tools, clothes or other property; watching or besetting his house or place of work. The Act seemed to make it clear that attendance 'at or near a house or place where a person resides or works or carries on business' in order to 'merely obtain or communicate information' was not deemed an offence of 'watching and besetting' under the common law.

Yet much to the surprise of many in the legal profession, that 1875 Act did not prove sufficient to protect peaceful picketing. There was no explicit admission that the law allowed pickets to carry out peaceful persuasion. This was made perfectly clear in the case of Lyons v. Wilkins (in 1896 and 1899) where the plaintiff, Wilkins, was found guilty of trying to persuade workers not to join the leather merchants where a strike was in progress. The judges insisted his action went far beyond what the 1875 Act intended, which was no more than the communication of information to anyone wishing to cross a picket line, if he was willing to receive it. That decision was one of a number in the courts during the 1890s that revealed the open hostility of many judges to the trade union movement and helped to undermine the legal foundations which the TUC thought had been achieved for unions in the legislation of the 1870s. The most important result was the formation of the Labour Representation Committee in February 1900. As an influential pressure group for the labour interest in Parliament, they managed to get the law revised with the return of the Liberals in 1906. Section 2 of the Trades Disputes Act of that year said it was lawful 'in contemplation or furtherance of a trade dispute to attend at or near a house or place merely for the purpose of peacefully obtaining or communicating information or of peacefully persuading any persons to work or abstain from working'.

This strengthening of the picketing position by Parliament appeared to settle the matter. No further change has taken effect since. Section 134 of the 1971 Industrial Relations Act took out any immunity for pickets outside a person's house during a strike, but the point was reaffirmed in the 1974 Trade Union and Labour Relations Act. Section 15 states:

It shall be lawful for one or more persons in contemplation or furtherance of a trade dispute to attend at or near a place where another person works or carries on business or any other place where another person happens to be, not being a place where he resides, for the purpose only of peacefully obtaining or communicating information or peacefully persuading any person to work or abstain from working.

But court judgments over the past fourteen years seem to have undermined picketing yet again. In the case of Piddington *v.* Bates in 1960 a police constable told Piddington, a picket outside Free Press Ltd in Islington during a printing strike, that two pickets at the front and back entrances of the premises were enough. When Piddington challenged this, he was arrested for obstructing a policeman in the execution of his duty. Lord Parker upheld the police action with the words: 'I think that a police officer charged with the duty of preserving the Queen's peace must be left to take such steps as, on the evidence before him, he thinks proper.' During an unofficial strike of draughtsmen in 1964 at English Electric in Liverpool, forty pickets walked round in a circle in a service road leading to the firm's entrance. Harold Tynan, the picket leader, was arrested for obstructing the highway – though, as the court report said: 'It was a well-managed strike, entirely lacking in disturbances or bad temper and all the strikers were decent, well-mannered people who maintained good friendly relations with the police.' Yet in 1966 when the Tynan *v.* Bulmer case reached the Queen's Bench, the judge backed up the police. This seemed to suggest that the 1906 Act did not allow pickets to carry out the means of making sure they were able to peacefully persuade and communicate information.

On 5 September 1972, during the building workers' strike, J. E. Broome, a union picket in Stockport, held up a poster on the highway in front of a lorry coming towards the picket line. Broome asked the driver to pull to the side of the road – which he did – but Broome was unable to persuade the driver not to make the delivery to the nearby building site. At this point, Broome stood in front of the vehicle to stop it moving forward. The driver asked him to stand aside, but did not try to run him down. The police arrested Broome for wilful obstruction under section 121 of the Highways Act 1959. It was agreed no angry words nor violent action had occurred. Broome said he was exercising his right to picket peacefully under section 134 of the 1971 Industrial Relations Act. In December 1973 the case of Broome was discussed on appeal in the House of Lords, where their lordships all agreed Broome had carried out an unlawful action. Lord Dilhorne said the law gave no right to a picket to stop anyone or any vehicle in order to try and persuade people not to work. But he added: 'It may be that unless the right to picket includes and extends to stopping people against their will, pickets will be unable to exercise their powers of persuasion as they wish.' Lord Salmon denied there was any right of picketing, only 'a narrow but real immunity'. Only attendance at the entrance to the workplace was covered by the law apparently. Lord Reid likened a picket to a hitch-hiker: 'One is familiar with persons at the side of a road signalling to a driver requesting him to stop. It is then for the driver to decide whether he will stop or not. That, in my opinion, a picket is entitled to do.'

The picketing position was eroded even further in the spring of 1973. This arose out of an incident on 28 March 1973 outside St Thomas's Hospital, London, during an electricians' strike. Between thirty and forty electricians were at the gate, four of them wearing armbands as official pickets. It was known that at 5.00 pm a coachload of black-legs was due to drive out of the hospital. The police decided to put a cordon round the entrance, so that when the coach appeared nobody was in a position to speak to the driver. At this point Peter Kavanagh of the TGWU became angry and pushed forward. PC Hiscock told the pickets to 'keep moving and stop pushing'. Kavanagh replied, 'You can't tell me what to do, you little squirt'; and he pushed Hiscock in the back. Later Kavanagh added, 'You can't fucking move me. I'm a trade union official and I want to talk to the driver of the coach.' Queen's Bench failed to support Kavanagh's view of what it was permitted to do under the law. The judge argued: 'Where a police officer reasonably anticipates that in the circumstances obtaining in the particular case the consequences of any peaceful picketing may be a breach of the peace, either by the pickets or the spectators, it is the duty of the police officer to take such steps as are reasonably necessary to prevent that anticipated breach of the peace.' In other words, obstruction is possible, before obstruction occurs. This judgment, like the others, has strengthened the discretionary powers of the police over the rights of picketing.

These cases have been explained in detail in order to illustrate the real limitations under the law for the unions, no matter what potential legal safeguards are protecting them in their activities under the 1974–6 labour law. Picketing provides a graphic illustration of why unions still dislike courts of law, while wishing to remain law-abiding bodies. They retain a firm belief in the autonomy of industrial practices, in the wisdom of the empirical way of logic, which lacks the precise clarity of a legal constraint. In the words of Professor Kahn-Freund, the unions remain believers in 'collective *laissez-faire*'. Social norms and sanctions count in the last resort not the *obiter dicta* of learned, class-biased judges. A rule-of-thumb approach upsets the legal mind, but it usually works. As Winston Churchill, Home Secretary of the day, told the Commons in 1911: 'It is not good for trade unions that they should be brought into contact with the courts, and it is not good for the courts. Where class issues are involved, it is impossible to pretend that the courts command the same degree of general confidence.'

The labour laws of 1974–6 have provided unions with new rights, but in practice they are likely to drag the trade union movement into an area it has always sought to keep at arm's length. The interminable wrangles over recognition with ACAS, EMA and TASS under the Employment Protection Act illustrate what happens when unions seek to use the legal system to extend their memberships and influence. As Harry Urwin warned the 1977 Congress: 'We must not allow ourselves to be shackled by legal rules and regulations. The law we have is a fall-back, not a weapon of first resort. We have not reached the highest ever membership of $11\frac{1}{2}$ million in this country by relying on the law.' The do-nothing view prevailed in Congress House during the late 1970s, and not without good reason.

Amendments to the legislation in favour of the unions might make it much more difficult to keep the law in future out of trades disputes. Nevertheless the TUC did give its support to two Labour private members' Bills in 1978, designed to remedy some of the alleged defects of the recognition provisions of the Employment Protection Act. One measure, moved by Mr Ted Fletcher, was specifically designed to avoid any repetition of the Grunwick affair. This would enable ACAS to make a report without the cooperation of an employer and to absolve

ACAS from having to consult non-independent bodies or to take into account the views of employees who wished to be represented by such organizations. It also sought to enable ACAS to use questionnaires rather than organize formal ballots.

Ian Mikardo's Bill was even more controversial. Its primary aim was to permit ACAS, if it so wished, not to proceed with matters in a dispute involving TUC affiliated unions that fell within the scope of TUC rules. This was clearly designed to bring maverick unions like EMA firmly to heel. But neither measure made any headway in Parliament.

It looks most unlikely that the laws will be radically changed in a union direction during the early 1980s. Recent episodes have done nothing to ease union doubts about the use of the law in industrial relations. As Jeremy McMullen has argued in his invaluable Pluto handbook (*Rights At Work*, 1978): 'Union organization, collective bargaining and industrial action are the pre-conditions for individual rights.' Putting it simply: don't sue – organize. In his words, 'Workers and their families have always distrusted the law, and rightly so. It is not an instrument geared to our needs and the people who administer it are unrepresentative, out of touch and antagonistic to our demands.' It is not merely the undeniable risks attached to going to law that concerned McMullen such as the likelihood of defeat and massive financial costs, but the time wasted, the exposure of workers to publicity and harassment, the tendency of the law to harden attitudes, above all the fact that resort to legal processes means unions have handed over to the courts of the land their ultimate sanction – that of industrial action.

Can the law be made any better – to help unions? There is an obvious danger that legal sanctions and codes of conduct backed up by the rigours of judgments in the courts could emasculate free trade unionism. The *laissez-faire*, common law tradition still survives in our collectivist society and judges like Lords Widgery and Denning have been less than sympathetic to the purposes of the unions. For the most part, unions have sought immunity from prosecution, safeguards by Parliament after well-intentioned laws have been rendered worthless by judicial decisions. The balance of arguments over the use of the law (with punishments) in the conduct of industrial dis-

putes is surely weighted against any further attempt at limiting
union activity in such a way. The experience of the 1971 Industrial Relations Act suggests that this can polarize attitudes,
inflame trade union opinion, and fail to ensure a peaceful settlement of vexatious issues.

But this should not be the end of the matter. The new rights
of trade unionists, enshrined in the 1974–7 laws, should be built
on during the 1980s in line with Western European practice.
Over a wide range of issues collective bargaining has simply
failed to provide Britain's unions with the powers and responsibilities enjoyed by their contemporaries elsewhere in
Western Europe. The TUC is pressing for compulsory
planning agreements, much greater disclosure of company information to unions, a radical measure of industrial democracy. Without legislation, none of these aims are achievable.
Properly worded and clear in its purpose, the law can
strengthen, not weaken the unions. There is much to be said
in taking a positive view of the value of law in industrial relations, if the aim is to strengthen not weaken the unions at
every level.

But we must be realistic. Old habits of mind die slowly. The
1969 *In Place of Strife* crisis and the legacy of the 1971 Industrial Relations Act provide apt warnings of the dangers of
rushing in laws with the intent of a reform of the unions. Yet
will our unions accept change without some outside stimulus
to action? The answer is surely – No. The limited improvement
in their legal position during the 1970s has led too many people
into the mistaken belief that they are now overmighty subjects whose arrogance and power need to be curbed. In fact,
the opposite is the truth. The laws have done little more than
provide trade unionists in Britain with rights enjoyed by others
in the Western world over the past decade. Moreover by innumerable decisions in courts and industrial tribunals they
have been circumscribed, in some parts rendered quite ineffective. The full apparatus of our legal system is deeply
antagonistic to the unions. It needs precise, iron-tight legislation to ensure judges do not hinder the will of a democratically
elected Parliament. Surely such a suggestion is not beyond the
wit of union reformers to accomplish, without reviving fears of
legal sanctions and punishments.

Certainly the present half-way position – neither within nor without a defined legal framework – cannot continue indefinitely. Much to their obvious chagrin the unions have put themselves on the legislatory road. The results are producing many self-doubts and anxieties. But there is only one way to go now and that is forward. If the unions are to become a powerful and effective force in Britain during the 1980s, they must drop their old suspicions. The philosophy of 'ourselves alone' makes no sense today. More far-sighted union leaders now recognize that they cannot achieve their aims merely through their own efforts. Seventy-eight years ago many unions in the TUC recognized that they required a political voice, if trade unionism was to survive intact from the threats of employer power and the legal system. The birth of the Labour Party and its early growth owed a great deal to the arbitrariness of court judgments. Contrary to the *laisez faire* critics, the unions remain just as vulnerable to the whims of judges today as they did at the turn of this century. This is why the social contract – if it is to grow and prosper – requires a new relationship between unions and the law.

The issue of trade union 'power' is once more in the forefront of British politics. But the long, tangled relations between the unions and the law suggest no clear, easy answers. The threats about changing the balance stem from the assumption that the law has given the unions immense privileges which make them irresponsible. As Professor Kahn-Freund has written: 'The law has important functions in labour relations, but they are secondary if compared with the impact of the labour market (supply and demand) and with the spontaneous creation of a social power on the worker's side to balance that of management.' The reason for immunities for unions in trade disputes is not because governments wish to give unions extra-legal powers to menace society, but to ensure unions are allowed to exist at all. The fact is that the law remains primarily concerned with individual, not collective rights, and judges never cease to disclose their hostility and insensitivity to the purposes of trade unionism. Without legal immunities, the unions would simply be unable to continue as effective, independent bodies. Employers would be able to take them to court successfully for damages in any breach of contract and thereby destroy any right to strike. In short, the 1974–6 labour laws did little more than restore the position prior to 1971 and extend to workers and unions certain minimum rights on issues like lay-off pay, time off for union duties, maternity leave (if they are willing to try and enforce them), but without sanctions against employers to ensure these all become well established. In truth, in 1979, far from being overwhelmed with strong new legal powers, unions felt they were ill-digested, badly phrased, and in the face of tough employers usually ineffective.

By the standards of the countries of the industrialized West, British unions have so far failed to exercise constructive let alone radical power and influence. Recent trends, traced in the first part of this book, suggest the picture is complex. Some developments – more the result of new labour law rather than collective bargaining – hold out the promise of a better future. Potentially massive changes for good are now within the grasp of the unions, if they choose to exercise their new legal rights. Britain's unions – after generations of negativism and insularity – have an opportunity to make a lasting and progressive impact on our society.

Whatever happens in the next decade or so, the unions will have only themselves to blame if they do not shoulder those burdens. Allan Flanders once wrote:

Trade unions may be a force for progress, but in their actual functioning they are, in the literal and unusual meaning of the word, 'reactionary' bodies. They react very closely to their members and their members react in the main to their everyday industrial experience. That is how union traditions have been formed over the years to express the lessons of group experience. They can only be changed by different experience when those who carry the final responsibility for running industry and politics, that is management and governments, are willing and able to provide it.

Thanks to the collective power of the state, the unions can now extend, not a tyrannical, ignorant monopoly, but a benign influence over our society. If this restores a lost idealism, based on justice and freedom, so much the better.

Yet the sheer diversity and cultural richness of the British unions make it unwise to generalize. The movement is not everything, only the sum of its disparate parts. This is why we have the most comprehensive trade union movement in the Western world. It is to those individual unions, with their tenacious belief in their own autonomy, that we must now turn.

Part two

Varieties of unionism

10 One industrial union

The 2,250,000-strong Transport and General Workers' Union (TGWU) bestrides the trade union movement like a colossus. One in five of all Britain's trade unionists are now within its ranks. 'Everyone listens to this union – employers, government, other unions. It is amazing what we can get done,' one national official told me. There is a belligerent self-confidence, a belief in the rightness of the TGWU way of doing things, shared by officers at every level.

Under Jack Jones (1969-78), the elected boss of the union, the mighty monolith played a crucial role in the TUC and the Labour Party. Jones was the chief architect of the Social Contract between Labour and the unions. The creation of the Advisory, Conciliation and Arbitration Service (ACAS) was very much his idea. His influence was massive on the Bullock Committee on industrial democracy. During the Jones reign in Transport House (the union's headquarters in London's Smith Square, opposite Conservative Central Office) the TGWU enjoyed a greater power and prestige than at any time since it was ruled by the union's founder – Ernest Bevin – between the wars.

Not every Jones cause triumphed by any means, even if prime ministers liked him on their side in an argument. His support for an investment reserve fund to help regenerate British manufacturing was effectively emasculated by the Bank of England and the Treasury. His advocacy of import controls found few supporters in governing circles either. Nor did Jones's highly personal commitment to see Britain out of the European Common Market make much impact, going down to total defeat in the July 1975 referendum. On the other hand, the successful defence of the living standards of the old age pensioners during the early 1970s owed much to Jones's campaign for their cause. No TUC Congress was complete in those years without a march of the pensioners led by Jones.

Jones headed a union where the pyramid of power ends at the top. The TGWU was welded together in 1921 as a highly centralized body and the basic structure remains the same to this day. The union was founded through the unification of fourteen separate unions under the ingenious, persuasive direction of Ernest Bevin. Its general secretary holds unique authority. As Alan Bullock, Bevin's biographer, has explained:

The general secretary represented the unity of the union. He was the man who held it together and resisted the particularist tendencies of the trade groups. It was to the general secretary that the executive looked for guidance in formulating policy and under his supervision that the officers carried out the executive's decisions.

Bevin stamped his personality on to the new massive general union, but he was in no sense a dictator. In Bullock's words:

Without leadership, democracy is an inert and feeble form of government, a truth still imperfectly comprehended by many who regard democracy and the exercise of power as mutually exclusive. The difference between autocracy and democracy is not that the first provides leadership, while the second eliminates it; the true distinction is in the character of the leadership, the conditions under which the power is exercised, arbitrary in the first case, responsible and liable to account in the second.

TGWU stalwarts in the days of Bevin and Deakin regarded the union as a rigid structure, where full-time officers controlled every level, shop stewards threatened internal unity, and plant agreements were barely tolerated. Yet the picture of an unbending, tough bossdom in the early years, transformed under Frank Cousins and particularly Jones into a democratic instrument of rank and file opinion, is pure mythology. Whoever rules in Transport House, there are no effective sanctions to impose on rebellious members. The centralized character of collective bargaining twenty years ago needed the concentration of decisions among a small praetorian guard of national industrial officers; but it also required the assent of those many thousands who were not active in the union's affairs. Increased local bargaining since Deakin's day was more the result of technological change at the workplace than any union initiative started from the centre. The secret of the TGWU is that it has somehow managed to elect general secretaries who fitted the mood of different times. More important, the union enjoys a unique structure, flexible enough to withstand abrupt changes of direction without falling to pieces (see figure 10.1).

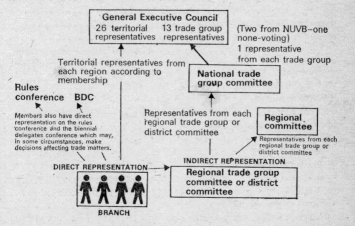

figure 10.1 The TGWU – how it works (*TGWU Shop Stewards' Handbook*, 1975)

The general secretary of the TGWU is responsible to the biennial conference of the union, but more realistically to the 40-strong General Executive Council. That body is made up of 26 territorial representatives from the 11 regions of the union and 13 from the 11 national trade groups. All members of the Executive Council are elected for two years, but they only meet four times a year. The rule-book sets out in detail what the responsibilities of the Executive Council are. It is the most important lay body in the union and no general secretary can govern without its consent. Divisions exist within the Executive Council on policy issues, even if it tends to provide a stolid phalanx of unity to the outside world.

The union is dualistic in character. Its national trade groups, with their lay committees, are paralleled by the regional organization. Internally the TGWU is an umbrella which encompasses a number of virtually separate industrial unions. The breakdown of the membership in 1976 indicates the multiplicity of different interests covered by the TGWU (see table 10.1).

All the national industrial officers are responsible to the general secretary. Like the rest of the 500 or so staff they are appointed centrally by the Executive Council. In practice the

table 10.1 Where the TGWU strength lies (December 1978 figures)

	National officer	Membership
Vehicle building and automotive	G. Hawley	193,428
Power and engineering	T. Crispin	278,407
Chemical, rubber manufacturing and oil refining	J. Miller	145,494
Docks and waterways	T. Cronin	51,153
Commercial services	J. Ashwell	226,290
Passenger services	L. Smith	144,501
Public services and civil air transport	M. B. Martin J. E. Collier	188,233
General workers (building materials, packaging, textiles, cement, brick)	P. Evans	269,845
Food, drink and tobacco	H. A. Ray	231,796
Building, construction and civil engineering	G. Henderson	375,000
Association of Clerical, Technical and Supervisory staff group (ACTS)	A. C. Sullivan	149,801

general secretary has a major say in the choice of full-time officials for local, regional and national work. But the union is flexible enough to tolerate change without massive purges. The rule-book remains a guide, not a bible.

Under Jones, much of the power and prestige of the trade group secretaries in Transport House was chipped away. Some of the former praetorian guard disliked the change. 'All we hear about these days are the stewards,' one grumbled to me. Others have accepted the new situation with relish and gone on to prove they still have a vital function to play in these days of localized bargaining. John Miller is responsible nationally for the TGWU in chemicals, rubber manufacturing and oil refining. He has encouraged active participation in the major plants, but also sets a high standard of negotiation himself. His work for ICI's manual workers has meant sophisticated analysis of the company's profits. It has brought far more say for TGWU members in that firm's decisions.

National bargaining remains crucial in the public services (where the TGWU remains predominant), particularly in passenger transport. All the trade group secretaries are active bargainers at national level on the various joint national councils, wages councils and Whitley bodies, where the union is represented. It is these which lay down national minimum wage rates and fringe benefits. This involves drawing up claims in the office at Transport House. The full-time trade group secretary often finds himself negotiating across the table at company or industry level, though it is much rarer nowadays for agreements to come into force without the members ratifying them first by ballot.

The spread of power to lower levels of the union – under the Jones philosophy – has brought more not less work to TGWU officials, most of whom have come up through the union's shop steward movement. This is particularly true of the regional secretaries, of which there are eleven. These cover the following areas:

Region
1 London and the Home Counties
2 South of England (including Channel Islands)
3 West of England
4 Wales
5 Midlands
6 Lancashire, Cheshire, Wirral, Isle of Man
7 Scotland
8 Northern region (including Cumberland, Durham and Teesside)
9 Yorkshire
10 Humber and East Coast
11 Ireland (north and south)

Brian Mathers is responsible for the Midlands (Region 5) which stretches from Derby to Oxford, from Northhampton to the Welsh border. Apart from London, it is the TGWU's main stronghold with 334,701 members in 1974. Since the war, the union has made heavy inroads into the region's engineering and car workers – where it now claims to have more members than the AUEW. Mathers has only a handful of full-time officers to help him in the regional office, fifty more in the seventeen district offices, thirty clerical staff and a couple of researchers. He is the region's chief administrator, looking after all the office needs 'from light bulbs to salaries' and paying various benefits to members. But Mathers is no faceless bureaucrat. 'The facts of life make sure that I get involved in every serious matter that arises in the region. If anyone has a problem, he does not go to London, he comes to me. My phone never stops ringing,' he said when I interviewed him in February 1975. Mathers tries his best to get to branch meetings, but with 928 of them in his region it is difficult. Mathers is an articulate backer of the Jones view of trade union life. In his opinion the full-time officials are there 'to train people to do the job of being good trade unionists themselves'. Mathers has to work with the regional trade group or district committees and meets once a quarter.

The personal dedication of a handful of full-time union officials keeps a union going. The work of the TGWU's district secretaries makes the point. Take the case of David Buckle, the able district secretary for the TGWU in Oxford since 1964. His responsibilities cover the Leyland car plants at Cowley, Witney blankets, the local cement industry, commercial transport and civil aviation. Apart from presiding over annual wage negotiations, Buckle leaves the stewards at Cowley to get on with their job, unless an emergency requires his attention. But there are not enough experienced lay activitists in the union, acting as stewards, in other sectors where Buckle works, so he must often act as a surrogate steward, preparing and negotiating the annual claim with workplace representatives sitting alongside him. 'I'm working harder than ever nowadays. Expectations among our members have gone up and the bargaining has grown more complicated. Ten years ago you had a few weeks to settle a problem. Now it has to be solved by tomorrow,' Buckle told me in an interview in February 1975. He showed me his diary. During the week I met him he had averaged 150 miles of travel a day and he usually worked until

11.00 every night. Two out of four Sunday mornings a month are taken up attending branch meetings.

The devolution of more power to the shopfloor under the Jones regime has not meant an easier life for the full-time officials; quite the opposite. The old structure of authority in the TGWU is less clear-cut than it used to be. The district secretary can no longer rely on the instant support of his superior full-time officials at a higher level in any conflict with the stewards, but most members still count on him to provide a strategy and take the burden of negotiation, if the situation requires. In the TGWU most full-time officials are recruited from among the union's stewards, so there is less of a gulf between the union's local officers and the factory organization. Both have mutual respect and understanding for each other's problems. The district secretary can no longer expect to enjoy instant obedience from members when he issues instructions. He must win the confidence of the rank and file, if he hopes to make a mark.

Under Jones the TGWU tried to make more of a local impact by pulling down the barriers separating the members of the different trade groups. In 1969 the old trade group committees were scrapped in most regions of the union. These used to bring together only a limited few in the same industry to discuss common problems. Instead, the district committee has been revived. Delegates are elected from branches within the district to sit on the new body. Here busmen, car workers, lorry drivers, engineers and any other groups in the union can meet usually once a month. It is the one level of the TGWU where activists can find common cause outside their occupational base. One romantically inclined member called them 'little Soviets', but they really resemble trades councils and only have advisory functions. The district committees have proved useful platforms for TGWU propaganda campaigns, like those on behalf of the old age pensioners or against the EEC. They can only work effectively if enough of the faithful fill the places. Here is the nub of the matter, for the union can be a rickety infant at branch level. A major effort is now being made to ensure branches are organized on a factory, not area, basis, making them more relevant to the shopfloor worker, but this is not always possible as a result of many scattered units of membership. 'If we have as many as one in every 1,000 of our members playing an active part, I'd be very surprised,' a steward told me in Birmingham in February 1975.

The TGWU still provides insufficient union education to meet the needs of its stewards. In the summer of 1976 the Eastbourne centre was opened for the union faithful to use mainly for holiday and recreational facilities, though it will also be used for education courses. This adds to the five weekly summer courses held every year at the Royal Agricultural College in Cirencester, and shorter sessions at regional, district and factory level. But in 1977 education cost £154,319, compared with £166,133 spent on accident benefit, over £3 million on disputes benefit and £803,508 on legal costs for members. A local TGWU official told me in Birmingham he reckoned less than 2 per cent of those in responsible lay posts in the region had ever experienced any union training. Of course, most stewards and branch officials learn on the job through experience and common sense, not from textbooks. Full-timers assured me that the most sophisticated wage claims were drawn up by the lay activists with minimal help from the union's own organization. Yet this can prove a very patchy affair. Engineering has a long tradition of plant bargaining, but the same is not true of the newer recruitment areas. The union needs to fill the gap, if it is to turn the laudable ideal of a self-confident, aggressive shop steward movement into a reality across the whole of British industry.

What Jones tried to do during his period as general secretary was to provide more chances for initiative from the shopfloor activists by opening up the TGWU machinery to new ideas. Yet perhaps this amounts more to a change in style. So far the union has failed to provide the muscle and resources to transfer power and effectiveness down the union's structure to the lay membership. It is the TGWU's sheer size and reputation for getting things done, far more than Jones's enthusiasm for industrial democracy, which has provided the union with such enormous influence and respect in the outside world. There is an undoubted sense of pride and purpose at every level of the TGWU. This can sometimes lead to a rather arrogant assumption that everyone would be far better off in the union. Jones strengthened that trend. He made sure the union's structure of regions and trade groups were reshaped to meet the conditions of contemporary bargaining.

There was a wide gulf between the Jones rhetoric of all power to the shopfloor and the reality of an apathetic membership in many areas of the union. Moreover, it looked odd to the outsider that the union could have been radically changed from the old popular bossdom it was under Bevin, Arthur Deakin and Frank Cousins into a workers' democracy under Jones. As the union's mighty bloc vote is wielded at the TUC and Labour Party conference, differences in style or method are hard to see. Jones could be a difficult man to cross words with, as some members of the TUC General Council found to their cost. He was quite ready to mobilize his huge organization behind the causes he believed in. Unlike other unions, the TGWU has experienced no fundamental internal reform. In a real sense, there was little need for such a step. Bevin's superb structure, with its subtle blend of regional and industrial layers, gives the man at the top enormous power to shape the union the way he wants. It is the lack of rigidity in the TGWU organization which has made it much easier over the past few years to attract smaller unions with financial or other problems to throw in their lot with the mighty giant.

The TGWU has grown at an astonishing rate since the early 1960s. Much of its success stems from its appeal to smaller unions, who believe they can retain some kind of identity within the larger organization. Alex Kitson became an influential executive officer in the union – close to Jones – when his Scottish Commercial Motormen's Union merged with the TGWU in 1971. The big breakthrough for the union was the amalgamation with the National Union of Vehicle Builders in 1972. This proved a major setback to the AUEW and boosted the TGWU's position as the main union voice for Britain's car workers. Table 10.2 underlines how the TGWU has spread its power and influence across almost every occupational interest over the past fifteen years. Over eighty unions have joined forces with the TGWU since its foundation in 1922. No wonder many of its officers believe it makes sense for all other unions to link up with the TGWU.

Early in 1977 the union elected a new general secretary to succeed Jack Jones. His successor was Moss Evans, a 51-year-

table 10.2 Come and join the TGWU – new arrivals since 1966

United Fishermen's Union	1966
Scottish Slaters, Tilers, Roofers and Cement Workers Society	1968
National Association of Operative Plasterers	1969
Process and General Workers' Union	1969
Irish Union of Hairdressers and Allied Workers	1970
Port of Liverpool Staff Association	1970
Sheffield Amalgamated Union of File Trades	1970
Scottish Commercial Motormen's Union	1971
Watermen, Lightermen, Tugmen and Bargemen's Union	1971
Chemical Workers' Union	1972
National Union of Vehicle Builders	1972
Iron, Steel and Wood Barge Builders and Helpers Association	1973
Union of Bookmakers' Employees	1974
Union of Kodak Workers	1975
File Grinders' Society	1975
National Association of Youth Hostel Wardens	1978
Staff Association for RAC Employees	1978

old Welshman, who is likely to be leading the Transport and General Workers from now until 1990. Evans won 349,548 votes at the branches on a 39.1 per cent turnout of the members. The runner-up, John Cousins, polled 119,241 votes. It was a clear and decisive victory for Evans.

Born in Cefn Coed near Merthyr Tydfil in the year of the General Strike, the son of a miner, Evans knew the hard times of the 1930s. His father was out of work for nearly 14 years and he never had a pair of shoes until he was 16. Evans claims he never had a full cup of tea until he started working on a paper round after the family had moved to Birmingham, where his father was seeking a job. In a moving and emotional speech to the 1976 TUC, Evans left no doubts about his feelings of unemployment.

As he told delegates: 'We knew what it was like then. We knew how degrading it was. We knew the morale-sapping fears of unemployment and how undignified it was. When we think of the unemployed we think of the young man or young woman and the parents being unemployed, but there are the children of the unemployed as well. They wear a different quality of clothes at school, sitting next to the kid of a person who is at work and who can dress his child differently. They are deprived of holidays. I remember my first holiday as a kid was under the auspices of the British Legion.'

Evans started work at 16 as a trainee with the engineering firm of Joseph Lucas in Birmingham. He was taught how to cut carbon for use as lightning conductors in aircraft and became a member of the Engineering Union. After the war he moved to work at Bakelite, where he joined the TGWU and became a shop steward there in 1947. During the late 1940s Evans cut his political teeth in local Birmingham politics. He used to speak outside factory gates for the Labour cause. At the age of 29 he was appointed engineering and chemical officer for the TGWU in east Birmingham and in 1960 he was promoted to become a regional trade group secretary. Evans soon proved himself as a formidable negotiator – tough and fluent. He also won a reputation for being a humorous and mild-mannered man, who enjoys nothing better than being one of the boys. Unlike Jones, he is approachable. A devotee of real ale. Evans is likely to give the TGWU a friendlier image to the outside world, though none the less effective.

In 1966 he was appointed engineering national officer in head office and three years later took on the important job of looking after the TGWU's members in the motor car industry. Evans transformed collective bargaining at Ford, where he brought in the assistance of the Ruskin College Trade Union Research Unit to help in drawing up pay claims. This new sophisticated approach became a model envied by union negotiators in other companies. Evans is a great admirer of the American methods of bargaining, particularly those of Walter Reuther.

In 1974 he was appointed the TGWU's national organizer. This helped to broaden his experience in the union outside his power base in the Midlands and the car industry. Evans became a highly successful salesman for the TGWU in hitherto weak areas of trade unionism and his work helped to push up the membership figures. There is no doubt that he was helped to the top through the kind of important jobs he was asked to do by the Executive Council, but it would be wrong to see Evans as merely a 'Yes' man for Jack Jones. In the years ahead he will imprint his own personality on British trade unionism, but it is far too early to decide just what his impact will be.

Evans is an unrepentant champion of free collective bargaining. He hates the idea of being a boss figure and stresses the need for union officials to be strictly accountable to the rank and file at all times. Though he sometimes suggests he is on the left in the Labour movement, Evans is a pragmatist, more at home at the negotiating table than at party conference. He believes in the need for more public ownership, but adds that he does not want to take away initiative or abolish the corner shop down the road.

A chunky, loquacious Welshman, Evans is a proud family man. He lives modestly in Hemel Hempstead. The father of six children, he likes to enjoy home life at weekends – going down to the local to down three pints before lunch and then putting up his feet for a snooze. It is unlikely that he will ever lose touch with the mood of his members. After the traumatic experience that Jack Jones had to suffer at the 1977 TGWU biennial conference, when his plea for orderly collective bargaining went down to defeat, no leader of the TGWU can hope to exercise an unquestioning sway over the union, as was so common in the past.

Evans is an interesting mix of joviality and toughness. His contrasting qualities were on display during the tragi-comedy involving the Fox and Goose public house at the 1977 TUC, when delegates voted to suspend the TGWU because it had failed to implement a disputes committee ruling, involving the Licensed House Managers. Evans began by treating the whole issue in a light-hearted manner. When this failed to please Congress, he lost his temper and made some rash remarks about the tiny union that was trying to humiliate the mighty TGWU. The adverse vote against the TGWU was a reflection of the widespread dislike for the union in the TUC. Those delegates who insisted on suspending the TGWU (albeit for an hour until the Engineering Workers had sorted out their internal confusion about how they should have voted) came from unions who had bitter memories of being worsted by the TGWU on previous occasions. The Fox and Goose may leave a nasty taste in the mouth for some time to come, but it looks unlikely to impede the onward march of the TGWU. Bevin's unique creation is as strong and influential as ever and no matter what style or policies Evans pursues in the years ahead, the TGWU will stay out in front – envied and despised by its jealous rivals, but the major force on the shopfloor and in the wider trade union and Labour movements.

11 All men are brethren

The Engineering section of the Amalgamated Union of Engineering Workers (AUEW) (1,199,465 members in 1979) is still Britain's second biggest trade union. Despite recurrent political in-fighting and membership stagnation since the early 1960s, it remains at the heart of manufacturing industry. Under the forceful, belligerent leadership of Hugh Scanlon (elected president in 1967; re-elected three years later and retired in October 1978 taking a peerage in the 1979 New Year's honours list) the union won a deserved reputation for uncompromising militancy. The AUEW fought tooth and nail against both Labour's plans for industrial relations legislation in 1969 and the 1971 Industrial Relations Act. Until the summer of 1975 the union was also implacably opposed to any incomes policy – whether voluntary or statutory. During Scanlon's presidency, the union proved a highly effective force in the TUC, though in retrospect it will be remembered far more for successful obstructionism than as the source of new ideas.

Terry Duffy, who was elected president of the AUEW in April 1978 by 169,168 votes to 122,251 for his left-wing rival Bob Wright on a postal ballot of 32.2 per cent of the membership entitled to vote, has enjoyed one of the most spectacular climbs to the top in recent trade union history. Only nine years before he was still a shop steward at Lucas Aerospace in his home town of Wolverhampton. A friendly man with a flat Black Country drawl and trim sergeant-major moustache, Duffy has been under-rated by friends and foes alike. 'I am no intellectual,' he said, 'but just an ordinary working-class lad from the shopfloor with simple tastes. I am president today because I can feel the pulse of the shopfloor'. He was born in 1922 in a back-to-back house in the Wolverhampton slums, the second child in a family of 11. He lived in a semi-detached council house before being elected president, with his wife Joyce who worked as a school-meals attendant, and they have two teenage children; their son works as an insurance agent and their daughter in a department store. Duffy used to drink with his mates at the local workingmen's club on a Friday night, take his mongrel dog for walks in the park, play snooker or golf.

Duffy can be maladroit and astonishingly gauche at times. His latest half-baked idea of giving manual workers one year off in every 10 on full pay is unlikely to be his last *faux pas*. Duffy often gives the alarming impression that he talks before he thinks. He can be incoherent and fail to grasp the guts of an issue. He has yet to make any reputation as a bargainer and his handling of the toolroom revolts at Leyland and Lucas in 1977 was tough, but less than assured. Duffy's delighted but anxious friends in the AUEW believe he has the capacity to grow as president.

Physically he is very tough, as befits a former boxing champion and PT instructor. He fought through the Second World War as a sergeant in North Africa, Italy and Greece (which cast him against the Communists for the first time). After 'the most terrible time' of his life, trying to get a job when he was demobbed, he became a skilled turner in the local aircraft firm of Hobsons, later Lucas Aerospace, where he worked for 20 years. Duffy is a Roman Catholic. He says he is no zealot, but believes in the motto 'I am my brother's keeper' – that the strong must help the weak. He has a deep, unyielding hatred of communism and he also dislikes political chameleons who change their views as the climate dictates. Recalling his time as a Midlands official in the early 1970s, when he faced the derision of the broad left which then dominated the area, he says: 'I came out of the jungle.' His breezy resilience and surprising self-confidence have helped him enormously. It is this mixture of pugnacity and sheer ordinariness that has given Duffy an unexpected strength to survive and prosper in the tough inner world of the AUEW politics where no prisoners are taken. In 1975 he won the Executive Council seat for the enormous number five region that stretches from Manchester to the west Midlands from Bob Wright, a clear sign of the in-built advantage to the right-wing faction of the postal ballot system. Duffy tipped George Butler, Coventry divisional organizer, for the right-wing presidential ticket. But he will be hard put to have the same kind of impact on the trade union movement as his predecessor Hugh Scanlon had.

The left turn of the Engineers between 1967 and 1977 was not entirely unexpected. Lord Bill Carron found it an increasingly difficult task to keep his union behind the Labour and TUC establishment by the mid-1960s. His bullying use of the bloc vote at conferences became legendary. As Harold Wilson explained:

The congress [of 1967] went badly for the government with the passing of hostile resolutions on Vietnam, prices and incomes and unemployment. The majorities were not all that large, mainly because the president of the Engineers, Lord Carron, insisted on using Carron's law – where as president of the union he claimed to decide what general union policy meant on any congress or Labour conference vote – to throw a million votes on the government side. He would not be there another year.

Wilson found Scanlon's 'tanks' on the lawn at Downing Street in 1969, when the militant AEU president took a forceful stand against the proposed industrial relations legislation. But with his genuine devotion to the ideas of shopfloor democracy, Scanlon was never able to turn the national committee of the union into an obedient instrument of his personal authority. In 1973 he even found – much to his embarrassment – that the National Committee refused to let him attend the TUC–government Downing Street talks on economic policy. The AUEW president was – more than any other union boss – responsible for the total defeat of the Conservatives' Industrial Relations Act. Not only did the AUEW position at the 1971 Congress over instruction not to register win the day, but the union refused to attend and defend itself in the National Industrial Relations Court when under attack. Such an *à l'outrance* position steadied doubters in the TUC over the wisdom of the non-cooperation strategy, though it brought a number of troublesome cases with heavy fines for the AUEW. Most notable were the affairs of a tiny engineering firm in Surrey called Con-Mech, which nearly led to a national engineering strike in the spring of 1974.

Scanlon was far less successful in gaining higher wages for his members in the engineering industry, despite the militancy.

He came to office as a result of growing rank and file frustration
with pay restraint. His predecessor, Lord Carron, had taken an
openly cooperative line with the employers. The 1964 agreement at national level was hailed by Carron as 'one of the most
outstanding events in nearly seventy years of engineering negotiations'. In return for wage rises, a 40-hour working week by
July 1965 and more paid holidays, the unions in the Confederation agreed no national or local claims would be lodged for
three years on wages or conditions unless they were to cure
anomalies or inequities within a firm. The unions even conceded that the guaranteed week should be suspended in any
company if work was disrupted by a strike in another firm in
the Engineering Employers' Federation. In 1968 Scanlon wanted
to take a tough attitude, but he was over-ruled by his National
Committee and an agreement was signed to last another three
years. Under the threat of a national strike the engineering
employers conceded skilled men should receive a minimum of
£19 a week in 1971, unskilled men £15 and women £13. Everyone was to have two all-round increases of 6s a week and holidays were increased to three weeks a year. Scanlon was an
outspoken critic of the rather convoluted procedures for resolving industrial relations issues in the engineering industry,
which were enshrined in the 1922 York Memorandum.

As AUEW president, Scanlon led the union negotiating team
from the Confederation of Shipbuilding and Engineering
Unions (CSEU) in the annual national pay negotiations with
the Engineering Employers' Federation. The AUEW dominates
the nineteen affiliate unions in the Confederation, which has a
small full-time secretariat under Alex Ferry, the general secretary, in London's Walworth Road. In the autumn of 1971 the
Confederation submitted a militant claim to the employers for
a £25 a week minimum skilled time rate, a 35-hour working
week, four weeks' holiday, increased overtime and shift payments and no productivity concessions. Negotiations broke
down in January 1972 and the AUEW National Committee
agreed to pursue their struggle at plant level. District initiatives
were taken in Manchester and Sheffield. As many as thirty factories were occupied by their workers in the spring of 1972, but
the union found local employers too well organized. The
AUEW lost as much as £2,500,000 in strike benefit as a result

of the local strikes. The eventual settlement with the engineering employers amounted to only a 7 per cent pay increase. Militancy went down to humiliating defeat.

Indeed, during Scanlon's years at the head of the AUEW, engineering workers suffered a severe relative decline in their earning power. By 1977 the pay differential for a skilled engineering worker was the lowest it had been for twenty years. In 1975 the take-home pay of a skilled married craftsman with two children under 11 was a mere 23 per cent above that of labourers, compared with 32 per cent in 1963. The skill differential has virtually disappeared in the motor car industry. In the south-east of England a semi-skilled worker was actually getting more than a man with a craft skill. No wonder the numbers of workers being trained from five to seven years as apprentices fell off sharply in the early 1970s. In the mid-1960s the annual intake averaged around 18,600. By the late 1970s it was running at around 10,500. Over the last decade craftsmen have declined in the engineering industry from 754,000 to 566,000.

Most of the anger and frustration among toolmakers and other skilled men in Leyland between 1977 and 1979 stemmed from the erosion of their skill differentials. It led to the emergence of Roy Fraser and his unofficial Craftsmen's Organization with the clear threat of breakaway. Two years of flat rate pay policy, dictated by the needs of the low paid, had undermined their position. The AUEW leadership must share some of the blame for this. Scanlon and the National Committee (moving rightwards after 1974) were more ready to stand by a Labour government through loyalty than press for higher wages for their membership. But there was one achievement during the Scalon years, which reduced the power of the employers. The notorious *status quo* clause of the 1922 memorandum was modified, so that union members did not have to wait until the exhaustion of the long disputes procedure before resolving a problem.

The AUEW has a dual leadership. There is a refreshingly blunt quality about John Boyd, who won a resounding victory over Bob Wright to become general secretary in the spring of 1975. He is no equivocator, ready to trim and appease the powerful broad left, which dominated the Engineering section from the late 1960s until the mid-1970s. Ever since his early years as an apprentice in the Lanarkshire town of Motherwell in the late 1930s, Boyd has fought a long, often lonely struggle against the always vocal and well-entrenched Communist faction in his own union and their band of Labour left allies. 'In all the countless elections I have had to face in my life, only Communists or their friends have opposed me,' he said in an interview in June 1975. Not that he has proved any the less a forthright, courageous fighter for the rights and welfare of engineering workers. Indeed in 1937, at the precocious age of 19, Boyd was leading a revolt of Clydeside apprentices against the miserable levels of pay that youngsters earned in the industry at that time. 'Our action was a necessary response to oppressive wages,' argues Boyd. That particular militancy proved highly successful. The mighty Engineering Employers' Federation – the toughest, most effective employers' organization in the country – was forced to concede negotiating rights for apprentices through the industry's national agreement and a 30s increase in their basic weekly pay packet.

Boyd acquired an early reputation as a keen union activist. He was elected an official door-keeper in the local AEU branch when he was only 16. His job was to keep out strangers from the meetings. In those days branches met in the backroom of pubs and served as centres of social life. Boyd also had to collect the subs from members at the door. Boyds' rapid promotion by election through the union hierarchy paralleled his advance as a skilled engineering worker. At 21 he became a convenor at Moss End engineering works outside Motherwell. Six years later he moved on to a job at Philips Radio in Hamilton, where he was also a union convenor and helped to recruit the entire 1,500-strong shopfloor into the AEU. By that time Boyd was also an elected member of the union's local Lanarkshire district committee. When 28, he won an election to the post of assistant divisional organizer on Clydeside. In his new job Boyd found himself surrounded by Communist officials who were determined to squeeze him out. But within two years he had foiled their efforts by defeating the Communist incumbent for the top job of divisional organizer. Boyd was then only 31 – the youngest person ever to be elected in the AEU to such a high position. Two years later in 1953 he was elected to the Executive Council for Region 1 – Scotland and the north-west of

England. Until his recent triumph, Boyd held that job for over twenty years. 'I have always had to defend my position, though my constituency has always been over 400 miles from where I work,' he said, for Executive Council work has meant constant attendance at the AEU's Peckham headquarters. Constant re-elections failed to unseat Boyd. 'Last time the Communists trooped round Scotland like circus clowns,' he recalled. 'They brought in folk groups, and Jimmy Reid and Jimmy Airlie, living in the pseudo-glory of the Upper Clyde work-in, addressed the meetings. But it made no difference.' Boyd was returned with a massive majority in an area where the AEU's membership has grown from 24,000 to 66,000 during his time on the Executive Council.

General secretary Jim Conway's death in the DC10 crash in 1974 gave Boyd a belated opportunity to recoup his political fortunes in the union. He beat left-wing contender Bob Wright easily. The job of general secretary lacks the publicity and potential glamour of the presidency, but its clearly defined functions in the rule-book provide plenty of scope for Boyd to demonstrate his talents. He is now the hirer and firer of the 650-strong union administrative staff. It is his task to make sure the Engineering section operates as an effective unit – a point Boyd stressed in his election manifesto. He also edits the union's monthly journal. His signed leading articles provide a platform for right-wing Labour views. Not that Boyd can behave like an autocrat, even if he wanted to, which he doesn't. 'I believe in fighting for policies which I think are correct,' he said in 1975. 'But when the National Committee takes a decision, I won't try to sabotage it in the journal. I'm nothing, except for what the members have made me.' Much to his obvious annoyance, the Executive removed him from the TUC General Council, where he had sat since 1967, and replaced him with the eccentric Maoist member, Reg Birch.

Some AUEW members believe Boyd is too obsessed with the need for efficiency, but he inherited a serious financial problem when he came into office. The Scanlon policy of sanctioning local strikes with payment of individual benefits from the central fund hit the union's assets very badly. The sum in the central fund dropped from £17 million in 1967 to £11.7 million in 1973. There was a falling away in membership contributions with arrears owed of nearly £2,000,000. Under Boyd's management finances have improved, though only slowly. Inflation has not helped to remedy the Engineering section's financial troubles. The arrears problem was still serious. But the position improved in the late 1970s. By 31 December 1978 the value of the combined funds totalled £18,149,228, with £5,378,724 paid out in benefit, just over £2,000,000 in dispute pay.

Bitter internal strife between right and left over the direction the union should take alienated potential members. No other union in Britain allows its members the chance to elect all their full-time officials down to district level like the Engineering section. Nor, once one of them is elected, can they enjoy the certainty of holding office for life. Any newly elected official faces another contest within three years and if again successful, elections every successive five years. This unique method of accountability dates back to the ultra-democratic craft traditions of the union's pioneers in 1851 when the Amalgamated Society of Engineers was first founded. It is one method of trying to prevent the growth of a permanent, unfeeling bureaucracy, out of touch with the rank and file, and it stops the rise of boss figures who can hold undisputed sway over the union machine. The checks and balances enshrined in the structure of the Engineering section ensures no person or faction dominates its proceedings. It is a prescription for paralysis. This remains a real cause of weakness in the union. The unique separation of powers, that would have found favour with the American Founding Fathers, has institutionalized a two-party system in the AUEW Engineering section and bred severe deadlock.

The primary policy-making body of the section is the fifty-two-strong National Committee, which meets annually. Its members are all rank and file members of the union and they are presided over by the president in the chair who once had a casting vote. With him is the general secretary and three or four of the executive councillors on a yearly alternating basis, who can take part in the discussion but do not vote. Two members are elected annually from each of the twenty-six organizing divisions to the National Committee. Unlike other parts of the union, those serving on the National Committee are not elected directly by ballot through the rank and file but indirectly at the first session of each divisional committee when it meets, following the annual election of branch officers and delegates every November. As the rule-book states, the National Committee 'shall discuss past and future policy of the union, with a view to giving the Executive Council instructions for the ensuing year, and may initiate any policy which they think would be beneficial to the union. Every fifth year after 1980 the National Committee will consider any changes in rule that might be suggested under a rules revision conference.'

The balance of political power on the National Committee is usually very close but it does not faithfully mirror the moods of the membership, as emphasized in postal ballot voting. During the late 1960s and early 1970s the broad left were in the ascendancy. After 1974 the pendulum swung slowly the other way. Every May there is a trial of strength between the highly organized if unrecognized political factions within the National Committee. The tedium of procedural wrangling and ritualistic debate often mask a real power struggle. Who sits on the Standing Orders Committee is vital, for it is they who decide the order of business. At the 1976 National Committee get-together in Scarborough, Scanlon was forced to toss a coin when Jimmy Reid, the militant from Clydeside, and John Weakley, the moderate from Llanelli, both collected twenty-six votes for a place on the Standing Orders Committee. Reid won the call but it made no crucial difference to the balance where the right won a majority of the five members. This proved a crucial success for out-witting the left that year.

The seven-man Executive Council is responsible to the National Committee. Each is elected by postal ballot by the registered members through seven electoral divisions. Executive councillors face the prospect of fighting for re-election once every three years until they reach the age of 60. The rule-book lays down precise details of what they have to do. Take Rule 15 (3), for instance. This states: 'The Executive Council's hours of business shall be from 9 am to 5 pm with one hour allowed for dinner, Mondays to Fridays.' Any councillor who fails to attend stipulated meetings or neglects his duties without giving a satisfactory reason can be fined 75 pence for a first offence and £1.50 for the second. Ultimately a negligent councillor can be removed from office. The union also has two assistant general secretaries, who are elected in the same way, and expected to help the general secretary in his work.

At divisional level the rank and file in each elect a full-time officer, once every three years, as divisional organizer. He is responsible for recruitment, negotiating with employers at works and local conferences, and carrying out the various stages of the procedure agreement in engineering. The divisional organizer also acts as secretary for each of the twenty-six divisional committees. Those bodies are made up of delegates elected by the district committees on the basis of two delegates for each district of 1,000 members or more, with one delegate for each smaller district. The divisional committees serve two basic purposes. First, they discuss resolutions which are passed from branch and district level, and if they approve them they go on the agenda of the National Committee. Second, they pick from among their own number two representatives to go to the National Committee in the summer.

A more crucial level in the working of the union is the district committee. There are around 267 of them, made up of representatives for every two branches in the district up to a maximum of twenty-five representatives alongside shop stewards in the ratio of one to every 5,000 members. The whole committee is elected every year – half on the last meeting-night in June and the rest in November when the branch officers are also elected. Every district committee member is supposed to report back to his branch on what is going on at district meetings on pain of a 5 pence fine. There is also a 25 pence fine if what happens at district committee is leaked to the outside world before the branch gets to know. The rule-book lays down that all district committee members are paid 37.5 pence for attendance and refunded for second-class return fares to and from home to the meetings. Unlike other unions, the Engineering section treats the district committee as a very important layer in the labyrinthine structure of the union. It is provided with considerable power. According to the rule-book the district committee can summon any member working at the trade in the district under its control to acquire information on working conditions or to investigate allegations against any member of the union. There is a fine of 50 pence if a member disobeys a summons to attend by the district committee. But the committee is not a secure, tyrannical oligarchy. The branches have the power to remove a representative at any time, if dissatisfied with his or her conduct. The president and secretary of every district committee must be elected by ballot every three years.

The district committee has the power, subject only to Executive Council approval, in dealing with and regulating rates of pay, hours of work, overtime terms, piecework and general conditions in its district among the rank and file. It can also enter into negotiations with employers in the district to enforce a closed shop of members. Some of the rules look like affirmations of the ideal rather than reality. For example, it is stated: 'Systematic overtime shall not be allowed in any district, and district committees shall see that this is strictly enforced and endeavour to minimize overtime as far as possible.' The district committee also has the power to approve strikes. It can hold a ballot vote of the members in the district to have a local levy and this can be done without Executive Council approval in London. No strike can be called affecting district members without a three to two majority of support by those voting in a ballot. A majority vote must be reached before a strike settlement can be reached. The district committee keeps a register of members who are out of work in the district. It also authorizes the appointment of stewards and their committees in the plants. No steward can be recognized – even if elected by the shopfloor – until he or she has the approval of the district committee. The rule-book tries to ensure the union structure keeps a close rein on the stewards. They are expected to report regularly – at least once every three months – in writing to the district committee on what has been happening at their particular workplace. For its part, the district committee must convene a stewards' meeting once a quarter and those not turning up are fined.

There is also a final appeal court of the union, made up of eleven rank and file members, elected triennially from eleven divisions. It meets every October, usually for a fortnight, to adjudicate on complaints, but as this body is also a highly political organization, those seeking justice often find it better to go to a court of law for redress of a grievance about the union.

The net result of this complex organization, where Duffy and Boyd (president and general secretary) sit together in reasonable cooperation, is the in-built existence of political intrigue. It legitimizes the party system in the union and as neither faction can hope to gain a complete stranglehold over all levels of the union, the section is condemned to a permanent struggle, where there are no total victories. Boyd likes it that way. 'Constant election creates a degree of interest in the Engineers. We have no need for constitutional or secret political disciplines. We are a hotbed of political debate, the foremost union for argument. Elections are the basic fabric of our union,' he said to me in June 1975.

The union has always been very conscious of its origins as a craft body for the skilled men of the 1850s, the labour aristocracy of mid-Victorian Britain. From its beginnings in 1851, the Amalgamated Society of Engineers (ASE) took pride in its democratic structure, founded on the ruins of the Journeymen Engine Makers Society and the Old Mechanics. The ASE claimed high subscriptions and a controlled entry into the engineering trade. Its prudence and respectability were matched by a stubborn independence. The early days were scarred by industrial conflict over the abolition of piecework and sytematic overtime. There was a three-month lock-out of ASE members by engineering employers in London and Lancashire. This was no red revolution. Even Lord Goderich – later the Marquis of Ripon – donated £500 to the ASE strike fund. But the ASE was no mere friendly society with high benefits for its members and a willingness to defend the interests of engineering craftsmen from arbitrary treatment from employers. There was also a wider idealistic vision, best exemplified in the columns of the union's journal, *The Operative*, edited by William Newton, the first general secretary. As he wrote on 9 August 1851:

Behind these reforms, greater ones, affecting society as well as politics, rise up from the darkness of the future – that future which may be the beginning of a bright and glorious end, when those who make the wealth of the world shall be treated as justly as the ox which was not muzzled when treading the corn.

In their evidence to the 1867 Royal Commission the ASE acknowledged the division of interest in industry: 'It is in their [the employers'] interest to get the labour done by as low a rate as possible and it is ours to get as high a rate of wages as possible and you can never reconcile these two things.' But the ASE spurned Marx's attempt to get them to join the First International and for its first forty years it became a bulwark of craft respectability and independence. However technological change in the engineering industry began to undermine the ASE's position, particularly in the machine shop with its fitters and turners who lay at the heart of the union's élitist empire. New machinery like the capstan and turret lathe and the external and surface grinder did not need broadly skilled craftsmen to operate them. There was a growing fear of 'dilution' in the skills of engineering workers. This was coupled with a much tighter form of managerial supervision. The ASE went on the defensive by trying to impose a ban on piecework and limit overtime, but these attempts were not often successful. After 1892 unemployment proved an added problem. A new militancy based on socialism began to gain ground in the union, through the influence of Tom Mann and John Burns. In the 1891 election for the ASE general secretary's post, Mann came a close runner-up to assistant secretary John Anderson, and in the following year the militants triumphed at the union conference with a radical organizational reform involving the creation of an executive of full-time officials elected by eight electoral districts and the appointment of full-time organizers and negotiators to act as go-betweens from the centre to the district committees. Membership was widened to bring in other skilled groups.

In 1922, efforts to commit the new union to a more manifestly ideological programme failed. A call for industrial unionism and reference to the class struggle were not included in the rule-book. Nor did a demand for workers' control win many votes on the National Committee. It was agreed by twenty-eight votes to seventeen that the AEU's primary aim should be 'the control of industry in the interests of the community'. A later sentence adds that the union is also dedicated to 'the extension of cooperative production to assist in altering the competitive system of society for a cooperative system'. In practice, both right and left remain very conscious of the craft tradition, even though skilled workers now make up a minority of the labour force in engineering. It was not until 1926 that the AEU opened its doors to male unskilled workers and 1940 before junior workers learning their skill through an apprenticeship could also become members. Women were admitted to the union two years later, a belated recognition of their value in the war effort on the shopfloor. There were 166,457 women in the Engineering section in 1976.

The Engineers have five different membership categories with varying subscription rates and benefits, but it remains section one that dominates the union. To join that section you have to produce satisfactory evidence of having worked four years at one or more of the fully skilled trades, except where fewer years' apprenticeship is the established rule, or to have worked three years at any trade other than fully skilled trades. As the rule-book says: 'A candidate into section one who has worked three years in the workshop in addition to at least four years in the engineering department of a technical school shall be eligible.' Potential members of the section must be at least 19 and under 35. Once they are over 30 they must provide clear evidence of their age. The rules explicitly exclude anyone suffering from 'a major disability or a constitutional disease unless he/she can produce a medical certificate to the effect that his/her failing is not detrimental to him/her in his/her capacity as a worker'. The Executive Council has to examine the medical certificate of any candidate in those cases. In December 1978 there were only 293,727 members in section one. Far more popular are sections five (437,575) and five A (390,558). Anybody between 18 and 50 employed in the engineering trade is eligible for membership of those sections, which broadly cater for the less skilled workers in the engineering industry. Section four (67,140) cover the apprentices and junior workers between the ages of 16 and 20 employed in any branch of the engineering trade.

The arrogance of craft power was well conveyed by Sir Bill Carron, the AEF president, in his verbal evidence to the Donovan Commission in 1967, when he was asked about restrictions on training. He informed the Commission:

My own industry, without any logical reasons, is entitled to as many rings of protection as any in the United Kingdom. We are entitled to our views, whether logical or not, and our view is that for our protection we are going to keep the situation which has

existed in a fairly satisfactory way.... I am not going to justify
this at all.

There was a similar disdain in the summer of 1975 when Hugh
Scanlon refused to come and give evidence to the Commons
Select Committee investigating the motor car industry. The
quixotic Maoist, Reg Birch, was sent along instead and he
earned a rebuke from the Committee in their report for his
eccentric behaviour.

The Engineers were attacked for their narrow craft mentality
by the Brookings Institution in its study of Britain in 1968, but
more recent research qualifies the assumption that the AUEW
is unsympathetic to the spread of engineering skills through
training and dilution. Ziderman and Walder tried to discover
whether government training centre trainees in engineering
found it hard to get a job with their freshly acquired skill. Of
the sample of 1,000 who left a GTC in April 1972, a third of
the trainees were given less than fully skilled acceptance in
their first job, while about a fifth were granted fully skilled
status at once. Only one trainee out of five believed that the
unions had played any role at all one way or the other. Of
those who mentioned the unions, as many as 60 per cent said
they were helpful. Less than 8 per cent of the sample believed
that the unions made it difficult for trainees to get jobs. The real
power of obstruction or cooperation rests with the AUEW district committees. Anthony Rees found local officials in the
AEU's division 6 Sunderland district refused to let GTC
trainees into occupations regarded as skilled, but he also discovered the Scotland division took a far less rigorous attitude.
As many as 72.2 per cent of Hall and Miller's sample believed
that union acceptance was 'very good'. But in recent years the
national leaders have backed widening skill opportunities. The
appointment of Hugh Scanlon as chairman of the Engineering
Industry Training Board in the spring of 1975 was an indication
of the erosion of the old craft resentments. His public backing
for training is a good example of how responsibility breeds
realism and compassion.

The AUEW has acquired a reputation in recent years for being an ineffective union. Its education services remain rudimentary, with no more than a handful of residential schools a

year. The Research Department at Peckham is little more than a source of basic information, rather than an instrument of policy formation. Leaders of other unions are often embarrassed by the calibre and lack of preparedness of AUEW executive members in collective bargaining. The union has failed to make any inroads into new areas of recruitment, and over the past fifteen years it has virtually stagnated.

The amalgamation with the constructional engineers (CEU), the foundrymen and DATA, which took place after ballots, has yet to be carried through to a successful finish. On four separate occasions before 1979 the AUEW National Committee turned down full amalgamation proposals, so that the so-called AUEW is still made up of four virtually separate parts with four rule-books, sets of benefits, union structures and financial systems. All of them come together every year in the national conference, but the AUEW speaks with an ineffective voice. The big setback was the failure of the union to attract the 82,000-strong National Union of Vehicle Builders into a merger in 1969. It joined forces with the TGWU instead. This meant the AUEW lost considerable ground in the British motor industry.

Negativism is in part due to the traditions and unique structure of the union, where partisan political warfare usually outweighs purely trade union matters. Yet this is not the whole cause of the failure to achieve a successful amalgamation. The lack of progress towards full amalgamation also stemmed from the lack of trust between the Engineering section and the 200,000-strong Technical, Administrative and Supervisory Section (TASS), led by a fluent and tough young Communist, Ken Gill. TASS was formerly known as DATA (Draughtsmen's and Allied Technicians' Association) and, when it was founded on Clydeside in 1913, the Association of Engineering and Shipbuilding Draughtsmen (AESD). Until the post-war period the union was a mild, exclusive organization with an undemocratic structure and an apathetic membership, concentrated almost entirely among draughtsmen and tracers in the drawing offices of engineering and shipbuilding firms. It did not join the CSEU as an affiliate until the mid-1940s, but over the next fifteen years the union left captured control with a militant programme. Jim Mortimer's appointment as editor of *The Draughtsman* in 1948 was hailed as a left victory and so was the election of George Doughty to the general secretaryship in 1952. Six years later, Graham Wootton has written (*Parliamentary Affairs*, vol XXIX, no 1), the left replaced the right as the 'controlling decision-makers'. The numerical expansion of the union – to be known as DATA after 1960 – did not widen the participative element. In Wootton's words:

At times conference is more like a professional wrestling match than a parliament: the activists prefer the playful kick in the teeth to the serpentine wrigglings and elaborate courtesies of politicians anxious to go down in history as 'good parliamentarians'. This increased measure of democratic control within the union, which has not been accompanied by any consequential weakening of its bargaining strength *vis-à-vis* the employers, does not seem to have involved a greater degree of rank and file participation, judged merely by numbers, than before the war. Despite every encouragement from headquarters, the number of members who play an active role is still small, even tiny.

During the 1960s DATA gained a reputation for its guerrilla-style militancy in pressing for higher wages. Dispute benefit was fixed at 100 per cent of the member's wage. Companies were selected as targets by the union for wage push. New militant tactics such as work-to-rules were introduced to drive the point home. Firms often found themselves helpless to combat such a strategy. In 1969 the shipbuilding employers staged a lock-out of DATA members in response to a massive wage claim, but the union imposed a national subscription levy on the entire membership to ensure their rank and file did not suffer and the employers were forced to give way. DATA members voluntarily donated their first week's increase into union funds to ensure they did not become depleted. Rolls-Royce in Derby was the scene of a bitter and successful DATA strike in the summer of 1970. In the previous three years the union grew from 73,024 members to 105,418.

Such activity was not entirely without cost to the union. In 1970 DATA paid out nearly £450,000 in dispute pay compared with less than £200,000 in 1969, largely because of the Rolls-Royce stoppage which was said to have cost them £250,000. In addition, DATA were for the first time faced with a heavy burden of benefits to unemployed members. By the end of

1970 some 1,600 were out of work and more than £55,0 had
been paid in unemployment benefit during the year. Less on
members were not enough to keep DATA's funds buoy, so
the 1971 conference reduced the strike pay to 60 per c of
the basic wage and it asked the rank and file to allow the le r-
ship to decide what disputes to promote and not launch 'u s
and expensive' adventures. None the less, the newly n
TASS was ready to take militant action, when necessar
still remains one of the most aggressive and uncomprom
unions in the TUC, even if the majority of the members
contract out of the political levy.

During the early 1970s the Communist Party strengthened
grip on the union. Under the amalgamation plans the Engine
ing section of the AUEW has tried to establish the principle
election for all full-time officers by the postal ballot method f
all sections of the AUEW. Gill, who was not elected but a
pointed to his top post in TASS in 1973, resisted such a pro
posal, if it was to be applied to those full-timers already in office
in TASS. In the opinion of the right wing in the Engineering
section, Gill helped to turn TASS into a highly disciplined
monolith under Communist domination. Under its internal reform, the TASS leadership appointed more than thirty full-time
officials for newly created regional offices. Over half of them
were said to be Communists; the rest were of the 'broad left'.
They were also reputed to have an average age of only 40 and
they were to keep their jobs for life under the amalgamation
proposals. Mrs Judith Hunt, a member of the Communist Party
Executive, was made women's officer in 1975. In January 1975
International Socialism published an analysis of the structure
of the union, in which it was suggested that 'without any doubt
the success of the Communist Party in TASS has been more
spectacular than in any other union since the war'. At least
seventeen out of the present twenty-eight organizers were believed to be Communists and two of the four national officers.
In 1975 TASS abolished its old twenty-six-strong Executive
Committee, which was elected by the membership every three
years. It was replaced by a new executive of fifteen, each member representing the twelve regions (a group of divisions),
elected every three years by an 'electoral college' on rotation.

Gill and his colleagues have already illustrated their deter-minion to push for militant policies in the AUEW, even if this leads to an embarrassment for the Engineering section. At the 19 TUC, Scanlon was compelled to twist Gill's arm publicly to get him to withdraw his motion attacking the social contract. Efforts to convert TASS to the principle of election through postal ballots in future for existing full-time officers failed. It is estimated that TASS has enjoyed a 90 per cent increase in full-time organizers compared with only a 15 per cent rise in its membership. At no time will any of these full-time officials have to face the problem of re-election through the ballot box, as their colleagues in the Engineering section are required to do. It is not surprising that the broad left on the AUEW National Committee have a difficult time in defending the Gill version of union democracy, when it comes to amalgamation debates. Perhaps TASS and the AUEW should part company, but this would be a sad blow to the ideal of one union for the engineering industry. On the other hand, all the merger proposals so far suggested would give TASS a disproportionate number of seats on the expanded National Committee (as it would the CEU and the Foundry Workers). If Gill and his colleagues swallowed the principle of postal ballot re-elections, the problem would soon be solved. But such a system would probably ensure the eventual defeat of Communist rule in TASS.

12 The loyal brothers

The 965,000-strong General and Municipal Workers' Union (GMWU) has always proved a bastion of loyalty and 'moderation' to the TUC since its formation in 1924. Today is no exception. Since January 1973 it has been led by the quiet, stooping, fluent David Basnett. Born in Liverpool in 1924, he spent twenty-five years as a full-time GMWU official before being elected to the top job. His placid, faintly academic approach belies an inner toughness. In a very short time, Basnett has become a major influential figure in the inner group of the TUC. More at home arguing in private with ministers and civil servants than declaiming from the public platform, Basnett is now a key TUC negotiator, one of the NEDDY six. He has sat on the TUC General Council since 1966, is now a part-time director of the National Enterprise Board and was a member of the McGregor Commission on the newspaper industry.

Basnett grew up in the shadow of the GMWU. His father was the union's district secretary in the Liverpool, North Wales and Irish region for many years. He became a district officer himself in 1948 and in 1954 got the post of national education officer – the first appointee to a newly created job. Six years later, Basnett became GMWU national officer covering the chemical, glass and rubber industries. He stayed in that post until his election to the general secretaryship in November 1972. Basnett is not a 'moderate' for its own sake. He has pulled the GMWU back from the right-wing isolation in which it was marooned under Lord Jack Cooper (1962–73). It now stands more in the centre of the TUC fulcrum, close by the TGWU. Basnett has no time for what he calls 'passive organizations that do not fight for their members' interests', for unions that 'make sweetheart agreements with companies to impose an artificial industrial peace'. In his view 'the trade union movement is one of the principal democratic elements in our society', 'a counter-balance and check on arbitrary actions' by employers.

As Basnett wrote in *Socialist Commentary* (September 1973): 'Our job as trade unionists is not merely to haggle about slices of the economic "cake". We are in politics. We are concerned about where power lies and concerned that that power is not abused.' This is not the kind of language that his predecessor, Jack Cooper, used to deploy. Under Cooper, the GMWU treated its members more like clients than participants. The members paid their dues. In return they expected certain services – provided they did as they were told.

Nobody can deny the union's professionalism grew impressively during the 1960s. Its headquarters moved out to a large country house – Ruxley Towers, in the midst of the Surrey stockbroker belt. In 1965 the reserves of the GMWU totalled around £5,000,000; by 1974 they had risen to just under £13,000,000. The Research Department, now under the direction of Larry Whitty, was made into one of the most effective in the trade union movement. A financial information service, advice bureau and legal section have all been started up at head office. Education of stewards and lay activists has been boosted with the opening of a residential college at Woodstock – in Surrey. Another was opened in Cheshire in 1976. Every region (there are ten of them) has its own education officer and many run courses of their own. In 1974 as many as 6,000 students went on such courses, three times the figure of a decade ago. There is a competitive spirit in GMWU education. The courses are closely linked to the provision of a professional full-time officer élite. In the GMWU the joint union/management approach to industrial relations has proved a success. Around 4.0 per cent of the total GMWU budget now goes on education, but this will have to be increased in the future.

As a way of making itself look more attractive to potential recruits, the GMWU under Cooper boosted its fringe benefits, notably introducing an accident benefit and new retirement gratuity. Big increases were also made to the fatal accident benefit and the disablement grant in return for a sharp rise in contributions. The Cooper proposals just scraped through the 1963 Congress on a close vote of 172 to 161. During the 1960s the GMWU was rarely involved in disputes of any kind. In

1967 the union spent only £17,746 on dispute benefit out of benefit payments totalling £756,595. In 1973 the dispute benefit totalled as much as £348,431 out of benefit payments amounting to £1,310,039. The GMWU is changing from a benefit to a service based union.

The GMWU was founded in 1924 through an amalgamation of the National Union of General Workers, the National Amalgamated Union of Labour and the Municipal Employees' Association, but its roots go back to the militant Gasworkers' Union founded by the socialist Will Thorne in 1889, with its demand for an 8-hour working day. Eleanor Marx was an enthusiastic champion of the Gasworkers' Union, serving on its Executive Committee. The Gasworkers were among the most prominent supporters of the Labour Representation Committee before Taff Vale accelerated trade union affiliations to the new body – to be transformed into the Labour Party in 1906.

The union has rarely let its hair down during the fifty years of amalgamation. It did so in 1959 when GMWU delegates at Congress upset the Labour leadership by voting by a narrow majority for unilateral disarmament. Tom Williamson, general secretary of the time, had to call a special Congress of the union together within weeks to get that decision reversed. For the most part, the GMWU has provided loyal, stalwart backing for every twist and turn of Labour orthodoxy. In 1950 the union even stood behind Sir Stafford Cripps's pay restraint policy after the TUC had abandoned it. The GMWU was a determined opponent of Bevanism in the Labour Party, and supported German rearmament. It was one of the very few big unions which espoused the cause of the European Common Market during the 1960s and early 1970s.

Such was the 'moderation' of the GMWU that Lord Cooper was even quite ready to register under the 1971 Industrial Relations Act. Only a threat of revolt from the union's Executive Council held him in check. In the TUC the GMWU stood as a stubborn, ineffective right-wing voice, which the world had passed by.

The bitter seven-week unofficial strike of glass workers at Pilkingtons in St Helens in the early summer of 1970 shook the GMWU to its foundations. The rank and file revolt was as much against the slothful ways of full-time officialdom as the company. Basnett remembers it well, for he was the national officer for the glass industry. Pilkington proved a watershed in the union's history.

It was not just pressure from the shopfloor that began to push the GMWU into internal reform. Far more central to change was the unmistakable fact that union membership was stagnating. The old regional-based structure of the GMWU with its praetorian guard was unattractive to other unions, who might be seeking a merger. There was no public opposition to the 1968 Congress decision to investigate 'the possibility of a trade group structure with vertical and horizontal integration'. Lord Cooper explained what he had in mind when he addressed delegates to the following year's Congress in the Isle of Man. There was no need to carry through root and branch upheaval. What Cooper argued was that 'the best course would be to graft on to what we already have such changes as current circumstances warrant'. The union's aim should be to discover a way of 'improving our industrial communications which preserves our system of overall control and regional flexibility while encouraging greater membership participation and identification'. The industrial conference was seen as the instrument to achieve that reconciliation. This was to parallel, not usurp, the old structure. The annual industrial conferences were to be entirely consultative and not rival centres of power to challenge the regional secretaries. The 1969 change was a tentative first step towards a more industry-based general unionism, but it was made with some reluctance. As Cooper confessed to delegates:

While we were carrying out our investigations we became even more convinced of the merits of our way of organizing ourselves. If a union is not to disintegrate, it needs central decision-making. On th other hand, over-centralization can lead to rigidity. Our structure, in my view, gives us the best of both worlds.

Cooper did not appear to envisage that the industrial conferences could be integrated into the collective bargaining system of particular industries. In his opinion, such matters must be left to the full-time officers to determine. As he explained: 'Your national officers who negotiate centrally and your district officers whom we have to negotiate specially on a district basis have got to make their own judgement and make up their own minds as what kind of wage application or conditions application to promote.'

More than most major unions, the GMWU under Cooper began to face the serious problem of matching an emphasis on self-reliance with the provision of professional back-up services in the full-time organization. A report to the 1971 GMWU Congress revealed that only a third of the full-time officials in the union were trained at the union's Woodstock residential college between 1965 and 1969, while of the 4,000 new stewards coming forward every year (80 per cent unelected) no more than a quarter even attended a basic course in the regions. Cooper was alive to the difficulty of devolving power and responsibility down through the union hierarchy to lower levels, if those upon whom the new tasks fell were incapable of maximizing the opportunities. He explained this to the 1972 Congress:

It is no use demanding and developing devolution and responsibility unless those who are taking on new responsibilities are capable of carrying those responsibilities. In fact we can do more harm than good if the new negotiators are not capable and knowledgeable about all the modern managerial techniques in relation to which they have to do their bargaining. There must be a new concept of shop stewards far and away from the old cloth cap image.

'Our trouble was we were not attuned to expansion. The leadership was simply unaware of what was going on,' said David Basnett in November 1976. Despite the cautious changes, the GMWU failed to enjoy the growth its union competitors achieved in local government and the national health service, between 1969 and 1974. Under Basnett, much greater emphasis has been placed on the need for membership expansion. Areas of major growth for the GMWU during the early 1970s were hotels and catering, and white-collar staff (in MATSA – Managerial, Administrative, Technical and Supervisory Association).

In a quiet, unobtrusive way Basnett has been chipping away at some of the powers and prestige of the regional barons. The 1975 internal reforms extended the role of the lay activists in the decision-making process of the union. It was decided to abandon the old two-tier executive system and replace it with a single Executive Council, made up of the general secretary, the chairman and treasurer of the union and three representatives from each region, two of whom are lay members and the other the regional secretary. Those serving on the Executive Council are elected every two years from each regional council from within their ranks. The council meets six times a year with a special session to deal with union business at the TUC Congress. The working party that looked at how to improve the organization did not feel that industrial representation was

table 12.1 Where the regional strength of the GMWU lies
  (December 1963 and December 1978)

	1963	1978
Birmingham and West Midlands	96,000	98,400
Lancashire	106,000	99,774
Liverpool, North Wales and Ireland	59,000	78,936
London	96,000	87,630
Midland and East Coast	62,000	71,964
Northern	75,000	112,444
Scottish	72,000	104,695
Southern	80,000	81,000
South-West	42,000	47,396
Yorkshire and North Derby	71,000	85,176

table 12.2 The industrial power bases of the GMWU

	1963	1977
Food, drink and tobacco	37,000	56,000
Chemicals and allied	35,000	34,000
Engineering and shipbuilding	195,000	173,000
Glass	15,000	17,000
Other manufacturing (eg rubber)	31,000	37,000
Public service industries (gas, water, electricity)	115,000	101,000
Health service	20,000	23,000
Local government	145,000	190,000
White-collar (MATSA)	9,000	28,000
Hotels and catering	4,000	9,000

needed for the new council nor a place for women members. Clearly a compromise was reached between the national leadership and the regional barons. On the Finance and Organization Committees of the union, there are one representative from each region, seven of whom are lay activists, and three regional secretaries. The numerical balance is slightly different on the Services Committee, where six lay members from the regions sit alongside four regional secretaries. Those three subcommittees report to the Executive Council and meet every two to four months.

At the same time, in 1974 and 1975, the role of the industrial conference was strengthened and integrated more closely into the union structure. At the 1975 Aberdeen Congress as many as eighteen separate industrial conferences were proposed to be held regularly under the auspices of the appropriate industrial officer under the authority of Basnett. It was agreed that national industrial conferences should be called by national officers as negotiating forums and 'sounding boards for lay reaction to industrial developments'. The aim is to convene at least one industrial conference for each sector annually. Its composition is made up of delegates from the regional industrial conferences with each one entitled to send three elected lay delegates to the national get-togethers. For those regions with more than 5,000 financial members (at the preceding June quarter) in the appropriate industry or sector, members up to a maximum of six delegates are elected. It is the job of the regional secretaries to organize the regional industrial conferences with a maximum of forty delegates to attend. Systematic reporting of what goes on at industrial conferences goes to the Executive Council. The idea of creating industrial committees in the GMWU was turned down in 1975 on the grounds that such bodies would involve an overlap with the National Executive and the conferences themselves. Nor was the proposal that national industrial conferences should have the power to mandate officers in negotiating taken seriously by the reformers.

These changes have not drastically changed the internal power structure of the GMWU. Regional secretaries remain semi-autonomous centres of influence and authority. Derek Gladwin is the southern regional secretary. From his tasteful, wall-to-wall carpeted office in Surbiton, he covers a vast tract of territory – from Land's End to the white cliffs of Dover, up to the Thames Valley and across to Bristol. There are 81,000 GMWU members in Gladwin's area, covering a multitude of industries in the private and public sectors. Any outbreak of trouble becomes Gladwin's immediate concern. He is not merely there to administer the books and supervise the union machine. 'No national officer would come into my region to examine a problem without telling me,' he said when I interviewed him in 1975. With a staff of eighteen he has to keep a close eye on all the key industries in the region. He has to preside over the regional committee and enjoys considerable power in appointments of full-time staff. Gladwin champions the often discredited branch system for elections and dislikes the idea of postal balloting. 'Voting for a man or woman to go to Congress or a regional council meeting – this is a matter for discussion in the union and the best forum for that is the branch.' In his view a geographically based branch is the way to bring groups of workers from different industries together. 'We can't simply form a Congress out of people who work for particular factories or local authorities.'

Gladwin is fluent and tough, affable and thoughtful. He commands attention by his ability, not through pulling rank. His background is impeccable – Ruskin College, Oxford, and the London School of Economics where he collected a certificate in personnel administration. He worked for British Rail for a while and later in the fishing industry in Grimsby, his home town. It was in 1956 that he came south as a district officer in southern region, until he was appointed a national industrial officer in 1963, covering local government water supply and the health service.

Gladwin does not believe the prudent extension of more lay involvement in the decision-making process of the GMWU will erode the power of the regional secretary. In his view, there is no genuine division of interest between the full-time officials and the rank and file. He speaks of a 'fallacious antipathy between bureaucrats and lay members. At regional council or at the branches there is no real tension nor any grass roots demand to clip our powers.' What Gladwin does detect is 'a clear demand for involvement in things meaningful to collective bargaining'. He finds the time in his crowded working life for a few extra-curricular activities. Gladwin sits on the board of British Aerospace and he is a governor of Ruskin College, chairman of the Labour Party's Standing Orders Committee, a Justice of the Peace and a member of the English Tourist Board. The new reforms in the GMWU have added to and not lessened the work load.

There is a constant pressure in the union to increase self-sufficiency, but the burden put on us as a result is the greater. My main job is motivation. Our members are good, solid citizens. In a tragedy who do they turn to? They come to us or they suffer in silence. The steward or the branch secretary can help out but the expert is appreciated.

This is why in the view of the GMWU more union democracy does not mean a lesser role for the full-time official. The new climate in the union does require a more tolerant and patient regional secretary than was necessary in the past, more a diplomatist than a commander.

There are no strong trade union traditions in many parts of the southern region. 'It is difficult getting the barricades up in south-east Kent,' argues Gladwin, but he often finds the best branch secretaries work in those places. 'They are the local ombudsmen of the public services.' Gladwin admitted that he could do his job as regional secretary perfectly well without ever meeting a member, but he makes sure he gets out to a branch meeting once a week. 'The members won't believe in the union unless they see the whites of your eyes.' Keeping the branches from becoming empty shells is a constant preoccupation. 'We must try and see they stay alive. Otherwise the union will become nothing more than a gigantic insurance company.'

A new layer of full-time officialdom has been introduced into the GMWU structure since 1974 – the district officers. They have two main functions to perform – to improve branch servicing and contact and intensify recruitment drives. Gladwin has a handful of the new officers in his region who are responsible to him. What constitutes a district is defined by the region for organizational and recruitment potential. As the 1974 reform proposal explained of the district officer:

He will provide regular and direct contact between the branch and

the union. He will be their first line of access to its services.
Although the District objectives must be to encourage them to
become as self-reliant as possible in the handling of their own
industrial relations problems.

The idea is that the district officer will prove a more effective
force in the union than the old branch administrative officer
turned out to be in practice. The emphasis has moved from
the routines of administration to recruiting, servicing and negotiating. This provides the union with a more dynamic presence
at the grass roots, although it will be surprising if the new
arrangement provides the necessary impetus to invigorate
branch life and the activity of the rank and file. By the summer
of 1976, fifty-three district officers had been appointed.

Burly, bespectacled John Edmonds is the very model of a
modern trade union boss. During the early months of 1973 he
was leading the cause of Britain's gasworkers for higher pay
from his spacious carpet-lined office. Edmonds is one of the
eleven national industrial officers of the union. He took over
from Sir Fred Hayday after that stalwart's retirement in 1972.
With an earthy common sense and broad cockney accent, Edmonds looks as though he must have worked his way up to the
top of the union the hard way from the shopfloor. But he is
still a sprightly young man in his early thirties. It is not just his
comparative youth, among the usual greybeards of the trade
union movement, which makes Edmonds something of an
oddity. He also happens to be one of the very rare breed – a
trade union boss who is also a university graduate.

Edmonds was born in Camberwell, where his father works
in a warehouse as a supervisor checker. As a boy, he won a
scholarship to Christ's Hospital, and from there he went on to
Oriel College, Oxford, where he read modern history. On his
graduation in 1965, Edmonds took a job in the GMWU Research Department. He specialized in the local government
sector and took an active part in the 1969 and 1970 local government manual worker strikes. Edmonds made a highly favourable impression on the GMWU bosses, so he was taken
out of the Research Department and given a post as a trade
union officer in the southern region of the union. After two
years, under union rules, Edmonds faced election by the members. He won handsomely. Not long afterwards he was re-

called to Ruxley Towers to take charge of GMWU's 42,000 gasworkers.

Edmonds does not believe the fact that he went to university is anything of a handicap in his job, nor does he accept that it is a disadvantage not to have had any shopfloor experience. In his view, the full-time union officer and the steward perform different roles. By the very nature of his work the steward is really only familiar with his own workplace, but the officer must keep his eyes on wider priorities. As Edmonds explained when I interviewed him in March 1973: 'I must balance the long-term interests against the short-term, the demands of one group of workers against the demands of another group.' Before he became an officer, Edmonds had no clear idea of what the job involved, but he admits he has never felt more satisfied or comfortable. What made him go into trade unionism? Edmonds is unsure himself. He thinks a psychologist might be able to explain, but he puts it down vaguely to a 'deep sense' of wanting to get back to his origins. He finds the job of trade union officer a 'peculiar' one, for he must be accountable to 'a large number of people through a smaller number of people'. It is personal contact and confidence that counts in working with and through the stewards and members. Edmonds thrives in an atmosphere of 'constant argument and persuasion'.

Edmonds is lucky to be in a general union, which has always taken a keen interest in recruiting bright young men and women from the universities to staff the Research Department, such as Giles Radice, now Labour MP for Chester-le-Street, David Winchester at Warwick University and Dianne Hayter, the Fabian Society's general secretary. Most unions with research departments tend to keep their young men in the backroom to carry out the spade work under often clumsy and tight supervision. The GMWU has not done that. The leadership has successfully integrated its researchers into the general structure of the union, so that each of the present half-dozen research assistants (most now equipped with an MA degree in industrial relations from somewhere like Warwick University) services one or more of the industrial officers. Derek Gladwin – himself a Ruskin College graduate – believes 'it is essential that the research officer should know the atmosphere in which pay negotiations are going on'. This means the graduates (Gladwin employs a couple in his own regional office) are in from the start on the formulation of a pay claim, so that he or she 'knows what the lads want'. This closer integration between research work and wage bargaining at national level ensures a much smoother path for someone like Edmonds to make the big leap into an active trade union post. Basnett is not hostile to graduates in the unions. In his opinion, a university training enables the development of not only critical questioning and an ability to assimilate vast mounds of material, but the capacity for reasoned, coherent argument. If somebody has acquired those skills and at the same time comes from a working-class background and retains an active interest in the Labour movement, then Basnett sees no reason why such a graduate should not prove a real asset to any union's effectiveness.

Over the coming years Basnett's union is likely to grow in numbers and influence. More than most, the GMWU realizes the new opportunities in the growth of industrial democracy and the labour legislation of 1974–6. But a sharper political edge and a more constructive voice in the TUC's inner counsels is not going to dilute the GMWU's commitment to professionalism. Whether the modest internal reforms will recover lost ground due partly to the GMWU's inflexible structure is another matter.

13 The new public sector giants

NALGO

The TUC's style and ethos is still dictated by the big general
manual unions, but new giants have arisen in the past decade
who will change the balance of influence in the trade union
movement in the future. The most prominent of them is the
National and Local Government Officers' Association. With
well over 700,000 members it is now the fourth largest union
in the TUC and the biggest white-collar union in the Western
world. Ever since it first affiliated to the TUC in 1964, NALGO
has played a quiet, unobtrusive role. It was represented on the
General Council in the autumn of 1978 by two members –
Geoffrey Drain, the rotund, affable, cigar-smoking ex-Bevanite
and general secretary since 1973, and Miss A. W. Maddocks.
'Greater involvement in the trade union movement is a slow
process,' said Drain, 'but the pace is accelerating. Our influence
in the TUC is growing greater all the time.' In 1978 he joined
the inner group of the TUC – the so-called gold plated NEDDY
six.

NALGO has come a long way since the early 1960s, when
the union's arrival in the TUC was prophesied as a significant
boost for the forces of 'moderation'. The *Economist* in 1965
remarked that NALGO was 'the kind of trade union a general
secretary must dream about – nearly 400,000 votes solidly for
moderation and a near guarantee of no awkward personalities'.
A picture of what the old NALGO used to look like was painted
by Scorpio in NALGO's journal, *Public Service*, in May
1975:

Comfortable, uncomplaining and isolated from the trials and
tribulations of the world outside. Once in a job you stayed in.
NALGO itself had an air of destiny: if the Almighty was a card
holder in a union then NALGO would hold his ticket. No strikes,
no trouble and a quiet fusty-dusty daily round that meant wearing
a dark suit from Monday until Friday. The world extended as

far as the town hall steps and politics were as welcome as smallpox.

This is certainly the kind of union NALGO's founding fathers must have envisaged at the inaugural conference at the Inns of Court Hotel, in London's High Holborn on 29 July 1905. The inspiration of the new organization for local government workers was Herbert Blain, who founded the Liverpool Municipal Officers' Guild in 1896 when only a 26-year-old clerk in the city's town clerk's department. Its avowed aim had been to eradicate jobbery, ignorance and inefficiency in local government, 'to provide the means for social intercourse amongst its members and for their improvement, advancement and recreation'. By 1918 NALGO was a respectable organization with sixty vice-presidents, including Lord Derby and Neville Chamberlain, but it took many years for it to achieve its original objectives.

NALGO's first major campaign was to win a retirement pension for every local government officer, but it took twenty-one years to get it. Much of the problem stemmed from the anti-union prejudices among council staff. 'Anything savouring of trade unionism is nausea to the local government officer and his association,' complained Levi Hill, assistant secretary in 1909. NALGO placed great emphasis on its range of social benefits. In 1910 it created a benevolent and orphan fund and two years later introduced sickness benefits for members. A legal advice centre was set up, but it was not until 1920 that NALGO decided to appoint a full-time general secretary. The catalyst which helped to change NALGO was the arrival of the Whitley council bargaining system in the years after the First World War. This provided the need for a comprehensive reorganization of the staff in local government. The autonomy of local councils was hard to change. NALGO pushed for nationally agreed salary scales, holidays, working hours and overtime pay – on the lines of the civil service. But councils, ever aware of the pressure from the ratepayers, resisted such a move. It was not until 1938 that NALGO was even able to gain precise information on what salaries local councils paid their staff. The association fought a rearguard action through the interwar period in the face of widespread indifference and council cutbacks.

NALGO realized its objective during the war. The Churchill coalition introduced legislation which made industrial arbitration compulsory. It also required all employers to observe pay and conditions agreed by 'substantial portions of workers and employers'. Bolton Corporation refused to implement a district Whitley award and NALGO took the case to the House of Lords, who found in favour of the association in July 1942. As a result a National Joint Council was established and the first acceptable national salary scales for local government officers were laid down.

There are at present thirty-five union representatives on the National Joint Council, twenty-six of them from NALGO. The secretary to the staff side is NALGO's national organizer for local government staffs, Alan Jinkinson, who is a non-elected full-time official. Drain is also a member. The rest of the NALGO representatives are drawn from the lay members, fifteen of whom are appointed from the provincial councils of the association and three from the Scottish, with the other eight nominated by the National Local Government Committee. Of the present twenty-six members, sixteen are currently on the NALGO Executive Council.

The key NALGO committee is the National Local Government Committee, for it is to this body that the NALGO members of the staff side of the National Joint Council remain answerable. There are twenty-seven at present on the Committee. All but one of them are lay members, with nineteen nominated by district local government committees and the other seven from the National Executive Council.

Yet as we have already seen in the chapter on democracy in the unions, NALGO enjoys a substantially higher participation than others in its Executive Council elections. Ballot papers enable the candidates to provide brief statements of their policy outlooks and this gives some hope that the rank and file know who they are voting for. The fact is that the majority of the seventy-strong National Executive Council, elected from twelve districts, tend to be more senior, long-standing members of NALGO, and they do not provide a representative cross-section of the membership as a whole. In a union as big as NALGO, with its wide recruitment area, there is a continual tension between the desire to widen differentials and protect increments with percentage-type pay increases and the wish of the lower paid for flat wage settlements.

But the social composition of NALGO's rank and file has changed dramatically over the past thirty years. As long ago as 1950 at least half the clerks employed in both the public and private sectors came from working-class families. 'The effect of the 1944 Education Act on the immediate post-war generation has increased this percentage,' writes White. 'These new workers entered white collar work with stronger trade union traditions and have expectations not found in the first generation of NALGO members.' So far these social changes have not drastically transformed NALGO, where even at branch level senior figures still usually hold sway.

table 13.1 Votes on NALGO's affiliation to the TUC

	% Voting	For	(%)	Against	(%)
1942	57.4	40,733	(58.7)	28,715	(41.3)
1948	71.2	46,200	(35.6)	83,443	(64.4)
1955	63.9	73,151	(48.5)	77,592	(51.5)
1958	75.5	82,618	(43.2)	108,615	(56.8)
1962	77.5	111,489	(48.7)	117,312	(51.3)
1964	77.7	138,120	(53.8)	118,531	(41.2)

The struggle of the NALGO activists to gain the support of the majority for TUC affiliation was a long, arduous affair. The successful ballot of 1964 was the outcome of over forty years of struggle (see table 13.1). The first attempt at trying to affiliate NALGO to the TUC was in 1921, but the case was not even heard by the annual conference. In 1936 NALGO's conference turned down a motion calling for membership of the TUC, but after 1947 NALGO agreed 'to observe all recognized trade union practices and subscribe to Bridlington'. The continual balloting of the membership reflected the determination of a growing activist minority in NALGO who believed the association should come out of its self-imposed isolation and turn into a fully-fledged trade union. The Executive Council was evenly divided over the issue, but came down strongly in favour of joining the TUC for the 1964 ballot. Jack Cooper of the GMWU suggested affiliation of NALGO was the equivalent of fixing a stablizer to the *Queen Mary*, but the first action of the association's apolitical general secretary, Walter Anderson, was to second a militant anti-pay-freeze motion, moved at the 1966 TUC Congress by Frank Cousins.

In retrospect, membership of the TUC did not prove to be the real turning-point for NALGO. More significant were the events of 1969 when the rank and file criticized the performance of NALGO's local government negotiating team at the specially convened conference held in London. Many NALGO members believe that get-together was 'a watershed' in the union's history. The majority of delegates turned down the idea of taking industrial action to better their pay claim, but they accepted a toughly worded resolution from the Northumberland county branch which instructed the negotiators to go back to the employers and get a better deal. The 1969 special conference revealed just how far the old guard on the Executive Council had become out of touch with the membership and it brought a perceptibly tougher attitude in future negotiations. In 1970 the union sanctioned its first-ever strike, when eighteen staff struck in Leeds. In the same year NALGO threatened to boycott the administrative chores needed in the general election, if the local government wage settlement did not prove satisfactory. The radicalism of a growing section of NALGO activists brought a new stridency into the union. In 1970 the militancy paid off with a 12.5 per cent increase for all local government staff.

The long and bitter NALGO campaign for a substantial improvement in the London weighting allowance for members in the capital during the spring and summer of 1974 was a further indication of the union's willingness to take industrial action in furtherance of its demands. Selective strikes in inner London boroughs such as Camden and Islington brought real hardship to many poor people as services in the town halls were disrupted. The solidarity took the leaders of NALGO by surprise. As the executive reported to the 1975 conference:

There was revealed the fact that a number of NALGO members, when called upon to do so by their union, acted collectively against their basic traditions, either of previous action on a small scale or against the general absence of industrial action over a period of many years. The action also proved that at the membership level there is a large reservoir of members with the ability to undertake organizing work in circumstances unfamiliar to them and, in many instances, alien to their outlook.

But the fact remains that the volunteers were all from inner London, while less radical members in outer areas like Richmond and Bromley stayed at work.

The dispute proved a heavy burden for NALGO's finances, because the union agreed to make up the full wages of all those who struck. This amounted to as much as £1 million. A total of 25,000 cheques were drawn in strike pay during the London weighting strike. By the end of 1974 only £1.3 million was left in the reserve fund, not a very sizeable sum for a union of NALGO's size and potential. As the Executive Council admitted in its report to the 1975 conference: 'The reserve fund needs to be substantially increased before further major industrial action is undertaken.' Indeed, it is highly questionable just how successful the London disputes were in bringing about a substantial rise in the weighting allowance. It was far more the Pay Board's last report, rather than NALGO's action, which determined the final outcome. Labour-controlled councils were unwilling to break ranks and defy the newly elected Labour Government and Phase Three of the incomes policy, which was still in force. NALGO now appears to have few scruples about taking militant action, when it thinks fit. It has gradually become aware of the power it can wield to paralyse society.

Outsiders often have the impression that NALGO represents a privileged élite, immune from the strains of economic life in non-productive service work. But the union covers a wide diversity of workers – from city chief executives with incomes of over £15,000 a year controlling budgets bigger than some members of the United Nations, to £30-a-week school-leavers in the typing pool of the district council office. In the 1975 NALGO salary survey it was found that as many as 69 per cent of the membership earned less than £2,538 a year, while only 9.5 per cent were in the principal officer grade and above, starting on 3,690 a year.

The union has certainly managed to grow without making any concessions. It is the passive beneficiary of the explosion which took place over the past decade in public sector service jobs. Between 1965 and 1975 NALGO grew by 68 per cent. In 1975 alone it acquired 83,245 new members, a rise of 15.36 per cent. This took the size of the association up to 625,163 by that October. Slightly more than 60 per cent of all NALGO members work in local government. But the union is expanding at a rapid rate in allied services. The universities are a big growth area. In 1975 membership there rose by a third to 8,308. NALGO's members in the water services totalled 20,470, in gas 40,161 and in electricity 37,869. The numbers in the National Health Service grew to 72,277.

Yet despite its unwillingness to identify with 'party' politics and the doubts of the old guard on the Executive Council, NALGO swung leftwards in the 1970s. The union attacked the Conservative Housing Finance Act and it came out in favour of the nationalization of all development land. It supported increased family allowances, and higher redistributive taxation. In the health service, NALGO campaigned, like the other unions, for the end of private paid beds in NHS hospitals. 'With all the difficulties of so complex and many-sided an organization, we are becoming much tougher and less patient,' said Drain. The union caused uproar among the more conservative members when the Executive Council decided to provide financial assistance to the striking miners in 1972 and again in 1974. Angry letters flowed into head office in protest. NALGO also started to take up attitudes on foreign policy. The Executive Council joined in the campaign against the military regime in Chile and even agreed to provide money to the rescue fund set up to help Chilean political refugees by the International Confederation of Free Trade Unions.

The early retirement of Walter Anderson from the general secretaryship of NALGO was an indication of the new winds blowing through the union. Whether or not to register under the 1971 Industrial Relations Act provoked impassioned debate within the union. Anderson was willing to cooperate with the measure, but the majority of his executive were not and they were backed by a substantial number of the delegates at the 1972 annual conference, mainly after Vic Feather had delivered a persuasive address. Anderson wanted to cooperate with the Pay Board – a body that the TUC was boycotting. Again he was over-ruled by his Executive Council on the eve of the special February 1973 TUC conference after getting the support of the majority on NALGO's Economic Committee. He decided to leave his post early as a result. 'The days have gone when the annual dinner was the main event on the NALGO calendar,' as a senior executive member told me in 1974. 'Local government is not such a wonderful place now. Before the war it was a Mecca for full and safe employment. Up to sixty grammar school boys would be trying to get the one job. Now they have to put out bait to get recruits,' said Glyn Philips, a stalwart council member and chairman of the Local Government Committee of NALGO in the early 1970s, and chief environmental health officer with Neath District Council.

Yet NALGO is far from being a union for the underdog. It still provides innumerable perks for its white-collar members, unheard of in most manual unions. NALGO's own building society merged with the Leek and Westbourne (assets of over £450 million in 1974). The union's members can borrow money to buy houses on far better terms than other people, with lower interest rates. NALGO runs its own insurance company, offering a wide range of cover from motor policies to retirement plans, from with-profits endowment assurances to mortgage protection. It still retains a holiday centre for members at Croyde Bay in North Devon. NALGO members can even get a reduced rate subscription fee to the Royal Automobile Club, as well as discount offers from a wide range of shops. It runs a convalescence old folks' home for ex-members near Lytham St Annes. NALGO moved into a new £3 million national headquarters in early 1976 near London's King's Cross station. It is one of the few unions in Britain with the resources to build and occupy a prime site in the central area of the capital.

NUPE

The National Union of Public Employees has enjoyed even more rapid expansion in the public sector during the past decade. It recruits local government manual workers, nurses and hospital ancillary staff, as well as canteen workers and caretakers, who service public authorities outside the civil service. In the summer of 1979 NUPE boasted a membership of nearly 730,000, compared with 257,460 twelve years earlier. Under the flamboyant, articulate leadership of Alan Fisher (appointed general secretary in January 1967) NUPE has gained a militant reputation for its defence of public services in its role in the battle on behalf of the low paid.

The union was founded in 1888 as the London County Council Employees' Protection Society, changing to its present name in 1928.

As Bob Fryer and his colleagues wrote (in their 1975 internal survey of NUPE): 'Probably the most noteworthy aspect of NUPE's early history is that the union should have survived at all. From its inception under Albin Taylor, through the split with the Municipal Employees' Association and into the 1920s, when the union first adopted its present name, NUPE always faced the combined hostility of employers and rival trade unions.' It was very much the work of Bryn Roberts, a militant Welshman, which enabled NUPE to grow and prosper. When he became the union's third general secretary in 1933, NUPE could boast no more than 13,000 members, a full-time staff of nine and a deficit of £450. Roberts turned the union round in only five years. By 1938 it had 50,000 members, 542 branches (compared with 143 in 1933) and an income of £48,000. A year later NUPE made its first important breakthrough, gaining recognition from the county councils where the union organized the dustmen. It was not until 1941 that a national joint council was formed to cover them. The GMWU and TGWU fought bitterly to restrict Roberts's growing influence and he was kept off the TUC General Council by the bigger battalions. It took much persuasion and arm-twisting for NUPE to be allowed four seats on the regional joint national councils at the 1942 TUC. In 1945 a national joint council was formed for hospital and institutional domestic staffs – another NUPE achievement.

During the late 1940s the union extended its recruitment among cleaners and caretakers in the public services.

Alan Fisher is an aggressive and persuasive public speaker, who does not endear himself to the inner coterie of TUC leaders. He was born in Birmingham in 1922 and started work as an office boy in the headquarters of the Heating and Ventilating Engineers' Union. Fisher moved to NUPE's office in Birmingham as a clerk in February 1939, where the future general secretary, Sid Hill, was area officer. In April 1946 he became area officer of the Midlands division and six years later divisional officer. Fisher went to head office as assistant national officer in 1956 and became assistant general secretary in 1962, succeeding Hill as general secretary in 1968 at the young age of 44.

It was an appropriate moment to come to the top of NUPE. The public service was expanding rapidly and frustrations at the Labour Government's incomes policy were growing more intense among the low paid workers. The bible of NUPE militancy became the Prices and Incomes Board report of March 1967 (no 29) on the pay and condition of manual workers in local authorities, the national health service, gas and water supply. That study revealed the average weekly earnings of manual workers in those sectors were 'well below the average for all industries'. Apparently, 'In none of the 129 industries covered by the Ministry of Labour's list were earnings lower than in local government and only in six lower than in the NHS.' The report emphasized the extensive under-utilization of labour, the lack of shift allowances, incentive payments and service increments. It revealed that only 7.5 per cent of the workers in England and Wales were covered by any incentive scheme.

In 1969 NUPE and the other unions on the National Joint Council for Local Authority Services put in a claim for a 15s a week increase, better overtime rates and an improved service supplement. There was also a call for a new grading structure in the service based on job designation. It was Fisher's public admission to the members that the pay talks were in deadlock that provoked Hackney NUPE dustmen to stop work unofficially on 23 September in support of a basic wage of £20 a week. By the start of October the strike had spread over London. Piles of refuse gathered in the streets as the dustmen demonstrated their power to make life unpleasant. On 11 October the strike was called off. The employers bowed to the unexpected pressure and conceded the bulk of the union's demands.

In 1970 NUPE spearheaded the local government manual workers' strike with the GMWU and TGWU playing subordinate roles. It proved to be the first major test of the new Conservative Government's resolve to reduce the level of wage deals. The eventual settlement outraged the Cabinet and the Prime Minister, Edward Heath, denounced it on television. At the time it was seen as a major breakthrough for the low paid in the public sector, even though its fruits were later eroded by the onward march of inflation and pay restraint. The 1970 strike cost NUPE as much as £201,604 in strike pay, but it

table 13.2 The rise of NUPE, 1968–78

	Total membership	Women members
1968	283,471	153,734
1969	305,222	173,058
1970	372,709	220,768
1971	397,085	236,782
1972	443,354	271,745
1973	470,172	294,640
1974	507,826	321,302
1975	584,485	382,638
1976	650,530	433,650
1977	693,097	457,444
1978	712,392	470,179

was seen as worth every penny, for it put the union firmly in front of the public gaze. 'Before that time a lot of workers had never heard of us. It was the first time people realized NUPE was a union to be reckoned with,' Alan Fisher told me. 'We became well-known at last. The effect of all that television publicity boosted membership. You've got to keep your union's name in front of the public.' Table 13.2 charts the soaring increase in NUPE members.

NUPE is the first major union which has called on outside academic experts to examine its structure and make proposals for modernization. The Warwick University team made numerous criticisms of NUPE in its report of August 1974. It spoke of the 'remoteness and isolation' of the organization with its emphasis on national negotiations. There was particular concern expressed about a constant problem of the large unions – how to knit together local and national levels in a coherent whole.

The creation of a national committee system has been used as one way to overcome a lack of collective identity with the union by the rank and file. There are national committees for local government, the health service, the universities and waterworks with an advisory committee for the ambulance service. These are linked to the twenty-six-strong NUPE Executive Council, and all are made up of lay activists elected every two years from the union's divisions. Those national committees have failed to establish an important role in the NUPE structure. Only 19 per cent of the branches told the Warwick team that they had communicated with one of the national committees since 1970. The very nature of the union's recruitment area, and the structure of local public services, places the main burden on NUPE's full-time centralized direction from headquarters in Blackheath, south London. The dependence of the lay members on the full-time organizers was seen by the Warwick team as a real problem for NUPE. As they wrote:

Excessive dependence on paid officials not only imposes narrow limitations on membership involvement, it may also limit the effectiveness of the union and its officers to the eventual detriment of the members. The more officers are called upon to settle grievances and problems which could better be settled locally with the advantages of local knowledge and the benefits for local confidence, the less are they able to give their attention to issues which confront the membership across a wider front.

The recent moves towards a more democratic NUPE have risen, not from a groundswell of opinion from below, but from the political perspectives of those who run the union at the top. This amounts to a form of 'sponsored' democracy.

The Warwick team suggested that the stewards (all 15,000 of them) should be brought more fully into the union's machinery. They were to be the majority voice on the service-based district committees alongside the branch secretaries as well as being primarily responsible for the organization of the union at workplace level. Those district committees negotiate with management above the workplace level. Stewards also predominate on the sixty area committees (twenty each for local government and the health service; ten each for water authorities and the universities) within NUPE's ten geographical divisions. It is at divisional level that union activists from the differing occupational and service interests meet to discuss overall union policy. In this way NUPE hopes to avoid the threats of sectionalism and breakaway. The four national committees are elected by the areas and these have been given a more crucial role in the preparation and progress of national negotiations including annual pay claims. The twenty-one-strong Executive Council elected from the divisions is the major decision-making body between biennial conferences.

'We believe we have reached a position where the size and type of membership makes it quite possible for members to do more day-to-day bargaining than previously,' Fisher told me. NUPE has made an effort to get the dispersed and passive rank and file more involved. The establishment of bonus incentive schemes by local councils made local organization more vital than before. Regular delegate conferences have enabled members to have pay settlements referred back to them for ratification. In the summer of 1976 NUPE balloted its members on their support for the incomes policy and the social contract.

There are now a statutory five women elected to the union's Executive Council, but the level of female participation in NUPE is still very low. 'We tend to get women in our union who are married but unable to move away from home,' said Bernard Dix, the influential deputy general secretary. 'This makes it very difficult to appoint any of them as officers. You don't need women to recruit women. During the last five years we have achieved equal pay for the women. In terms of results they've seen what we [the men] have achieved for them.'

NUPE was the main militant union defending the social wage and public expenditure from attack since the mid-1970s.

Much to the annoyance of TUC colleagues, Alan Fisher and his Executive gave their active support to a mass lobby of the TUC in September 1976 and they inspired a 40,000-strong march on the Commons by public service workers on 26 November that year – the biggest demonstration by trade unionists since the TUC march against the Industrial Relations Act in February 1971. In the campaign against pay beds in national health hospitals, NUPE also took a strong stand. Above all, over the battle for the low paid the union has always adopted a radical strategy, though the relative position of its members has not improved dramatically over the past few years. It is often fashionable to disregard NUPE and suggest the union carries no influence in the TUC. Fisher's style is certainly less impressive in private meetings than it is at the rostrum at Congress, but the organized strength of NUPE is a force any sensible government will have to recognize before it decides on any major cuts in public service expenditure again in the future. The potential of NUPE to create chaos in hospitals and schools was made manifest during the industrial action of January and February 1979 in support of a 40 per cent pay claim for a new basic minimum wage of £60 for a 35 hour week. It is true that the GMWU, the TGWU and COHSE coordinated their campaigns for local government manuals, hospital ancillaries, ambulancemen and university manual staff in an unprecedented winter offensive across the public services, but it was NUPE that set the pace and the tone. 'We are a thrusting, campaigning union', said Fisher. NUPE's militancy is often the envy of others who lack the drive and aggression to copy its methods. 'We are the only union who can put 60,000 workers on to the streets of London at almost a moment's notice,' claimed Fisher. But the NUPE pickets who blockaded hospitals and schools did grave damage to the reputation of the trade union movement. The government was compelled to move substantially towards the unions' demands, with agreement on a 9 per cent pay rise plus £1 in advance from a staged comparability exercise under the standing commission chaired by Professor Hugh Clegg. The sensible aim is to guarantee the low paid public service workers an agreed position in the national earnings table around two thirds of average industrial earnings, but NUPE will find it very difficult to maintain this, when the defence of differentials and relativities is a hallowed tradition among the unions. Workers at the bottom end have hardly improved their relative position since accurate labour statistics began in the 1880s. For all NUPE's panache, ruthless tactics and flair for publicity, it is by no means clear that the union has achieved a better deal for its low paid members than others have for theirs.

COHSE

The Confederation of Health Service Employees was also a major beneficiary from public service sector expansion in the late 1960s and the new mood of militancy among low paid workers. It was founded in 1946 through a merger between the Mental Hospital and Institutional Workers' Union and the National Union of County Officers, but until the late 1960s its main recruitment base hardly extended far beyond the mental hospitals. In 1969 the association had only 75,183 members; but by the end of 1978 it was approaching 215,000. The public expenditure cuts of the coming years will ensure that the rate of COHSE's growth will decline, but there are still many thousands of nurses in the National Health Service ripe for recruitment. With twenty-eight members on seven of the ten Whitley councils, COHSE is in a good position to consolidate its strength. Unlike its rivals – NUPE and the GMWU – its interests are strictly confined to the health service.

Albert Spanswick, the burly general secretary – elected to the top job in COHSE in the spring of 1974 – has brought a more militant style to the association. 'We are not any pseudo-professional body but a fully fledged trade union,' he insists. The rise of COHSE has been meteoric since the early 1970s.

There is clear evidence of a correlation between COHSE militancy and improved recruitment into the union during the early 1970s. The 1973 ancillary workers' dispute, which was a fiasco, and the 1974 agitation among the nurses, both contributed to an improvement in COHSE's strength. In June 1974 at the height of industrial action over nurses' pay the association received as many as 14,882 members. With an annual turnover of around 20 per cent, COHSE has been successful in holding its own and making rapid improvements. Clearly the staid, 'responsible' image of the Royal College of Nursing no longer appeals to many young nurses. The 1973 ancillary strike cost

COHSE as much as £39,198 in benefit to its members, but the amount of strike pay handed out in 1974 was only £272 and in 1975 it was £346.

It took years of mounting frustration among the nursing profession over poor pay and low status to ignite COHSE. In 1972 the union decided to register under the 1971 Industrial Relations Act and it was expelled from the TUC as a result. But the new militancy began in the winter of 1973–4. COHSE's National Executive Committee agreed unanimously to de-register under the Act and rejoin the TUC. In December 1973 the Conservative government announced £42 million worth of cuts in the NHS. 'This was the final blow,' claimed COHSE. In the following February issue of the union's journal, Spanswick, then general secretary elect, asserted: 'Unions have a reputation for getting things done. COHSE is determined to fight.' The union settled – as the other bodies in the NHS did – under Phase Three of the Heath pay policy that very month, but after Labour's victory COHSE led the battle for a complete review of nurses' pay and an interim wage increase. On 8 May, eleven nurses at Storthes Hall Hospital in Huddersfield took unofficial action by striking for an hour and closing three wards. Eight days later COHSE's National Executive agreed to call industrial action among their members, if the government produced no 'cash on the table'. At the end of May an overtime ban and other measures were begun to disrupt hospital life, including short and selected stoppages of work. Barbara Castle, then the health minister, announced a review body under Lord Halsbury to examine the nurses' case, but she refused to make any interim payment. This was not enough for the unions. As many as fifty hospitals were closed by the end of the first week of industrial action. The unions agreed to suspend their activities on 29 June and Halsbury reported on 17 September. The report was a major acceptance of the nurses' case and resulted in massive pay rises, averaging 35 per cent. This was a vindication of the COHSE approach. Industrial action had 'given the nurses their self-respect', claimed Spanswick.

As the report to the 1975 delegate conference argued: 'Health Service staff have become increasingly more organized in COHSE, the NHS trade union, and are no longer satisfied with taking second place to the powerful industrial groups on pay

and conditions of service agreements.' The upsurge in support
has brought major internal reforms in the union. Conference
has now become an annual affair. The size of the full-time staff
was increased. By the end of 1978 there were twelve at head
office in Banstead, Surrey, with a further twenty-nine based on
thirteen regional offices.

But COHSE is likely to experience a virtual standstill in its
growth for the rest of the 1970s with the massive cutbacks in
public expenditure. The National Health Service is once more
in crisis. In the battle over political priorities, it seems probable
that COHSE will not be able to flex any serious muscle power.
Yet with the other wholly public sector unions, it is a new and
permanent force to be reckoned with in the TUC.

Teachers – NUT and NAS

It was only in the late 1960s that any teachers' union joined
the TUC. The 111,566-strong National Association of School-
masters and Union of Women Teachers led the way in 1969
under the direction of its rotund general secretary, Terry Casey.
'We are the ASLEF of teaching,' he told me. The union's main
recruitment area lies among specialist teachers in secondary
education. The Association's decision helped to force a change
of mind in the much larger 291,239-strong National Union of
Teachers, which joined the TUC a year later. The NUT's general secretary, Fred Jarvis, now has a seat on the General
Council. His union has its main membership strength in the
primary schools and it has a sizeable number of women in its
ranks. Outsiders might wonder why there is not one union for
the whole of the teaching profession, but it looks an unlikely
development at present. Both major bodies in the profession
mirror the attitudes of their distinctively different power bases.
The National Association stresses differentials and the need to
reward the skill and expertise, while the NUT concentrates
mainly on a flat rate approach to pay and efforts to make the
starting salary more attractive. While the National Association
pushes the idea of the career-based teacher, the NUT has a
more egalitarian flavour, though its executive is still dominated
by head teachers.

Both have a difficult time trying to reconcile their claims to
be fully fledged unions as well as professional associations. But

Jarvis believes there is no conflict between the two ideas. 'We have never taken the view that one excludes the other,' he said. With sixteen seats on the staff side of the Burnham negotiating panel for teachers (compared with three for the National Association), the NUT boasts an impressive back-up service for its members. It has a full-time headquarters staff numbering around 200 with fifteen full-time officials. There are twelve regional offices, most with two full-time officials. In 1974 the NUT's account balanced at over £1 million and its assets totalled over £3 million. It runs a benevolent fund for members as well as a building society (started in 1966), assurance agency and publishing house. But in recent years, the NUT has become more militant. As many as 150,000 members (more than half the membership) took some form of strike action in 1969–70, protesting against a low Burnham pay award. The NUT won that particular struggle, as the Labour Government's incomes policy crumbled away in the face of an upsurge from the public sector. Recent public expenditure cuts and rising teacher unemployment have been far less successfully resisted by the union. With the falling birth rate and worsening teacher–student ratio, the NUT will have a difficult job holding its own.

The union has a highly vocal left wing, mobilized in Rank and File, but it would be misleading to assume the NUT is very political. It was an early champion of the comprehensive system, but the bulk of NUT members have little sympathy with the Labour Party. An NOP survey at the time of the October 1974 election discovered 37 per cent of the sample intended to vote Conservative, 27 per cent Liberal and only 30 per cent Labour. Most opposed any statutory incomes policy, but a majority also expressed opposition to the elimination of grammar schools and the raising of the school-leaving age to 16. As we have seen in the chapter on union democracy, the NUT has a relatively high level of participation in decision-making, but its annual conference gives an unequal voice to the union's different segments, with a bias to the more conservative county areas and an under-representation of members from the inner cities. Executive seats for the twenty-seven districts are hotly contested every year. 'We believe in one union for all teachers,' says Jarvis, but the NUT, like the National Association, has failed to enjoy the full benefits of the massive expansion in the numbers in teaching since the mid-1960s. This is one area of the blossoming public sector where trade unionism has not grown at such a rapid rate.

With as many as 1,561,000 people working in educational services in 1974, the teachers' unions (as well as NUPE and NALGO among ancillaries and administrators) might have been expected to benefit. It is true that the National Association doubled between 1969 and 1976, but the NUT actually fell in membership from around 310,000 in 1971 to 281,000 five years later. This does not suggest increased employment is automatically being translated into union growth.

14 The miners' revival

This is the period of our greatest strength. It is the eve of our greatest achievements. (*The Miners' New Charter*, NUM, Scottish area, 1973)

The capitalist society belongs in the dustbin of history. The ideal of a Socialist society belongs to the youth of today and to the future. I have seen the vision of the socialist tomorrow and it works. (Arthur Scargill, 1975 presidential address to the Yorkshire miners)

The 255,887-strong National Union of Mineworkers is once more a mighty force in the land after its victorious strikes in 1972 and 1974. As the blunt NUM president, Joe Gormley, told delegates at the 1975 NUM Conference: 'We have proved in the last three to four years that this union has great industrial power.'

Only a few years ago the NUM was regarded as an ineffective union without a future. The rundown in coal as a basic fuel during the 1960s put the NUM firmly on the defensive. All that changed in 1972 with the national miners' strike. Two years later the NUM was instrumental in bringing about the downfall of the Heath Government, with the coming of the three-day working week for British industry and a sudden general election which ended with an indecisive result, but the return of a minority Labour government. Now every utterance by a miners' leader sends a shiver down the stock exchange index. Cabinet ministers woo the NUM in a way they never used to do. What goes on at NUM headquarters in London's Euston Road now matters to the outside world. There is a belligerent self-confidence about the NUM these days. The militancy of recent years has been vindicated, but the union often remains sharply divided.

Joe Gormley, the NUM's president, remains something of

a mystery. Ever since he beat the Scots miners' leader Mick McGahey in the election for the top job in 1971, his behaviour has often proved difficult to fathom. Of course, it is said Gormley's heart is in the right place. He retains a deep, though not always unquestioning loyalty to the Labour Party. In his younger days Gormley served on the Ashton in Makerfield District Council in his native Lancashire, before being elected secretary of the Lancashire miners in 1961 and joining the NUM National Executive two years later. Gormley used to sit on the Labour National Executive, where he chaired the International Committee, until he was defeated by the left in 1972.

But Gormley is no pale pink moderate. Far from it. 'I am an expensive man,' he told me. Putting Britain's miners at the top of the national earnings table and keeping them there remains his aim. He made that clear in a speech to his area conference in 1970. 'I do not want to be regarded as any less of a trade union leader than anyone else,' argued Gormley. 'I am sick and tired of fighting on my knees. I like to stand up fighting. I am not going to be a miners' leader if I cannot claim a bigger minimum wage for the lads who go underground than the lads carting dustbins round the streets of London are getting. We have been acquiescing too long. We have been too much part of the scheme of things.' Gormley's blunt, militant rhetoric was well timed. It reflected a new mood on the coalfields which had not been seen since the early 1920s.

The growing frustration and anger among the miners by the end of the 1960s was not hard to understand. Between 1957 and 1972 the size of the labour force in the coal industry was cut back sharply – from over 700,000 to under 390,000. The number of pits in operation fell over that same period of time from over 800 pits to under 300. As Lord Wilberforce's report in 1972 explained: 'This rundown, which was brought about with the cooperation of the miners and of their union, is without parallel in British industry in terms of the social and economic costs it has inevitably entailed for the mining community as a whole.' The union had collaborated with the Coal Board in the massive contraction. Coal was in retreat as a major fuel and union leaders believed that militant resistance to decline would merely speed up the process and worsen the position of the miners. By concentrating on the more productive collieries, productivity went up sharply. In 1957 output per manshift amounted to under 25 cwt; by 1971 it had climbed to 44.2 cwt – a 77.5 per cent increase. This impressive performance took place despite a radical change in the industry's wage system. During the early 1960s the union agreed with the Coal Board to substitute the old local piecework rates with a day wage system of national rates. Wilberforce explained the reasons for the reform:

The NUM had long desired to remove regional differentials on grounds of equity. It had also objected to a piecework system of payment because geological conditions often resulted in an inverse relationship between output and effort. The NCB for its part had aimed to reduce disputes and control wage drift by removing wage bargaining from pit and area level to national level.

The old piecework system had benefited miners in highly productive coalfields like Nottinghamshire and South Yorkshire, but worked to the disadvantage of those who mined difficult seams in South Wales and Scotland. Localized, unofficial strikes were endemic as a result of piecework. Between 1944 and 1964, 28,168 separate strikes occurred, an average of 1,409 a year, and they accounted for more than half the total number of strikes in all industries during those years. The introduction of the Power Loading Agreement in phases from 1966 had a severe impact on the earnings of many miners. Up until then miners had stayed fairly near the top of the national earnings table. In 1960 they were third out of the twenty-one industry groups with £16.28 a week, compared with the average in industry of £15.16, which was 7.4 per cent less than the miners. Ten years later the miners had fallen drastically down the table to twelfth position, earning on average £28.01 a week, 3.1 per cent less than the average in manufacturing industry. Many individual miners took a sizeable cut in their pay packets as a result of the day wage system.

The first symptoms of the new militancy occurred in the winter of 1969 when miners took unofficial action in Yorkshire and South Wales. The stoppage lasted a fortnight and cost the Coal Board 2.5 million tons in lost production. Lord Robens, the NCB chairman, talked darkly about political extremism on the coalfields. But in the following year the NUM passed a motion at the annual conference for a massive wage increase.

This involved an extra £5 a week for surfacemen (up from £15 to £20), £6 a week for underground workers (from £16 to £22) and between £5 3s and £2 7s 6d for the power-loading teams (from £24 17s to £27 12s 6d to £30). All the Coal Board offered in response were increases less than half that figure. The union decided to ballot the members for industrial action, but the 55.5 per cent vote in favour of a strike fell far short of the two-thirds majority required under the constitution.

In 1971 at the Aberdeen conference the union cleared the way for industrial action, if it became necessary. Joe Gormley moved for the change in union rules that lowered the majority needed to call a strike to 55 per cent. This was carried by 215 votes to 98. A strike reserve fund was also created on a motion from the Northumberland area. There was unanimity on the toughly worded wages resolution moved by Yorkshire and seconded by South Wales. This called for £26 a week for surface workers, £28 for those underground and £35 a week for the power-loading teams. The Coal Board – under pressure from the government – was only prepared to give wage increases ranging from £1.80 to £1.70 a week. The union decided on a national stoppage to back its claim.

The 1972 national coal strike stands as a landmark in post-war labour history. After a bitter eight-week struggle, the miners achieved a total victory. Edward Heath's Cabinet was forced to abandon its abrasive policies of the first nineteen months of office and seek cooperation with the TUC. For the miners, it brought a sudden end to the long retreat of the 1960s.

What happened in 1972 is already blurred by mythology. No history of the strike has yet been written, but autonomy in the NUM ensures that each area office keeps its own records. In the chaotic archives of Yorkshire's gothic area headquarters in Barnsley lie a few battered exercise books. They provide a patchy but unique record of the role that the Barnsley area, led by Arthur Scargill (now area president), played in the 1972 strike. Here are the authentic handwritten messages scribbled down from telephone conversations to the Barnsley strike committee office by flying pickets at the power stations and coal depots. In January 1972 the Yorkshire coalfield was in a militant mood. Over 75 per cent of the area voted for strike action in the union's national ballot.

Most Yorkshire miners had had recent experience of striking. In 1969 almost the whole area erupted in unofficial action in support of a 40-hour week. Pickets were dispatched to the pitheads in nearby Derbyshire and Nottinghamshire to spread the revolt. Again in 1970 the majority of Yorkshire miners defied their leaders and struck for higher pay against the NUM's acceptance of the employer's offer. The area's panels – democratic joint pit committees of lay activists – had already become a focus of opposition to the men of restraint in Barnsley head office. Neither Sam Bullough, the president, nor Sid Schofield, the general secretary and NUM vice-president, had much heart for leading their fiery troops into battle. Reading the official minutes of the area for the period, it is often difficult to realize a strike was on at all. Events simply passed the Yorkshire area machine by. It was the four area strike committees in Yorkshire who took over the running of the strike. On 17 January Scargill and the Barnsley men literally forced themselves into area headquarters and set up their campaign office in a ground-floor room. Messages were sent upstairs to the officials to keep them in the picture.

When the strike started at midnight on 9 January, no grand strategy had been devised by Gormley and Daly in London. The National Executive was ill prepared and uncertain of what to do. 'They hadn't a clue,' Scargill told me in December 1975. An NUM circular went out to the areas on 4 January. This provided a list of ports where coal was being unloaded. But a similar document on the whereabouts of the country's power stations – both oil and coal fired – was held back by the leadership, who always hoped for a last-minute settlement. It was not until 12 January that Daly's written instructions for the picketing of all power stations and coal depots were issued from headquarters. By that time the Yorkshire miners had already brought most movements of coal and oil in their area to a halt.

On the first morning of the strike, Scargill and his colleagues at Woolley pit were out in the swirling snow picketing their own collieries. Clerical and staff members still at work were leaving the pithead at 7.30 that morning in response to the determined picket line. The men then moved on to the coking plant at nearby Barrow, where they found lorries being loaded with coke and the cokemen (members of the NUM) working as normal. Apparently their strike notices did not come into effect until a week later. Over 300 miners tried to stop the plant's operation. Scargill headed a delegation to see the manager. 'The phone rang in his office. The manager's face went chalk-white when he heard what had happened. The lads were stopping the oil deliveries. The Transport and General Workers' Union drivers were turning back at the gates,' said Scargill. Management explained that oil was needed to keep the ovens warm. Without it, they would crack. The miners agreed to let oil supplies through on condition that the plant only operated priority cases under the NUM permit scheme for coke deliveries to schools, hospitals and old people.

The National Strike Committee agreed to spread the pickets outside the coalfields to power stations and ports elsewhere. The Barnsley miners were allocated the whole of East Anglia to picket. At first there was a division of opinion on the area strike committee. Against Scargill's advice, the majority favoured sending pickets across East Anglia to the different power stations at the same time. After a week that tactic was abandoned. Too few men were being spread over too large an area. It was Scargill who pushed for mass picketing at each point in turn. On 19 January the Barnsley logbook notes:

Three buses to East Anglia. One to Peterborough power station. Two to docks at Ipswich and Colchester. Two coaches to Bedford, transferred to the docks. We are tending to move away from power stations to cover coal at the source, ie the docks. In addition today two cars and one mini-bus to Great Yarmouth. Local TGWU helping with accommodation. Our lads have established an office in Norwich and have stopped unloading at Great Yarmouth and are now proceeding to Lowestoft.

Next day Don Baines, the Barnsley panel secretary, reported in from Norwich:

Assurances from other unions no movement of coal, other than that in stock in Peterboro power station. Gone to Wisbech docks (boat arriving). From Norwich some members gone to Kings Lynn (boat coming in). Problem of accommodation getting very difficult. TGWU trying to get trade unionists to cover the accommodation problem. Local students are helping, as far as we know.

On 22 January the Norwich strike office phoned through to

say that all coal movements in East Anglia seemed to be at a standstill, but the situation in Ipswich was a cause for concern. A message lodged that day at 5.20 pm read:

Conditions at Ipswich require a greater number of men, police reinforcement increased to 150. Contacted A. Phillips at Woolley who has arranged to see men at colliery Friday and will then contact stike HQ with any arrangements he has made for his men's return to Ipswich.

The logbook entry for 24 January reads:

Cliff Quay, Ipswich – despite intense picketing, only limited success achieved. Information suggests that success will only be achieved by picketing in strength. If this one can be rendered ineffective, a major success can be recorded. Propose to gain cooperation of oil tanker drivers as shortage of oil appears to have immediate effect on operation of power stations.

Through political contacts, Scargill had organized many pickets to stay on the campus at Essex University; but the students proved a mixed blessing. Baines rang in from Ipswich, where seven bus-loads of picketers were in action on 24 January: 'Generally all movement of coal stopped and now turning oil tankers away. It is reasonably quiet. Students in attendance are reported prepared to "storm" power station.'

Essex University authorities were now trying to evict the miners from the campus. At 5.00 pm on 24 January the university registrar phoned Scargill in Barnsley to say a 'bus-load of men had arrived there [at Wivenhoe] and he said it looked as if they were going to stay the night at the university. He reported talk of students clearing all staff out of the university to accommodate any other miners arriving.' In the early days as many as 1,000 miners passed through the university. 'And many got all their home comforts,' adds Scargill. The pickets did not confine themselves to the big towns. A party was sent scouting around the Stour Valley. According to a message on 23 January: 'They hired a boat and travelled six miles up the river but saw nothing at all. The local TGWU have suggested that scouts be sent out to have a look at two small ports – Wivenhoe and Brightlingsea.' The cooperation of other unions at local level was crucial to the success of the picketing. The footplatemen's union, ASLEF, threw its muscle behind the miners in a positive way. On 27 January a message came in from Norwich asking for ASLEF's help, 'to stop oil tankers coming into Norwich power station. Coming in from Thames Haven. Had eight 100-ton tankers in today. Could this be stopped at source?' Barnsley passed on the message to Jim Wheeler on the full-time staff at Euston Road. Less than two hours later came the reply: 'Wheeler rang back after speaking to Ray Buckton [ASLEF general secretary]. Answer? All power stations are blacked and no oil should get in.'

By 5 February there were 11,000 miners (scarcely 5 per cent of NUM members) on continuous picket duty every day throughout Britain and three weeks' supply of coal left at the power stations: but there were still large depots where the picketing had so far proved ineffective. The most important was at Saltley in Birmingham, where over 1,000 lorries a day were piling up with coke unhindered. News of this came to Scargill from Frank Wattis, Birmingham Communist Party official, on 4 February. He phoned London for confirmation. Head office was already aware of what was happening at Saltley, but the Midlands area of the NUM refused to do anything about it unless the union at national level agreed to pay their pickets for turning up. This view was received badly in Euston Road, and at 4.00 pm on the following day Scargill was contacted in Barnsley. As the logbook states:

Urgent message received from London. They require 200 pickets in Brum to prevent 1,000 lorries per day leaving Brum Gas Works. As many branches as possible contacted by car and phone: first bus 49-seater left at 6.40 pm, K. Newton in charge: Second 40-seater left at 8.10 pm, third at 8.20 with 25 on board to pick up 24 men at Brodsworth.

Scargill travelled through the night by car and reached Saltley at 3.00 am on Sunday morning. He rang back at 11.45 am:

All movement of coal has been suspended but after meeting management they had been informed that coal would be moved again 10.00 am Monday. Contacts had been made with A. Law [TGWU] who had informed all drivers they would be blacked if they broke the picket line. Three men had been injured by a lorry ... as many pickets as possible would be required.

On 8 February Scargill phoned in that 'police kicking hell out of our lads. Urgent require support – send more pickets – ring Schofield and other panels.' But the Yorkshire area leaders opposed more men being sent to Saltley. Scargill made an impassioned appeal on television for miners to come quickly.

It was the Saltley incident that provided Scargill with a national audience for his fiery politics, but it also revealed his formidable organizing abilities. Within three hours of that message from London, 200 miners had arrived at the depot's gates. The local Communist Party Social Club was turned into the headquarters for the first night, then it was moved to the Labour and Trades Club. Sleeping bags were obtained from the Co-op and the Conservative-controlled Birmingham City Council chipped in with 4,000 blankets. There was no phone for the strike office. 'A Post Office Engineering Worker suddenly walked in. Would we like some help?' said Scargill. 'The Post Office said no phone could be installed at such short notice. He rang his manager. Unless one was received quick, the engineers in Birmingham would do no more repair work. Within an hour the phone was installed.'

The flow of lorries leaving Saltley was cut from 1,000 to less than 30 a day by mass picketing, but the scene outside the plant was a battle-ground. At 1.30 pm on 7 February the message came through:

600–700 police on duty. Police stopping lorries in the first place to let pickets have a talk with them, but now they are letting them go straight through and there have been four or five arrests – not all ours and the police are keeping them there so that they will not go back to the picket lines. Full cooperation from TGWU.

That day the police in Birmingham were placed on emergency extended alert to deal with the hundreds of picketing miners who had arrived not just from Yorkshire but also South Wales. Over 3,000 pickets faced a similar number of police outside Saltley depot. On the evening of 9 February, Scargill urged local leaders of the AUEW to call their men out on the picket lines in support of the miners. He spoke to them for forty minutes and demanded action. They agreed. So did the TGWU, the Electricians and the Vehicle Builders.

At midday on Thursday 10 February the news came through

from Birmingham into the Barnsley office. 'All Brum stood. 10,000 trade unionists jammed the picket lines. All roads to power station jammed. Police had no alternative but to close power station.' Scargill called it 'an historic day'. Chief Constable Sir Derrick Capper shut the Saltley gates 'in the interests of public safety', on the advice of NUM headquarters in London. The closing of Saltley led to an enforcement of a state of emergency and three-day working. It was also the moment when Lord Wilberforce's court of inquiry was set up to examine the miners' claim. It reported on 18 February and accepted the union's demands. The strike had been vindicated. But the union Executive went on to reject the Wilberforce proposals. Further concessions were squeezed out of the Cabinet during marathon talks at Downing Street on the night of 18–19 February 1972.

In retrospect, it is easy to say that the miners were bound to win their struggle, but most of the NUM leaders at the time did not believe that they would. If Heath had persisted with lorry convoys into the power stations guarded by the police, the strike could well have gone down to defeat. In a trial of strength, the NUM had not seemed entirely invincible. The massive, practical help from other trade unions and the general public as well as trades councils was crucial. The success of those flying pickets depended on the support of the many. But the ultimate reason for victory was the spirit of aggression and zeal displayed by rank and file miners. And here the men of Barnsley were at the forefront. Scargill provided an *élan* and strategy which mobilized the anger and frustrations of the area. That spring of 1972 he was elected area compensation agent easily. Within a year the amount paid out by the Coal Board to injured miners doubled and Scargill proved a masterly advocate before the inquiry into the Lofthouse pit disaster. In May 1973 Scargill became Yorkshire area president at only 36 years of age on a massive vote of 26,130 to only 14,916 for his two opponents combined. By the time of the 1974 national coal strike, unofficial committees no longer ran operations. The militants were now in control of the area machine. They look like being so for the near future.

The composition of the twenty-seven-strong National Executive Committee of the NUM is a continual course of conflict.

table 14.1   How the miners voted, 1970–8

For a Strike	%	Against %
1970	55	45
1971	59	41
1973	37	63
1974	81	19

Against	%	For %
1974 (productivity)	61	39
1975 (pay limit)	39	61
1976 (pay limit)	48	52
1977 (early retirement, 2nd ballot)	55	45
1978 (pit incentive)	55	45

Table 14.2   Where the miners are (December 1978)

	Members	Seats on the NEC
Cokemen	5,138	1
COSA	18,980	1
Cumberland	914	1
Derbyshire	11,617	1
Durham	16,258	1
Kent	2,759	1
North-West	8,798	1
Leicester	3,241	1
Midlands	13,973	1
Northumberland	7,767	1
North Wales	1,052	1
Nottingham	34,275	2
Scotland	16,373	1
South Derbyshire	3,269	1
South Wales	26,092	2
Yorkshire	64,060	3
Group Number One	9,371	1
Group Number Two (Scottish enginemen)	4,638	1
Power group (1)	4,982	1
Power group (2)	1,230	1

Those who now sit as representatives no longer accurately reflect where the membership lies on the coalfields. In 1944 areas were given representatation on the NEC according to their membership so that each area had at least one NEC member, but, as table 14.2 illustrates, this means coalfields with large workforces such as Yorkshire are now under-represented on the NUM Executive, while others, notably North Wales and Cumberland, have members on the executive though they now only have one pit each. Understandably such disparity upsets many militants, who come from the larger coalfields, but periodic attempts to carry through any readjustment have failed to make any headway. As Owen Briscoe from Yorkshire explained to the 1973 NUM conference: 'As the principle of the NEC is one man one vote, vital policy issues can be decided by votes of men who represent tiny areas.' An added curiosity is the presence of a member of the General and Municipal Workers on the National Executive to represent 2,000 members in Yorkshire, mostly in a coking plant. 'The occasion can arise when representatives of the NUM on the EC are not masters of this union's destiny,' argued Briscoe. 'I suggest the streamlining of the union will not be brought about by a voluntary basis and until it is we will remain as we are, a federation or in other words a mini-TUC.' Executive members are elected every two years in their areas, though many return without a contest.

The annual conference is a more representative voice of the union. It is held in the first week of every July. Each area of the union is entitled to elect two delegates for the first 10,000 members with a further delegate for each additional 5,000 members, up to a maximum of twenty. The rule-book states that the conference is the government of the union. Rule 8 explains:

In the periods between conference the National Executive Committee shall administer the business and affairs of the union and perform all duties laid down for it by resolution of conference, and it shall not at any time act contrary to, or in defiance of, any resolution of conference.

In recent years the embattled leadership has bypassed conference effectively by holding pithead ballots, as it did in 1975 and 1976 over the government's incomes policy. But the effort to appeal over the heads of the lay activists is not always a sure way of achieving success, particularly when the Executive is so often narrowly divided.

The NUM is still extraordinarily decentralized. The areas remain a law to themselves. Head office in Euston Road is not even always sent full records of what the areas are doing during the year. Most of them hold area delegate conferences in the spring during the run-up to the NUM conference itself. These set the tone of those later proceedings. The areas are responsible for collecting subscriptions from the membership and they pass on a capitation fee to Euston Road. While they exercise complete autonomy in the use to which they put the rest of their finances, NUM rules forbid the areas to finance strikes, lock-outs or other forms of industrial action. Men like Ray Chadburn in Nottingham and Arthur Scargill in Yorkshire are major union leaders in their own right. The level of benefits differs from one area to another, just as it did in the days of the Miners' Federation before 1944. Ultimately all the area officials and their committees are responsible to the National Executive for their activities, but this usually means rule with a loose rein.

Every pit has its lodge or branch and each lodge is governed by the rules of its constituent association. Those who run the lodge are part-timers, who work in the pit. The lodge committee consists of officers, plus six to fifteen other workers. All of them are elected every year or biennially. Each lodge elects a delegate to the area council. Unlike most union branches, the NUM lodges are vital and active parts of the union, and they practise a degree of democratic involvement unknown in many larger unions. Miners live in tightly knit communities close to the pithead. It is true that modern transport and rehousing has dispersed many farther away from their workplace, but the solidarity and comradeship of the pit village is still strong on most of the coalfields.

The NUM is an industrial union, one of the few in Britain, but it does not cover all those who work for the National Coal Board. Rule 3(a) calling for a single union for the whole industry remains unrealized. The 20,589-strong National Association of Colliery Overmen, Deputies and Shotfirers (NACODS) stays aloof, as a TUC affiliate, proud of its independence from the mighty NUM. Relations between those two unions remain patchy. There are also growing numbers of members in the colliery officials and staff section (COSA) of the NUM.

For all its militancy in recent years, the NUM failed to achieve the fringe benefits and rights enjoyed by miners in most industrialized countries. The threatened conflict over early retirement in the winter of 1976-7 provided a good example of the backwardness of past NUM leaders in championing the rank and file, but the final settlement showed the NUM is a force to be reckoned with, for our underground miners now have the most generous early retirement scheme (on up to 90 per cent of earnings) of any country. Since 1972, the old caution and defensiveness has vanished. The miners have become a militant force and no government can ignore their demands.

Yet the massive wage increases of the 1970s failed to improve productivity in the pits. Indeed, output per manshift was worse in 1976 than five years earlier, despite the massive capital investment poured into the pits and the constant government reassurances that coal has a long future. The Coal Board and many union leaders (notably Gormley) blame the lack of incentive payments in addition to the basic wage. In the autumn of 1974 a pit-by-pit incentive scheme was turned down in a ballot by a three to two majority, one was introduced in 1978 with massive pay rises (over £27 a week for the underground workers). The NUM now looks liks emulating the philosophy of the American miners' boss – John L. Lewis – of a high wage, high productivity industry. Militants saw such an incentive system as a return to the bad old piecework days when men fought men and industrial injuries were widespread. It would also help to reduce the possibility of an annual confrontation over pay between the NUM and the Coal Board. Lawrence Daly, the eloquent and literate NUM general secretary (a Scotsman who grew up on the West Fife coalfield) spoke out forcefully against such a scheme in 1974. He disagreed with Gormley on that issue, but for the most part the two men work closely together. Daly, a firm believer in the Social Contract, was elected in 1969 (defeating Gormley in the contest) as a man of the left, but the militants in the NUM believe Daly has drifted to the right. He remains one of the most eloquent and effective speakers in the trade union movement.

There are around ten inflexibles on the NUM Executive, who

are usually opposed to any policies agreed to by the union leadership and the Coal Board. Only around five members are in any sense floaters, whose minds are open to persuasion on the merits of an issue. This means delicate diplomacy, arm-twisting and flattery, to ensure the Gormley/Daly leadership stays in control. The NUM is likely to move farther leftwards in the next few years with unforeseeable consequences for the union and the British economy. There are those who believe a showdown on the coalfields is inevitable. The miners have shown what they can do when they flex their industrial muscles. The grim question remains. Is this country ungovernable without their blessing?

15 White-collar rivals

ASTMS

It is not hard to understand why so many of the staider brothers on the TUC General Council find it difficult to stomach Clive Jenkins, flamboyant and witty general secretary of the 471,000-strong white-collar union, the Association of Scientific, Technical and Managerial Staffs. He thrives on his success in the cut-throat world of white-collar union competition, combining a sharp left-wing political philosophy with a love for the good things of life. Jenkins has a town house near Regent's Park canal and a country cottage in Essex. His taste for good wine and haute cuisine fails to impress the manual union bosses, who still often believe the irrepressible Clive is simply too clever by half. He was kept off the General Council for years, because he got under the skin of the big battalions. It was not until September 1974 that the TUC establishment capitulated by forming a new trade group section on the General Council for the area of membership growth where Jenkins has excelled – among private sector services and white-collar staff in manufacturing industry. Jenkins reached the inner circle at last, or least its outer rim. He will eventually get on to the more important TUC committees under the rules of Buggins's turn. His enthusiastic contribution to General Council debates, particularly on education for the unions, has already enlivened many a dull session.

Drinking gin and tonic at 11.00 in the morning in his trendy office, with its modish furniture, the Hi-fi playing Fats Waller records, and a copy of the *Good Food Guide* in the in-tray, Jenkins looks more like a successful whiz-kid salesman than a serious union boss. For years few in the TUC were prepared to take him seriously. Even now, the knowledge that dear old Clive is raising an issue or exploiting a loophole can raise the hackles of the more cautious union leaders. Yet this charming, imaginative, voluble Welshman, with his portly stomach and

well-cut suits, has been invigorating white-collar trade unionism since the early 1960s. Like him or not, Clive Jenkins has
been the progenitor of a social revolution. He has made trade
unionism successful with an aggressive, radical driving spirit
among the class-conscious, stuffy conservative ranks of
Britain's white-collar élites. 'Organizing the middle classes' is
what Jenkins includes as one of his few hobbies in *Who's Who*.
The statistics show just how big an advance he has made with
ASTMS – up from 70,000 in 1968 to over 430,000 nine years
later.

ASTMS revolves round the Jenkins personality. He is the
second son of a railway clerk from Port Talbot in South Wales,
who left school when he was 13 to be trained as a metallurgist.
The young Jenkins joined a union – the Association of Scientific Workers. He was elected branch secretary in his home
town at the tender age of 18. Two years later Jenkins met
Harry Knight, general secretary of ASSET (the Association of
Supervisory Staffs, Executives and Technicians), who offered
him a full-time job in his union. By the age of 34 Jenkins
reached the top job in ASSET. He has never looked back since.
Much of the astonishing growth of ASTMS comes from
shrewd mergers and amalgamations. ASTMS itself was the offspring of the marriage between ASSET and the Scientific Workers in 1968. Others to join the rapidly expanding Jenkins
empire were the National Union of Insurance Staffs, the Medical Practitioners' Union and the Guild of Pharmascists.

ASTMS is sensitive about publishing a breakdown of its
membership, so that sceptics believe the union inflates its true
size for reasons of prestige. The criticism is unfair. In the highly
competitive market place of the white-collar world, ASTMS
has to protect itself against innumerable rivals. The following
figures are merely estimates supplied by the ASTMS Research
Department in 1975, but they provide a rough guide to the
multiplicity of areas where the union has won a substantial
stake. Around 44 per cent of ASTMS members are in the engineering industry. While TASS recruits in the drawing offices and
ancillary professions, ASTMS specializes in the scientific and
research side as well as the managerial. It battles with the
clerical union, APEX, over the office staff. In 1974 there were
around 150,000 members in that important sector, where the

union is governed by national engineering agreements as a member of the Confederation of Engineering and Shipbuilding Unions. Between 40,000 and 50,000 ASTMS members are in the insurance business, with a further 17,000 in banking. The decision of the Midland Bank Staff Association to merge with Jenkins's union in 1973 widened the ASTMS bridgehead into that sector. Over recent years, ASTMS, particularly under the shrewd leadership of Mrs Muriel Turner, one of Jenkins's deputy general secretaries, has been recruiting at a furious pace in the highest citadels of capitalism. Between 5,000 and 6,000 members now exist for ASTMS in the shipping companies such as P & O, Lloyds and general commerce.

The union has a 1,000-strong publishing branch. It has over 8,000 members in civil air transport with full representation on the collective bargaining machinery of the industry. ASTMS is also growing fast in the chemical industry. In its first negotiation on behalf of 7,000 scientific workers at ICI in 1975 it achieved a 26 per cent increase plus improvements in fringe benefits. The union also has a sizeable membership among staff in the car, telecommunications and aerospace industries; and the union is fairly strong in certain parts of the public service sector. It has 10,000 members in oil and petro-chemicals. Around 20,000 are in the National Health Service, including doctors, speech therapists and medical laboratory technicians. ASTMS has also made inroads on to the university campuses, where it represents academic staff (disillusioned with the Association of University Teachers) as well as laboratory technicians and office staff. In short, ASTMS is pursuing an aggressive strategy of becoming a general union for all white-collar workers, those who work more with their brains than their hands.

The union grows inexorably, but as in all unions, the inward and outward flow of members is a constant problem. Turnover is small by union standards. In the first four months of 1975, 30,503 members were recruited into ASTMS, but the union lost 22,833 through membership lapses at the same time, giving a net gain of 7,670. The average annual growth is 30,000.

ASTMS operates in a highly competitive, cut-throat market, where resistance to unions remains strong, but Jenkins has won a reputation for highly effective bargaining. Contrary to first appearances, ASTMS is not a rich union. In 1975 its total assets were only just over £5 million. Twelve national officers cover the various areas where ASTMS have members and they are backed up with twenty divisional full-time officers, based on 26 offices.

ASTMS is something of a contradiction. It recruits in the citadels of capitalism from the status-conscious middle class, but the union lies on the left of the TUC. This does not mean that Jenkins has not proved highly adept at exploiting every advantage for his union's benefit. Though it boycotted the Industrial Relations Court like other TUC affiliates, ASTMS was always ready to turn up at the Commission on Industrial Relations and accept its recommendations when it brought increased membership for the union.

In fact, Jenkins is a pragmatist with an eye for the main chance. He is also one of the few union leaders who think more widely than the confines of his own union. Jenkins is a passionate champion of manpower planning – Swedish style. He was an early supporter of flexible working hours and he is one of the lone voices who pushes for more resources being put into union education in the TUC. In 1975 ASTMS opened a residential college called Whitehall in Essex, where it trains lay members in techniques of bargaining and the intricacies of new labour law. Over 1,000 students a year pass through on residential courses. This rate was to be doubled from 1978. The ASTMS Research Department produces periodic economic reviews, which are of a high standard. Jenkins is a powerful advocate of the 'alternative strategy' of import controls, public ownership and the control of capital movements. He has always been a firm anti-Common Marketeer, though this did not stop him setting up a consultancy link with a telex machine in Brussels to keep in touch with what the EEC is doing.

But as his union grows apace, there is a danger that the Jenkins strategy will come under fire. The twenty-two-member executive was deadlocked in its attitude to Labour's plans for the nationalization of the banks and insurance companies in 1976, so ASTMS abstained from victory at the party conference as a result. There is a threat of Conservative infiltration into the executive, though this does not give Jenkins cause for worry. 'We find Tories are just as militant as anybody else when it comes to higher pay and better conditions,' he says.

His union is loyally affiliated to the Labour Party and it uses its twenty-nine-strong contingent of MPs very effectively on the floor of the Commons with regular briefings. Nobody who visits the annual ASTMS conference can fail to be impressed by the tough way in which Jenkins rules the union. His blend of entrepreneurial energy and broad left politics has not yet brought any conflict within the union. As long as ASTMS delivers the goods to the disgruntled and militant members of the white-collar salariat, it looks unlikely that the union will find itself taken over by impassioned Tories, anxious to curb its militancy. But ASTMS is no longer alone in the white-collar area. It acts as a catalyst, and there are others who now believe they are better equipped to woo the skilled and privileged into trade union membership.

APEX

The Association of Professional, Executive, Clerical and Computer Staffs (APEX) has grown at a much slower pace (up from 79,200 in 1964 to 150,000 in 1978). The union is led by a mild-mannered, bespectacled, moderate, pro-EEC Labour loyalist – Roy Grantham – who lost his seat on the TUC General Council in 1975, falling foul of the big union barons. APEX organizes in the offices of affiliate unions. In 1974 there was a bitter strike at the Peckham headquarters of the Engineers. It did nothing to improve APEX's reputation with that union. Moreover, the union's decision to take the issue of union recognition at General Accident to court in 1975 – defying a TUC Disputes Committee ruling – lost APEX more friends at Congress.

The union was founded in 1890 as the National Union of Clerks. It claims to be the oldest white-collar union in Britain. In 1920 the words 'and administrative workers' were added to the union's title and it merged with the Women Clerks' and Secretaries' Association. This was later transmuted into the Clerical and Administrative Workers' Union in 1941, before the new name of APEX was established in 1972.

The union won its first procedural agreement in the engineering industry as long ago as 1920 and two thirds of its present membership are from that sector – in the administrative and clerical grades. In 1963 the union had 44,250 members in engineering; ten years later the number had risen to 87,500.

'White-collar staff are the last feudal bastion,' said Grantham in an interview. 'We have had to educate them to a new approach in trade unionism.' APEX is a strong believer in plant bargaining, pressing for grading schemes for clerical staff, the enlargement of rank and file rights over redundancies and sick pay. In recent years it has launched fairly militant campaigns for the implementation of labour legislation, notably the Equal Pay Act. APEX has fifty-six full-time officials who spend most of their time in negotiation with employers. The union claims to have a staff representative for every twenty-five members. The APEX annual conference lays down broad policy and it expects those who bargain at office level to be limited by those conference decisions.

In recent years the union has broadened its recruitment base with a big campaign for new members in the textile industry among clerical staff. Progress has also been made in carpet-making, distilleries and chemicals. Around 5,000 members are now in the food industry in firms like Rowntree, Cadbury and Fry. APEX is competing fiercely with ASTMS in the insurance sector. It is also active in civil air transport, electricity supply and coal mining among clerical workers. 'A union needs to be strong in a number of different industries. Having strength in one sector can help the union in others,' argues Grantham. He has practical experience of a number of industries. Grantham was a laboratory assistant with a Birmingham engineering firm for a year before he entered the civil service, where he became an active secretary of the local district committee of the Inland Revenue Staff Federation. At the precocious age of 22 Grantham was appointed Birmingham organizer for the Clerical and Administrative Workers' Union. In 1963 he was appointed by the fifteen-strong Executive Council to the post of the national full-time official, responsible for negotiations in engineering. In January 1970 he became general secretary of the union. 'We are a low profile union most of the time. We like to get on with our job and not sound off all over the place,' says Grantham. 'The best test for a union is getting a good agreement for the members and not spending your time on matters of ephemeral interest.' But in the highly competitive atmosphere of white-collar unionism, a touch of flamboyance and *savoir-faire* does not go amiss. This is what APEX lacks at present.

EPEA

Another potential ASTMS rival is the 47,000-strong Electrical Power Engineers' Association (EPEA), which plans to transform itself from being among the smallest of TUC affiliates into one of its largest. Under the shrewd and highly effective leadership of its pipe-smoking general secretary, John Lyons, the EPEA is seeking to extend its recruitment base beyond the electrical industry where it organizes the highly skilled engineers into the ranks of professional engineers as a whole. Between 150,000 and 300,000 engineers in middle and upper income jobs are thought to be ripe for membership of this responsible and able organization. Other white-collar leaders like Ken Gill and Clive Jenkins argued that the EPEA was in no position to launch any recruitment drive among professional engineers, for in most industries agreements already exist which carved up the recruitment area among specific TUC-affiliated unions and the EPEA was not one of them. In the spring of 1976 ASTMS and the TASS section of the Engineers reached agreement with the Engineering Employers' Federation on recruiting professional engineers among the 4,000 federated firms. Clear-cut agreements also exist with large companies like Ford, Chrysler and Massey-Ferguson.

The impetus for the EPEA decision to change its rules came from a December 1975 report by the Council of Engineering Institutions, which advised its members to join a union and mentioned the EPEA as the one to which they should belong. 'ASTMS is a Hoover union sucking up white-collar workers from all over the place,' claimed Lyons. 'The EPEA is the best geared to look after the interests of engineers.' In his view, his association has two big advantages over others. 'We are a politically non-committed union, but at the same time we are a thoroughly effective one in the TUC.' Certainly the EPEA has been totally transformed over the past few years, with major organizational reforms and a new militant edge to its industrial relations activity. This was best exemplified in the EPEA overtime ban during the winter of 1973–4, contributing to the 'crisis' that eventually brought down Heath. Lyons has proved an eloquent champion of the downtrodden ranks of middle management, and those with skill, who have been hit by inflation and incomes policy. His union, along with ASTMS, was one of the few to oppose the Social Contract in 1976.

The EPEA transformed its rules in November 1973, when the National Executive Council agreed to bring the organization up to date. An annual delegate conference was introduced for the first time in 1975 and Eric Varley, the Energy minister, turned up for the occasion to address delegates. The EPEA was founded in 1913 at a meeting in London's Fleet Street, with twenty-one engineers in attendance. It was decided to set up the new body to raise the efficiency and general status of the profession. Local groups came together with a programme of demands including a six-day week for all workers in electricity stations, a 48-hour week and time off for public holiday working. But it was not until the mid-1920s that the EPEA won recognition in the electricity supply industry. 'We are the most powerful union in the country,' Lyons assured me. 'The members have only realized this in the past five years, but we are responsible for the lives of the whole community. Our members have seen industrial unions winning through muscle power, while their loyalty has been taken for granted.' But Lyons's efforts to recruit among managerial ranks ran into difficulty after 1976 particularly with the TUC and the Engineering Employers' Federation. The hopes of rapid growth were quickly dispelled in inter-union wrangles, the lengthy procedures of ACAS and an eventual writ issued by Lyons against the TUC. The decision of the 1,600-strong Shipbuilding and Allied Industries' Management Association (SAIMA) to have a transfer of engagements to the Engineers' and Managers' Association, part of the EPEA (EMA), at the end of 1977 was a breakthrough and TASS's efforts to prevent the union winning recognition in the newly nationalized shipbuilding industry were not successful, though the British Shipbuilders' Board took a long time to accept EMA's position. A number of cases, most notably that concerning managers at GEC/REL at Whetstone in Leicester and Hawker Siddeley Power Transformers Ltd, brought EMA into a head-on collision with the TUC Disputes Committee. The TUC insisted that the Bridlington principles made it impossible for EMA to recruit members in areas of the engineering industry, where collective agreements existed for other groups of workers, even if the relevant groups agreed by ballot that they wanted EMA to represent their interests as a bargainer. In Lyons's opinion, this behaviour constituted a pre-membership closed shop, because it prevented managers belonging to no union from choosing a union for themselves. Unfortunately for Lyons the employers have been unwilling to risk any damage to existing industrial relations practices by giving EMA the green light. In Lyons's opinion they would rather their managers belonged to no union at all than EMA. A number of ACAS recognition ballots in 1977 and 1978 testified to the popularity of EMA among managers, but by early 1979 there were only just over 6,000 members in its ranks.

BIFU (formerly NUBE)

There are now over a million workers in what is officially categorized as 'insurance, banking, finance and business services', but only the Banking, Insurance and Finance Union with 110,000 claimed members in 1979 solely concentrates its efforts in that highly competitive sector, where belonging to a trade union is still often viewed as a subversive act. ASTMS was seen as a threat by the bank staff associations and NUBE in 1974, after Clive Jenkins had scored an unexpected triumph with the decision of the Midland Bank Staff Association to throw in its lot with ASTMS, retaining its virtual autonomy. 'Clive has been very useful to us,' said Leif Mills, the young and able Balliol College graduate, BIFU general secretary. 'He woke people up to the dangers of multi-unionism in banking.' But Jenkins was not a strong enough menace to enable the bank staff associations and NUBE to reach agreement on a confederation, however hard they tried to achieve unity. Talks were eventually broken off in 1975 and NUBE returned to the TUC after its expulsion three years earlier for staying on the register under the 1971 Industrial Relations Act.

Surprisingly, for a white-collar union in the private sector, NUBE first affiliated to the TUC as long ago as 1940, although the union has never won representation on the General Council. The Bank Officers' Guild was formed in 1917, provoking the banks into the creation of staff associations as a protection against any incursion of full-blooded trade unionism into their preserves. Between the wars the banks were successful in keeping any unions at bay. Most bank staff were from the middle class and hated trade unionism. Widespread discontent at salary levels in the 1940s gave a boost to NUBE (as the Guild became after the 1946 merger with the Scottish counterpart), but the union's struggle for employer recognition was hard and painful. In the early 1950s the banks strengthened the staff associations through large wage settlements and the institution of domestic arbitration agreements in all but one of the major clearing banks. In February 1956 national machinery was agreed between NUBE and the Central Council of Bank Staff Associations, but it came to nothing. By the early 1960s the main resistance to NUBE no longer came so much from the employers, but the staff associations, who had begun to adopt a more aggressive attitude with the rejection of pay offers from their employers. It was now the banks themselves who realized the sense of a more formal joint wage negotiation at national level, something NUBE had been campaigning for over the past two decades. In 1960 NUBE established a strike clause in its constitution, making industrial action now possible if a simple majority of members in a particular section of banking agreed. Five years later the Cameron Report drew public attention to the bad industrial relations in banking. During 1967 NUBE mounted a vigorous campaign for recognition and astutely linked the issue to poor pay and conditions for bank staff. Between September and November 1967 NUBE membership rose from 57,000 to 70,000. As a result nine of the clearing banks (excluding the Midland and Coutts) agreed to recognize NUBE through national negotiating machinery without waiting for the Donovan Royal Commission to report. On 22 May 1968 official ratification was given to NUBE after a fifty-year struggle for recognition.

'The attitude of the management has always been in the best imperial tradition,' Mills told me; 'well-meaning, paternalistic and clever.' The creation of a joint negotiating council for banking, which decides maximum and minimum rates for staff below junior management level, minimum salaries for branch managers on first appointment, territorial allowances, working hours, overtime, holidays and the aggregate amounts payable under basic salary scales, should have worked to the advantage of NUBE. The union expected that it would in fact soon absorb the staff associations. Initially membership did grow, but it failed to overtake the joint numerical predominance of the associations, which enabled them to deliver the final vote on any decision in the Banking Staff Council, made up of NUBE and the staff associations. The failure of NUBE to attract more members than the staff associations was a major setback for the union, but perhaps not wholly unpredictable.

True, the new situation should have strengthened NUBE; clearly the union had been the major force on the staff side in pressing for higher pay and better conditions. Mills can look back with some satisfaction at what the new machinery achieved for bank staff. Job evaluation proved a big success. Working hours were reduced to 35, the lowest in 1974 for banking in Western Europe. Saturday closing would not have come about so quickly or easily without the existence of national machinery. Equal pay for women was negotiated long before it had been achieved in other sectors. Yet ironically those visible advances in bank staff pay and benefits weakened NUBE's position. The reason was simple enough. Now that the union and the staff associations work together nationally and jointly in the individual banks, neither side can really claim special credit alone for the negotiated improvements. In the 1960s the distinction between the two forces was clear: NUBE was willing to use the strike weapon. It still is. In fact, the union has been far more ready than the staff associations to go for higher wage increases in joint negotiation. But the ordinary bank clerk is in no position to see the difference any more. BIFU's problem is that its subscription rates are higher than those of the staff associations. So in 1974 NUBE faced an insoluble dilemma. It could not survive as a viable trade union without the existence of centralized machinery; but that very machinery kept NUBE in a permanent minority position and made it look less attractive to non-members among banking staff.

The danger was that NUBE would surrender its own position in the planned get-together with the staff associations in a new body. It was in the interests of NUBE to establish a highly centralized structure, but the staff associations wanted a loosely organized federal system, where power lay with the affiliates and not the skeletal national body. Moreover Clive Jenkins made a powerful argument against NUBE revealing the active role played by the employers federation in the merger talks, whose director took the chair during the meetings. The danger was that the Association of Banking and Finance Unions (ABFU) – as planned – would prove a grandiose-sounding name for a hollow façade behind which the staff associations recouped their power under a new guise. By 1978 ABFU looked a moribund concept.

BIFU, as the union has been known since 1978, is strong in the Trustee Savings Bank (12,000) and the Co-operative Bank. It has around half the employees of Barclays in its ranks (25,000) and around a third in the Midland Bank. Between 35 and 40 per cent of the staffs of National Westminster and Lloyds are also in BIFU. The union enjoys sole negotiating rights at Williams and Glyn, but in the other major banks it has to compete with the staff associations and other unions such as ASTMS. In May 1971 NUBE changed its rule to allow it to start recruiting in financial institutions outside banking. In November 1973 the union claimed to have 1,300 members spread over thirty-one building societies. BIFU is run on a shoe-string. It is therefore surprising the union can afford to employ nine full-time officials and sixteen regional organizers and run a Research and Publicity Department from its tiny Surbiton headquarters. Over the next few years BIFU may find it hard to grow rapidly.

16 The hammer of the left

EETPU

Frank Chapple believes he is fighting in a 'battle for survival'. As general secretary of the 420,000-strong Electrical, Electronic, Telecommunications and Plumbing Union since 1966, he is the trade union movement's hammer of the left. On the TUC General Council – where he has sat since March 1971 – Chapple's truculent anti-communist causes irritation. In the age of so-called *détente* he has the uncomfortable habit of reminding his TUC colleagues that the Soviet Union and its satellites are far from sweetness and light. Such behaviour isolates Chapple on the General Council, but he does not seem to mind, and he makes no effort to rally any fainter-hearted moderates to join his ideological crusade. In fact, Chapple finds it difficult to disguise his utter contempt for the TUC establishment, particularly Jack Jones of the TGWU. As he wrote in an editorial in his union's journal *Contact*, in September 1973:

Sitting and listening at the TUC often resembles watching a play. The actors strut across the stage mouthing their lines, breathing defiance or simulating sympathy, every now and again glancing at their prompter for assistance. Off stage most of them revert to ordinary human beings facing ordinary human problems in the empirical and reasonable way that trade unionists always have done.

This is hardly the language calculated to endear Chapple to other union bosses. He stands in splendid isolation, unwilling to swallow the TUC orthodoxies. To Chapple, the main enemy is not so much the employer class but Soviet communism, and he devotes much of his considerable energy to combating that menace within his own union's ranks and elsewhere. Chapple's union critics believe his zeal for import controls stems from a belief that Eastern European regimes have been dumping cheap

shirts and shoes on Britain, but this is not true. The plight of
the electronics industry was the main reason for his protec-
tionist stand. The EETPU has banned members of the Communist Party from holding full-time office in the union since
1965. The rule was reaffirmed by the rules revision conference
in 1973. 'The obstacle to unity in this union and indeed to the
Labour movement is the Communist Party,' Chapple told delegates to the 1973 biennial conference; 'its hatred of democracy,
its hatred of all those people who oppose its views, its character
assassinations of anyone who dares to differ from it.' In his
opinion, there is no room for compromise in the war against
communism. In August 1974 Chapple wrote in the union journal:

All around us unscrupulous but persuasive people are waiting in
the wings to frighten the dispossessed and confused to follow the
flag. The trade union movement must provide the bastion of
democratic values which will preserve our way of life. Even within
the movement there are those who seek to undermine our resolve,
who would push us a little further down the slope that leads to
chaos or dictatorship. For evil to triumph it is only necessary for
good men to do nothing.

To many trade unionists that kind of language seems to come
from a bygone age when Stalin ruled supreme in the Kremlin.
Chapple regrets that his main support outside the EETPU comes
from the Conservative press. But his virtual one-man war
against Soviet communism and its influence in the unions is the
result of hard, personal experience. For nearly twenty years
Chapple was a dedicated Communist himself. He was one of
the disciplined comrades who helped to establish an iron grip
over the Electrical Trades' Union (ETU) in 1947. In the late
1950s, after the trauma of the Red Army's invasion of Hungary, Chapple joined the union's Reform Group to work with
former Communists like Les Cannon and Mark Young in
wresting control of the union from the Communists.

This is not the place to detail the events of those years. C. H.
Rolph, in his account of the 1961 Old Bailey trial (*All Those in
Favour?*), and the biography of Les Cannon (*The Road from
Wigan Pier*), do ample justice to the most disreputable episode
in post-war trade union history. The whole affair threw little

credit on the TUC, which dragged its feet for over three years. Resort to the law courts in the search for justice against the Communist ETU leaders, who had rigged the union elections in favour of themselves, displeased many TUC worthies who wanted to pass in silence over what was going on. The EETPU reformers won their battle through self-reliance and inner convictions, with only a few friends (notably Vic Feather who risked his career, Walter Padley of USDAW and Trevor Evans of the *Daily Express*) to aid them.

It is not therefore surprising that Chapple and his union should keep their distance from the rest of the TUC. In 1972 he was even ready to defy the TUC's instructions and register under the Industrial Relations Act. Only the imprisonment of the five dockers in Pentonville held the EETPU back. Chapple lacks the more philosophical approach of his predecessor Les Cannon, who died of cancer in December 1970. But he is a forceful speaker with a biting turn of phrase. As a hammer of the left his enemies are innumerable and he often thinks he gets a raw deal from industrial correspondents. There are no grounds to believe Chapple's rough, tough style upsets the majority of his members. He won a landslide victory in his re-election as general secretary in the spring of 1977 with over 70 per cent of those who voted doing so for him. Tom Breakell, the union's president in 1975, did himself no harm either with his attack on the Shrewsbury building pickets that so aroused the wrath of the gallery at the TUC. Though the left retain an irritant value inside the union, they are no longer a menace for the movement, to the ever-vigilant eyes of Chapple.

There is no doubt who rules at Hayes Court, the EETPU's country house in suburban Kent. Chapple's spiky personality dominates everything. He has only had three real holidays in the past fifteen years. His workload is formidable and he finds less and less time for his favourite hobby – pigeon breeding. Chapple lays great stress on the need for administrative competence. He believes lack of financial sense and a tendency to proligate waste are the 'Achilles' heel' of the trade union movement. Unlike some other union bosses, Chapple lives frugally and he keeps a close watch on the expense accounts of his full-time officials. His proudest claim is the rise in the union's total assets over the past few years. At the end of 1974 they totalled nearly £4,750,000. In 1961 when the Communists were ousted, the union was almost bankrupt. Chapple is a keen supporter of the mixed economy. He sits on the NEDDY Finance for Investment Committee. Unlike most union leaders, Chapple is ready to nurture the EETPU's finances through dealings on the stock exchange. In 1977 the union had equity stakes in numerous companies including Reed International, Tube Investments, General Electric, Tate & Lyle and Courtaulds. Education for union members has a high priority in the union, ever since the Communist leaders founded the residential college at Esher in 1952. In 1975 the EETPU purchased a house near to Hayes Court called Culham with a large tract of land for further development. In 1974 the union spent nearly £76,000 on education. Chapple's belief in the virtues of joint union–management training courses is not shared by other union leaders who believe employer involvement can distort 'true' union education programmes.

This is not to say that he is a weak and ineffective bargainer on behalf of his members; far from it. 'We are not prepared to see our people, who are among the highest skilled workers in this land, fall disastrously behind anybody else's wage,' he assured the 1974 biennial conference of the power workers. Chapple is well aware of the enormous power his union holds to paralyse the economy. Just a handful of striking supply workers could bring the country to its knees. Since 1972 Chapple has made it perfectly clear that he will not tolerate his members falling behind the living standards of the miners. As he argued in his 1974 speech to the supply workers' conference:

The warning I give both to the miners and to everyone else who thinks they have the country by the throat, if anyone wants it by the throat and to use it on their own behalf, this union and the electricians in this land can do just that and they will do just that if it is the only alternative to getting some common sense into our industrial relations.

The power workers were heavily criticized for their work-to-rule during the winter of 1970–1 which led to black-outs, but the Wilberforce Court of Inquiry backed up their pay claim. The statistics paraded in the Wilberforce Report were impressive. The power workers went along with productivity bargaining and made no attempt to resist technological change. Under Cannon's influence the union agreed to an improved status for the supply workers in return for changes in working patterns. In 1964 annual salaries were introduced as well as an extension of the industry's sick pay scheme to the manual workers. The following year brought the 40-hour working week, better holidays and revised shift working. Work study methods were agreed in 1966. As a result, there was an impressive increase in productivity, but earnings fell behind the national average for manufacturing industry. As Wilberforce conceded: 'Up to and including the 1969 agreement the great majority of workers had not in our view been adequately compensated for the changes they had willingly accepted.' The power workers won an estimated 20 per cent pay increase as a result of the Wilberforce settlement. As Chapple explained to the 1972 power workers' conference: 'This is among the largest percentage increase ever achieved by any industry for such a period.'

It is often not realized that the bulk of the EETPU's members no longer lie among supply or electrical contract workers. The union has turned into a general one with members being recruited across the breadth of British manufacturing industry, many of whom have no electrical skills. In 1968 the Plumbers' Union merged with the ETU. There have been no further sizeable amalgamations with Chapple's union, though talks have been held with the Engineers and the GMWU.

The Electricians' Trade Union was founded in 1890 as a result of a merger between the Amalgamated Society of Telegraph and Telephone Construction Men and the Union of Electrical Operatives. It adopted an ultra-democratic rule-book similar to that of the Engineers. The union did not appoint any full-time general secretary until 1901, but it took an early interest in political action with representation at the 1900 Memorial Hall meeting that founded the LRC. One of the first decisions of the full-time leadership was to donate money to electricians on strike in Australia. During the 1940s the Communists proved highly successful in manipulating the organization for their own political purposes, so that when they lost control of the union in 1961 the reformers decided to carry through a major reform of the ETU's structure.

Before 1962 the only regular gatherings of the union had been the annual conference and an infrequent conference for rules revision. Both assemblies had been limited to a chosen few lay activists with no more than 350 attending the conference and 50 the rules revision get-togethers. The first changes were made at the 1962 conference. It was agreed to change the method of union elections from voting at the branch to voting by postal ballot under single transferable vote, all to be administered by the Electoral Reform Society. A Final Appeals Committee was also established, made up of rank-and-filers. It was their function to hear members who believed they had been treated unfairly by the Executive Council. The 1962 conference also agreed to hold biennial conferences of the whole union, instead of once a year, and have rules revision once every six years. On top of this, industrial conferences for particular occupational groups in the union were to be held in the intervening years, where it was believed necessary. An attempt to extend the term of office for elected executive councillors from two to five years was defeated, but carried three years later. In his impressive, well-argued evidence to the Donovan Commission, Cannon spelt out in considerable detail the *raison d'être* of the union's reforms. The aim was not merely to cleanse the leadership of corruption and political extremism or the rank and file of subversive elements, but to provide the ETU with a more effective and relevant structure to the needs of the times. As Cannon argued: 'The answer to trade union power – where it exists – is not to deprive it of that power but to impose checks and balances against the abuse of that power.' He was convinced the main obstacle to efficiency in the past had been the 'tortuous lines of communication between the various units of the union'. Branch meetings held once a fortnight were not seen as the quickest way to act upon instructions from head office. Cannon and the reformers wanted to see union organization concentrated more on the shopfloor and less at branch committee meetings outside the place of work. This is why the ETU was one of the first unions to integrate the stewards into the organization of the union. Rule 15 sets out the functions of the steward, who is responsible to the area full-time official and under the directions of the Executive Council. The ETU have around 7,700 stewards at present. The

1968 survey for Donovan reckoned there was on average one EETPU steward for every thirty-five members and a senior steward for every 200. Those ratios are far smaller than for most other large unions.

A controversial decision, which aroused heated debate, was the abolition of the area committees in 1965. Those bodies had been hotbeds of political intrigue and manipulation and, with the new emphasis on industrial-based unionism, it made sense to remove the layer from the union's organization. Benefits were extended to widen the appeal of the union with a new fatal accident benefit, and cheap holidays. Administrative efficiency was stepped up with the installation of a computer to keep a closer control over membership figures and the spread of the check-off system for paying union dues. In 1965 the union agreed in a ballot by 42,187 votes to 13,932 to ban members of the Communist Party from holding office in the union and the decision was upheld in 1971. The eleven-man Executive Council was turned into a body of full-timers, who must face the members for re-election every five years. The purpose of the reforms, which continued in 1977, was both to make the union more effective and to keep the extremist minorities in frustrated isolation (see figure 16.1).

Electricians tend to be independent-minded, assertive people. They know they have become indispensable. The economy would collapse without them. The tenacity of their attitude is often demonstrated in industrial disputes. Electricians have a reputation for being tough and argumentative. 'We are such an awkward bunch all round that we can never do even the most beneficial things from our own point of view easily,' says Chapple. Electricians are skilled craftsmen in growing demand. A good electrician needs to have a head for figures and to understand mathematics to calculus level. He also must be literate and have the ability to think theoretically. Above all, he must have initiative, the ability to improvise. The man with his own bag of tools, moving from job to job with little personal contact with the employer, is still very common. In private contract work the hours can be long. The more ambitious and foot-loose are ready to travel from one end of the country to another on a job, if the money is good enough. Jobs on muddy building sites of new power stations can be arduous, requiring

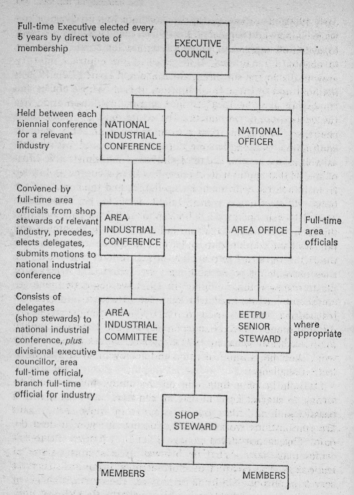

figure 16.1 The industrial structure of the EETPU

brawn as much as sense. It is not surprising that contract work tends to appeal to younger men, who have finished their apprenticeship – which they can now do by the time they are 18. The average age of a contract worker is no more than 30. In the early 1960s the private sector was a vicious jungle of competing wage claims and frequent strikes. Electricians were even known to switch off supplies to employers with whom they were trying to negotiate a pay deal. Both sides of the contract industry grew to dislike the cut-throat atmosphere. As part of the 1966–9 national agreement a Joint Industry Board was set up by the employers and the EETPU in January 1968. Each side has twelve representatives on the JIB which has an independent chairman. This is an attempt to bring order and coherence to contracting. Nationally agreed rates of pay were established, as well as recognized hours of work and overtime rates. Most of the 34,000 contract workers enjoy JIB privileges and move from job to job with their stamped JIB card to show they are bona fide electricians with the right certificate for each grade. The JIB even operates a labour pool to help employers find the men they want. Inflation and successive government pay policies have combined to undermine the model cooperation of the JIB in the past few years. Electrical contract workers on big sites or building power stations have found that bricklayers, plasterers, even those making the tea, have negotiated huge increases at the site level with complete disregard for national restrictions. The JIB tried to remedy this through paying additional money to electricians on larger sites. The men I talked to in electrical work in 1973 expressed satisfaction with the work they did, a sense of pride and achievement and an intellectual challenge.

Chapple keeps a tight rein on the union, but it would be wrong to suggest he is merely an old-style union boss with a passive rank and file obeying orders from above. Electricians are rumbustious workers, ready for fierce argument and debate. This is not stifled in the EETPU, whatever Chapple's critics may claim. What he believes in is a strong sense of leadership. The creation of more democratic union structures serves no purpose if it leads to drift and indecision, a gaggle of divided and uncertain voices. This is why the EETPU constitution does not lay final, irrevocable power in the hands of its conferences. Outside electrical contract work, the union has sole bargaining rights nowhere. As a member of the CSEU, it must cooperate with other unions in reaching collective agreements.

17 The weaker brethren

USDAW

The 462,178-strong Union of Shop, Distributive and Allied Workers has a hard job merely standing still. It estimates that it loses as many as a third of its members every year. In 1973 USDAW recruited 123,525 members. This only amounted to a net gain of 1,436. In 1976 the union launched a vigorous recruitment campaign through public display advertising, but weak areas like retail distribution are notoriously hard to organize. A 1974 report by the Commission on Industrial Relations reckoned that no more than 10 per cent of all those working in retailing were in unions. There were estimated to be as many as 1,900,000 people employed in the retail trade in 1973 in Britain with total sales of over £20,000 million. In the past, USDAW (founded in an amalgamation in 1947) had its main strength in retailing. It was very strong in the Co-operative societies – thanks to a closed-shop agreement; but during the 1960s and early 1970s that centre of USDAW strength contracted at a rapid rate. Between 1966 and 1971 alone the labour force of the Co-ops fell by nearly a quarter from 173,458 to 131,521, while the number of shops almost halved. Consequently USDAW experienced real decline during the 1960s. By 1973 it was estimated only 59 per cent of the union's members worked within the scope of the retail wages councils, with 43 per cent in the Co-ops and 16 per cent in the private trades. Back in 1961 the Co-ops alone accounted for as much as 55 per cent of the union's entire membership. Yet with 94 out of the 134 union seats on nine wages councils, USDAW is a major influence on the bargaining over wages and conditions in the retail business.

Over recent years USDAW has made company agreements with a wide range of large multiple stores. The most notable are Lewis's, Selfridges, Littlewoods, Woolworth, Tesco, and Fine Fare. The union also negotiates on behalf of employees at multiple tailoring chains such as Burton, John Collier and Hepworths. But, as the CIR survey discovered, small retail outlets remain dominant. In its study, as many as 49 per cent of establishments were single-establishment firms and 83 per cent of workers were employed in establishments with fewer than ten on the payroll. The very smallness and scattered nature of the retail trade hampers trade unionism. As the CIR commented: 'Without fundamental changes to the prevailing situation no union will be able to make much impression in the area or establish a viable organization.' High labour turnover is not the only added problem. As many as 75 per cent of all those working in retail trade are women and as many as 40 per cent of workers in retail only do part-time, ranging from a third in retail drapery to two thirds in the newspaper trade. Moreover, the bulk of them are young people with around a third of those in retail aged under 21. As many as 51 per cent of all male employees in distribution (including wholesale) were between 15 and 19. Such factors are hardly conducive to stable and effective trade unionism.

It is not surprising therefore that USDAW has done its best to widen its catchment area over the past few years and by so doing transform itself into more of a general union for the semi-skilled and unskilled in the private sector. The obvious growth points have proved to have close links with the retail trade in food processing, wholesaling, credit trading and mail order business. A large number of USDAW members work in the Co-operative Society's mills, factories and dairies. There is an USDAW presence in the retail meat trade and the bacon-curing industry as well as milk (Unigate, United Dairies). The union negotiates for workers in restaurants and clerical grades in the NAAFI. It is also active in flour milling, cocoa, chocolate and confectionery, and the brewery industry, as well as the laundry trade, chemicals and tobacco.

USDAW is not a militant union. The annual conference even voted to register under the 1971 Industrial Relations Act, a decision which had to be hastily reversed by a narrow majority at a recall conference in 1972. This was after the union faced the threat of suspension from the TUC. Yet USDAW's political stance has not always been so moderate. In the late 1940s the union was a major critic in the TUC of Ernest Bevin's foreign policy. Walter Padley, MP, and the general secretary of the time, Alan Birch, fought a hard battle against communist influences in the union until the mid-1950s. In 1951 USDAW was the only non-communist trade union to support the call for an investigation into allegations that the USA were using germ warfare in Korea. From 1951 until 1955 the union was a stalwart supporter of Bevanism over German rearmament and the need for nationalization. But by 1958 the left tide had turned in the USDAW rank and file. As Martin Harrison wrote at the turn of the 1960s: 'No union meeting has a wider variety of opinion. Most conferences produce a boring succession of speeches in which the only argument is between the more and the less extreme.' In recent years, USDAW has been a supporter of British entry into the Common Market and its old left line on foreign policy issues has been much less obvious.

Under Lord Allen (1962–79), USDAW became a moderate, restrained force in the TUC. Bill Whatley took over in 1979. The union invariably backs the Labour leadership and the General Council line, but not in an aggressive way. To judge by the temper and quality of debate at the union's annual delegate meeting, there was only a small, ineffective opposition to the Allen way of doing things. The union has not gone in for any drastic internal reform. The 1971 annual delegate meeting debated the issue and it was referred to an executive subcommittee, but progress proved slow and indecisive. An eight-page discussion paper went to the 1973 meeting, but the outcome was insubstantial.

USDAW has over 1,300 branches with the majority of them organized on either a single-employer or a trade basis. Only in districts or towns with only a few members does USDAW organize mixed branches. On top of this, the union has eight territorial divisional councils, each made up of ten members who are nominated and elected by the branches in each division every two years. The councils meet once a month together with the divisional officer who is a full-time official and appointed by the Executive Council. The functions of the divisional councils are to plan and strengthen union organization and recruitment, negotiate local agreements, and maintain contact with the branches. The Executive Council is made up of the president, general secretary and sixteen executive councillors (two from each of the eight divisions) elected by the branches in those divisions once every two years. Full-time officials have a perfect right to stand and be elected to the council, but the body is overwhelmingly dominated by lay activists.

The union's head office in Manchester has seven separate departments and the whole of USDAW was serviced by over 368 staff (126 at HQ and 242 elsewhere) in 1975. The supreme policy-making body is the annual delegate meeting, which gathers for three days near the end of April. Every branch is entitled to a delegate and those with over 500 members are entitled to a further delegate for every additional 500 members. USDAW also has federations consisting of groupings of union branches in a locality or region. These provide a forum for members from different industries to come together once a quarter. There are also the trade conferences, which were first introduced in 1950. Held annually or biennially for each of the main trades or industries where USDAW has a large membership, they play a substantial role in the union's machinery. As the union's guidebook explains: 'Their character is consultative and advisory and their decisions are subject to endorsement by the union's Executive Council.'

One of Labour's steady allies during the 1960s and 1970s, USDAW failed to make an impact on the low pay problem. But in 1976 and 1977 it began to overcome the severe recruitment difficulties for a union seeking membership in the highly vulnerable unskilled private labour market. Perhaps, in retrospect, we can see it as something of an achievement that the union has held its own during a period when the Co-op (that old bastion of USDAW strength) fell into deep decline.

UCATT

'This system turns men into animals,' said a building worker outside Leach's site in the London suburb of Mitcham. He was picketing the front entrance with a handful of his mates, who were on official strike against the company which they claimed was hiring 'lump labour' to do the sub-contracting work on flats being built there by Merton Council. The 'lump' is that vivid phrase used to describe the self-employed in the construction industry who provide their labour on a sub-contract basis, as compared with those workers who are directly employed by a contractor and are bound by national agreements. They get a lump sum of money by the week or the day – even by the hour – for specific pieces of work. 'This place was alive with lumpers a few weeks ago. We chased most of them off,' another Leach worker told me. 'Some of them were nothing but thugs. One had been charged for breaking and entering. Another carried a gun. They smashed through our picket lines in columns of three. One of our union blokes asked for protective clothing on the job and he got belted in the mouth. There are still thirty of the buggers dossing around, trying to bust this strike. They spend their time charging round the yard in their fast cars. And they're getting paid ratepayers' money for doing it.'

Douglas Reed, the contracts manager, denied he was using lump labour; but this did not convince the 270,000-strong builder's union UCATT (Union of Construction, Allied Trades and Technicians). Leach is a family contracting firm operating in west London. It joined the employers' federation for the industry in 1973 and is therefore bound by the regulations which are supposed to govern construction. The company took the union to the national joint council over the issue. 'The entire inquiry was a whitewash,' said Brian Tatham, UCATT's London organizer.

The Leach strike in 1975 illustrated a new, more determined mood among the unions (in UCATT as well as the Transport and General Workers) to do something to outlaw the lump system. Coordinating committees were established throughout the country, made up of full-time officials and stewards. Their main function was to search out sites where lumping was rampant and try to stamp out the practice through persuasion, or if necessary by industrial action. Lumpers anger the directly employed workers in a fragmented industry where unionism is on the defensive. The intensity of emotions aroused by self-employment on the building sites erupted into scenes of violence during the official 1972 national building strike. This was why the trial and imprisonment of the Shrewsbury strike militants – Des Warren and Ricky Tomlinson – for their antics on sites against lumpers aroused so much feeling. 'The union is on a merry-go-round,' said Lou Lewis, a well-known Communist militant in UCATT who was elected on to its executive early in 1976. He led strikes at the Barbican in the late 1960s. The lump problem is intractable. The very fluidity of construction jobs, where men move from site to site in gangs or as individuals for only short stretches of work, make the industry very hard to organize.

The startling fact is that there were reckoned to be more lumpers than union members in construction early in 1975. Some union officials reckoned the figure could be as high as 600,000. The lump practice began to spread out from traditionally recognized sectors like repair and maintenance into primary craft jobs like bricklaying, plastering and carpentry in the middle of the 1960s. The introduction of the selective employment tax in 1965, and the 1968 increase in its rate, helped to stimulate the system, by encouraging contractors to start shedding their work to sub-contractors as a way of avoiding added expenses.

There are those who believe the unions must take a major share of the blame for the spread of the lump. Lou Lewis believes union leaders were far keener on combating the militancy on sites than meeting the challenge of the lump. Others feel union concentration on the need for national bargaining with the employers lay at the root of the trouble. UCATT was cobbled together in 1970 as a merger of the Amalgamated Society of Woodworkers, the Amalgamated Society of Painters and Decorators and the Association of Building Technicians. In 1971 the Amalgamated Union of Building Trade Workers and the Amalgamated Union of Sailmakers joined the new enlarged union for the industry. There was pressure, as a result, for the erosion of skill differentials in construction. 'The lump was seen as a way for the craftsmen to get their own back. Many brickies and joiners broke out of a system which was under-valuing their talents,' a government adviser told me. Perhaps far more important was the labour shortage of the time, where men were in a position to bid up their labour power far above basic rates. Faced with a fixed-price contract with a time clause, employers were more willing to take on small groups of workers for short periods of time to carry out particular jobs. It is still not unknown on a building site for thirty sub-contracting firms to be at work with 170 men between them.

The 1971 Finance Act made a plaintive attempt to combat the tax evasion of lump workers. A contractor who made payments for sub-contract work had to deduct 30 per cent of the payment, unless it was made to a limited liability company or to an individual who held a tax exemption certificate. That 30 per cent was remitted to the collector of taxes, and it was up to the sub-contractor to apply for the appropriate refund. In theory, those certificates were issued at local tax offices under stringent controls, once the tax inspector was satisfied that the sub-contractor had either paid tax before or was liable to meet future tax obligations. The law laid down that those certificates had to be produced every time payments were made and every self-employed person or partnership required one.

The lump brings severe problems to the construction industry. It has had a serious effect on training young men through apprenticeships. 'No lumper has got the time to teach a lad a skill,' one worker told me. The numbers being trained in the industry dropped sharply in the late 1960s from 16,369 in 1966 to 8,793 in 1971. There has been some improvement since then, but not much. The lump produces a spiral effect. As an NEDC paper explained, 'Self-employment leads to inadequate training, a consequent shortage of craftsmen and an added stimulus to self-employment.' Lump workers are not covered by sickness benefits, redundancy pay or pension rights. Nor are they liable for any compensation if they injure themselves on the job, and construction remains a dangerous business. Over 200 men were killed on sites in 1976. It is reckoned half the injuries in the industry never get reported at all.

The slump of the mid-1970s hit construction worse than any other industry and the lumpers worse than anybody else. In the autumn of 1978 the industry reckoned there were 220,000 unemployed building workers in Britain, getting on for 20 per cent of all the jobless, and business was running at 30 per cent below its 1973 level. Government action through the issuing of identity cards for building workers, complete with photo and address, have been issued to those who can justify bona fide self-employment and thereby get on the register. Since the summer of 1974 the Inland Revenue has stepped up its drive in tracking down the tax liabilities of lumpers. There was a rash of well-publicized court cases, which helped to discourage the practice. Threat of imprisonment and heavy fines have pushed many lump firms underground. 'It has become even more of a secret society,' one worker told me. The 1975 pay settlement for construction workers bargained by the unions helped to push up basic rates substantially and make the rewards of self-employment less attractive. Efforts were also made to improve the industry's slender fringe benefits with the introduction of a pension scheme for the workers and better sick pay. But it is the catastrophic slump in the industry which has done most to blunt the threat of the lump. The government has helped with the creation of a register and the provision of a levy for employers to pay out of the cash sums made to those not on the register. Yet market forces are what count in construction.

Some experts would like to see far more union responsiveness to differential pay on the sites and the willingness to absorb lump gangs into the union structure itself. Union dislike of the lump is not hard to understand. It is a threat to trade unionism in a weakly organized and scattered industry, with a reputation for abrasive, cowboy employers and chronic conditions. As long as construction is subjected to the violent economic ups and downs of the market place, the powerful forces of the market are likely to prove far stronger than those who hate the lump appreciate.

UCATT endured a troubled youth under the leadership of Sir George Smith. He died in 1978 to be replaced by Les Wood. Its origins in the mergers of 1970 stemmed from a desperate need for unity in the face of a rapid disintegration of trade unionism in the construction industry. The 1968 Phelps Brown Report estimated that half the building workers employed by medium and large firms and less than a third of those belonging to small companies were members of a union. There was very little evidence in Phelps Brown of a widespread union structure at the site level. Among larger companies as many as 77 per cent had sites with shop stewards on them, while a further 13 per cent only claimed there were a few. A mere 4 per cent of small firms claimed to have any stewards at all on their building sites. Yet this was a conservative figure based on head office estimates. The report found 11 per cent of the sample of company sites and 47 per cent of the local authority sites had at least one steward representing the main contractor's direct workers. Two out of every five sites with over fifty direct workers claimed to have a shop steward. Contact between the unions and employers was virtually non-existent. In the case of 52 per cent of the large firms and 80 per cent of the smaller ones there was no contact more frequently than once a year.

Many construction workers are the direct heirs of the railway navvies who built Britain's railways in the last century. They value their sturdy self-reliance and freedom. Rugged individualism remains a severe obstacle to the growth of trade unionism. The rapid labour mobility and the scattered nature of the work, as well as the chaotic hiring system, were all seen as key factors by Phelps Brown in the inability of the unions to grow or even stand still. The laws of supply and demand weakened any urgent necessity for collective action through a union. This hardly creates a climate conducive to trade unionism or collectivist attitudes.

During the early 1970s George Smith and the leaders at national level fought to retain control at the centre, a policy which came into head-on collision both with the self-employed and a militant left group, made up mainly of Communists, known as Building Charter. Those divergent opponents of centralism sought wage negotiations at site level. Until the 1960s the Amalgamated Society of Woodworkers had placed particular emphasis on the virtues of district control; before 1956 the union's district management committees exercised wide autonomy with the power to raise their own finances and even appoint their own full-time officials. This was paralleled by the National Federation of Building Trade Operatives, with its considerable control over its affiliates. It was these which negotiated the rates and earnings actually made on the site, especially when the demand for labour was high.

In 1970 UCATT was the trade union answer to the deep fears of break-up and decline. The NFBTO was disbanded with the creation of UCATT. During the early years the union was top heavy with full-time officials at headquarters, but in 1976 UCATT underwent radical internal reform. It was decided to ensure the periodic election of all full-time regional officials, more frequent meetings of regional councils and the delegation of power down to regional council committees. Under the new rules it was also decided to streamline the eleven-man executive into a seven-strong body by 1981 to more accurately reflect geographical distribution of the membership. Out-dated restrictions on who could be a member were also done away with and a white-collar section – STAMP – was also founded.

Lacking muscle in a sector where trade unionism has found it very difficult to hold its own in face of market forces, UCATT will continue to face the dangers of decline in the years ahead.

Farmworkers – NUAAW

It was a highly emotional time down at the village hall at Kelmscott, Oxfordshire, that warm September evening in 1973. Charlie Brown, local regional secretary of the National Union of Agricultural and Allied Workers (NUAAW), was about to retire after over twenty years in the job and old union members had turned out to wish him well. Old Bill Harris, the branch secretary, had brought his wife along to present Charlie with a handsome barometer as a parting gift from the Kelmscott branch. It had been set for 'fair'.

Bill Harris started work on the farm when he was only 11, just before the outbreak of the First World War, for 3s 6d a week. Those were hard, difficult days. 'You often never knew where the next week's wages were coming from,' remembers Harris. The terrible threat of eviction hung over the heads of all farmworkers in tied cottages. The fact that a worker's home is owned by his employer gives the boss enormous power over his workforce, if he chooses to use it. In the past, it was a familiar sight to see a man and his family turned out into the road with their furniture at the whim of the farmer.

Memories bind the farmworkers together in their scattered isolation in the English countryside. Every July union stalwarts gather in the tiny village of Tolpuddle in Dorset for the annual rally in commemoration of the events of 1834 when six farmworkers were deported to serve seven years' hard labour in Australia for daring to organize themselves as a union. A leading Labour politician heads the procession of gaily coloured banners through the main street of the village to the churchyard where a wreath is laid on the grave of James Hammett, the only Tolpuddle 'martyr' actually buried in the village. When Hammett was laid to rest at that spot in 1878 the local squire stood by the graveside to make sure nobody spoke for or on behalf of trade unionism. The brass bands play and the assembled faithful munch cucumber sandwiches and reminisce, beside the row of martyr memorial cottages built in the 1930s. Tolpuddle – like the Durham miners' gala – has a hallowed place in Labour's commemorative history.

Today, as always, trade unionism has a difficult struggle to stay alive on the land. The National Union of Agricultural and Allied Workers only has around 85,000 members, no more than 35 per cent of the 220,000-strong labour force qualified to join. Founded in 1906, the union reached its peak of strength in 1947 when it had over 162,000 members. The NUAAW's main strongholds are in East Anglia, the region of high capitalist farming where Joseph Arch's ill-fated agricultural union grew rapidly in the 1870s. It was in Norfolk and parts of Suffolk that over 10,000 farmworkers struck in 1923, in what the union's history calls the 'great strike' against wage cutting. Over 37 per cent of farmworkers in East Anglia are estimated to be trade unionists, and there are relatively large numbers in the NUAAW in Lincolnshire and Essex. The extent of union growth seems to have little impact on the well-being of the farmworkers. East Anglia remains the area with the lowest average weekly earnings in the country. Wage rates are much higher in the East Midlands and Yorkshire where the lure of factory jobs in the towns ensures that farm pay rates must stay competitive.

'Free' collective bargaining has never made much sense to most farmworkers. It is the Agricultural Wages Board – founded in 1947 in its present form – that determines the basic rate of pay for all farmworkers in Britain. This is a tripartite body made up of union representatives, members of the National Farmers' Union, and five independents, who meet once a year to determine the national wage level for the industry. The NUAAW usually finds itself in a difficult negotiating position, for the National Farmers' Union remains rich, powerful and persuasive in the furtherance of its interest. In face of the most effective pressure group in the country,

NUAAW has to rely on the detailed arguments prepared for them in the claim by the Ruskin College Trade Union Research Unit. There is no doubt that farmworkers remain among the lowest paid. In the autumn of 1976 the basic weekly rate was only £36.50 – far below the national average earnings. There was on average a 23 per cent gap between agricultural and industrial wages in 1975, compared with one of around 32 per cent three years earlier. Thanks to overtime working and premium payments (all but 4 per cent of farmworkers get that from their employers) a farmworker reckoned to be getting between £42 and £46 a week in 1975. Rates are much higher for skilled workers like dairy cowmen, stockmen and tractor drivers.

On the larger capitalist establishments in East Anglia farm income levels averaged between £20,000 and £30,000 a year. Between the late 1960s and 1974 farmers' basic incomes rose by twice to three times as much as the total weekly earnings of their workers.

The union makes little overall impact on the fragmented membership. The 1975 Tavistock Institute study found only a quarter of its representative sample of 803 were actually NUAAW members. Of that minority 14 per cent said they often attended branch meetings and 58 per cent admitted they never went to such gatherings. The union operates on a shoe-string. It only employs thirteen full-time organizers to cover the whole country. The subscription rates, at 80 pence a month, remain derisorily low. Between 1968 and 1972 the union was actually running in the red. It took staff cuts and economies as well as an increase in fees to get the union back in balance. There is little more than £½ million in the union's general fund and just over £200,000 in investments, mainly government securities and local authority mortgages.

The NUAAW leadership has no wish to give up the struggle and merge the union with some mightier force in the movement such as the TGWU. But it would make real sense. For too long, Britain's farmworkers have been the victims of the cheap food/high profit doctrines of farming. Their wages and conditions will remain the lowest in the country, though the industry they work in is one of the most efficient and productive, as long as the cause of trade unionism fails to win converts

among the agricultural labour force. In the EEC, particularly
France, the peasant farmers have often demonstrated their
highly effective power over governments through direct action.
Here the NFU has held sway, championing the farmers' interests with aplomb. If the NUAAW were part of a bigger
union it is possible the farmworkers would stop getting a raw
deal.

18 Industrial unions on the defensive

NUR and ASLEF

The marble corridors of Unity House on London's Euston Road resemble the inside of a Victorian gothic town hall, recalling the great days of the railwaymen in the age of steam. Even twenty years ago the National Union of Railwaymen boasted a membership of over 400,000. It was a major force to be reckoned with in the TUC. Now it has shrunk to around 174,000 members. The union's chirpy general secretary, Sid Weighell, a Yorkshireman from Northallerton, finds his main task is to defend the remains of Britain's railway system from its enemies in government and the powerful road lobby. The publication of the government's 1977 White Paper on transport underlined the sharp decline in the fortunes of the railways. Ever since the early 1960s and the cuts of Dr Beeching, then head of British Railways, the NUR cooperated in the contraction of the system, but now the union – along with its two companions in railway unionism, the Associated Society of Locomotive Engineers and Firemen (ASLEF) and the Transport Salaried Staffs' Association (TSSA) – faces an uncertain future with rising fares, falling custom and cutbacks in the government subsidy to public transport.

The NUR is very conscious of its place in the Labour movement. It was on 26 November 1871 at a meeting in Leeds that the Amalgamated Society of Railway Servants was born. Its early years witnessed a bitter struggle to gain recognition from autocratic, reactionary railway companies who detested the whole idea of trade unionism. Richard Bell, general secretary of the ASE, moved the crucial motion at the 1899 TUC which led to the formation of the Labour Representation Committee, progenitor of the Labour Party. The famous 1903 Taff Vale judgment proved vital in the growth of union backing for the new body. In 1901 an unofficial strike for a 2s a week increase in wages on the Taff Vale railway in South Wales provoked the company's general manager to import blackleg labour. The railwaymen retaliated and the union decided to provide financial support to its members under threat. The company took legal proceedings against the ASE, which ended up in the House of Lords, where their noble Lordships proceeded to judge that the ASE was liable to pay damages for the actions of its members in the Taff Vale company. The union was obliged to pay £23,000 damage to the company and costs amounted to another £19,000. The whole legal security of British trade unionism, supposedly guaranteed by the 1871 and 1875 Acts, was now endangered. Taff Vale convinced the many union doubters that they needed to organize a separate pressure group in the House of Commons to champion the labour interest. It was the Railway Servants who provided the necessary stimulus for the Labour Representation Committee.

At a special general meeting of the ASRS in January 1903 it was decided to levy 1s a year from every member to provide financial assistance to the fledgling LRC. But in July 1908 Walter V. Osborne, secretary of the Walthamstow branch, took legal proceedings to restrain the union from using any of its finances for political purposes. The House of Lords upheld Osborne's appeal. This deprived the unions of the right to support their MPs, though employers continued to provide financial aid to their supporters at Westminster. The railway companies had a major pressure group in Parliament. In the 1900–6 period as many as fifty-three railway directors sat in the Commons. As a result of the Osborne judgment the 1913 Trade Union Act was passed which enabled the unions to spend money for political purposes, with the right of any members to contract out of paying the political levy if they wished to do so.

That same year the ASRS amalgamated with the United Pointsmen's and Signalmen's Society and the General Railway Workers' Union to form the NUR. In 1913 the National Union of Railwaymen was hailed as a new form of industrial unionism by the Webbs, while G. D. H. Cole believed its structure promised to be a model 'as influential for the twentieth century as the Amalgamated Society of Engineers had been for the Victorian age'. In the labour unrest of the years before the First

World War the railwaymen played a prominent part, many of their leaders influenced (if only partly) by the ideas of syndicalism. The NUR became a crucial partner in the triple alliance with the miners and the Transport Workers' Federation, founded in the spring of 1914. That *entente* failed to live up to expectations and it fell apart under the pressure of events in the early 1920s, but the NUR displayed an impressive solidarity with the miners during the 1926 General Strike, when its members obeyed the strike call without hesitation and despite the real threats of intimidation from the railway companies. That sense of unity has not been eroded over the years. In 1972 all the railway workers supported their unions in the compulsory strike ballot enforced by the Heath Government under the Industrial Relations Act.

The rule-book of the NUR retains a strong socialist flavour. One of its stated aims is 'to work for the supression of the capitalist system by a socialist order of society'. But on the whole, NUR general secretaries have been on the right rather than the left of the Labour movement and they have never found much difficulty in justifying their outlook to the rank and file. The most colourful example is Jimmy Thomas, who kept one foot at the top of the NUR and the other in the inner leadership of the Labour Party, until he followed Ramsay MacDonald into the 1931 National Government. Under Sidney Greene's long stretch in power – from 1958 to 1973 – the NUR was a faithful supporter of the prevailing orthodoxies. Yet the union has known its militant periods, particularly from the Second World War to 1958. In 1943 the NUR even came out in favour of progressive unity between Labour and the Communists and it remained loyal to that policy as late as 1946. At the TUC the union was a major critic of the 1949 voluntary pay freeze, and led the attack on wage restraint to final victory in 1950. The NUR was one of the first unions to call for the withdrawal of foreign troops from Korea and it proved a sturdy champion of Bevanism, strongly opposed to German rearmament. Jim Campbell, general secretary of the time, denounced any suggestion that Labour should dilute its commitment to full nationalization, what he called 'the rich red blood of socialist objectives'.

Sid Weighell is unlikely to carry the union back into such a left position, but this will depend on the mood of his members. He is a jolly, sprightly man with a blunt way of speaking and considerable self-confidence about the rightness of his cause. Before he was elected to the top job in the NUR, Weighell spent twenty-one years as a full-time union official. He comes from a railway family. His grandfather was a railway guard and founder member of the Northallerton branch of the union, while his father was a railway signalman. Unusually, Weighell was an engine driver who did not belong to ASLEF. The vast majority of his members work as porters, signalmen, guards, and on what is known as the permanent way maintaining the railway track. In his youth Weighell was a professional footballer with Sunderland for a couple of years, and an active Labour Party member. He spent five years as Labour agent in the rock-solid Conservative seat of Richmond in Yorkshire.

Weighell's scope for introducing reforms within the NUR is strictly limited. The rank and file have a far more effective voice in his union than they do in most others. 'I sometimes think we have democracy run mad,' said Weighell. All twenty-four full-time officers are elected by the membership through the ballot box under the single transferable vote system with the whole process administered by the Electoral Reform Society. Recently the union dropped individual voting at the branches in favour of the bloc vote system. This means the whole branch votes for one candidate, even if only a handful have turned up to the meeting. Even Weighell admits no more than 10 to 15 per cent of eligible branch members really play an active role in the life of the union. Every man who wants to hold a permanent post in the NUR must satisfy the union he is capable by passing a tough written test which includes accountancy, English and mathematics. There is no danger of the tiny oligarchy at Unity House losing touch with the rank and file. With its 680 branches, twenty-eight district councils and twelve annual grade conferences for differing occupational sections, the NUR attempts to bridge the gap between the national leaders who carry out the main bargaining with the Rail Board and the depots, stations and workshops where the members work. The annual general meeting attended by seventy-seven elected delegates and the full-time officers gathers every year in the second week of July for a fortnight of intensive debate on every aspect of railway affairs.

Even though the bulk of the bargaining is conducted at the centre, the NUR has one of the most articulate and effective shop steward movements in British trade unionism. The Parker/McCarthy survey for the Donovan Commission in 1968 found as many as 90 per cent of NUR stewards paid the political levy, with fifteen hours of work a week on average for the union. In the early 1970s the NUR was relatively passive. It was left to the footplatemen's union, ASLEF, to set the pace in labour militancy on the railways. Weighell came into office with a dogged determination to champion his members in a more flamboyant and aggressive way. 'My members are key workers like the miners,' he said. 'Railwaymen once had a pride in their job. I mean to restore that pride.' Weighell compared his men with surface workers in the coal industry. 'Rail employees often form part of a society dominated by miners,' argued the NUR in its 1975 claim. And despite the rundown of the railways over the past twenty years, the railwaymen are responsible for transporting three-quarters of all the coal consumed by the power stations and in the coke ovens of the steel industry and foundries. The headquarters of the Mineworkers is almost opposite Unity House on the Euston Road and Weighell is keen to establish close ties with his more powerful neighbour. Unfortunately for the NUR the government has accepted there is a real future for coal in Britain, but doubts persist about the railways. The NUR's membership has been halved in less than fifteen years, but it will prove well-nigh impossible for the union to stop the rapid decline, let alone put it into reverse.

Yet even the threat to the continuance of a sizeable railway network has failed to bring the rail unions together in harmony. The 70,000-strong Transport Salaried Staffs' Association displayed no opposition to the escalation in fare increases in 1975 and 1976 and only took a half-hearted part in the anti-rail cuts campaign. Sid Weighell decided to launch a separate NUR propaganda drive. A major headache is the stubborn presence of the 28,000-strong Associated Society of Locomotive Engineers and Firemen (ASLEF). Under Ray Buckton's friendly but militant leadership, the union has pursued a quixotic policy of left-wing socialism mixed with craft élitism. Between 1972 and 1974 the union took industrial action to further its demand for higher wages and brought misery to thousands of London commuters as a result. ASLEF opposed the voluntary pay policy. It is a stalwart defender of 'free' collective bargaining. The union makes out a strong case for special treatment for rail drivers.

Under the 1965 Penzance Agreement provision was made for a reduction in manning levels with a scale of productivity payments agreed on the basis of minutes' pay for miles worked, but from 1968 onwards a pay and efficiency exercise froze all bonus and mileage payments. As a result, the relative position of the driver deteriorated. It was not until the 1974 settlement that this was rectified. 'Today in this country there is insufficient reward for those men prepared to undertake responsible work and to acquire knowledge and skills which are an asset not only to their employers but the nation as a whole,' said Buckton. With its ornate headquarters in Arkwright Road, Hampstead, ASLEF keeps aloof from the other rail unions. Buckton and his two assistant general secretaries were elected by the membership and they are responsible to a nine-man executive elected every three years. It is the forty-four-strong delegate conference, elected through the districts, that governs ASLEF. The left have a majority both on the executive and in conference. Yet the campaign for higher pay is bound to conflict with the needs to preserve the railway network. Now the government is cutting back on subsidies, the system's labour costs will have to be borne by train users. ASLEF's militancy is likely to mean big pay for fewer drivers.

The rail unions find it very hard to coexist in friendship as the tragi-comedy over bonuses for drivers in 1978–9 illustrated. In February 1978, British Rail caved in to pressure from the NUR and agreed to the re-introduction of bonus payments for pay-train guards on rural runs. Only about 1,600 out of 12,000 guards were affected, but their union had instructed them not to collect money from passengers until they won a bonus and this was causing a loss of revenue to BR. The concession upset ASLEF. The ink was scarcely dry on the agreement when Buckton was in to see BR chairman, Sir Peter Parker, demand-

ing the same for all his drivers. If Parker had surrendered to
Buckton's demand, then Weighell would have demanded that
all his members should have the same. After much argument,
the TUC general secretary Len Murray persuaded the rail
union leaders to turn over the whole problem to Lord Mc-
Carthy and his railway staff national tribunal. Early in November 1978 McCarthy announced his decision: high-speed drivers
were to have an extra £3.14 a shift, but other drivers were to
get nothing more. The verdict was rejected by both ASLEF
and BR, while Weighell and the NUR accepted it. Buckton
suggested his members should get a 10 per cent rise as a sign
of 'goodwill' by the Board, but BR came up with the idea of
a joint working party with the unions to look at ways of paying drivers more through productivity improvements. Tom
Jenkins, general secretary of the TSSA, then stepped in to say
his clerks wanted a similar exercise done for them. As a result, all grades were covered by separate working parties.

With a series of unofficial one-day strikes due by drivers on
Southern Region, Buckton and his colleagues issued an ultimatum: unless agreement was reached on a deal for drivers by
7 January 1979, official industrial action would follow. This
brinkmanship seemed to harden Weighell's attitude. The joint
working party on drivers' bonuses dragged on through December without any apparent progress, for Weighell made it clear
Buckton's drivers were not going to steal a march on his members. Agreement was eventually reached on a national productivity scheme to cover all railway workers. This provided a
crudely devised bonus based on the increase in the volume of
traffic divided by the numbers employed, and it did nothing
special for the drivers.

When Buckton was told by BR that he was getting 'nothing
for nothing' his executive suddenly agreed that he could talk
about efficiency savings as a way to produce a bonus for the
drivers. The Board could hardly believe its ears. Here was
ASLEF apparently dropping its old Luddite views that the jobs
of drivers were sacrosanct. Buckton's new position was hedged
about by caveats but it looked like a breakthrough. 'We suddenly saw a beach-head opening up,' said one official. 'Astonishingly it came from Mr Hyde, not Dr Jekyl.' But on the
very next day Weighell, who had been ill, arrived from his sick

bed to pull the rug out. He made it clear that his union was not in the business of trading jobs for money. After reading what the Board intended to offer the NUR in return for efficiency improvements, Weighell walked out of the joint working parties. He claimed 20,000 jobs would be lost and his union had made enough sacrifices during the past 20 years to help the railways. Weighell's attitude made it impossible for Buckton to carry on talking about a deal for his drivers. While in the public's eye Buckton was the villain, Weighell was not blameless either. Weighell insisted that his members would not let the drivers have a separate deal. 'If I gave an inch, I would have a hurricane about my ears.' But thanks to the tough diplomacy of Len Murray, Weighell persuaded his executive to swallow their pride and refer the matter back to McCarthy, who eventually came up with a formula to provide most drivers with a bonus.

Boilermakers

The 131,000-strong Amalgamated Society of Boilermakers, Shipwrights, Blacksmiths and Structural Workers sums up much that used to be wrong with British trade unionism. The union remains highly sectionalist, with a proud tradition of defending the skilled craftsmen of the shipyards from any dilution or threat to their position as the élite of the shipbuilding industry. The Society organizes a variety of different skills in the yards such as welding, plating, caulking and boilermaking, drilling and riveting. Nearly a third of the 70,000 workers in the industry in early 1977 belonged to the Society. In the bigger yards like Govan Shipbuilders, Cammel Laird and Harland & Wolff the Society claims up to 40 per cent of the labour force in its ranks. In the smaller ones it is not much more than half that figure. With its headquarters in Newcastle upon Tyne, the Society is one of the few unions in Britain whose centre lies in an industrial heartland, not the capital.

In 1968 the Society amended its rule-book, so that it could recruit beyond its old craft boundaries, but so far this has brought no dramatic increase in membership. Both the General and Municipal Workers and the AUEW are the other main unions organizing among the semi-skilled and unskilled workers in shipbuilding. As many as ten unions are signatories to the national procedure agreement and they work together through the Confederation of Shipbuilding and Engineering Unions. Shipbuilding remains a closed shop with 100 per cent pre-entry for the skilled men and post-entry for the rest.

During the 1960s mergers and amalgamations thinned down the number of unions in the industry. In 1961 the United Society of Boilermakers, Shipbuilders and Structural Workers joined forces with the Associated Blacksmiths, Forge and Smithy Workers. Two years later they were amalgamated with the Ship Constructors and Shipwrights' Association to form the ASB. Full integration between all three sections was reached in April 1969. The 1971 study by the Commission on Industrial Relations found joint working within the Society had developed widely, though unresolved areas of tension remained among workers, particularly between welders and men in other trades. Most yards have signed interchangeability agreements, which has brought some (though not much) flexibility into the work done by skilled workers. Low productivity – as much a result of rigid demarcation lines and restrictive practices as lack of investment – still hampers the progress of many yards, and there is often a serious division of view between what union head office thinks and what happens in the yard. Shop stewards' committees, particularly in the Society, retain considerable power over day-to-day affairs.

The CIR report was highly critical of what it saw as the 'sectional behaviour' of unions in the shipyards, particularly the Society. It argued:

The members of the ASB think of themselves not only as being divided from their helpers and the semi-skilled but also as being divided from other craftsmen. Indeed, their sense of separateness is the strongest and deepest of the divisive forces in the industry and more than any other single factor militates against comprehensive negotiating machinery at company and yard level.

Technological changes have eroded many of the traditional lines of demarcation, particularly those between steelwork and fitting-out, but the special position of the Society in the yards remains strong. Moreover conflicts within skilled groups persist, even though they are within the same union now. In the words of the CIR,

Sectionalism perpetuates the uneconomic use of labour, it stands in the way of wider job opportunities, it prevents differences over pay being settled with the interests of all employees being taken into account at the same time, and it stands in the way of arrangements for collective bargaining which take the long- rather than the short-term view. In the long-term, sectional behaviour could destroy what it seeks to protect, the continuing security of employment opportunities.

The shipbuilding industry is in the midst of a severe crisis, which threatens its entire future. The nationalization of the yards was seen by the Labour Government as a sensible way of giving the industry a viable policy. The unions, notably the Boilermakers, believed public ownership would ensure the preservation of existing jobs. It took months of painful persuasion by the organizing committee of British Shipbuilders to persuade union leaders that the downturn in orders for new ships and the overcapacity in the industry worldwide were not a familiar trough in the cycle, but involved long-term structural changes. The Boilermakers were the least willing to face harsh realities. This is not altogether surprising, for the ASB has gained its main organizational strength from domination of the skilled trades in the shipyards. Proud craft traditionalism does not take kindly to thoughts of decay and possible collapse. The Boilermakers' leaders sought a merger with the General and Municipal Workers in 1977 but their union conference turned down the idea. Old traditions die hard.

19 Public service malaise

Civil servants

The British civil service is not what it used to be. The cartoon stereotype of the non-industrial civil servant – a middle-aged man in a bowler hat and pin-striped trousers – can still be seen striding down Whitehall with furled umbrella heading for his Pall Mall club, but most of the vast majority of the 570,000 who staff the ministries down to the local social security offices are not among the élite mandarins of the administrative grade.

Times change rapidly. By 1978 public sector workers, particularly civil servants, were being envied their high pay, security at work, inflation-proof non-contributory pensions and generous sick pay. In the depths of the recession, working for the government looked attractive again, but this may prove only a temporary attitude.

Concern at sagging Whitehall morale after the sporadic strikes over pay in 1973 led to the creation of a Wider Issue Review Team to examine what was happening to the service. The report argued 'the character and atmosphere' of the civil service had changed markedly. As it pointed out:

Older civil servants joined when recruitment was highly competitive; before the war some schools would inscribe on the honours-board the name of a boy who was accepted into the civil service as an executive officer; he had joined a small élite by open competition – in one year for example fourteen eligible candidates were turned away for each one who was accepted. But other jobs have become attractive and more widely available to those who meet the service's recruitment standards, and today the very much larger numbers of executive officer entrants do not regard the civil service or themselves as very special.

The Wider Issues Review Team, reporting in 1975, revealed that over a third of the staff were born after the end of the Second World War. In the Department of Health and Social Security nearly half the staff are under 30 years of age. The younger you are, the less likely it is that you will either swallow or tolerate the stuffy red tape of the older generation with set rules and regulations. The Wider Issues Review Team wrote:

Today a large proportion of the staff in the civil service were born and brought up in the post-war world and naturally their values, assumptions and attitudes have been shaped by the existence of the welfare state and the security it provides, by the changes in our educational system which encourage a more questioning outlook, by the wider horizons of the television age and the greater awareness of what is happening in the outside world.

The massive number of younger people in the civil service with no career commitment to staying there for the rest of their working lives, and the tension which has grown up between the public service ethos of the system and its harsher realities, have helped to strengthen the appeal of trade unionism among civil servants at all levels. As the Wider Issues Review Team reported in 1975:

Seeing the material success of organized labour in industry, the civil service staff associations – like those of some white collar workers in other public services – have tended more to resemble other trade unions; for example industrial action was unheard of in the non-industrial civil service ten years ago.

In recent years the civil service unions have moved closer together, but the concentration of negotiations in the hands of the national and departmental staff sides of Whitley has opened up a gulf between the individual civil servant and those negotiating on his or her behalf.

Nearly all civil service pay is determined through national Whitley Council agreements, based on a doctrine of fair comparison, as laid down by the 1955 Priestley Report. That Commission came to the conclusion that the equitable way of assessing civil service pay was to compare the rates with staff doing comparable work in good firms in the private sector. The Pay Research Unit, made up of civil servants, carries out an annual exercise to ensure there is no wide disparity between salaries in and outside the civil service. In recent years the whole system has come under considerable criticism as the gap widened between the comfortable, protected life of the civil servant and the uncertain, deteriorating position of workers outside government employment. Massive pay rises in 1974 and 1975 ensured fair comparisons pushed civil service wages above what was perceived to be the norm in private industry. This contrasts with the mounting frustration and militancy over wages, which hit the civil service in 1973 and 1974, as a result of government incomes policy. It was felt by most of the civil service unions that government determination to apply pay restraint rigorously to the public sector had undermined the Whitley system and its arbitration procedures.

On 24 February 1973 civil servants struck for the day all over Britain. As many as 9,000 civil servants marched through the streets of Glasgow in protest, drawing the admiration of the local militant trades council. 'I don't believe that the one-day strike came as a trauma to my members,' said Gerry Gilman of the Society of Civil and Public Servants. In his opinion, there is a new breed of younger executive officer, different from previous generations in the service.

For most of those who enter the civil service as a clerical or manual worker, it is merely another job, not a vocation or a secure post for life. Levels of staff turnover are no greater than in private industry, but there is not much pride in being a civil servant now. The old sense of public duty has gone. As the Wider Issues Review Team confessed, civil servants 'do not have traditional white-collar attitudes and do not aspire to them'.

These social changes have added to the strain of the consultative machinery governing the civil service. Ever since 1916 the Whitley system has regulated staff relations. In the words of the Wider Issues report: 'It is an outstanding system of staff relations, based on a formal framework but flexible enough to adapt to changing conditions; it operates, as it can only be operated, in a spirit of mutual trust and cooperation between the two sides.' Without that sense of common purpose, however, Whitleyism could fall to pieces, because it is the collective obligation to ensure increased efficiency and staff well-being that perpetuates the system. Can such a consensus survive the social revolution that has hit the civil service since the war? The Civil Service Department has gone to some lengths to strengthen the staff associations. At the end of 1974 agreement was reached on the provision of office facilities for association representatives.

This allows them the use of rooms, furniture and equipment, typing and telephone services and time off to carry out union functions. Annual branch meetings for the election of association officers can now begin within office hours. Check-off has also reached the civil service. Efforts are being made to ensure work is more rewarding by reducing the number of jobs that are 'narrowly specialized, repetitive or grinding'. As the 1975 report argued:

Although work ought to give people a sense of fulfilment, a good many jobs in the civil service can be unrewarding; checking entries on forms or compiling statistical returns can easily become monotonous or seem pointless; interviewing a succession of clients with complex human problems can wear down the patience and human feelings of the person who does it all day every day. It is not surprising if those who do those jobs do not come whistling to work.

Whitleyism tried to take the cutting edge off any assertive trade unionism by institutionalizing close staff–management relations at all levels of the service. The national Whitley Council was founded in 1920. There are twenty-four members of what is known as the official side (made up of senior civil servants from major departments) with nine unions on the staff side occupying twenty-three seats. The union representation is calculated roughly on a basis of relative size and capacity of each union. The composition is as follows:

Civil and Public Services' Association	7
Society of Civil and Public Servants	4
Institution of Professional Civil Servants	4
First Division Association	1
Association of Inspectors of Taxes	1
Inland Revenue Staff Federation	2
Civil Service Union	2
Prison Officers' Association	1
Association of Government Supervisors and Radio Officers	1
	23

There are seven separate committees in the Whitley system at national level. The most important is known as Committee A, which deals with major policy issues from pay to industrial relations. It is made up of all the union general secretaries and meets every Tuesday morning. No other group of union leaders in the same sector have such close and continuing contact with one another. Committee B covers the range of service conditions such as overtime and sick leave and it is composed of the deputy general secretaries of the Whitley unions. There are committees for personnel management, management services, superannuation, welfare and accommodation and training.

The staff side of Whitley has a small full-time secretariat, made up of four officers and a research officer with a further staff of eight. All are located on the top floor of an office in London's Rochester Row, close to Victoria Station. Despite sporadic attacks on Whitleyism, the unions support the present system. As a Whitley staff side report in April 1974 explained:

There can be no doubt that the steady development of the negotiating role of the national staff side has immensely strengthened the effectiveness of the trade union movement within the civil service. It has provided the machinery through which common policies can be hammered out by representatives of individual constituent associations coming together round the national staff side committee table.

Bill Kendall, former general secretary of the CPSA, took on the torrid job of secretary general of the Whitley staff side in June 1976. He is chief spokesman for the civil service employees. 'Everybody wants easily identifiable villains in an economic crisis,' Kendall told me. 'There is a touching belief that a sure, simple answer exists to it all. Five years ago you could show we lagged behind everybody else's pay. Now I can't really think we're substantially ahead.' His old union, the Civil and Public Services Association (CPSA), only covers the relatively low-paid clerical grade, where early in 1976 the average pay was around £2,000 a year. Kendall spent twenty-four years at the CPSA's headquarters in Balham, south London – first as an assistant secretary and after 1967 as general secretary – fighting a long struggle for better pay and conditions for typists and clerks. In his new post at the head of Whitley he has to speak up for the whole civil service – from the under-secretary to the cleaning woman.

Kendall spent his childhood in the depressed north-east of the 1930s, where his father worked as a labourer for South Shields Council. 'I was a humble Young Communist Leaguer,' he told me. Kendall left the party in August 1939 over the Nazi–Soviet pact and he spent the war years having a 'boring stretch' in the Royal Air Force. He joined the CP in 1945, but left for good in 1951. Kendall originally wanted to be a teacher or a journalist, but he got a job in the Ministry of National Insurance in 1946 'in order to live'. Within two years he had become secretary of the ministry's CPSA branch, the biggest of its kind in the country. Kendall is a devout Roman Catholic – disliking services in the vernacular but 'progressive' on birth control. He was converted in 1952. 'I was always fascinated by religion, even when I said I was a daletical materialist.'

The nine civil service unions still negotiate pay separately, but other issues, from fringe benefits to office conditions, are dealt with collectively through the Whitley staff side. 'Everything is getting far more centralized. The members do not like it, but that's where the action is,' said Kendall. He will not defend every Whitehall absurdity. 'We have no interest in creating a swollen bureaucracy. We want people to work more efficiently on decent rates of pay,' he said. As the first CPSA general secretary to be appointed to the Whitley staff side top job, Kendall can be expected to champion the many thousands of civil servants in the civil service outside the power and glamour of the mandarin élite highlighted by the Fulton Report. But whether he can bring all the unions together in a unitary organization, even a loose confederation, remains problematic.

The 1974 Whitley plans for an umbrella organization got nowhere in the face of sectionalist intransigence from many staff unions, notably the CPSA and the Society of Civil and Public Servants. The main problem is that any reform would involve much more power to the centre with a revamped, larger Whitley staff secretariat. Some recent mergers have reduced the number of unions in the civil service. The Ministry of Labour Staff Association and the Court Officers' Association merged with the CPSA, while the Customs and Excise group joined the

Society of Civil and Public Servants. Yet the prospect of one union from top to bottom of the government bureaucracy still looks remote.

For the most part, civil service union leaders work harmoniously together through the Whitley system. They meet regularly at Rochester Row to discuss important matters and the Whitley committees do so less frequently. Working together ensured the smooth negotiation of the civil service's superannuation scheme in 1972 and the 1975 review of transfer terms from one job to another. The Whitley system has parallel structures down to local departmental level. One major problem has been the lack of liaison between what happens at the centre and down below.

The chief unions in the civil service are as follows:

First Division Association. This covers the top administrative grade, the élite of the service. It is a non-militant body, and in 1977 joined the TUC. In 1979 it had 8,149 members.

Civil and Public Services' Association (CPSA). This is the recognized association for clerical, typing and allied trades in the civil service. Its origins lie in the formation of the Assistant Clerks' Association in 1903, which later became the Clerical Officers' Association in 1920 and two years later merged with two similar unions to form the Civil Service Association. At the end of 1978 it had 224,780 members. General secretary Ken Thomas won a General Council seat in 1977.

Society of Civil and Public Servants. This union covers the executive officer grades of the service. It also now recruits custom and excise officers. Under the leadership of Gerry Gilman, the Society has grown more militant. It joined the TUC in 1975, and now has 106,903 members.

Inland Revenue Staff Federation. This covers skilled grades in the inland revenue. It originated in 1892 as the Association of Tax Clerks. Between 1936 and 1937 the association amalgamated with the Association of Assessors and Collectors of Taxes (1904) and the Valuation Officers' Clerical Association (1919). At the end of 1978 it had 67,614 members.

The Civil Service Union. This was founded in 1917 by messengers, employed by the Ministry of Education and reorganized under its present title in 1944. Its aim is to organize all the non-industrials outside the clerical grade and above. The CSU strength lies with messengers, museum attendants and miscellaneous grades. At the end of 1978 it had 46,928 members.

Institution of Professional Civil Servants (IPCS). The union caters for the specialist grades within the civil service – mainly scientists. Under the leadership of Bill McCall, it joined the TUC in 1976. At the end of 1978 it had 99,051 members.

The largest civil service union is the CPSA. Its structure is inevitably shaped by the Whitley system into national, departmental and local machinery. The union's National Executive is made up of twenty-six members who are all elected annually at the union conference from among the branches. The president and the two vice-presidents serves for three years before they have to face re-election. The full-time staff of the CPSA (this includes Ken Thomas, the general secretary, his deputy and the treasurer) are appointed to office by the executive, subject to approval by the annual conference where ultimate power lies. The National Executive, meeting once a month, is a mixture of lay representatives and full-time officials. Alongside the three chief officers are the twelve assistant secretaries, but they have no voting rights on the executive.

The CPSA has gained a reputation for unreliability with the TUC establishment. But Thomas won a seat on the General Council in September 1977. 'The CPSA is the best-organized and potentially most powerful white-collar union in the country. It has 800 workplace branches (up to 9,000-strong) organized around a single basic grade,' said an article in *International Socialism* (31 May 1975). 'The government and the big private employers are becoming increasingly terrified by this situation. The civil service is a crucial part of their state machine. Loyalty to the "values" of their society is crucial if they are to stay in control. Until recently, they have always looked on the trade unions in the civil service as tame poodles of the government.'

The CPSA is bitterly divided by political in-fighting. The Red Tape faction represent the ultra-left with a handful of seats on the executive. The broad left (an alliance of Communists and Labour left) hold an uneasy sway over the union, and there is a less powerful anti-Communist group, which dislikes the intrusion of politics into CPSA affairs.

Certainly the union leaders often find themselves face to face with an unruly rank and file at conference time and it is quite common for CPSA orthodoxy to be swiftly overturned, but rumbustious antics once a year do not constitute a breach of national security. Only a handful of the CPSA's executive are on the ultra-left and what stirs up the members is not political action but wages and conditions. The turnover in the CPSA is massive, as abler members are promoted up the civil service ladder into the executive grades where they join the Society of Civil and Public Servants. Over 30 per cent of the union's branch officers are lost every year as a direct result of promotion. Staff turnover adds to the problems of ensuring a stable membership. The CPSA has one of the youngest rank and files of any union.

To a much larger extent than other unions, the CPSA has very few full-time officers. There are nineteen altogether: the general secretary, deputy general secretary and general treasurer; twelve assistant secretaries with mainly negotiating roles; and four supporting officers, editor of the *Journal*, national organizer, research officer and accounts officer. This ensures a ratio of one official to 14,000 members, compared with a union national average of one to between 4,000 and 5,000 members. All the CPSA full-time staff are centralized at union headquarters in Balham, south London. Considerable power and influence is exercised by the lay activists at branch, regional and section level of the union as a result. Robert Price of Warwick University has carried out a survey of the Department of Health and Social Security section of the CPSA, which emphasizes the strength of the lay members in the administration of their union. In the massive branches running the CPSA, organization is a full-time occupation. As Price has written:

It is not unrealistic to describe the full-time lay officials as playing both full-time officer and shop steward roles. In the manner of convenors and/or stewards, they remain employees of the civil service, they are subject to recall at regular intervals, they work in close physical proximity to their membership and they are normally the first union representative to deal with any issue coming up from the shopfloor. But in the absence of any first-line paid officials, they might equally well be considered as performing the functions that such officials perform in other unions.

Periodic attempts are made to form one union, between the CPSA and the Society of Civil and Public Servants, but so far they have proved abortive. It would make sense for a grand confederation embracing everyone from permanent secretaries to the office cleaners. Yet vested interests remain strong. The militancy of recent years has made civil servants at all levels more conscious of their rights, but if they are now thinking more as trade unionists, this does not mean they place less value on sectionalism. The logic of Whitleyism may be one union. It looks a long way off.

Post Office workers

In 1979, at only 54 years of age, Tom Jackson, general secretary of the 197,000-strong Union of Post Office Workers, was already one of the old guard on the TUC General Council, eighth in the seniority order. He was elected to that august body in February 1967 and now has a seat on its three most important committees – Finance and General Purposes, Economic and International. Unlike most union leaders, Jackson does not limit his interest or activities to Post Office affairs. He tries to see the wider interests of the unions. This has often led him to make frank speeches at TUC Congresses that have failed to endear him to the faint-hearts.

The seven-week-long Post Office strike in 1971 nearly bankrupted the union. It was a bitter watershed in the history of the UPW, as Jackson's militant, loyal members went down to total defeat at the hands of Edward Heath and his n-minus-one pay policy. The UPW was forced to borrow heavily and received some aid from other unions, but not enough. The union had to push up its subscription rates by 25 per cent and cut back on its education budget. It took two years for the UPW to recover financially from the débâcle. The 1971 strike had a sobering impact on Jackson's members and made them adopt a more cautious approach, though chronic staff shortages impelled a massive catching-up operation on pay during 1974 and 1975. That dispute demonstrated in a rather painful way just how incorrigibly sectionalist the British trade union movement still is. Just after the strike ended, Jackson urged a special TUC conference of public sector unions to coordinate their pay strategies, so that all of them could bargain and organize collectively in a united front against their common employer. He found little support from his colleagues in other unions for such a radical idea, which ran up against the desire of unions to preserve their basic autonomy at all costs. At the 1972 TUC Jackson tried unsuccessfully to popularize the issue again. As he argued: 'Unity is not a word on a banner to be carried into Trafalgar Square and then stowed away for another occasion.' Jackson's presence at the rostrum seemed like a standing rebuke to those union leaders who stood idly by and let the UPW go marching to defeat.

The UPW took a surprisingly hard line against the 1971 Industrial Relations Act. Jackson backed the Engineers' motion at the 1972 TUC instructing unions to de-register and thereby boycott the new law. He poured scorn on those union leaders who were anxious about the resulting loss of tax concessions for taking such a step: 'There are those of you who talk about the £5 million and wanting to get your share of it and make sure you do not lose it. Well brothers, it is not crinkly pound notes you will be getting in your hands; it is thirty pieces of silver.' But for the most part, Jackson is not a man of the far left, far from it. He supports the idea of an incomes policy, though in the late 1960s he and his union were militant opponents of Labour's. In 1973 he was one of the few voices on the TUC General Council who spoke up for pay restraint as part of the union's contribution to the battle against raging inflation. 'I used to be alone in the middle of the four-poster bed. Now you can't move, it's so full,' said Jackson to me in April 1976. But he still champions causes which his TUC colleagues oppose. Jackson was the last supporter of free trade and critic of import controls as a vital weapon in Britain's industrial recovery. He speaks up against excessive public expenditure, which does not endear him to the other public sector unions.

Jackson has spent a lifetime in Post Office work, since he began as a messenger boy in Leeds at the age of 14. After naval service during the war he joined the Communist Party. 'I wanted radical change and quickly,' he says, but he left within eighteen months as a protest against Stalin's treatment of Tito's Yugoslavia and its expulsion from the Cominform. It was not until 1964 that Jackson was made a union national official. He is critical of his predecessors at the UPW. 'In the 1950s we had bloody awful wages and the leaders did not push hard enough,' he says. By 1967 when he took on his union's top job 'it was like a bottle of champagne being opened'. The UPW was once a stronghold of syndicalist thought. Its constitution, drawn up in 1920, still enshrines belief in the need for 'effective participation' in all decisions affecting the members. In 1976 the UPW pressed the Post Office to introduce a two-year experiment in industrial democracy, which started in January 1978, though Jackson believes the UPW founding fathers were 'a lot of idealistic dreamers'.

Twenty years ago his union was virtually para-military, the home of ex-national service NCOs, who valued the security of Post Office work with a solid pension for old age. 'All sense was knocked out of many of them with all that clicking of heels and saluting,' said Jackson. He remembers the bullshit of morning parades for the messenger boys in Leeds in the 1930s. That kind of internal discipline has gone now. Indeed, many of Jackson's members are demoralized for their employer has become rather a sick joke with the general public. 'We had to absorb four years' inflation in one year's price increases,' argues Jackson. This was the result of government price restraint distorting the finances of the Post Office Corporation.

Jackson believes the separation of the Post Office from the civil service in 1969 has done little to make the organization any different. 'We have frustrated expectations. The red tape of the civil service ethos still hangs about.' Jackson finds the time to carry on other work outside the union and the TUC, where his moderating voice has often found few supporters. His moustachios are a familiar sight on television current affairs programmes and he is now a regular contributor to *Any Questions*. He had a spell as a govenor of the BBC and sat on the Annan Commission looking into broadcasting. He is a non-executive director of British Petroleum, but waives his fee for that job. A few years ago Jackson was offered the job of running the Post Office, but he turned it down. 'Union disciplines do not fit us for playing managerial roles.' Jackson is a good example of what the leader of a medium-sized union can achieve in the TUC, not entirely dominated by the general union bosses.

The 121,000-strong Post Office Engineering Union, under the general secretaryship of Bryan Stanley, is one of the most progressive and far-sighted unions in Britain, though it rarely gets publicity. The new £2 million headquarters – Greystoke House – close to Hanger Lane tube station in west London suburbia looks more like a high-class motel than a union headquarters. Most of the POEU's members are employed in telecommunications and cover the grades from labourers to technical officers. The union also has some members in the engineering trades in the postal business and staff in the Post Office motor transport, supplies and factories departments.

The union's motto is 'For social and technological progress' and it has lived up to those ideals over the past twenty years. The POEU can rightly boast one of the best productivity records in the country. As it revealed in evidence to the Carter Committee on the Post Office in 1976: 'Between 1965 and 1974 when the number of telephones in service increased by 104.3 per cent and a number of new services were introduced the Post Office engineering workforce grew by only 20.9 per cent from 79,431 to 100,310.' The union was among the first to participate in productivity bargaining. In the old days it took eight men to install a new telegraph pole. Now it only needs one. Manpower required for installation has also been cut from an average of four to one. The idea of a second mate for the skilled engineer was also cut out with union support.

The POEU estimates that without such union cooperation the Post Office would have had to employ getting on for 43,000 more workers. Such willingness to embrace new technology annoys a minority of the POEU activist membership, who believe the union has given away too much for very little. In the coming decade the old, increasingly defunct Strowger telephone exchange system is being phased out and replaced by the TXE4 system and eventually a wholly electronic exchange network known as System X. This involves a massive public investment and it will entail a dramatic cutback in the manpower requirements, perhaps by as much as half. The POEU refuses to contemplate any idea of redundancy. In the union's view better marketing and zeal from the Post Office should boost consumer demand and allow the Corporation to redeploy the workers who will have no maintenance work on to the new telecommunications network. Of course, the POEU members have benefited from their productivity record in higher wages. Craftsmen had a 140 per cent increase between 1966 and 1974 on their basic rate. The Post Office was even able to convince the Pay Board that the union's increased productivity merited a further rise in 1973 on top of the £1 plus 4 per cent formula in phase two of Heath's income policy.

The POEU's structure is shaped to parallel that of the Post Office from national to branch level. The twenty-three members of the National Executive Council are elected annually at conference (eleven occupational; twelve regional). There are 290 branches in the union, varying in size from 30 to as many as 4,000 in some of the larger Post Office establishments. The interests of the members are divided into 'external' (those jobs involving outside construction and maintenance) and 'internal' (working in the exchanges). The union affiliated to the Labour Party in 1964 and Bryan Stanley has a seat on the National Executive. Like most white-collar unions, the POEU's general secretary is appointed and not elected. Though the Post Office left the grip of the civil service in 1969, the Whitley system still tends to be reflected in the outlook of the union. As Frank Bealey, the official historian of the POEU, has written, it is unique 'as a civil service union which recruited technical workers'. 'Because of civil service privileges and conditions, it has been disinclined to undertake industrial action.' Over the years the POEU has kept its distance from other postal unions. It is an élitist body for skilled workers, who believe they are a cut above postmen and telephonists, and is more concerned with status and wide differentials. In the early 1950s the POEU was faced with threats of breakaways, so it has tried to marry strong central control with a wide occupational representation on its committees. It has become a more 'open' union with a big influence on Post Office policy. Of course, technological progress has meant more jobs, better pay and security, so the POEU displays an enlightened self-interest. More than most, it has spurned Luddism.

The Council of Post Office Unions (COPOU) was formed in October 1969 and it represents 98.8 per cent of the 433,000 Post

Office staff in both rank and file and management grades. It provides a collective voice for all the constituents except on pay, which is still negotiated by the unions separately. The creation of the Post Office Corporation proved a stimulus to merger and rationalization with a reduction in the number of unions in the industry from twenty-two in 1968 to nine in 1975. These are: Society of Post Office Executives (19,000-strong). The union is affiliated to the TUC and it covers supervisors and managers in the engineering field as well as telecommunications traffic and telephone sales supervising grades. The Civil and Public Services Association, posts and telecommunications group with a membership of 34,887. This covers clerical staff, typing and machine operating grades. The National Federation of Sub-Postmasters with 20,142 members. The Post Office Management Staffs' Association (POMSA), consisting of 18,104 members among supervisory staff in the postal, telephone, telegraph and counter and writing fields. Both the UPW and POEU are also dominant voices on the Council. Associate unions are Telephone Contract Officers' Association (TCOA) (1,025 members); the Society of Civil Servants Posts, Executive and Directing group (5,200); and the Institution of Professional Civil Servants have 300 members.

The Council has modest offices off London's Tottenham Court Road, not far from Post Office headquarters. Its general secretary is Tony Carter and it employs three full-time officers. There are twenty-one separate COPOU regional councils throughout the country. It also operates in every head postmaster's and general manager's area as well as in regional and area offices. There are over 300 of these area committees, which are all staffed by voluntary part-time unionists, elected by the unions.

The close and highly integrated industrial relations system in the Post Office made it easier to introduce an experiment in industrial democracy in the Corporation. In February 1977 unions and the Post Office announced agreement on a two-year scheme to introduce worker directors on to the top board. Six trade unionists were to be chosen through union machinery to sit alongside six executive directors and four independents on the Corporation's main decision-making body. A joint working

party took many months before reaching agreement. The first
step came in April 1974 when Tony Benn, Industry minister of
the day, asked the Corporation and the unions for their views
on industrial democracy. The main impetus for a radical
change came from the unions. The UPW and POEU joined
forces in putting forward a scheme. Initially the unions wanted
a two-tier board with half the seats on the supervisory board,
but they eventually dropped the idea and plumped for a single-
board scheme. The unions made it clear from the start that 'the
area of decision-making must be extended at all levels to the
point where there can be no unilateral application of executive
action by management'. They never accepted the Post Office's
view that it was difficult, if not impossible, to separate participation in top decision-making for the unions from collective
bargaining. An internal document the unions submitted to the
Corporation explained: 'Union nominated board members may
well find themselves in the position of having to defend an unpopular decision. This is a well-known hazard of trade union
life and there is no reason to suppose that any union nominee
would baulk at it.'

The next few years will prove whether such a system is the
harbinger of things to come elsewhere in British industry or a
temporary aberration. But if industrial democracy has any
future, it needs to be tried in the public sector and there is nowhere better than the Post Office in which to begin.

20 The Fleet Street follies

People take print for granted, until their morning newspaper fails to drop through the letterbox. Yet print is everywhere. It covers packaging, cartons, beer labels, banknotes, stamps, stationery as well as the more obvious books, periodicals and newspapers. Print is also one of the most accurate barometers of Britain's economic health. It remains the first to catch a cold in bad times and to enjoy the sun when a boom arrives. The industry is also gripped by a painful and drastic series of technological changes that will transform its face over the coming years. Print has been an old traditional craft industry, imbued with all the pride of the skilled craftsmen who remain its highly paid élite. Now it is becoming a technology. The man sweating over the hot type may eventually be replaced by the man pressing buttons on the automated machine.

Less than a decade ago William Caxton would have not felt a stranger in a composing or machine room. The processes of print had hardly changed in principle since the fifteenth century. Now innovation is making a dramatic difference. Type is increasingly being made up with electric keyboards. Computers are being used in make-up and in the lay-out of the type. Hot-metal type is being replaced by photo-composition, where an image of the matter to be printed is produced photographically. Traditional letterpress printing (the use of type or blocks on which the image to be printed stands out on raised surfaces) is being rivalled by lithographic printing, which uses a plate on which the printing and the non-printing parts are on the same level and the latter are kept damp and so free from ink. Litho produces less precise an image than letterpress, but it is increasingly being used in illustrative and glossy productions. The 1973 labour survey produced by the British Federation of Master Printers (the non-newspaper employers' organization) revealed, for the first time, that less than 75 per cent of their members were using letterpress machines any longer. The trend to litho started in 1964. It has involved retraining crafts-men in the new techniques. The ratio of craft to non-craft worker is being reduced by litho and there has been a noticeable increase in labour productivity with the long-run, fast-moving machines, almost all imported (like letterpress) from West Germany and Austria. These changes, and others like the 'web-offset' process and more automation in finishing and binding, have eroded craft skills. The old distinctions with-in the labour force no longer make much sense with the new technology.

The 1967 Cameron Report, looking into the problems caused by the introduction of web-offset machines into the printing industry, emphasized just what the changes meant for the workforce. It would involve retraining and redeployment as well as a reduction in the manpower. British printing has never been short of critics to attack its alleged inefficiencies, such as poor management, lack of investment and, above all, poor pro-ductivity. In 1970 a little NEDDY contrasted British with American and European performances and it reached the con-clusion that web-offset and gravure machines were handled more efficiently with smaller manned crews producing a higher output anywhere but in Britain.

The trade unions have a peculiarly strong hold over the 320,000-strong industry. They control entry into the profession and in many cases (particularly in the national newspaper in-dustry) exercise control over the apprenticeship system. But times are changing among the unions. The bad old ways (even of Fleet Street) no longer find many union defenders in the new harsh climate – born of soaring paper prices, falling adver-tising revenue and shaky corporate finances.

The furious, destructive demarcation disputes between dif-ferent unions still erupt on national newspapers, where workers have a considerable control over the means of production; but mergers and rationalization have thinned down the number of unions over recent years. In 1960 there were still fifteen unions covering the British printing industry. By 1976 that number had shrunk to seven.

The National Graphical Association is the main craft union in print with 110,000 members in 1979. It's present general secretary is Joe Wade, a dapperly dressed man with frizzy hair. He was elected to the top job by a big majority in a 77 per cent poll of the membership in the winter of 1975. His union covers craftsmen in print in England, Wales and the Irish Republic, but not in Scotland in any large number. The NGA dominates the composing department of print firms. These are the men who set copy in hot metal or lino. The union also organizes wireroom and telephoto operators as well as readers and machine managers. The NGA is made up of a series of mergers. It began in 1964 with the marriage of the London Typographical Society and the Typographical Association to form the NGA. In the following year the National Union of Press Telegraphists and the Association of Correctors of the Press joined the organization. In 1967 the National Society of Electrotypers and Stereotypers became part of the NGA too and a year later so did the Amalgamated Society of Lithographic Printers. During the winter of 1976–7 serious merger talks were going on between the NGA and its rival craft union, SLADE, as well as a union for the semi-skilled, NATSOPA. The eventual aim is one union for all print workers. After generations of inter-union wrangles and bitter personality feuds this would be a major advance for the industry, if it eventually succeeds.

The NGA raised considerable conflict within the industry when it registered under the 1971 Industrial Relations Act, after the majority of members supported such action through a ballot – in defiance of the wishes of their leaders and the annual conference. It was not until 1976 that the NGA was back in the TUC, because of a disagreement over how much the union was expected to pay in arrears for its years outside. With its plush headquarters in Bedford, the NGA is run highly efficiently. A modern computer keeps a close check on when the members change their jobs and who is in default in paying his dues. But the NGA is on the defensive. Its whole *raison d'être* is under threat through the new technology.

Wade is the son of a Blackburn compositor, who has spent over twenty years negotiating at national level in the industry, and he is no Luddite. During the 1960s the NGA cooperated with the provincial press when they introduced photo-composition and computer type-setting, even though these new methods imperilled the traditional demarcation lines of skill. 'Our members recognize something has got to be done on the national newspapers, but like me they are concerned it should be socially just and humane,' said Wade in an interview in December 1975. 'Since the days of Northcliffe every paper deliberately fostered overstaffing to put rivals out of business and stop new ones starting.' In Wade's opinion, voluntary redundancy must be the answer, not wholesale sackings. 'You are not going to get cooperation from people in putting them out of work. There must be gradual change. The lessons from the United States are those who run into greatest difficulty have tried to rush the technological change through too quickly.'

SLADE (the Society of Lithographic Artists, Designers, Engravers and Process Workers) is a craft union founded in 1885 at the height of William Morris-style socialism. It represents workers mainly in the process departments. In 1979 the union had just under 25,600 members. In recent years SLADE and the NGA have fought some fierce battles over demarcation. The Society of Graphical and Allied Trades 1975 (SOGAT), with 203,352 members, is the largest union in the printing industry. Its general secretary, Bill Keys, is a man of the broad left and a member of the TUC General Council. He was elected with a comfortable majority by the members in 1975. SOGAT 1975 is the product of a bewildering series of mergers and break-ups. It used to be known as the National Union of Printing, Bookbinding and Paper Workers until it merged with NATSOPA in 1966 to form a single union for all the non-craftsmen in print, but the liaison fell apart in bitter acrimony in 1970. The Paperworkers held on to the SOGAT name. About a third of SOGAT's members are in papermaking. There is a craft element in packaging, with 30,000 workers. There are also SOGAT journeymen in bookbinding. Outside London the members make up the majority of machine assistants in general print. The strong London branch consists of non-skilled men in the publishing end of Fleet Street, binders, warehousemen and van drivers, where they dominate the distribution and wholesale trades.

NATSOPA (the National Association of Operative Printers, Graphical and Media Personnel) is a similar union with around 60 per cent of its 55,000 members working in Fleet Street, where

they are machine assistants, clerical staff, ink and roller workers
and administrative personnel. NATSOPA members are also the
cleaners, doormen and messengers on national newspapers.
The union is strong on Manchester and Glasgow newspapers.
NATSOPA's origins lie in the formation of the Printers
Labourers Union in 1889. The union is recruiting in the computer and photographic side of the industry, which leads to
sporadic inter-union wrangles. Although NATSOPA rules insist that the general secretary should be in office for only three
years at a stretch, Richard Briginshaw during his long reign at
the top of the union from 1951 to 1975 was never opposed.
'Brig' won a reputation as the scourge of Fleet Street, with his
blunt if muddled outlook. His successor, Owen O'Brien, is a
more moderate man. He lacks the abrasive qualities of Brig,
who now sits in the House of Lords and has a job as a part-
time director of the British National Oil Corporation.

The print unions are not run by autocrats; quite the contrary. They suffer all the strengths and weaknesses of ultra-
democracy. Over the years, they have usually failed to find
common ground. Union wrangles have broken up almost every
joint body in the industry. The joint Industrial Council folded
in 1965, and both the Joint Board for the Newspaper Industry
and the Joint Manpower Committee went two years later. The
little Neddy for print and publishing collapsed in 1970. The
Printing and Kindred Trades Federation – a forum for the resolution of inter-union disputes as well as the bargainer on basic
hours, holidays and apprentices' wages – fell apart in 1974 with
both SOGAT and NATSOPA refusing to participate any
longer. But in the same year the TUC Printing Industries Committee was established. As ACAS explained in its evidence to
the Royal Commission on the Press in 1976, the TUC committee is 'a forum for information exchange between the unions
on claims and settlements and its activities encompass health
and safety, the work of industry training boards and monitor-
ing developments' in the industry. All the print unions belong,
as well as the other unions with members in newspapers. These
include not just the National Union of Journalists, but also the
general ones. The majority of maintenance workers are in the
EETPU and the AUEW Engineering section. There are also
members of the construction union (UCATT), the GMWU,

COHSE, and the Sheet Metal Workers in Fleet Street's inflated labour force. As a result of the crisis at the *Observer* newspaper in the summer of 1975, most of the unions came together with the employers on the national newspapers in the formation of a joint standing committee. This drew up *Programme for Action*, ground rules covering redundancy terms for the gradual rundown of the manpower on the nationals on a voluntary basis with the introduction of the new technology. The issues were put to the entire Fleet Street labour force in a ballot held early in 1977 but the document was turned down. The pressure of events had pushed erstwhile bitter rivals together, though time will tell whether this augurs well for a new climate in the industrial relations of the industry.

What union leaders at head office say or do is more important than it used to be, but the power and autonomy of the chapels – those ultra-democratic voices from the shopfloor – remain supreme. This is not to say they are entirely a law unto themselves. The vetting of chapel draft agreements must take place in the branches of every print union. Nor are chapels empowered to take strike action without the approval of their union officials though, as ACAS admitted, 'the range of sanctions other than a full stoppage of work a chapel can employ in pursuance of a claim of grievance may be equally effective'. Every member of the union is automatically a member of a chapel.

The rule-books confer enormous power on the chapels. All members must turn up to meetings. If they do not, then they are fined for non-attendance. Over the years print chapels have accumulated considerable control over production. They draw up work allocation, overtime and shift rotas in some chapels. The chapels (there are as many as 360 on national newspapers) have their own funds to cover administrative costs, but also sickness payments and even death benefits. Although it is untrue to say chapels are a law unto themselves outside the control of their union branches and full-time officials, the power to halt production ensures they are in an effective position to seek extra payments and privileges on top of what is negotiated centrally.

Fleet Street is a jungle of competing wage rates and conditions for its overmanned printing operations, but all workers earn well above the manufacturing average (in April 1975 as much as 39 per cent more, though a good deal less than a few years ago). It remains virtually impossible to keep a close eye on the different payments made to keep production going. Many Fleet Street observers in 1977 agreed that most print chapels had broken through the social contract pay norms. Around 35,500 people work in the national newspaper industry, with as many as 12,200 full-time regular production workers and 4,600 casual part-timers. The ACAS survey found as many as 21.5 per cent of production workers were over the age of 60 in October 1975 in Fleet Street and 6.5 per cent more than 65. Union rules guard entry into employment and it is virtually impossible to move from one newspaper to another. The 1966 *Economist* Intelligence Report into the newspaper industry was a devastating attack on the malpractices and abuses practised in Fleet Street. Little has changed since then, despite the efforts of the Newspaper Proprietors' Association (the NPA) to encourage comprehensive agreements to buy out restrictive practices and the overmanning on machines and in the publishing room. Leap-frogging of claims persists between one house and another. A 100 per cent difference can still be found between the pay of a machine-minder on one newspaper and that at another where a man is carrying out exactly the same kind of work. The 'ghosting' system remains, whereby men take on the extra work which another man could have done, if he had been recruited. Overtime payments are made for work done on the daily shift. The 'blowing' practice still goes on as well, with men working two hours on the job and then taking one or two hours off on full pay through the day or night. Work studies are unknown. Job evaluation is non-existent. Fleet Street remains a secure closed shop where the family connection or old boy network can provide a meal ticket for life. No lay-off clauses exist in agreements. This means employers must pay everybody if a small group stops production. The 17-hours-a-week man being paid well over £100 is still common. The NPA would like to cry a halt to this anarchy and build a common front among newspaper proprietors, but in the competitive world of Fleet Street such solidarity is very hard to achieve. Inter-union rivalry is a good way of pushing for more pay up the escalator. No wonder it used to be said that the waiting list for entry would stretch three deep from the NPA offices in Bouverie Street to St Paul's.

The financial troubles of most national newspapers and the urgent need to introduce the new technology is putting immense strain on to the antique industrial relations system that has ruled Fleet Street since the war. Union leaders have seen the writing on the wall and they want to cooperate in a humane demanning, but their members are less willing to swallow such a solution. The economic logic is a more capital-intensive industry with fewer production workers trained in new automated skills. It looks like being a battle royal to convince most print workers that this must come, as the protracted showdown at Times Newspapers in 1978–9 illustrated.

21 The unions into the 1980s

The character of organizations is very much the product of
their ancestry and the circumstances of their early growth.
British trade unions, more than those of most countries perhaps,
are historical deposits and repositories of history. (H. A. Turner,
1962)

Society today is so organized that every individual group
almost has the power to disrupt it. How is their power to be
channelled into constructive channels? That is a question for
the government. But it is a question for the trade unions too.
(Jim Callaghan, Labour Party Conference, 3 October 1978)

It is a truism to say that Britain's unions are the product of the
industrial system which has developed over the last century and
three quarters, but in the familiar exhortation for union reform that simple fact is too often overlooked. Nobody who
ever visits the annual conference of a trade union and wit-
nesses the archaic rituals and procedures can ignore the deep
respect for past achievements, the sense of pride and respectability, which is handed down from one generation of union
activists to the next.

All our institutions are exceedingly hard to change. It is not
simply the trade unions who resist the challenge to their settled
ways of doing things. The boardrooms of many of our companies are dominated by the pampered offspring of the entrepreneurs who fought their way to the top in the days of a more
buccaneering capitalism. The senior echelons of the civil service
remain firmly under the debilitating, arrogant control of Ox-
bridge graduates with arts degrees, despite the Fulton Report
and the cult of scientific management and the widespread demand for open government. The House of Commons still resembles more a gentleman's club than a workshop for action
and custodian of the people's liberties. The upper house remains an indefensible bastion of class privilege. The City of

London and the Bank of England continue to enjoy enormous power and influence.

It is untrue that our unions are overmighty subjects with a lust for power and a contempt for freedom. Economic and social changes in Britain do not allow the unions to merely stand still, to resist blindly. Most unions have to stay dynamic in order to keep alive. But at present many of them have lost touch with their old ideals. Those who carry out the burdens of office either in the full-time organization or on the shopfloor have a difficult task in reconciling the materialistic aspirations of the members who look to the union as a guarantee of better wages, conditions and job security, and the wider, invariably socialist ideals of the activist minority. This produces a familiar tension between the doctrines of free collective bargaining and the collectivist aspirations for which unions claim support. Here is the real, intractable conflict that lies at the heart of British trade unions. Their purely economistic purpose is often in conflict with wider political perspectives.

The breakdown of the 5 per cent pay policy under the strain of widespread strikes in the private and public sectors during the winter of 1978–9 suggests that nobody has yet learned the lessons of the past twenty years. It may seem rather pointless to advocate familiar nostrums for the cure of the illness, but there are no easy answers, panaceas that can overcome deep-rooted social problems that lie at the heart of our society.

However painful it may turn out to be in practice, the Labour Party and the unions, if they are to live together in partnership during the 1980s, will have to find a way through on wage determination between the horrors of the jungle free-for-all and the rigidities and tyranny of a statutory policy imposed by dictate from Whitehall. The 'social contract' must work towards the creation of a new consensus based on realism and a sense of social justice. The attempt to reconcile freedom with responsibility in the tangled area of pay is very difficult, but both the concerted action idea in West Germany and the solidaristic approach in Sweden suggest that there can be successes which fall far short of any imposition of a rigid pay norm on an unwilling people.

Britain needs an annual public debate on the country's economic prospects before the start of the pay round where all sides (government, unions, employers, consumers and other relevant interest groups) sit together and discuss and argue about what the indicators show on profits, prices, balance of payments, investment, employment, wages. At national level we need to know the parameters of the possible. This should take the form of a nationwide teach-in, perhaps its sessions should be televised. In this way we might go some little way to the establishment of more consensus on economic objectives, and alternative critiques would have a real chance of being aired publicly.

Yet this is not enough. Governments in Britain cannot escape the need for an incomes policy, mainly because of the ever-present difficulties of the public sector. Leaving private employers to settle on a high going rate for wage settlements that in many cases will be paid for through an increase in their prices is a prescription for chaos in industrial relations, because of its immediate and damaging impact on what happens in the public sector. Any inequality of treatment between the two will create insoluble problems for any government. Consequently we need to see the initiative on reform coming from the public sector. As I have argued elsewhere in this book it makes a good deal of sense to introduce synchro-pay in the public sector, with active encouragement for private firms to follow suit. The most appropriate time for the bargaining season would be April after the annual budget, with the previous three months taken up with the 'great debate' on the economy's prospects that year. Changes in tax rates should become a vital part of the bargaining process, so that governments can make trade-offs between pay and tax.

The main thrust of these suggestions implies a greater centralized control or influence on wage determination; but it is no use disguising the fact that this runs in the face of the continuing devolution of bargaining down to plant and company level. If all pay is negotiated in a national forum, there remains a grave danger of inflexibilities and frustrations building up with dangerous results for longer term stability. The creation of some kind of tripartite relativities board may help to ease much of the tension, but it would be foolish to suppose it can fully remove the difficulty. In Sweden and West Germany there remains substantial wage drift. The same would be true in any more rational and harmonized pay bargaining here as well, but perhaps even more so. Clearly companies in monopoly markets or healthy profits are better able to provide their employees with higher rates of pay than firms in a more competitive position with narrow profit margins. What we must expect to see is a two-tier pay system, whereby a general increase for all is reached through national bargaining with individual workplaces enjoying further rises to be negotiated at the place of work. The crucial need is to avoid too great a disparity between the winners and losers in the market economy.

And here the union activists should play a vital part. We cannot treat incomes policy in isolation from broader social and economic objectives. It must become an integral part of a growth strategy. Moreover, unions need to generate a wider perspective, a sense of collective solidarity between different groups of workers. Through a common awareness of mutual problems, the trade union movement might start to abandon the old negative sectionalism that has always hampered any moves towards a voluntary incomes policy.

It will not be easy for union leaders to drop their unthinking, instinctive belief in the virtues of free collective bargaining as at present conducted. But the illusions need to be shattered. Those who suffer from voluntarism are not the rich or those on above average incomes, but the low paid, the old, the unemployed and those who do not belong to a trade union. In the war of everyone against everyone they remain the victims of a misguided sectionalist greed. There are two good reasons why union leaders have been reluctant to drop free collective bargaining. Ever since the 1949 pay freeze, incomes policies have always been introduced by governments as crudely drawn norms in the face of a desperate national crisis. By their very nature these attempts at introducing some stability to pay bargaining have been *ad hoc*, emergency measures dictated by the sheer speed of events. As a result, incomes policies have brought with them serious anomalies and injustices, which in turn have led to militant opposition within the unions towards their continuation and their eventual collapse under a flood of inflationary wage deals. This is what happened in 1969–70, 1974–5 and again in 1978–9. There has simply never been enough time available to politicians, union leaders and employers to construct a more flexible system based on consent that might endure for some years.

But this leads us on to the second, perhaps more important, reason why unions dislike pay policies. They take away from unions the freedom to pursue their primary function – that of wage determination. Without the autonomy to bargain about the members' pay packet, just what is a union negotiator left to do? The push for higher money wages in a stagnant or low growth economy has become a dangerous virility test in the incessant struggle between the unions for increased memberships in a highly competitive labour market. No union leader worth his salt can be seen to favour pay moderation in such rough and ready conditions since any genuine wages policy does require some outside intervention to curb the freedom of negotiators. Moreover, the all-important shop stewards need a *raison d'être*. As W. W. Daniel discovered in his 1976 and 1977 studies the lay activists were the main antagonists of further national incomes guidelines.

None of these arguments are conclusive vindications for the wisdom of the voluntarist approach. If the ultimate purpose of free trade unionism is not the pursuit of idealistic political objectives but the material well-being of the members, then we can say with certitude, free collective bargaining fails to deliver the goods. The leap-froggers calendar impoverishes, because it stimulates inflation, not real rises in living standards, where trade unionists are no better off than anybody else in a bankrupt economy. The ultimate test for the success of an incomes policy must lie through what John Hughes has called 'efficiency bargaining', a willingness to trade off genuine productivity increases in return for higher pay.

But a broader approach to wage determination should also provide a belated opportunity for the lay activists and the full-time officials to take a closer and more systematic interest in a greater, hitherto underdeveloped area of negotiation. This links up with the need for more union involvement in company decision-making through full disclosure of company information, closer union cooperation in manpower planning, investment decisions, fringe benefits and the indefensible inequalities between blue and white-collar workers that still scar

British industry. The more involved negotiators can become in these neglected, still too often forbidden, areas which are directly relevant to the needs and welfare of workers, the more exciting and fruitful are the potentialities for shopfloor bargaining.

But the future of pay bargaining in Britain during the 1980s looks gloomy. The possibility of a permanent incomes policy with recognized and acceptable institutions remains remote. No doubt under the pressure of sterling crises and high inflation, governments will try and impose crude, *ad hoc* pay restraint in the name of a national emergency. But this can only be an uncertain palliative that will not last very long. The grim cycle is likely to grind on with severe consequences for the standard of living of workers, whether they belong to unions or not.

The social climate of Britain is no longer conducive to a voluntary consensus on pay, but incomes restraint through statute will not work for very long either. So we look like having to endure what Thomas Hobbes called 'a state of nature' where it is war 'of all against all'. It would be quite wrong to blame the unions alone for this sorry condition. The values of our divided, unequal society are not mainly determined by them. But the nature of our chaotic bargaining system remains a major reason for instability.

A statutory incomes policy, backed by sanctions and punishments, cannot work for long in a free society. It is only possible where democratic institutions have been destroyed. On the other hand, a state of nature in an economy with next to no growth also threatens our liberties. The leviathan is an alternative that few wish to see; yet alarmingly few seem ready to fight against the self-destructive irrationalism of the present pay chaos.

The 'revolt' against pay policy in the winter of 1978–9 lacked any political perspective. It was not a challenge to the political and social system, but a reversion to a familiar acquisitive sectionalism. The people who suffered from the strikes were other trade unionists, the poor, the sick, the unemployed, not the well-off members of the community. What motivated those who took part in the stoppages was a deep anger, a frustration at falling behind in the earnings league table after three years of voluntary wage restraint. There were no grounds for optimism among the revolutionary theorists in those events. Organized labour was not launching a serious assault on the power of capital. Indeed, there was no coherent political explanation by the union participants for their actions, other than a simple demand for 'much more money now'. Once a satisfactory wage settlement was reached, the strikers returned to work without any obvious change in their relations with their employers.

More realistic Marxists today recognize the bleak prospects for revolutionary change. As Professor Eric Hobsbawm wrote in the September 1978 issue of *Marxism Today*, trade union militancy at the end of the 1970s had an 'increasingly sectional and economistic character'. And he went on: 'On the whole the level of generalized response is much lower even than in 1970. In the present period of fragmented and sectional struggle where the ideology of the "national interest" (and of keeping Labour in power to defend it) is dominant, to continue to fight for such a generalized response is to struggle completely against the stream.' The main political consequence of the upsurge in strikes during the early months of 1979 was not to rekindle a spirit of socialist militancy, but massively to boost the electoral prospects of Mrs Margaret Thatcher and the Conservatives. The labour militancy was aimed at achieving higher pay for some workers at the expense of others.

So what are unions for? What kind of a future do they have in the Britain of the 1980s? There is a temptation to try and impose new, restrictive laws on their activities as a way of disciplining their potentially anarchic internal relations. Certainly the hostile anti-trade union mood of 1979 does not suggest this would provoke any initial opposition from public opinion. But populist policies remain an inadequate and ultimately self-destructive reaction to fundamental problems that go deep into the social structure of modern Britain. There are simply no easy, sweeping solutions and it would be foolish to believe otherwise. Undoubtedly a voluntary, permanent incomes policy, the standing commission on public service pay comparability and an annual economic assessment make sense in a society based on agreed principles of reason and fairness. But we don't happen to live in that kind of country at the moment.

To a very large extent workers are responding to the values of our society, which are competitive, individualist and materialist. Ironically the main critics of the unions come from the liberal *laissez faire* wing of the Conservative Party, who seem unable to live with the remorseless logic of their own libertarian philosophy, when it is applied to workers not just entrepreneurs. What is so depressing about the outlook for the 1980s is that such a primitive view of life has gained an ascendancy and eclipsed older values of fellowship and solidarity, social justice and equality that used to shape – to a certain extent – the outlook of union leaders and their activist rank and file. An irrational scramble for higher money wages at all cost (including the well-being and the living standards of workers themselves) remains the nadir of free trade unionism.

The strong likelihood is that we shall lurch from side to side through the 1980s, through bouts of voluntarism to bouts of panic wage control, in an economy which is likely to suffer from continuing poor growth, low productivity and high rates of inflation, with lengthy dole queues. In this depressing scenario the unions will continue to battle in a half-hearted, unknowing way to keep some feeble grip on events over which they have virtually no control.

Yet this does not have to be our fate. We need only go back fory years to the beginning of the people's war to know that the British trade union movement is miraculously capable of exercising a progressive and highly effective influence on this country. It was between the formation of the Churchill coalition in the terrible spring of 1940 and Labour's great victory at the polls in July 1945 that a real and lasting social contract was forged between the unions and the politicians. Its fruits were seen in the creation of the welfare state, in the famous 1944 government White Paper with its ambitious commitment to the establishment of full employment in peacetime, in the Beveridge plan for social insurance, and the radical changes that took place in manpower policies through the joint production committees and the works councils that sprang up spontaneously in the factories with the dilution of proud craft skills and demarcations and even the compulsory direction of labour. The high levels of output and productivity achieved in Britain's armaments industry were the envy of the German war machine. This was done without any resort to terror and slave labour, but through a genuine idealism and commitment to total victory over the evils of Nazism and a social revolution once the war was won.

In the deceptively easier years of peace those basic, simple truths were lost. Labour governments have failed to change the values of our society, and the dogmas of voluntarism and *laissez faire* remain obstinately strong. During the 1970s important steps were taken towards a closer understanding between the unions and government, which imposed severe stress on the difficult, often tenuous links between union officials and their rank and file. By the end of the decade trade union 'power' and influence remains the central issue of British politics. Many of the constructive trends of the 1970s point in a more hopeful direction. The social contract was in many ways closer in conception to the highly successful partnerships achieved between the Social Democrats and the unions in mixed economies such as Austria, West Germany and Sweden. Bringing the unions into a closer, more representative role in the development of a democratic society lies at the heart of the Labour–union alliance. As this book has attempted to show the record of the 1970s has not been so negative as the innumerable enemies of free trade unionism like to suggest. Our unions have had too little influence in the past, not too much. Indeed, a good deal of the resistance to further pay restraint stemmed from a not altogether unjustifiable belief among the rank and file trade union activists that not merely had the pay policies become manifestly unjust in their application but that the government had simply failed to respond to trade union pleas on a wide range of social and economic issues, most notably public spending and import controls.

Walter Citrine's declaration at the 1946 TUC of entering the 'era of responsibility' was premature. There is one major indestructible barrier to any effective and radical trade union movement in Britain and nobody has found a way of removing it. The sheer diversity and number of unions in every industry lies at the roots of the problem. As we have seen, mergers and amalgamations have thinned down the union numbers, but in 1977 there were still 436 registered unions. The vast majority are little more than defunct friendly societies.

Most workers (70 per cent) are in the top ten unions. At factory level joint shop steward committees usually bring together activists from different unions where they can make common cause. But *ad hoc* informal arrangements are not always the best way of ensuring a unified union movement. The competition for members between unions in many areas of the labour market makes it difficult for them to demand realistic subscription rates to pay for the kind of servicing members require in their bargaining with management. Union monopolies do exist in established areas like printing, shipbuilding, mining and the railways. The spread of the closed shop has tightened up the freedom of workers to move from one union into another. The Bridlington Agreement of 1939 is supposed to stop poaching between unions and the TUC Disputes Committee adjudicates on vexatious cases, but this is an erratic check. Unions lay claim to areas of influence in recruitment drives, but they lack the sanctions to uphold them against competition. This remains a safeguard (for the moment) against any possible union tyranny.

Yet the lack of clear demarcation lines between unions means that union officials spend much of their time in duplication of effort as organizers and bargainers. In an industry like telecommunications, for example, no one union has a dominant voice, so its workers lack the kind of influence they would expect to wield if they were all in the same union. 'Structure is a function of purpose' were the wise words of Citrine, but for too long the unions have failed to respond to their logic. It is not hard to understand why. Three big manual general unions dominate. Any move to a more sensible, rationally streamlined trade union movement would require their virtual breakup. There is no chance that such self-sacrifice will ever happen. So the TUC will remain a weak, loose confederation. Its counsels will be dominated by the power brokering and personal rivalries which often cripple decisive action. More and more decisions will be taken on pay farther down the union structure. National agreements outside the public sector will bear little relationship to the realities of gross pay packets. The trend towards companywide bargaining (Ford, ICI, GEC) between combine committees, thrown together by necessity across the boundaries of individual unions, will grow more intense. This will bring further pressure to bear on the ossified structures of many union organizations. In the long run, it carries the dangers of breakaway, independent, company-based unions. Going through local, regional or national trade union machinery will be viewed as a recipe for inertia.

An added threat to the unions in the 1980s will come from the arrival of microprocessing technology, which is likely to transform the organization and content of work in our society. The TUC is taking a constructive view of the micro-chip, to judge by the interim report it published in April 1979 – *Employment and Technology*. There are no obvious signs of Luddism in Congress House; though the message of enlightenment may be harder to get over among workers, who fear the loss of their jobs as a consequence of technological change. As the TUC report argues: 'Collective bargaining, involving the whole workforce through established procedures, provides the most effective and suitable vehicle for the trade union response.' It talks about the introduction of new technology agreements, seeking to turn *status quo* and mutuality clauses into 'more positive provisions'. The TUC want to ensure management do not unilaterally introduce the new technology against the wishes of the workforce, but on the other hand the report talks about union negotiators being ready to take the lead in pressing for joint management/union assessments of the opportunities of new processes. The TUC has been quick to notice the impact these changes will have on existing union structures, making them more difficult to maintain in their present form. The report calls for the creation of joint union committees to examine the problems and while there must be 'a guarantee of full job security for the existing workforce', the TUC recognizes the imperative of internal transfers of jobs in the plant, more mobility, much more extensive training in new skills. In other words, microprocessing will make a nonsense of many of the customs and practices that are enshrined in so much of shopfloor life and the unions must bend to the pressures and reform themselves.

A handful of union leaders are painfully aware of the inadequacies of the present structure. Not enough have given it much thought at all. There are those (notably David Lea of the TUC) who believe industrial democracy (trade unionists on company boards) can provide the urgent catalyst for action. Without such a stimulus for change, it is argued, our shoe-string unions will fail to maximize the opportunities to play a decisive role in the shaping of Britain. Some form of industrial democracy remains perhaps the most hopeful development for the future. Through joint control, the unions could transform themselves, becoming instruments for change, not merely conservative bodies obsessed with the wage packet. As Flanders wrote, management and governments in Britain have for too long seen union leaders as 'mainly managers of discontent'. Within the severe limitations imposed by history, vested interest and apathy, we can expect the unions to become more the innovators, who will no longer say 'No' so often. But don't anticipate miracles. Britain remains a society divided rigidly by class and status. Contrary to popular mythology, it is not run by the unions; quite the opposite. Not until the power of big business, high finance and the civil service is curbed through democratic controls can we hope to see the unions enjoying the security and power of a new ruling caste, and there is no evidence at all to suggest the vast majority of union members would like to see such a state of affairs. Faith in the mixed economy and parliamentary politics among workers is much stronger than the fair-weather friends of democracy like to admit. The fantasy world of brutish union bosses dictating what we read or where we work belongs to fiction writers in Fleet Street.

Our protracted economic crisis has highlighted many defects in British trade unionism. The dangers of fragmentation are real. There is an often unappealing sectional self-interest about the motives of union leaders as well as members. Few think beyond the parameters of their own union about the movement as a whole. Union leaders are practical, hard-headed people, who devote long hours to union business and take their heavy duties seriously. Overseas observers are usually impressed by the calibre of those at the top. They compare favourably with union bosses in other countries. But our problems are more deep rooted and insuperable than other Western economies. The chaos of multi-unionism means the British trade union 'movement' is ill-prepared to modernize.

The very inter-union divisions undermine union effectiveness.

They enable many employers to divide and rule. As Richard Scase has shown in his study of British and Swedish workers: 'The TUC is not a manual workers' confederation in the same manner as the Swedish LO, with the result that it is less able to pursue policies intended to further the interests of manual workers as a class in society.' The fragmented structure of our unions, which tries to transcend manual and white-collar divisions, generates less awareness of the economic rewards and privileges of different groups of workers. Differentials and relativities, hallowed by custom and practice, bedevil our industrial relations. They make it much more difficult for union harmony on the achievement of a permanent incomes policy.

Divided unions often lead to a lack of solidarity on the shopfloor. Workers in the same factory often find it difficult to organize coherent action. Contrary to popular belief, unions have failed to become dynamic instruments of economic change or organizations with enormous power. More often than not, they try to act as agents of control over the workforce, seeking to bring order from potential chaos. As Richard Hyman has written: 'The remarkable fact about most industrial disputes is that, given the wide range of demands which could reasonably be raised by workers, union aspirations in bargaining are unambitious and the gap between disputing parties is thus relatively narrow.' Unions seldom question the existing power structures in companies, let alone demand much better fringe benefits, working conditions and worker rights be placed on the agenda for bargaining. In the opinion of Michael Mann, 'reformist unions tacitly abandon the wider issues of worker control. They fail to articulate the experience of work deprivation and are often prepared to sign away job control rights in return for wage concessions.' But the main and obvious reason for this indifference by the union officials is that the rank and file pressure is usually not strong enough to do otherwise.

For the most part, the unions have proved too weak and trusting rather than too strong. They have the potentiality to become a progressive force in British society during the next decade, if they grasp the opportunities provided by law. For too long, they have been treated as outsiders or enemies, not as vital partners in a programme of national recovery. Experience has taught them to be very suspicious of progress. Unions radiate insecurity about their position as a result of history. They are too much on the defensive, and unwilling to combat the grotesque distortion of their aims and behaviour which many of our media give to union affairs.

Yet in the final resort, unions mirror the strengths and the frailties of those they represent. Their often muddled but good-natured response to the need for sacrifice in the 'national interest' is an accurate reflection of the volatile, unpredictable mood of the rank and file. However wide the gap has become between leaders and led, it is quite wrong to believe a union boss can ignore the views and aspirations of his members in defence of what he thinks is the greater good. Mealy-mouthed views of the need for the 'moderates' to crush 'extremism' in the unions implies militant trade unionism should have no place in a free, democratic society. But a tough and determined union bargainer, getting what is possible for his members, is an essential ingredient in any industrial relations system based on consent. The strike weapon is a tactical last resort to be used sparingly, but in a disciplined way when necessary by any union worth its salt. Moderation should not stand for mild defeatism, an unwillingness to champion the interests of union members, and a toleration of low wages and poor conditions. Those who mindlessly chant the litany of 'if only the moderate majority would rise up and defeat the extremists running the unions all would be well' are doing a grave disservice to free trade unionism, but perhaps many do not really believe in it, preferring freedom only for employers to treat labour just like any other commodity in the market place.

In January 1969 the Labour Government produced a White Paper – *In Place of Strife*. Its introduction contains words of relevance for the 1980s. As the document argued:

Our present system of industrial relations has substantial achievements to its credit, but it also has serious defects. It has failed to prevent injustice, disruption of work and inefficient use of manpower. It perpetuates the existence of groups of employees who, as a result of the weakness of their bargaining position, fall behind in the struggle to obtain their full share of the benefits of an advanced industrial economy. In other cases management and employees are able unfairly to exploit the consumer and endanger economic prosperity. It has produced a growing number of lightning strikes and contributed little to increasing efficiency. There are still areas of industry without any machinery for collective bargaining at all. Radical changes are needed in our system of industrial relations to meet the needs of a period of rapid technical and industrial change.

This was Labour's attempt to create a 'more equitable, ordered and efficient system' to benefit workers and the community at large through 'the active support and intervention of government'. Tragically the narrow concentration on a 'short, sharp' Bill to outlaw unofficial strikes destroyed any serious use of the law to reform the unions in a positive way, to make them more effective as bargainers and more responsible to the wider needs of society. The February 1979 voluntary concordat between the TUC and the government was a politically inspired document to try and provide a more acceptable face to trade unionism after the industrial strife of the winter of 1978–9. But it relied on self-regulation, leaving it to the unions to control themselves unaided. Future events may make this approach impossible. We cannot rule out for good the use of positive law to provide our unions with rights and obligations.

Genuine conflicts of interest between capital and labour are inevitable in industrial societies. This is why trade unions remain crucial for the well-being of a democratic society. A flourishing trade union movement is a guarantee of liberty, not a threat to it. As this book has attempted to demonstrate the divisions in industry, the inequalities of power and influence, the threats of statutory controls and legal sanctions against the activities of unions and their members, reflect the divergent values and assumptions of a society where there is no consensus, no widely shared belief in the 'national interest' or agreement on what constitutes 'a fair day's pay for a fair day's work'. The ethics of social justice do not play a powerful role in the conduct of industrial relations and preaching will not alter that unpleasant but obvious fact of life.

My overall conclusion (despite the hopes for constructive change) is therefore a rather pessimistic one. In a country facing severe economic problems during the 1980s the unions look like taking the full force of the coming social stress. During the past twenty years they were blamed (usually mistakenly) for what went wrong with post-war Britain. As scapegoats of national decline, the unions have become objects of hatred, fear and derision. Many people are no longer susceptible to reason and common sense when discussing the role of the unions. But the unions have also grown in membership, despite those popular attitudes, and their influence, though much exaggerated, is greater than it was. Under the threat to living standards, people have naturally sought protection for themselves in trade union membership. After all, the primary function of trade unions must always be – not social or political change – but the defence and improvement of the wages and benefits of the members. We therefore tend to have a schizophrenic attitude to the unions, hating and needing them at the same time. We must expect a Jekyll and Hyde response to the unions from government in the 1980s as it tries to wrestle with Britain's underlying structural problems. The unions look like remaining an unstable, unpredictable element in a country whose future as a leading manufacturing power must now be in serious jeopardy. The better way does lie through incomes policies; the redistribution of income and wealth; tripartitism; enlightened labour law with positive rights for workers; a major internal modernization of union activity with more professionalism; industrial democracy; and a move to provide a 'new legitimacy' for the unions where they are closely involved in a 'social contract' with government. The close alliance between social democracy and trade unionism has worked elsewhere in democratic Western Europe to achieve economic growth and social justice in a market economy. Perhaps our own problems are too unique, too overwhelming to respond to the same answers. The inability to marry shopfloor realities with the stresses imposed on national union organizations by governments remains a serious obstacle to progressive change. This is not to argue that Britain's unions must have more centralized authority and less democratic accountability within their ranks. The age of the big union boss passing down orders from on high is over and it is unlikely to return, thank goodness. But it also means that the present drift, ad hockery, sloganizing and posturing can only impoverish not enrich the membership. The trends outlined in this book point in possibly two different directions. Past experience suggests the triumph of the Hobbesian scenario of sectionalist greed and strife as the most probable outcome. It will be a miracle if we display enough realism and determination to transform Britain into a high wage/high productivity country, like almost all our major competitors in the industrialized West.

Select bibliography

An invaluable guide is A. Marsh and E. O. Evans, *Dictionary of Industrial Relations* (London, Hutchinson, 1973). The best sources on today's unions are the newspapers, in particular the *Guardian*, the *Financial Times*, the *Morning Star*, the *Observer*, the *Sunday Times*, the *Economist* and the *Socialist Worker*. Other useful periodicals are *New Society*, *Management Today*, the *British Journal of Industrial Relations*, the *Industrial Relations Journal*, *Incomes Data Reports*, and the *Industrial Relations Review and Report*. The annual reports of the TUC are of major value, full of information on every conceivable subject concerning the unions. They remain a neglected source.

I found the following general studies of the unions of great help in the preparation of this book: Michael Shanks, *The Stagnant Society* (Harmondsworth, Penguin, 1960) and Eric Wigham, *What is Wrong with the Unions?* (Harmondsworth, Penguin, 1961). Both books have dated in some respect, but their critiques are still worth reading. Stephen Milligan, *The New Barons* (London, Temple-Smith, 1976) is a tough, rather oversimplified view of the unions, but highly readable. Innis MacBeath, *Cloth Cap and Beyond* (London, Allen & Unwin, 1974) is badly structured, but pointed. Hugh Clegg, *Trade Unionism under Collective Bargaining* (Oxford, Blackwell, 1976) is a useful essay. Clegg's *The Changing System of Industrial Relations in Great Britain* (Oxford, Blackwell, 1979) is a reliable and straightforward account. Richard Hyman, *Industrial Relations: A Marxist Introduction* (London, Macmillan, 1975) is both lucid and provocative. A good guide is T. Lane, *The Union Makes Us Strong* (Arrow, 1975). A hostile view of the unions can be found in J. Burton, *The Trojan Horse* (Adam Smith Institute, 1979). The most recent work that is closest to my own sympathies is Allan Flanders, *Management and Unions* (London, Faber & Faber, 1975). Flanders had a rare distinction; he was an impeccable scholar of industrial relations who could write beautifully. Also see K. Hawkins, *The Management of Industrial Relations* (Penguin, 1978).

The following books were of particular importance in writing this book in order of appearance.

Preface

The most recent attitudinal work is David Butler and Donald Stokes, *Political Change in Britain* (London, Macmillan, 2nd edn, 1971); J. Goldthorpe, D. Lockwood *et al.*, *The Affluent Worker* Vols I and II (Cambridge University Press, 1968); S. Hill, *The Dockers, Class and Tradition in London* (London, Heinemann, 1976); R. Scase, *Social Democracy in Capitalist Society* (London, Croom Helm, 1977); W. G. Runciman, *Relative Deprivation and Social Justice* (London, Routledge & Kegan Paul, 1966); and M. Moran, *The Union of Post Office Workers* (London, Macmillan, 1974). The survey of NUPE by R. Fryer and Warwick University colleagues in 1975 is available from the union on request.

Part one   Profile of the movement

The Department of Employment Gazette is packed with facts and figures every month. So is the annual year book of *British Labour Statistics* published by the Department. The historical context can be found in *British Labour Statistics*, Historical Abstract 1886–1968 (HMSO, 1971). The best up-to-date studies of recent union growth are in G. Bain and R. Price, 'Union Growth Revisited 1948–1974' (*British Journal of Industrial Relations* Vol XIV, No 3, November 1976). A theoretical explanation can be found in G. Bain and F. Elsheikh, *Union Growth and the Business Cycle* (Oxford, Blackwell, 1976). Other works on union growth worth reading include J. Hughes, *Trade Union Structure and Government* Parts 1 and 2 for the Donovan Commission in 1968. Hughes has also written two background papers in 1973 and 1975 to update those studies for the Ruskin College Trade Union Research Unit. G. Bain, *The Growth of White Collar Unionism* (London, Oxford University Press, 1970) and R. Lumley, *White Collar Unionism in Britain* (London, Methuen, 1973) are also of critical importance. Bain's book is unlikely to be superseded for many years. A seminal work is H. A. Turner, *Trade Union Growth, Structure and Policy* (Allen & Unwin, 1962).

More general studies that throw light on union growth are R. Bacon and W. Eltis, *Britain's Economic Problem: Too Few*

Producers (London, Macmillan, 1976); D. Jackson, H. A. Turner and F. Wilkinson, *Do Trade Unions Cause Inflation?* (Cambridge University Press, 2nd edn, 1975); A Shonfield, *Modern Capitalism* (London, Oxford University Press, 1968); A. Shonfield, *British Economy Since the War* (Harmondsworth, Penguin, 1958).

Two key articles on union organization are W. Brown and M. Lawson, 'The Training of Trade Union Officers', *British Journal of Industrial Relations* (Vol XI, No 3, November 1973); and G. Latta and R. Lewis, 'Trade Union Legal Services' (same journal, Vol XII, No 1, March 1974). The report of the Bullock Committee of Inquiry into industrial democracy, published in January 1977 by HMSO, is full of detail on the unions.

On the TUC there is very little worth reading on the modern period. W. Citrine's *Two Careers* (London, Hutchinson, 1967) remains vital. Also see E. Silver, *Vic Feather* (Gollancz, 1973). B. C. Roberts, *The History of the Trades Union Congress* (London, Allen & Unwin, 1968) is full, if pedestrian. The best source are the verbatim accounts of Congress published along with the annual TUC report.

On relations between the unions and the Labour Party there is a richer output. R. McKibbin, *The Evolution of the Labour Party* (London, Oxford University Press, 1974) is the best account of the formative years. The TUC's evidence to Donovan, *Trade Unionism 1966* (London, TUC, 1966) is quite an eloquent document. G. Dorfman, *Wage Politics in Britain 1945–1967* (London, Charles Knight, 1974) is useful on Labour/union relations on pay policy. Also valuable is L. Panitch, *Social Democracy and Industrial Militancy* (Cambridge University Press, 1976). Martin Harrison's *Trade Unions and the Labour Party since 1945* (London, Allen & Unwin, 1960) has not been updated, more is the pity. T. C. May, *Trade Unions and Pressure Group Politics* (Farnborough, Saxon House, 1975) is worth reading. S. Beer, *Modern British Politics* (London, Faber & Faber, 1966) remains of prime importance. E. Heffer, *The Class Struggle in Parliament* (London, Gollancz, 1973) is a view of the unions from the Labour left. J. Ellis and R. W. Johnson, *Members from the Unions* (Fabian Society, September 1974) is a rundown on the unions in the Parliamentary Labour Party. Also see W. D. Muller, *The Kept Men?* (Harvester Press, 1977). Works such as R. Milliband, *Parliamentary Socialism* (London, Merlin Press, 1961) and D. Coates, *The Labour Party and the Struggle for Socialism*

(Cambridge University Press, 1975) are highly polemical but worth reading for a disparaging view of the union influence. See also I. Richter, *Political Purpose in Trade Unions* (London, Allen & Unwin, 1973). H. Pelling, *The History of British Trade Unionism* (Harmondsworth, Penguin, 1963) is the standard work at present. Also of value are L. Minkin, *The Labour Party Conference* (Allen Lane, 1978), H. M. Drucker, *Doctrine and Ethos in the Labour Party* (Allen & Unwin, 1979) and R. Currie, *Industrial Politics* (OUP, 1979). T. Cliff, *The Crisis: Social Contract or Socialism* (London, Pluto Press, 1975) is a combative manifesto from the International Socialists. There are no good studies of the unions and communism, but see K. Newton, *The Sociology of British Communism* (Allen Lane, 1972), and the Conservative trade unionist remains a mysterious figure. R. McKenzie and E. Silver, *Angels in Marble* (London, Heinemann, 1968) is a pioneering work on the latter. Let us hope we don't have to wait too long for more. On the Tories see M. Moran, *The Politics of Industrial Relations* (Macmillan, 1978) and R. Behrens, *Blinkers for the Carthorse* (*Political Quarterly*, October–December 1978).

On union influence there is very little of real interest worth reading. K. Coates and T. Topham, *The New Unionism* (Harmondsworth, Penguin, 1974) is valuable. So is P. Brannen, E. Batstone, D. Fatchett and P. White, *The Worker Directors* (London, Hutchinson, 1976). On the closed shop see W. E. J. McCarthy, *The Closed Shop in Britain* (Berkeley, University of California Press, 1964).

Union democracy is also thinly researched at present. B. and S. Webb, *Industrial Democracy* (London, Longmans, 1902 edn) remains of immense importance. So does R. Michels, *Political Parties* (New York, Dover Publications, 1959). Newer works include J. D. Edelstein and M. Warner, *Comparative Union Democracy* (London, Allen & Unwin, 1975); J. Goldstein, *The Government of British Trade Unions* (London, Allen & Unwin, 1952); A. Carew, *Democracy and Government in European Trade Unions* (London, Allen & Unwin, 1976) and J. Hemingway, *Conflict and Democracy* (Oxford University Press, 1978). The shop stewards have been better served. Most recent works are W. E. J. McCarthy, *The Role of Shop Stewards in Industrial Relations* (for Donovan, London, HMSO, 1966) and the survey by McCarthy and S. Parker, *Workplace Industrial Relations, A Social Survey* (London, HMSO, 1968). Follow-up studies were

published by S. Parker in 1974 and 1975. A valuable article is
M. G. Wilders and S. R. Parker, 'Changes in Workplace Industrial
Relations 1966–1972', *British Journal of Industrial Relations*
(Vol XIII, No 1, March 1975). For the relationship between
shopfloor and union see I. Boraston, H. Clegg and M. Rimmer,
Workplace and Union (London, Heinemann, 1974). H. Beynon,
Working for Ford (London, Allen Lane, 1973) is illuminating. A
study of stewards in a particular industry is A. I. Marsh,
E. O. Evans and P. Garcia, *Workplace Industrial Relations in
Engineering* (Engineering Employers Federation, 1971). Various
reports of the defunct Commission on Industrial Relations are also
useful on stewards, most notably No 17, *Facilities Afforded to
Shop Stewards* (London, HMSO, 1971); No 85, *Industrial Relations
in Multi-Plant Bargaining* (London, HMSO, 1973); Industrial
Relations Study No 2, *Industrial Relations at Establishment Level*
(London, HMSO, 1974). G. D. H. Cole's *Workshop Organisation*
(London, Hutchinson, 1973 edn) was written as long ago as 1916
but retains its relevance. Also see J. Elliot, *Conflict or Co-operation*
(Kegan Page, 1978), G. Radice, *The Industrial Democrats*
(Allen & Unwin, 1978) and E. Batstone, I. Boraston and
S. Frenkel, *Shop Stewards In Action* (Blackwell, 1977) and *The
Social Organisation of Strikes* (Blackwell, 1978).

International studies that were useful in writing this book were
W. Kendall, *The Labour Movement in Europe* (London, Allen
Lane, 1975); T. Nairn, *The Left Against Europe?* (Harmondsworth,
Penguin, 1973); C. Tugendhat, *The Multinationals* (Harmondsworth,
Penguin, 1973); J. Gennard, *Multinational Companies and the
Response of British Labour* (British/North American Committee,
1972). E. Jacob's *European Trade Unionism* (London, Croom Helm,
1973) is a brief guide.

Many books already mentioned were of value in assessing the
effectiveness of the unions. It is also worth looking at A. Jones,
The New Inflation (Harmondsworth, Penguin, 1973);
W. W. Daniel, *Wage Determination in Industry* (London, PEP,
June 1976); A. Glyn and B. Sutcliffe, *British Capitalism,
Workers and the Profits Squeeze* (Harmondsworth, Penguin, 1961);
OECD, *Wage Determination* (Paris, OECD, 1974) and OECD,
Socially Responsible Wage Policies and Inflation (Paris, OECD,
1975); Dorothy Wedderburn (ed), *Poverty, Inequality and Class
Structure* (Cambridge University Press, 1974); A. Fisher and
B. Dix, *Low Pay and How to End It* (London, Pitman, 1974); Low
Pay Unit, *Trade Unions and Taxation* (London, Low Pay Unit,

1976); S. Mukherjee, *Changing Manpower Needs* (London, PEP, 1970); B. Weekes, M. Mellish, L. Dickens and J. Lloyd, *Industrial Relations and the Limits of Law* (Oxford, Blackwell, 1975); K. Hall and I. Miller, *Retraining and Tradition* (London, Allen & Unwin, 1975); F. Parkin, *Class Inequality and Political Order* (London, MacGibbon & Kee, 1971); M. Mann, *Consciousness and Action Among the Western Working Class* (London, Macmillan, 1973); F. Hirsch and J. Goldthorpe (eds), *The Political Economy of Inflation* (Martin Robertson, 1978); S. Britton and P. Lilley, *The Delusion of Incomes Policy* (Temple Smith, 1977). C. F. Pratten, *Labour Productivity Differentials Within International Companies* (Cambridge University Press, 1976) is important. On the unions and the legal system see O. Kahn-Freund, *Labour and the Law* (Stevens, 1977), W. Wedderburn, *The Workers and the Law* (Penguin, 1972), J. McMullen, *Rights At Work* (Pluto, 1978).

Part two   Varieties of unionism
Studies on individual unions remain few and far between and most of them seldom rise above hagiography. I found the following of particular value. V. L. Allen, *Trade Union Leadership* (London, Longman, 1970) and A. Bullock, *Life and Times of Ernest Bevin* (London, Heinemann, 1973) vol I. These, along with Goldstein, are musts on the Transport and General Workers. So are the monthly issues of that union's paper, *The Record*. The Engineers are less well served. J. B. Jeffreys, *The Story of the Engineers* (London, Lawrence & Wishart, 1946) remains the only major work and it is unsatisfactory. Also see *Trade Union Register*, No 3 (1973); F. Fletcher, *Union Democracy: The Case of the AUEW Rule Book* (Nottingham, Spokesman Books, 1970); and E. Wigham, *The Power to Manage* (London, Macmillan, 1973). On the General and Municipal Workers there is H. Clegg, *General Union in a Changing Society* (Oxford, Blackwell, 1964); E. A. Radice and G. H. Radice, *Will Thorne: Constructive Militant* (London, Allen & Unwin, 1974); and T. Lane and K. Roberts, *Strike at Pilkingtons* (London, Fontana, 1971). On NALGO, there is the very readable and solid A. Spoor, *White-Collar Union* (London, Heinemann, 1967); and on NUPE, A. Craiks, *Bryn Roberts and NUPE* (London, Allen & Unwin, 1964) as well as B. Roberts, *The Price of TUC Leadership* (London, Allen & Unwin, 1961). The recent history of the miners is not well covered. We await the last volume of their history from

Page Arnot. Michael Jackson, *The Price of Coal* (London, Croom Helm, 1974) is useful and so is J. Hughes and R. Moore (eds), *A Special Case?* (Harmondsworth, Penguin, 1972). C. H. Rolph's *All Those in Favour?* (London, Deutsch, 1962) gives a good account of the ETU trial, while J. R. L. Anderson and O. Cannon, *The Road from Wigan Pier* (London, Gollancz, 1973) is a favourable biography of Les Cannon, well worth reading. A reliable account of civil service trade unionism can be found in H. Parris, *Staff Relations in the Civil Service* (London, Allen & Unwin, 1973). On the railwaymen see P. S. Bagwell, *The Railwaymen* (London, Allen & Unwin, 1963). R. Grove's *Sharpen the Sickle* (London, Porcupine Press, 1947) is a rather romanticized view of the agricultural workers. The print unions are well if diplomatically handled in K. Sisson, *Industrial Relations in Fleet Street* (Oxford, Blackwell, 1975) and in the evidence from the Advisory, Conciliation and Arbitration Service to the McGregor Royal Commission on the Press published by HMSO in 1977.

Index

The following abbreviations have been used in the index:

Amal	Amalgamated	Dept	Department
Assn	Association	Fed	Federation
Assoc	Associated	Ind	Industrial
Brit	British	Inst	Institute
Comm	Commission	Nat	National
Conf	Confederation	Org	Organization
Cte	Committee	Soc	Society

Alastair Mant
The Rise and Fall of the British Manager £1·25

'Seeks to explain, in a vigorous style, why in this country we "downgrade so many of the jobs that really matter" ... Mant argues that the business of making and selling things, and doing these jobs well, has been submerged by the preoccupation with "management", as if it was something quite distinct from these humdrum activities' FINANCIAL TIMES

Peter F. Drucker
Management £1·95

Peter Drucker's aim in this major book is 'to prepare today's and tomorrow's managers for performance.' He presents his philosophy of management, refined as a craft with specific skills: decision making, communication, control and measurement, analysis — skills essential for effective and responsible management in the late twentieth century.

'Crisp, often arresting ... A host of stories and case histories from Sears Roebuck, Marks and Spencer, IBM, Siemens, Mitsubishi and other modern giants lend colour and credibility to the points he makes' ECONOMIST

You can buy these and other Pan Books from booksellers and newsagents; or direct from the following address:
Pan Books, Sales Office, Cavaye Place, London SW10 9PG
Send purchase price plus 20p for the first book and 10p for each additional book, to allow for postage and packing
Prices quoted are applicable in the UK

While every effort is made to keep prices low, it is sometimes necessary to increase prices at short notice. Pan Books reserve the right to show on covers and charge new retail prices which may differ from those advertised in the text or elsewhere.